Electoral Shocks

Electoral Shocks

The Volatile Voter in a Turbulent World

EDWARD FIELDHOUSE
JANE GREEN
GEOFFREY EVANS
JONATHAN MELLON
CHRISTOPHER PROSSER
HERMANN SCHMITT
CEES VAN DER EIJK

OXFORD
UNIVERSITY PRESS

OXFORD
UNIVERSITY PRESS

Great Clarendon Street, Oxford, OX2 6DP,
United Kingdom

Oxford University Press is a department of the University of Oxford.
It furthers the University's objective of excellence in research, scholarship,
and education by publishing worldwide. Oxford is a registered trade mark of
Oxford University Press in the UK and in certain other countries

First Edition published in 2020

Impression: 1

Published in the United States of America by Oxford University Press
198 Madison Avenue, New York, NY 10016, United States of America

British Library Cataloguing in Publication Data
Data available

Library of Congress Control Number: 2019954877

ISBN 978-0-19-880058-3 (hbk.)
ISBN 978-0-19-880059-0 (pbk.)

DOI: 10.1093/oso/9780198800583.001.0001

Printed and bound in Great Britain by
Clays Ltd, Elcograf S.p.A.

*To our respondents, who collectively gave up many
thousands of hours of their time to help us
understand British electoral behaviour*

Acknowledgements

The British Election Study (BES) is one of the longest running election studies worldwide and the longest running social science survey in the UK. It has made a major contribution to the understanding of political attitudes and behaviour over nearly sixty years. Surveys have taken place immediately after every general election since 1964. The first study conducted by David Butler and Donald Stokes in 1964 transformed the study of electoral behaviour in the UK. Since then the BES has provided data to help researchers understand changing patterns of party support and election outcomes.

The BES has been almost continuously supported by the Economic and Social Research Council (ESRC) since its inception as the Social Science Research Council in 1965. In 2013 the funding for the 2015 British Election Study was awarded to a consortium of the Universities of Manchester, Oxford, and Nottingham (grant number ES/K005294/). The scientific leadership team was made up of Professors Fieldhouse, Green, Evans, Schmitt, and van der Eijk, who were later joined by Drs Mellon and Prosser. The project was further supported by funding from the Future of the UK and Scotland programme chaired by Charlie Jeffrey (grant number ES/L005166), and later extended to include the 2016 EU referendum (in collaboration with Anand Menon and UK in a Changing Europe) and the 2017 General Election (grant number ES/P001734/1). The team gratefully acknowledge the financial support of the ESRC, without which the BES would not exist. We would like to thank all those at the ESRC who have supported the BES team and responded to changing political circumstances—and hence the need for more data—with an admiral degree of speed and flexibility. We are especially grateful to Samantha McGregor, Paul Meller, Alison Weir, and Doug Walton for their help and support over the last five years.

The 2015–17 BES has also been generously supported by the University of Manchester and Nuffield College, Oxford. We are hugely grateful for the moral, financial, and intellectual support provided by our respective institutions. At the University of Manchester we are especially grateful to (former) heads of the School of Social Sciences David Farrell, Fiona Devine, and Chris Orme; and former heads of Politics Andrew Russell and Francesca Gains for encouraging us to bid to run the BES and providing the necessary institutional support. At Nuffield we are grateful to Sir Andrew Dilnot, Nuffield Warden, who has supported the BES following the long line of Nuffield collaboration with the election study and its inception at Nuffield by College Fellow David Butler.

The Electoral Commission provided vital access to data and additional support for linking voter turnout and registration records to the BES data. We would like to thank Phil Thompson in particular for making the voter registration collaboration possible, and Emma Noyes and Davide Tiberti for helping with the important practicalities. We also want to thank all the research assistants who helped with the difficult and no doubt tedious task of linking electoral records: Arthur Hunter, Jac Larner, Charlotte Hargrave, Laura Sanchez Carboneras, and especially Jessica Smith, who not only led the effort in both 2015 and 2017 but also co-authored a report on the impact of the move to individual electoral registration.

ITN and ITV News—as well as other leading broadcasters—have recognized and valued the BES for its unique scope and possibilities for analysis. ITN and ITV News have been open, imaginative, creative, and ambitious in their use of BES data to lead analysis of the 2015 General Election, 2016 EU referendum, and 2017 General Election. We are especially grateful to Emma Hoskyns, Alex Chandler, Jon Roberts, Tom Bradby, and Julie Etchingham—and also to Professor Colin Rallings—for giving us the opportunity to learn how to use BES analysis in real time and communicate it during election night coverage.

We are also grateful to our colleagues at Manchester and Oxford for providing countless ideas, feedback, and moral support, especially Rachel Gibson, Rob Ford, Maria Sobolewska, and James Tilley. A special thanks also goes to those colleagues who have supported the BES team at various points including Sue Bailey and Pip Walker (Manchester) and Yani Moyse (Nuffield), each of whom have provided sterling administrative support. We are especially grateful to Mike Addelman who provided seemingly unlimited help and inspiration in promoting the BES and liaising with the media with boundless enthusiasm. Jack Bailey, William van Taack, Lawrence McKay, James Griffiths, Tom Loughran, and Kathryn Simpson all provided invaluable research assistance for various BES activities.

We would like to extend a special thank you to Ruth Dassoneville, Dick Johnson, Laura Stoker, John Aldrich, and Ted Brader, who were all participants in an American Political Science Association (APSA) panel in September 2018 who commented extensively on the draft of this book and provided incredibly useful feedback. We are also grateful to our advisory board members: Mark Franklin, John Aldrich, Rosie Campbell, Sara Hobolt, Bob Huckfeldt, Rob Johns, Richard Wyn Jones, Jeff Karp, Ian Plewis, Dave Sanders, and Patrick Sturgis; and to our impact stakeholder group: Greg Cook (Labour Party), Andrew Cooper (Populus Ltd/Conservative Party), Ruth Fox (Hansard Society), Katie Ghose (Electoral Reform Society), Peter Riddell (Institute for Government), Neil Serougi (Freedom from Torture), and Tom Smithard (Liberal Democrats).

We are grateful to Sage Publishing and Elsevier for permission to reproduce parts of two articles that feature in chapters of this book. Chapter 4 draws on an article by Evan and Mellon (2019) in *Party Politics* titled 'Immigration, Euroscepticism and the Rise and Fall of UKIP'. The 2015 portion of Chapter 7 draws heavily on the article 'The limits of partisan loyalty: How the Scottish independence referendum cost Labour' by Fieldhouse and Prosser which appeared in *Electoral Studies* (2018).

A note on the data used in this book

As might be expected in a book from the BES team, most of the data analysed in this book comes from the BES past and present. The 2015–17 BES included two major components: a post-election in person address based probability survey following the general elections in 2015 and 2017 (Fieldhouse et al. 2015; Fieldhouse et al. 2017) and an internet panel study with thirteen waves between February 2014 and June 2017 (Fieldhouse et al. 2018) both of which are drawn on heavily in this book.

The 2015 face-to-face survey was an address-based random probability sample of eligible voters living in 600 wards in 300 Parliamentary Constituencies in England, Scotland, and Wales, completed by 2,987 people. The fieldwork for the survey was conducted between 8 May 2015 and 13 September 2015 and achieved an overall response rate of 55.9 per cent.

The 2017 face-to-face survey is an address-based random probability sample of eligible voters living in 468 wards in 234 Parliamentary Constituencies in England, Scotland, and Wales, completed by 2,194 people. The fieldwork for the survey was conducted between 26 June 2017 and 1 October 2017 and achieved an overall response rate of 46.2 per cent.

Fieldwork for the 2015 face-to-face survey was conducted by GfK NOP Limited (now part of Ipsos MORI) and fieldwork for the 2017 face-to-face survey was led by GfK NOP in consortium with Kantar and NatCen. We are grateful to all those who worked on the survey, especially the field interviewing team who did a fantastic job in helping secure an impressive response rate, and to Claire Bhaumik and Adam Green who managed the 2015 and 2017 operations respectively. A special thank you also goes to Nick Moon and Richard Glendinning who oversaw the project at various points and helped ensure a highly successful operation.

The thirteen-wave 2014–17 internet panel is a non-probability survey of approximately 30,000 respondents per wave. Fieldwork for the BES internet panel was carried out by YouGov and we are enormously grateful to Joe Twyman and to Adam McDonnell who, over the last five years, have been incredibly accommodating and helpful in ensuring the ongoing success of the panel study despite many last-minute deadlines and unexpected events.

We also draw on the following historical BES surveys extensively in the book.

- Political Change in Britain 1963–1970 (Butler and Stokes 1969a)
- British Election Study 1969–1974 (Crewe, Robertson, and Sarlvik 1976)
- British Election Study 1974–1979 (Sarlvik, Robertson, and Crewe 1981)

- British Election Study Panel, 1983, 1986, 1987 (A. Heath, Jowell, and Curtice 1999)
- British General Election Panel Study 1987–1992 (A. Heath et al. 1993)
- British Election Panel Study 1992–1997 (A. Heath, Jowell, and Curtice 1998)
- British Election Panel Study 1997–2001 (A. Heath, Jowell, and Curtice 2002)
- British Election Study Internet Panel 2005–2010 (Clarke et al. 2014)
- British Election Study 2001 Cross-section (Sanders et al. 2002)
- British Election Study 2005 Cross-section (Clarke et al. 2006)
- British Election Study 2010 Cross-section (Sanders and Whiteley 2014a)

We also make use of the British Social Attitudes surveys running yearly since 1983 (NatCen Social Research and Social and Community Planning Research 2017).

Contents

List of Figures

List of Tables

1

Introduction

Observers of British politics have begun to expect the unexpected in British elections. The general elections of 2015 and 2017 were among the most volatile in British electoral history. The outcome of the 2015 General Election delivered the highest share of votes on record for parties other than the traditional big three (Labour, the Conservatives, and the Liberal Democrats). Only two years later, the 2017 General Election delivered the highest combined Labour and Conservative two-party share since 1970. Underlying these results, the electorate has become increasingly volatile at the individual level, as more and more people switch their party support between general elections.

Why have British politics and the British party system become destabilized? How can we explain the extraordinary election outcomes in Britain in 2015 and 2017 and the turbulent period of British politics in which we find ourselves? These are the questions we answer in this book.

Our explanation shows how long-term, gradual changes in voter volatility and the impact of electoral shocks have combined to radically transform the political landscape. We show that increased voter volatility is driven, in part, by a weakening of voters' partisan attachments—a process known as partisan dealignment—together with the growth of smaller parties (or 'party system fragmentation'). Party identities act as a stabilizing force. When voters interpret the political world through the lens of partisanship, they are less likely to be swayed and rocked by the political winds. The British party system now has less of this kind of ballast. Partisan dealignment means that, compared to previous decades, fewer people have strong identity-based attachments to political parties and are more likely to switch parties than voters in the past.

On its own, partisan dealignment does not explain the results of recent elections. Voters might be more likely to switch parties than in the past, but that does not tell us which voters are switching to which parties, and why. To properly understand political change, we need to consider the electoral shocks that have acted as catalysts for large-scale vote-switching in particular directions in the election outcomes we set out to explain. We focus on five electoral shocks, each of which had a major impact on either the 2015 or 2017 elections, or on both. These are: (i) the substantial rise in immigration after 2004, particularly immigration from Eastern Europe; (ii) the Global Financial Crisis prior to 2010; (iii) the coalition government of the Conservatives and the Liberal Democrats between 2010 and 2015;

Electoral shocks. Edward Fieldhouse, Jane Green, Geoffrey Evans, Jonathan Mellon, Christopher Prosser, Hermann Schmitt, Cees van der Eijk, Oxford University Press (2020). © Fieldhouse, Green, Evans, Mellon, Prosser, Schmitt, and van der Eijk.
DOI: 10.1093/oso/9780198800583.001.0001

(iv) the Scottish independence referendum in 2014; and (v) the European Union (EU) referendum in 2016. Each of these electoral shocks leads us to revise our understanding of recent British elections and how different variables have shaped vote choices over time, and why.

Electoral shocks are having a remarkable impact on election outcomes *now* because they are happening within an electorate less constrained by strong party loyalties. This need not be the inevitable state of play in the future if new political divides—such as those around Brexit—anchor voters to political parties, or if levels of partisanship increase in the future. However, our analysis of trends in partisan dealignment suggests that the decline may be unrelenting, as older cohorts with strong identities are leaving the electorate and being replaced with newer cohorts with much weaker partisan attachments. Electoral shocks look set to continue to play a major role in British elections, and individual-level volatility is likely to remain high. These factors are also present in a large number of other countries, as well as in Britain. Our arguments and analysis are not just relevant to British electoral politics, although the specifics in British election outcomes are driven by the electoral shocks and the choices on offer in British politics.

Electoral shocks are not defined by their consequences. A major electoral shock could occur within a political system and its effects be absorbed by existing political divisions. Whether a shock disrupts politics depends on the way in which shocks are politicized and how parties compete over the fallout. Electoral shocks offer politicians opportunities to which they may—or may not—strategically respond, and respond in different ways. Shocks create political and strategic uncertainty, and allow, therefore, for unanticipated consequences and opportunities.

Each of the electoral shocks in this book shares the same features in common. We define them by the following characteristics:

Electoral shocks are an abrupt change to the status quo. They are not necessarily exogenous to the party system, but they are more than simply the outcomes of normal everyday politics. They represent a significant and often unanticipated change.

Electoral shocks are manifest over prolonged time periods and are highly salient: they have the potential to be noticed and recognized even by people who do not have much interest in politics, and by people who might otherwise select into information that fits their partisan beliefs and preconceptions. Electoral shocks are, therefore, very difficult for voters and politicians to ignore.

Electoral shocks are politically relevant and they have the potential to change how parties are perceived and therefore to reshape the party system.

Electoral shocks vary in the degree to which they are short-term and longer-term. A shock, as we define it and think about it, differs from how the term has often been used in quantitative political science and economics. That is to say, we do not define a shock as a temporary and short-lived event that creates a sharp spike in a time-series which then quickly returns to its former equilibrium. We are interested in shocks that change a system—the British political system. Understanding the longer-term evolution and complex outcomes of electoral shocks is one of the contributions we offer in this book. None of the shocks we identify have had only short-lived consequences, and many are likely to last well into the future, and some have already had impacts spanning more than one election. This reflects the significance of electoral shocks, the varied ways in which voters and parties respond, and the way they are given attention in politics and in the media. Shocks may therefore alter the equilibrium.

Electoral shocks vary in their form. For example, they may be political events, campaigns, referendums, institutional changes, or the consequences of particular policies. The way in which a shock affects electoral politics varies too. The effect of the Global Financial Crisis was not just a high-profile shock to the economy and to Labour's reputation for economic competence; it was also the beginning of a long-term policy shift towards austerity and continued political competition around the level of national debt, political responsibility and blame. The EU referendum and Scottish independence referendum differed in their outcomes—the former leading to the outcome of Brexit, the latter to a vote for the status quo. However, both led to the electoral expression of identities made salient by the referendums and the realignment of voters to parties on these divisions. The example of Scotland illustrates how shocks are not necessarily independent in their effects. In 2017 the Scottish independence referendum and the EU referendum combined to influence the outcome of the General Election in Scotland.

Electoral shocks provide an overarching explanation that departs in a significant way from a focus on a single causal assumption, a fixed set of variables, a specific type of statistical model, or one particular electoral outcome. This is not a book about one particular party's rise and fall, a single election outcome removed from its wider context, or an argument for the supremacy of one set of bottom-up or top-down processes, distant or proximate in the causal chain of electoral choice. That would, we believe, be a mistake, given the broader and longer-term changes to the British party system that need to be explained and understood. Instead, building on the foundations of the existing literature, we are seeking to understand why the party system has been exhibiting considerable volatility and instability, offering an explanation that can cover both the pre- and post-EU referendum periods, that can account for the divergent fortunes of political parties across the political spectrum, and that can be applied into the future as well as into the past. An explanation of electoral shocks—combined with our empirical analysis of how, and why, electoral shocks are shaping political behaviour—offers an approach to understanding broad system-level change, and it applies across time, elections, and also across countries.

We offer a multitude of different insights into the routes to party choice in the two previous general elections within the broader context of volatility. We do not provide an exhaustive list of how electoral shocks may potentially shape electoral behaviour. We do not, after all, have a complete list of historic or future shocks on which to base our analysis. However, five broad important themes run throughout:

1   **The broader electoral context has become significantly more volatile**

There have been a number of long-term, gradual, social and political changes that have fundamentally changed the electoral context, making elections more volatile. The first key driver of volatility is partisan dealignment—the weakening of voters' attachments to political parties. As we explain in a detailed chapter on partisan dealignment and volatility, partisan dealignment is itself a more general phenomenon of generational change. The second key driver is party system fragmentation (the rise of smaller parties) which has contributed to greater electoral volatility because of the tendency of voters of smaller parties to switch from one election to the next. However, we cannot properly understand the increase in volatility in British elections without appreciating the role of shocks.

2   **Electoral shocks can alter party images, reputations, and perceived positions on issues**

The 2010–15 Conservative–Liberal Democrat coalition substantially reshaped voters' perceptions of the Liberal Democrats. Our analysis shows that the decision to enter coalition government with the Conservatives was a reputational turning point for the Liberal Democrats that was to continue through the 2015 and 2017 general elections. The impact of coalition helps explain not only the Liberal Democrat collapse in 2015 but also why the Liberal Democrats failed to make significant inroads in the General Election of 2017 off the back of the EU referendum result in 2016.

The EU referendum changed the image of the Conservatives. Having been divided during the campaign, but ostensibly pro-Remain in terms of Conservative leadership, the Conservative response to the referendum was to embrace the result of Brexit, such that voters began to perceive the Conservative Party as much more opposed to EU integration than they had done before the referendum. This meant that they were seen as *the* party of Brexit, allowing them to increase support among Leave voters in 2017.

When the Global Financial Crisis hit Britain, the effect on Labour's competence on the economy did not just influence vote choice in the immediate general election that followed in 2010. It also influenced vote choice in 2015. One way in which economic crises have long-term effects on electoral behaviour is via their lasting effects on party competence. The Global Financial Crisis also provided an opportunity for parties to compete and win votes subsequently around austerity, competence, and responsibility and blame for the level of national debt.

3 **Electoral shocks can shape the relevant dimensions of political choice**
European immigration—and its politicization—contributed to the rise in electoral significance of immigration, an increase in its correlation with attitudes towards the European Union, and in the overall importance of the cultural dimension in British politics. We chart how non-left—right issues became increasingly salient to the British public alongside the rise in immigration and the increase in media attention to immigration. This new set of issues has become increasingly related to electoral choice. This change preceded the 2016 EU referendum, but was then significantly accentuated in 2017 as large numbers of voters chose between parties on the basis of this newly salient dimension. The EU referendum caused a substantial increase in the electoral significance of liberal–authoritarian values alongside immigration attitudes and attitudes about Europe, deepening demographic divides based on age and education, but softening those based on income. In a different way, Scottish nationalism became more important to Scottish general election vote choice in response to the Scottish independence referendum in 2014, shaping the 2015 and 2017 election outcomes.

4 **Partisan dealignment conditions the effects of electoral shocks**
Since electoral shocks are not defined by their consequences, we can understand their importance by the context in which they happen, as well as the ways in which political actors respond and compete around them. There are some contexts under which electoral shocks should have weaker effects, such as in periods of strong partisan alignment, and others in which their effects will be magnified, such as periods of weak partisan alignment. One reason that shocks are having such destabilizing consequences in contemporary British politics is the context of weakening partisan attachments. Partisan dealignment has weakened the ties between voters and parties and led to increasing between-election switching in the British electorate (individual-level volatility). The impact of electoral shocks is therefore amplified by volatility, as unattached voters are more easily moved by the force of a shock.

5 **The effects of electoral shocks are contingent**
In all of our chapters and explanations about the effects of electoral shocks there is a story about the central role of politics: the ways in which parties

compete around shocks and offer voters a choice, and the degree to which the media contributes to the salience and politicization of new issues, identities, and party performance. This means that electoral shocks are not independent changes that always have the same potential to switch vote choices, or will do so in predictable or linear ways. Political actors may magnify the effects of a shock by competing around them, or they may not. Our story is therefore also about political supply: how the number of parties— and their policies, leaders, competence, and viability—offer voters a basis to choose based on a particular political issue. The effects of electoral shocks are contingent on the political response and competition around them.

1.1 Outline

The remainder of this book sets out to explain and demonstrate in detail how British politics has become more volatile, unpredictable, and turbulent.

Chapter 2 describes the key electoral outcomes we wish to explain and elaborates the changing patterns of volatility over consecutive elections, at both the aggregate and individual levels.

Chapter 3 sets out our concepts and expectations about electoral shocks in greater detail, how they work and the ways in which their effects are contingent on political competition and politicization.

Chapter 4 provides an explanation of how the wider context of voter volatility has come about over time. It demonstrates the role of partisan dealignment and the rise in voting for 'other' parties to account for the rise in individual-level volatility in British elections.

The remaining five empirical chapters each focus on one of the electoral shocks listed above: the rise in European immigration (Chapter 5), the Global Financial Crisis (Chapter 6), the Conservative and Liberal Democrat coalition (Chapter 7), the Scottish independence referendum (Chapter 8), and the referendum on Britain's membership of the European Union (Chapter 9). Each chapter demonstrates how a particular electoral shock shaped political attitudes and vote choices in the 2015 and 2017 elections. The order of our chapters is broadly chronological, focusing on the effects of each shock as they occurred over time, each chapter examining the effects upon the relevant general election(s). Our book is, then, organized around our explanations, rather than on vote choices for different parties, or separately on the elections of 2015 and 2017.

Our final chapter considers the implications of our broad explanation and analysis for the future of British politics. We cannot predict what will happen in future general elections, but we can identify the factors that will matter: the degree to which electoral shocks may further destabilize the party system, and the degree to which partisan—or perhaps Brexit loyalties—provide a context for greater stability or destabilization of the British party system into the future.

1.2 Conclusion

This book offers a novel perspective on the wider context of the British electorate, focusing as it does on the trend towards greater electoral volatility over time. It demonstrates how shocks have contributed to the level of electoral volatility, and also which parties have benefited from the ensuing volatility. As such this book follows in the tradition of British Election Study (BES) books. We provide a comprehensive account of specific election outcomes—in our case the elections of 2015 and 2017—and also a more general explanatory model for understanding electoral change.

Existing explanations of electoral behaviour in Britain have typically focused on explaining the outcome of one particular election or one party, the adoption of one particular variable-based explanation to assess against rival explanations, and pitting variables and explanations against each other to assess the primary importance of one explanation overall. Each of these approaches can give us valuable insights into different aspects of electoral behaviour, and each provides a foundation for an understanding and critique of the broad understanding of electoral behaviour. They have been a feature of research that is applied to periods of stability or 'normal' political competition. However, these kinds of analytic approaches are less well-equipped to explain wider features of the system and sharp changes in outcomes and electoral behaviour that span multiple vote-switching between different political parties over time. Our focus on electoral shocks offers an overarching explanation for the volatility in evidence in British elections, alongside the long-term trends that have led us to this point. It offers a way to understand the rise and fall of the UK Independence Party (UKIP), Labour's disappointing 2015 performance and its later unexpected gains, the unexpected Conservative majority in 2015, the collapse in support for the Liberal Democrats, the dramatic gains of the Scottish National Party (SNP) in 2015, and the importance of the continuing period of tumultuous politics that has followed the General Election in 2017. It provides a new way of understanding electoral choice in Britain, and also beyond, and a greater understanding of the outcomes of recent elections.

As befitting a book from the BES team, we draw heavily on BES data, including not only data collected as part of the 2015–17 BES but data collected by previous BES teams going back to 1964. This long-running series of cross-sectional surveys provides invaluable evidence for measuring and analysing the long-term trends we refer to. For much of our analysis we rely on BES panel data, including data from our own thirteen-wave 2014–17 panel study, and also from inter-election panels collected by previous BES teams (again going back to 1964). This reliance on panel data reflects the dynamic nature of electoral choice and the importance of electoral volatility in our story. At each election most voters do not arrive with a completely blank slate—they come with the baggage of a lifetime of political socialization and previous electoral choices. This book is about what drives voters to switch their electoral allegiances and more fundamentally about understanding profound electoral change in British politics; a topic that has central importance to an understanding of voters, elections, and the future of British political life.

2

Volatility and Electoral Shocks

The period of British politics spanning the general elections of 2010 and 2017 was
tumultuous, to say the least, and has been followed by an equally extraordinary
period in British politics. The seven-year stretch between 2010 and 2017 saw five
years of coalition government, three referendums, a general election in which
minor parties achieved their highest ever vote share, and another that delivered
the highest two-party vote share since 1970. In the space of two years, in 2015 and
2017, we witnessed first the heralding of the fragmentation of the British party
system, and then the apparent rebirth of the two-party system. Figure 2.1 illustrates the dramatic change that took place between these two elections in terms of
the total share of vote for the two largest parties. What seemed like an inexorable
decline in the vote share of the two largest parties since 1945 was followed by a
dramatic reversal in 2017. Likewise there was an abrupt halt to the decades-long
trend towards a more fragmented party system, as shown in Figure 2.2. Having
reached a high-point in 2015, the effective number of electoral parties (Laakso
and Taagepera, 1979) dropped to levels not seen since the 1970s. Despite this
pronounced shift, thanks to the nature of British electoral geography there was
little corresponding change to the effective number of parliamentary parties.

In this chapter we introduce the common factor that helps us make sense of
these seemingly contradictory outcomes of very high party system fragmentation
in 2015, and a very high two-party share in 2017. This common factor is the high
level of electoral volatility—by which we mean the degree of change between elections, either in terms of the votes received by political parties or by the amount of
switching by individual voters. We also reflect in this chapter on the key political
developments that help us understand why some parties rather than others were
the beneficiaries of this volatility between elections. In the next chapter we examine why individual-level volatility has increased. Subsequent chapters show how
electoral shocks, acting in this volatile context, have provided the catalyst for
rapid political change.

2.1 Aggregate-level volatility

When measured at the aggregate level, volatility is 'the net change within the
electoral party system resulting from individual vote transfers' (Ascher and

Electoral shocks. Edward Fieldhouse, Jane Green, Geoffrey Evans, Jonathan Mellon, Christopher Prosser,
Hermann Schmitt, Cees van der Eijk, Oxford University Press (2020). © Fieldhouse, Green, Evans, Mellon,
Prosser, Schmitt, and van der Eijk.
DOI: 10.1093/oso/9780198800583.001.0001

Figure 2.1 Two-party share of the UK vote 1964–2017

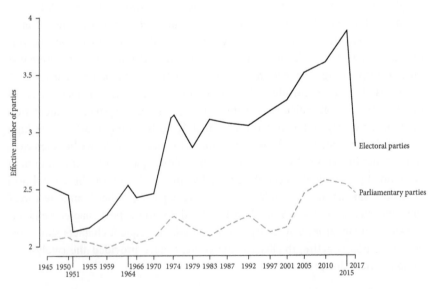

Figure 2.2 Effective number of UK electoral and parliamentary parties 1945–2017

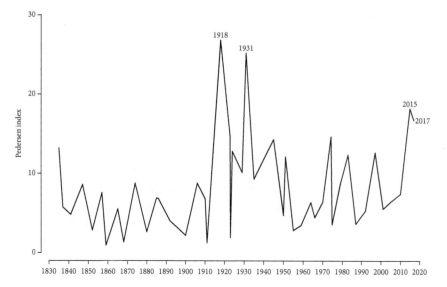

Figure 2.3 Pedersen Index of Aggregate Volatility 1835–2017

Tarrow 1975, 480). In other words, the system-level volatility is the aggregation of individual decisions.

Here we measure aggregate-level volatility by how much the national vote shares of parties have changed between two elections (Pedersen 1979).[1] Figure 2.3 shows over-time variation in aggregate volatility for British elections from 1835 to 2017. Taking this very long view of British elections allows us to place the 2015 and 2017 elections into context to see just how unusual they were. From the Liberal revival of 1974, the 1983 election which followed the Social Democratic Party (SDP) split, to Labour's landslides of 1945 and 1997, the twentieth century has seen many volatile elections. However, there have only been two UK general elections that were more volatile than 2015 and 2017, and both took place in very exceptional circumstances.

The first exceptionally volatile election, the 1918 General Election, followed the expansion of the franchise, giving women over the age of thirty the vote for the first time, and giving the vote to all men over the age of twenty-one. It came at the end of the First World War; a period of remarkable social and political change. The 1918 election, delayed because of the war, gave the coalition led by Lloyd George a landslide victory whilst the nascent Labour Party more than tripled its vote. The Liberals, who had not sided with Lloyd George, lost more than

[1] Aggregate volatility is measured using the Pedersen index, which is the sum of differences between each party's aggregate vote shares in the two elections, divided by two. It would have a maximum value of 100 if every previous party received zero votes in the second election and a minimum of 0 if every party received exactly the same vote share as in the first election.

70 per cent of their vote and the Irish Parliamentary Party was almost wiped out by Sinn Fein.

The second exceptionally volatile election, in 1931, followed the Great Depression and a budget crisis which precipitated the collapse and resignation of the Labour government. A National Government was formed at the request of King George V and, following the removal of the Pound from the Gold Standard, won the election—primarily with Conservative support—in a landslide. The Labour Party split into two factions and the Liberals into three. Against these two elections of 1918 and 1931, the 2015 and 2017 general elections stand out as the next two most volatile elections at the aggregate level: more volatile than the landslide elections of 1945, 1979, and 1997; and more volatile than the February 1974 election that failed to deliver a majority government.

Aggregate-level volatility is an important indicator of the dramatic changes that took place in 2015 and 2017. However, the aggregate picture does not tell the whole story. Aggregate volatility only captures the top level changes in vote shares, meaning that it is possible for an election to appear stable, even if a large numbers of voters switch parties beneath the surface, providing those vote flows cancel out. To give a simple example, if voters were split fifty–fifty between two parties at one election and *everyone* swapped parties at the next election, we would want to classify this as extremely volatile voting behaviour. However, the aggregate volatility would be zero, implying a very stable election. High aggregate volatility indicates many voters switching parties, but low aggregate volatility does not necessarily mean the reverse. A complete picture of this period of British politics requires attention to both aggregate-level switching and the switching that takes place beneath the surface among individuals.

2.2 Individual-level volatility

We measure individual-level volatility by examining the same voters in pairs of elections using the British Election Study panel surveys[2] and reported vote choices at the time of each election.[3] Our measure of individual volatility is the

---

[2] We also make use of British Household Panel Survey/Understanding Society (BHPS) data for available elections. The exact levels of switching differ slightly between sources, with the BHPS estimates consistently lower. There are a number of possible reasons for the gap. The BHPS tends to interview respondents considerably longer after the election than the BES. This may tend to lead respondents to forget behaviour that is out of line with their long-term partisan preferences (and therefore underestimate volatility). Alternatively, the BES may tend to retain more politically engaged respondents who may react to events more. Finally, the BHPS is a long-running survey, so the samples may skew older (we use unweighted estimates) and, as we will show in Chapter 3, older voters tend to switch at lower rates. Most importantly, however, both sources closely agree about the over-time trend in volatility.

[3] The data are derived from the British Election Study (and BHPS/Understanding Society) inter-election panels where the same group of voters are interviewed in two successive elections right after

proportion of voters who switch to a different party in the second election of each pair. Figure 2.4 plots this measure for every election since the 1960s, when the British Election Studies began with Butler and Stokes' (1969b) panel study of the 1964 and 1966 general elections.

While 12.5 per cent of Butler and Stokes' respondents (who voted in both 1964 and 1966) switched parties, this has ultimately turned out to be the lowest ever recorded level of switching. Individual volatility tells a different story of recent British electoral history to the spikey pattern of aggregate-level volatility we displayed in Figure 2.3. Rather than the pattern of peaks and troughs of volatility shown by the aggregate measure, the individual data shows the British voter becoming fairly steadily more volatile over time. The elections of 1966 and 2001 may look similar in terms of aggregate volatility, but Figure 2.4 shows that under the surface, voters were twice as likely to switch parties in 2001 as they were in 1966. Moreover, the 'landslide' election of 1997 does not look so different to the two elections either side of it. What really differentiates 1997 from 1992 and 2001 is not the number of voters switching parties, but the fact that much of the vote-switching was in one direction.

Using the measure of individual volatility, the 2015 election stands out as a clear high point: more than four in ten of those people who voted in both the 2010

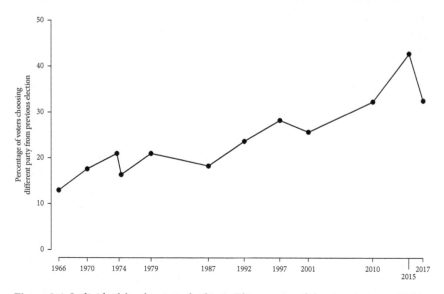

Figure 2.4 Individual-level voter volatility in Eleven pairs of elections between 1964 and 2017 in the British Election Study

each election, meaning we do not need to rely on respondents' recall of their previous vote choices, which previous research has shown are often unreliable (van Elsas, Miltenburg, and van der Meer 2016; Weir 1975).

and 2015 elections switched which party they voted for between the two elections. The 2017 election was slightly more stable, but only relative to the election of 2015. The level of switching between 2015 and 2017 still marks the second highest level of individual volatility in our data.

In order to understand this level of volatility in the 2015 and 2017 general elections, we revisit the political events of the period between 2010 and 2017 that contributed to these record levels of volatility and the resulting election outcomes.

2.3 Politics 2010–15

The 2010 General Election took place in the shadow of the Global Financial Crisis and the subsequent recession; events which had critically undermined Labour's reputation for sound economic management (Green 2010). The Conservatives also won over long-time Labour voters on the issue of immigration, which had risen in salience among the public (Evans and Chzhen 2013). Despite this, there were relatively low levels of aggregate volatility in 2010 (see Figure 2.3), with the Conservative Party failing to secure sufficient seats to form a government on its own. However, as Figure 2.4 shows, 2010 was a historically volatile election at the individual level, with large numbers of voters moving beneath an apparently tranquil surface. In 2010 these vote flows largely cancelled each other out, with voters moving in one direction being matched by others going in the opposite direction.

The degree of individual-level volatility in 2010 was a harbinger of the large changes to British politics that lay ahead. To give one example, the Liberal Democrat's vote share barely shifted between 2005 and 2010 (it increased by one percentage point). However, when we look at the individual-level BES panel data, we find that the Liberal Democrats lost 35 per cent of their 2005 voters between 2005 and 2010. It was only because they also recruited large numbers of voters in that period that their overall share was so stable. In fact, as we will see in Chapter 4, this is a fairly consistent pattern for the Liberal Democrats, who typically lose large proportions of their voters between elections and have to gain new voters to compensate.

The 2010 General Election also saw the continuation of a decade-long rise in voting for smaller parties. This was mainly reflected in the success of the Liberal Democrats, but was also evident in the rapidly increasing vote share of UKIP, the Greens (who also won their first seat), Plaid Cymru, and the SNP. UKIP achieved 3.1 per cent of the vote, which was their highest national vote share to that point. The 2010 General Election delivered the Liberal Democrats' highest ever vote share (23 per cent) and fifty-seven MPs, slightly short of the sixty-two Liberal Democrat MPs elected in 2005 (on 22.1 per cent share). By 2010, the combined Labour and Conservative share was just 65.1 per cent, whereas the Labour and

Conservative parties had consistently received a combined vote share of around 80 per cent in the 1960s (see Figure 2.1).

As a result of the narrow Conservative victory in 2010 and the Liberal Democrats' strong performance, British voters experienced Britain's first peacetime coalition government since 1922. After a short period of negotiation, the Liberal Democrats formed a coalition with the Conservatives, to the consternation of many of their voters, as we discuss in Chapter 7. The results did not in fact quite rule out a Labour-led coalition, but it would have required involving at least three parties to achieve a majority of even one seat.[4] Moreover, the Liberal Democrats were reluctant to be seen to be propping up an unpopular Labour government.

The hung Parliament and coalition government that ensued was only one of a series of shocks that contributed to an upturn in the fortunes of smaller parties in 2015. Eleven years previously, the establishment of the Scottish Parliament and Welsh Assembly had resulted in a substantial change in the UK's constitutional arrangements. Over the ensuing decade, the devolved governments gained further powers, increasing the importance of the devolved legislatures and the political significance of Scottish and Welsh elections. While the majoritarian Westminster system had just dealt a coalition at the 2010 General Election, a year later, in the 2011 Scottish Parliamentary elections, the mixed-member proportional system delivered a single-party majority government. The SNP won a landslide victory on a platform that included a promise to call a referendum on Scottish independence. The independence referendum that the SNP had promised was held in Scotland on 18 September 2014. Had the 'Yes' independence campaign won, the vote would have led to the break-up of the United Kingdom. The result was a 55 per cent vote in favour of the status quo, with a reported 85 per cent of registered voters turning out to vote.[5] Turnout for the Scottish independence referendum was the highest recorded turnout for an election or referendum in the UK since the introduction of universal suffrage, considerably higher than the 63.8 per cent turnout in Scotland in the 2010 General Election. This very high turnout is indicative of the importance Scottish voters on both sides had placed on this outcome. The referendum divided Scottish public opinion in visceral and

---

[4] Assuming Sinn Fein abstained, 323 seats were required for a majority in Parliament. Labour + Liberal Democrats + DUP = 323 seats. Alternatively (given the DUP's poor ideological fit for Labour and the Liberal Democrats), they could reach 324 seats with Labour + Liberal Democrats + SNP + Plaid Cymru. Various other arrangements were possible, but all involved reaching a tiny majority with an increasingly large number of parties. Politicians and observers generally considered these arrangements unlikely to be workable, given the large number of interests that would need to be reconciled and the small working majority that would result (Murray 2010; BBC News 2010).

[5] Figure for turnout as a percentage of registered voters are always underestimates in the UK, as they do not account for duplicate entries which inflate the denominator (Mellon et al. 2018b). The actual turnout in the Scottish referendum was therefore almost certainly considerably higher as a percentage of registered voters.

highly significant ways. These divisions would shortly reshape Scottish electoral politics, as we discuss in Chapter 8.

Parties other than the two largest in Westminster were also gaining support on specific issues including the environment, immigration, and Europe. Having previously found success in the 2004 and 2009 European Parliament Elections, where they had won around 16 per cent of the vote on both occasions, UKIP began to enjoy further electoral success with their opposition to immigration and the EU. First, they made significant inroads in the 2013 English and Welsh Local Elections, winning 147 local councillors (up from eight). Then, spectacularly, UKIP won 26.6 per cent share of the vote in the European Parliament election in June 2014, a higher vote share than either Labour or the Conservatives. UKIP also gained representation in the Westminster Parliament when the Conservative MP, Douglas Carswell, defected to UKIP from the Conservatives in 2014.

2.4 The 2015 General Election

The 2015 General Election campaign took place in the context of a recovering economy after years of sluggish performance and austerity policies under the Conservative-led coalition. The polls suggested that the most likely outcome was another hung Parliament with Labour as the largest party, but the SNP was in the ascendance in Scotland in the aftermath of the independence referendum in 2014, and also saw a rapid rise in the polls in Scotland throughout the campaign. The combination of these factors led the Conservatives to focus on two messages: Labour could still not be trusted on the economy, and if Ed Miliband became prime minister, any Labour coalition would be influenced by the SNP. The Conservatives promised 'competence with the Conservatives or chaos with Labour'. This framing was largely successful in setting the campaign agenda. Labour appeared unsure whether to apologize for, or defend, its former record in office, struggling to identify an effective counter-message. As we will show in Chapter 6, economic competence played a key role in the 2015 General Election. However, our analysis suggests little evidence that the threat of the SNP won the Conservatives votes (Jane Green and Prosser 2016).

The expectation that there would be a hung Parliament with Labour ahead was confounded, with observers and parties misled by inaccurate polls that substantially understated the Conservatives' lead (Mellon and Prosser 2017; Sturgis et al. 2018). In the end, the Conservatives increased their vote share by a tiny 0.8 percentage points but gained twenty-four MPs, and could therefore govern with an unanticipated Conservative majority (see Table 2.1). One implication of this surprise victory was that the Conservatives had to deliver on their election pledge to hold a referendum on Britain's membership of the European Union.

As shown in our earlier plot of aggregate volatility in Figure 2.3, the 2015 General Election was the third most volatile election since 1835. At the individual level, volatility was immense by relative standards, with 43 per cent of BES panel respondents reporting a different vote choice in 2015 to the one they reported in 2010. As Figure 2.4 showed, this level of switching was the highest seen across any pair of elections since the BES began in 1964. Unlike 2010, when individual switching mostly cancelled out, in 2015 the net effect of individual-level switching was large-scale changes in vote shares. In particular, there was a much larger increase in voting for minor parties, leading many commentators to announce the fragmentation of British politics. Table 2.1 displays the substantial increase in vote shares for UKIP, the SNP, and the Greens.

Were it not for the collapse in support of the Liberal Democrats in 2015, the combined vote share for the two largest parties might have been far lower. As it was, the vote share for the two largest parties increased very marginally, as shown earlier in Figure 2.1, whilst the vote choices split much more broadly across the smaller political parties, leading to a much more fragmented party system.

The flow of the vote between the 2010 and 2015 elections is illustrated in Figure 2.5. The size of each bar at either end of the ribbons representing the vote flow shows the total share of the vote each party received at the election (ordered from most votes at the top, to least at the bottom). The size of each ribbon represents the proportion of all 2010 and 2015 voters who voted for each pair of parties in 2010 and 2015. One of the most dramatic ways in which the large-scale switching manifested in 2015 was the collapse of the Liberal Democrat vote, as discussed. The Liberal Democrat vote share, which was 23.6 per cent in 2010, plummeted to 8.1 per cent in 2015, with the party losing a total of forty-nine of its fifty-seven MPs. The Liberal Democrats retained only 25 per cent of their 2010 supporters, compared to the equivalent figure of 65 per cent retained voters in 2010.[6] While the opinion polls had been very poor for the Liberal Democrats since entering the coalition in 2010, many MPs believed that a personal vote

Table 2.1 Results of the 2015 General Election. Figures shown are calculated for Great Britain (i.e. excluding Northern Ireland)

	% votes	Change in % votes	Total seats	Change in seats
Conservative	37.7	0.8	330	24
Labour	31.2	1.5	232	−26
UKIP	12.9	9.7	1	1
Liberal Democrat	8.1	−15.5	8	−49
SNP	4.9	3.2	56	50
Green	3.8	2.9	1	0
Plaid Cymru	0.6	0	3	0

[6] While the Liberal Democrats performed historically badly at recruiting new voters in 2015, they did gain a small percentage of new recruits (~2 per cent of voters).

would be enough for them to hold on to their seats. The modest incumbency advantage they actually enjoyed did not save many of them (Curtice, Fisher, and Ford 2016). The Liberal Democrats' greatest losses in 2015 were to Labour, but they also leaked a large number of voters to the Conservatives, the Greens, and even UKIP. While the Conservatives gained fewer Liberal Democrat deserters than Labour, those they did gain were disproportionately in marginal seats which they were consequently more likely to narrowly win.

Figure 2.5 also shows substantial flows of voters moving from the Conservatives to UKIP. In 2015, UKIP's vote share quadrupled to 12.9 per cent, representing almost 4 million votes. UKIP won votes most notably from the Conservatives, but also from Labour, the Liberal Democrats, and the British National Party (BNP). Importantly, many of the Conservative to UKIP switchers had previously defected to the Conservatives from Labour in 2010 (Evans and Mellon 2016b). UKIP also captured nearly two-thirds (63 per cent) of the BNP's 2010 voters (the BNP fell from half a million votes to fewer than two thousand between 2010 and 2015). While the electoral system deprived UKIP of equivalent representation in terms of parliamentary seats (retaining only the one MP who had previously defected from the Conservatives), they won their highest ever national share of the vote in 2015.

The Green Party won 3.8 per cent of the vote, increasing its national vote share from 1 per cent in 2010 and achieving the highest ever popular vote share for the Green Party in a British general election, retaining its one parliamentary seat (Brighton Pavilion).

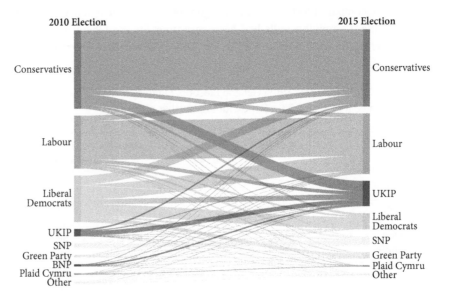

Figure 2.5 Vote flows between 2010 and 2015

The 2015 General Election was also remarkable for the result in Scotland (see Chapter 8). As shown in Table 2.1, the SNP almost trebled its GB vote share from 1.7 per cent in 2010 to 4.9 per cent. This equated to a huge increase of 30 percentage points in Scotland and a vote share of 50 per cent of Scottish voters; the highest share of the vote for any party in Scotland since 1931 when the Conservatives won 54.3 per cent of the vote. The SNP deprived Labour of forty of its former Scottish seats in 2015, the Liberal Democrats of all but one of theirs, and overturned more than fifty years of Labour dominance in general elections north of the border. It was Labour's lowest Scottish vote share since 1918.

Not only was the 2015 General Election volatile in electoral terms, it also had dramatic political consequences. For Labour, the election triggered a leadership election under new rules proposed by Ed Miliband, giving members and supporters a greater say. The outcome was the election of Jeremy Corbyn as Labour leader, a backbench MP for thirty-two years, one of the party's most rebellious MPs, a noted campaigner for nuclear disarmament, and a leader labelled the most left-wing since Michael Foot (Pickard and Parker 2017). The surprise outcome gave further rise to the conclusion that the mainstream political establishment was under challenge. Labour now had a leader that two-thirds of its MPs did not support and voters saw the party as increasingly divided.[7] The other hugely significant outcome was that the Conservatives, now forming a majority government against former expectations, committed to deliver on their manifesto pledge to hold the referendum on Britain's membership of the European Union.

2.5 The 2016 EU referendum

The Conservative EU referendum manifesto pledge was part of the Conservatives' attempts to stem the flow of votes to UKIP and manage decades of bitter internal Conservative parliamentary divisions over the question of Europe. However, rather than paper over the cracks in the Conservative Party, the EU referendum heightened them; first in the campaign and then, of course, in the resulting period of Brexit negotiations. High-profile Tories such as Boris Johnson and Michael Gove led the Leave campaign in 2016, while David Cameron and George Osborne campaigned for the Remain side.

The internal divisions were not limited to the Conservative Party. Despite strong support for Remain among Labour MPs and Labour voters, Jeremy Corbyn ran a low-key referendum campaign that many commentators believed reflected his long-standing scepticism about the EU. Labour's ambiguity on Brexit also

---

[7] Twenty-seven per cent of BES panel respondents said that the Labour Party was 'very divided' or 'fairly divided' in the pre-election wave in April 2015, but 45 per cent said the same by April 2016 (denominator includes don't knows).

served the strategic purpose of helping to avoid Labour losses in heartland seats, many of which went on to strongly vote for Leave. These splits left the Remain campaign in the odd situation of having one of its most prominent figures on paper offering only lukewarm support for EU membership.

The British public had never been strongly supportive of EU membership, even though 67.2 per cent of Britons in 1975 voted in the last EU referendum to stay in the European Community (Evans and Menon 2017). Nor had they developed a strong sense of European identity (Curtice 2016). The campaign therefore centred on practical questions of the costs and benefits of EU membership. On the Leave side this focused on the issues of immigration from the EU, and sovereignty; 'taking back control'. The Remain side focused on the economic benefits of EU membership and the costs of leaving the EU. These issues were also reflected in the reasons BES panel respondents gave for their vote at the time (Prosser, Mellon, and Green 2016).

The referendum took place on 23 June 2016 with the dramatic—and for many, surprise—result that Britain voted 51.9 per cent to 48.1 per cent to leave the EU. The vote was an endorsement of the most significant constitutional, economic, policy, and political change of direction in decades. It was another sign of the rejection of the status quo and of mainstream politics and politicians, especially as the vast majority of the political establishment had campaigned for Remain. The referendum also exposed deep attitudinal and geographic divisions that were emerging in the UK (Jennings and Stoker 2017).

Other than UKIP, none of the parties' 2015 voters overwhelmingly supported one side or the other in the referendum. The Conservatives' 2015 voters leaned 60 per cent towards Leave, while Labour's leaned 62 per cent towards Remain. The SNP faced a similar breakdown to Labour, with 67 per cent of their 2015 supporters backing Remain. The Liberal Democrats' 2015 voters were the most Remain leaning, but even among these, 27 per cent voted Leave. The EU referendum cut across the existing political divides in a way that would have substantial consequences for electoral politics (see Chapter 9).

The outcome of the referendum had immediate ramifications for the political parties. David Cameron resigned the morning after. Following a relatively short leadership contest, Theresa May was elected Conservative leader. Many Labour MPs felt let down by Jeremy Corbyn's weak support for the Remain campaign and triggered a new leadership election, with two-thirds of the Labour Shadow Cabinet resigning. This attempt to replace Corbyn ultimately backfired. In the ensuing leadership election, Corbyn expanded his majority among the Labour membership. Corbyn's second leadership win quelled the brewing civil war within the parliamentary Labour Party, at least temporarily. UKIP, meanwhile, was in internal disarray. Nigel Farage resigned immediately after the referendum, declaring that he had achieved his political goal. He was succeeded for eighteen days by Diane James (who then resigned) and subsequently by Paul

Nuttall. A series of internal disputes led to funders withdrawing, a fist fight between two UKIP MEPs, and UKIP's only MP leaving the party to sit as an independent MP.

The immediate aftermath of the EU referendum was a turbulent period in Britain's political history, during which the government needed to conduct crucial and complex negotiations for Britain's exit from the EU, and pass important legislation and key parliamentary votes. While the 2015 General Election had delivered a majority Conservative government, the result was a slender working majority of only seventeen MPs. After the EU referendum, however, the tide looked like to be turning in the Conservative's favour. A week before the election was called, one poll gave the Conservatives a twenty-one point lead over Labour (YouGov 2017). On 18 April 2017, with Labour and UKIP both internally divided and crashing in the polls, and the Conservative Party with a large lead, Theresa May called a snap general election.

2.6 The 2017 General Election

The 2017 General Election was almost universally expected to increase the Conservatives' majority, perhaps with a landslide. However, instead of increasing the Conservative majority, the result was a huge blow to May's leadership. The Conservatives increased their share of the vote, but they lost thirteen seats and with them, their parliamentary majority. A subsequent 'confidence and supply' deal was forged with the Northern Irish Democratic Unionist Party (DUP). At a time when the Irish border would be paramount in Brexit negotiations, the Conservatives relied on the votes of the Leave-supporting DUP.

The election had been billed as the Brexit election, but the campaign failed to focus very much on Brexit as an issue (Prosser 2018). Instead, the public debate focused on controversial Conservative manifesto promises on social care and fox-hunting, Theresa May's controversial policy U-turn on social care, and two terrorist attacks that took place during the campaign. Theresa May appeared as an ineffective campaigner as she repeated her campaign slogans with lacklustre performances and avoided taking part in a televized head-to-head debate with Jeremy Corbyn. By contrast, Jeremy Corbyn enjoyed a highly successful campaign and the two leaders' ratings had converged by election day. The campaign confounded expectations that short periods of campaign activity are rarely decisive for the outcome of the election. The 2017 General Election campaign was a highly influential campaign in which the main beneficiary of vote-switching was Labour (Mellon et al. 2018a). Once again, the outcome of the vote confounded the expectations of many observers. Corbyn, who many had written off as incapable of improving Labour's electoral fortunes, in fact led the party to an increase in their vote share of 9.8 percentage points (see Table 2.2), reaching

Table 2.2 Results of the 2017 General Election. Figures shown are calculated for Great Britain (i.e. excluding Northern Ireland)

	% votes	Change in % votes	Total seats	Change in seats
Conservative	43.4	5.8	317	–13
Labour	41	9.8	262	30
Liberal Democrat	7.6	–0.5	12	4
SNP	3.1	–1.7	35	–21
UKIP	1.9	11	0	–1
Green	1.7	–2.2	1	0
Plaid Cymru	0.5	–0.1	4	1

a level for Labour not seen since 2001. Labour enjoyed success in parts of the country that had not voted Labour in such numbers since Blair's historic victory in 1997. The Conservatives increased their vote by 5.8 percentage points to 43.4 per cent. Together, the two largest parties scooped up almost 85 per cent of the vote, but the large increase in Labour support cost the Conservatives their majority, turning the expected easy election victory into something that was widely perceived to be a disaster for Theresa May. Its consequences would overshadow the subsequent Brexit negotiations and weaken Theresa May's authority among her MPs in Parliament.

At the aggregate level, 2017 was nearly as volatile as 2015, making it the fourth most volatile election in British history (Figure 2.3). Nowhere was this aggregate volatility clearer than in the dramatic change in the two-party share of the vote (see Figure 2.1). The steady and significant decline of the two-party vote over many consecutive elections, which had culminated in the largest share for parties other than Labour, the Conservatives, and Liberal Democrats in 2015, was dramatically reversed only two years later. Because both major parties gained substantial numbers of votes at the same time, neither reaped a huge electoral reward in terms of seats.

The rapid change in the aggregate vote shares between 2015 and 2017 was reflected in large vote flows at the individual level. In total, 33 per cent of BES respondents reported a different vote choice in 2017 to the one they reported in 2015. This individual-level switching was lower than in 2015, but still somewhat higher than 2010, making it the second highest on record. Although the period between 2015 and 2017 was dramatic, including as it did the EU referendum and Britain's vote to leave the EU as a result, it was still only a two-year period in which we would normally expect overall switching to be lower than in a longer five-year election cycle when voters have more time to be persuaded to switch votes between parties. Given this, we can see 2017 as a highly volatile election, not least because of the dramatic change at the aggregate level.

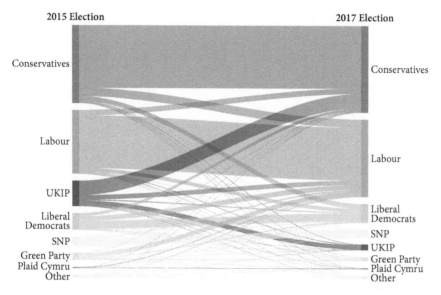

Figure 2.6 Vote flows between 2015 and 2017

Furthermore, the cumulative effects of individual-level volatility meant that of those that voted in 2010, 2015, and 2017, only 51 per cent voted for the same party in all three elections.

Figure 2.6 shows the flow of votes between the parties in the two-year period between 2015 and 2017.

In addition to the aggregate-level and individual-level amounts of volatility, the 2017 General Election also witnessed the highest levels of an unusual *form* of volatility in British politics: switching between Labour and the Conservatives. The usual view of British voters sees them as 'bounded partisans' who switch within party groups, but consistently reject one of the major parties (Zuckerman, Dasovic, and Fitzgerald 2007). In 2017, as Figure 2.7 shows, a more substantial proportion of Labour and Conservative voters switched to the other major party than in any previous election we can compare. This direct swapping between the major parties contributed to some surprising changes in the geographic distribution of the Labour and Conservative vote, resulting—for example—in Labour taking the highly educated Conservative strongholds of Canterbury and Battersea, and the Conservatives wresting working-class constituencies such as Mansfield and Middlesbrough South from Labour.

While Labour and the Conservatives gained large numbers of voters, including from each other, the Liberal Democrats failed to improve on their disappointing 2015 performance. As might now be apparent, this apparent aggregate stability hid substantial individual-level volatility: 51 per cent of 2015 Liberal Democrat voters defected to another party choice in 2017. The Liberal Democrats made up

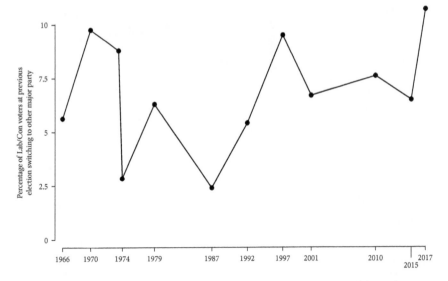

Figure 2.7 Combined switching from Labour to the Conservatives and from the Conservatives to Labour between one election and the next as a percentage of Labour and Conservative voters at the previous election

the difference by recruiting substantial numbers of 2015 Labour and Conservative voters. This individual-level volatility was also reflected in seats. While the Liberal Democrats ended the election with twelve seats—four more than in 2015—they won eight new seats in comparison to 2015 but also lost five (including the Richmond Park constituency they had won in a by-election the previous year).

Labour and the Conservatives also gained votes from the smaller parties. Most dramatically, UKIP's support fell from their 12.9 per cent high in 2015 to only 1.9 per cent in 2017. The earlier 2017 local elections had wiped out all of UKIP's local councillors, and the 2017 General Election, in which they fielded less than 400 candidates, largely eliminated their electoral base. The Conservatives were the major beneficiaries of this collapse, securing 56 per cent of all 2015 UKIP voters, according to our BES panel data. The Conservatives also gained votes from Leave-voting 2015 Liberal Democrat, Labour, and SNP supporters. Labour's success came from sweeping up huge proportions of 2015 Green and Liberal Democrat voters, as well as a modest portion of UKIP voters (Mellon et al. 2018a).

Labour to Conservative switching was especially strong in Scotland, where the Conservatives campaigned as the party of leaving the EU and keeping Scotland part of the UK. Their appeal to Unionist voters helped them gain 22 per cent of 2015 Scottish Labour voters along with 25 per cent of 2015 Scottish Liberal Democrats. Their appeal to Leave voters, meanwhile, meant that they even succeeded in attracting 8 per cent of 2015 SNP voters. The SNP's vote share fell from 50 per cent in 2015 to 36.9 per cent in 2017, the largest direct beneficiary being Labour, although these gains were mostly cancelled out by Labour's other losses. The net result of these shifts was a twenty-one seat loss for the SNP, with corresponding gains for Labour, the Liberal Democrats and, most notably, the Conservatives, who gained 28.6 per cent of all Scottish votes and twelve seats (see Chapter 8).

2.7 Conclusions

The General Elections of 2015 and 2017 marked a historically high level of volatility, both at the aggregate level and also at the level of the individual voter. In this chapter we described how this increased volatility is part of a long-term trend in British politics, but one which accelerated markedly after 2010. At the aggregate level, 2015 and 2017 were the two most volatile elections since 1931. At the individual level, they were the two most volatile elections for which we have data to measure. Unlike with aggregate volatility, which has changed erratically over time, we showed that individual-level volatility has been steadily and significantly increasing since 1964. The changes seen at the 2015 and 2017 elections were not the sudden, out-of-the-blue shifts that the aggregate results might suggest. They were the culmination of a fifty-year increase in vote-switching in British elections. The 2015 and 2017 elections were important—not only because of how much switching there was—but also the directions of that switching. Unlike many elections when vote flows favouring one party are compensated by counter-flows favouring another, voters in 2015 and 2017 moved systematically, first away from, and then towards the two major parties. The 2017 election saw record numbers of voters moving between the two largest parties.

The 2017 General Election is the endpoint of our analysis in this particular book, but it was only the beginning of another turbulent period of British politics. The period between 2010 and 2017 was extraordinary in many ways, as we highlighted in this chapter. The last few years have not just *felt* like a more tumultuous period in British politics than usual; this really *has* been an exceptionally volatile period in British political history.

Judged by our metrics, the elections of 2015 and 2017 are historically volatile. Both elections were remarkable in different ways, and each raises important questions about the instability in the British party system. They represent an intriguing puzzle: what can both account for dramatic gains for minor parties and nationalists in one election, and also the collapse of Britain's third party, but also account for the highest two-party vote share in almost forty years? What were the common factors and themes that led voters to reject the mainstream parties in 2015, only to subsequently be willing to vote for them again in large numbers only two years later? In short, we need to address the following question: what explains this instability in the British party system and in the British electorate? To answer that we need to pay attention to both the long-term trends that produced volatility in the system, and the electoral shocks that were able to have such a large impact in that volatile environment.

3

Turbulent British Politics

An Explanation

British politics has become less predictable and the party system less stable. More voters are switching their vote choices than ever before. This switching has led to dramatic changes in election outcomes and dramatic changes in political party support over very short time periods. What can account for this instability in British politics, and what does this instability tell us about the outcomes of the two most recent British general elections?

Our explanation focuses on the long-term and short-term antecedents of electoral choice.

We start with a foundation of the gradual and long-term changes that have made voters more likely to switch their support to different parties: the changing long-term context of volatility. Chapter 4 deals with these changes in greater detail and explains why they have come about. Here we explain why the gradual destabilization of the party system means that shocks can result in extraordinary political consequences; from the largest vote share for parties other than Labour, the Conservatives, and Liberal Democrats in 2015, to the largest two-party vote share since 1970 in 2017. However, there are still features of the system that provide stability, not least the advantages enjoyed by the major parties in retaining voters and the majoritarian electoral system.

The remainder of this chapter focuses on the mechanisms and consequences of *electoral shocks* in the context of increasing electoral volatility. We set out the reasons for focusing on the impacts of shocks, a definition of electoral shocks, and the mechanisms through which shocks affect voting behaviour. Our approach to the study of electoral shocks recognizes that the potential impacts of shocks are multifaceted and can have far-reaching, system-wide effects. Shocks do not have inevitable consequences, and are not defined by their consequences. They create political opportunities, and their consequences depend on how politicians react to them and compete around them, and how they are politicized in the wider media environment. The chapter also explains why the gradual destabilization of the party system means that electoral shocks are having increasingly dramatic consequences.

This account of electoral change departs from a focus on single explanatory factors or votes for a particular political party. It rejects a false choice between

Electoral shocks. Edward Fieldhouse, Jane Green, Geoffrey Evans, Jonathan Mellon, Christopher Prosser, Hermann Schmitt, Cees van der Eijk, Oxford University Press (2020). © Fieldhouse, Green, Evans, Mellon, Prosser, Schmitt, and van der Eijk.
DOI: 10.1093/oso/9780198800583.001.0001

bottom-up demand-based explanations and top-down political supply-oriented explanations. Political outcomes are more complex than this. Understanding the changing nature of the party system calls for an explanation that is broad and multifaceted. We need to understand how the structures and incentives that underpinned the stable party system have become weaker over time, what the consequences of that weakening are, how they account for instability in British politics, and what the prospects are for a return to greater stability in the future. This chapter sets out an explanation that considers relatively short-term but complex factors—electoral shocks—and situates them and their effects in the context of long-term gradual political change. We explain how these long-term and short-term factors interact: the impact of electoral shocks can be accentuated when party attachments are weak.

3.1 The long-term trend in volatility

In Chapter 2 we showed how sharp and trendless fluctuations in aggregate level volatility have been accompanied by a long-term and gradual increase in individual level volatility over the last five decades. The long-term trend reflects an electorate that is more fluid and potentially more responsive to the choices provided by political elites and parties.

The gradual rise in individual-level volatility can be explained by the combination of two other long-term trends, the evidence for which is set out in Chapter 4.

The first long-term trend is the gradual and sustained reduction in the strength and number of people identifying with political parties over time—a process widely referred to as 'partisan dealignment' (Särlvik and Crewe 1983; Dalton 2000). As people have become less attached to political parties—both in terms of the number of party identifiers in the electorate and the weakening strength of the attachment of those who still identify with a party—the ballast in the party system has been steadily eroded. Partisan attachments have the effect of stabilizing the party system. Conversely, partisan dealignment has the effect of destabilizing the party system. A system with strong social identities built around parties tends to reproduce itself for several reasons. First, in an electorate with strong party attachments, a higher proportion of voters have a default vote choice that they are likely to revert to at each election. In other words, voting can have a habitual element (Plutzer 2002), with voters demonstrating a 'homing instinct' towards a foundational party over consecutive elections (Butler and Stokes 1969b). Second, party identifiers tend to socialize their children into their own partisanship (Zuckerman, Dasovic, and Fitzgerald 2007), so that successive generations have some of the distribution of partisan leanings to their parents. This gives the system stability over the long term, such that there is 'memory' in partisanship, inherited over time. Third, partisan identification acts as a perceptual filter, which means that voters interpret political information through the prism of their pre-existing political commitments (Lodge and Taber 2013), making the system less vulnerable to disturbances, such as negative performance or policy change. Partisans are more likely to reject information that conflicts with their prior beliefs, by rejecting the message or the source (Zaller 1991; Zaller 1992), and attribute responsibility for problematic outcomes to other political actors or institutions (Tilley and Hobolt 2011). Indeed, some scholars see this filter as the primary way in which partisanship affects vote choice (Bartels 2002). Weaker party identifiers and those with no party identity, on the other hand, are more likely to consider other party choices because they are open to information from other parties. As partisan dealignment means there are now more people in Britain with weak attachments to political parties, or no attachment to political parties at all, this partisan dealignment creates the conditions for the system to become unstable because more people are available to switch between parties.

The second long-term factor is the increase in the proportion of votes won by parties other than Conservative or Labour between 1950 and 2015, which we refer to as fragmentation.

As the electorate has become increasingly 'dealigned', minor parties have seized opportunities to gain votes from a more fluid and available electorate. As we showed in Chapter 2, the share of the vote won by the two major parties declined steadily from the 1960s to 2015. However, 2017 saw a sharp increase in the two-party share of the vote and a drop in fragmentation. The fragmentation of votes in British elections has directly affected volatility because, compared to the major parties, smaller parties struggle to retain voters from one election to the next. We demonstrate the extent to which this is the case in Chapter 4. The fact that major parties are more likely to retain their voters successfully between elections is the reflection of a number of important and continued stabilizing features of British politics which create inertia and help maintain the party system over time, albeit with some major disturbances. Increasing returns to electoral success stem from the institutionalized advantages enjoyed by established larger parties including high start-up costs for new parties, funding disparities, differential media coverage, and advantages bestowed by the electoral system (Pierson 2000). Success leads to success, especially in the British majoritarian electoral system, as larger vote shares are rewarded with a disproportionate number of seats. This in turn provides a strong disincentive to 'waste' votes by supporting smaller, less viable alternatives (Duverger 1954). Major parties also have a significantly greater likelihood of being able to form a government, creating further incentives for voters to support them at the expense of minor parties (Green, Fieldhouse, and Prosser 2015). Additionally, major parties enjoy informal advantages of an established support base. By virtue of having more supporters and partisans, major parties benefit from habitual voting and the passing down of partisan preferences from generation to generation through political socialization, as discussed above. Similarly, this greater support base provides advantages in terms of interpersonal influence (Huckfeldt and Sprague 1995), mobilization (Rosenstone and Hansen 1993,) and normative pressures (Fieldhouse and Cutts 2016). Smaller parties have to overcome all of these built-in advantages that favour their larger rivals in order to attract voters and retain them in subsequent elections. Even those voters who are convinced that a smaller party is viable in one election are likely to grow disillusioned when success does not materialize, and then switch back to a more viable option in subsequent elections.

Taken together, these factors make it difficult for minor parties to attract and retain voters, and therefore to sustain their support from one election to the next. Because of the structural disadvantages facing minor parties, increased votes for minor parties in one election tends to lead to an increased level of volatility in subsequent elections, as smaller party voters are more likely to switch parties. In Chapter 4 we show that this effect is substantial, accounting for a large portion of the increase in individual-level volatility since 1964.

Partisan dealignment and fragmentation change the system in more ways than just the total amount of switching between elections. A dealigned electorate is one that has greater *potential* to respond to stimuli and political disturbances— the storms and headwinds of politics—because there are fewer stabilizing factors for these stimuli to overcome. The system has less inertia. Similarly, because minor party voters already have a high probability of switching between elections, a larger number of minor party voters means a larger pool of voters who are more vulnerable to the effect of shocks and other stimuli. This might be seen as normatively desirable, creating a closer connection between political actors and the mechanisms of electoral accountability. However, a more tumultuous and unpredictable electoral environment may have its own risks, particularly where parties miscalculate the likely outcomes of their policy offerings and where voters find it harder to anticipate the likely outcomes of collective voting decisions.

Our analysis in Chapter 4 suggests that volatility cannot be completely explained by partisan dealignment and fragmentation, however. This raises the question of how else we might explain the increase in vote-switching and the dramatic changes in British elections over a short period of time. An increase in the willingness of voters to switch parties is not sufficient to explain dramatic changes in support for particular parties at particular elections. To understand these outcomes, we need an explanation that can account for the choices that the more volatile electorate makes in a particular election. Furthermore, we need to explain how the long-term destabilization of the electorate provides the context for such shorter-term dynamics to have greater effects.

3.2 Electoral shocks

In economics, international relations, and public policy studies, systems undergo sharp changes in outcomes in response to shocks. In the absence of shocks, systems are expected to function in a relatively stable and incremental way. Economists state that system shocks 'interrupt and disrupt the process of economic growth and development' (Martin 2012, 3), leading to long-lasting societal implications and changes in public policy (Rodrik 1999). In international relations, system-level shocks can be necessary prerequisites for changes to otherwise intransigent tensions. 'A political shock is a dramatic change in the international system or its subsystems that fundamentally alters the processes, relationships, and expectations that drive nation-state interactions' (Goertz and Diehl 1995, 31). In public policy, major policy change comes in bursts in response to pressure accumulating, external events, or shocks, known as a process of 'punctuated equilibrium' (Baumgartner and Jones 1993). Shocks change policy paradigms and can have permanent, wide-reaching consequences (Hall 1993). These ideas can be very usefully introduced to the study of party systems and elections.

In electoral politics, we propose that electoral shocks are the disturbances that have the ability to lead to substantial and dramatic increases in vote-switching, and therefore to changes in the party system. They may alter the political system in the short-term, and potentially the long-term—cutting through 'normal' political ebbs and flows, loyalties, and levels of public inattention to politics. They are not, however, defined *by* their consequences.

Electoral shocks are unavoidable, high-salience changes or events that can prompt large sections of the population to update their political evaluations and party preferences. This is in contrast to more stable, 'normal', or uneventful periods in politics in which voters have fewer reasons to update their partisanship and when new information can be more readily rationalized into pre-existing beliefs. Shocks cannot be as easily avoided via partisan selection mechanisms of information and social networks, or through partisan rationalization. This is consistent with work showing that major economic shocks alter the relationship between partisanship and economics. In stable economic periods, economic evaluations are more likely to be endogenous to party preferences, driven by party attachments and voting behaviour. In times of exogenous economic shocks, however, partisanship is more likely to be updated in response to economic changes (Chzhen, Evans, and Pickup 2014).

A definition of electoral shocks

A electoral shock has the potential to be recognized even by people who might otherwise rationalize, ignore, or attribute responsibility to someone else (Green and

Jennings 2017). Electoral shocks are not the minor everyday routine political happenings such as misdemeanours, resignations, speeches, or announcements. A major event or discontinuity must be highly salient and relevant to party choice and competition to have the power to cut through traditional loyalties, inattention to politics, and cause dramatic political change. Shocks can cause people to re-evaluate their political preferences in a way that everyday politics should not. This means that shocks can lead to substantial volatility, shifting people out of their habitual voting behaviour.

Electoral shocks might not always have major consequences in terms of abrupt system-wide electoral change. They could occur within a very stable system that is resistant to the effects of external shocks, they could reinforce rather than cut across stable patterns of electoral choice, and their effects might be dampened by the failure of political actors to capitalize on them. If the concept of electoral shocks is to be theoretically and analytically useful, they must not be defined by their consequences. However, electoral shocks are *necessary* conditions for abrupt system-wide changes to occur alongside the broader context of a system less constrained by party loyalties.

In terms of their defining characteristics, electoral shocks: 1) represent a sharp change to the status quo outside the normal course of politics; 2) are highly salient and noticeable over prolonged time periods, and 3) are relevant to party politics.

We now elaborate on these properties in greater detail.

1.   Electoral shocks are an abrupt change to the status quo. They are not necessarily exogenous to the party system, but they are more than simply the outcomes of normal everyday politics. They represent a significant and often unanticipated change.

Electoral shocks are extraordinary political events or changes, representing a departure from the status quo. Many such events might be described as 'exogenous', originating outside of the political system. In reality, however, most events are not entirely exogenous. For example, wars, economic recessions, and major political crises usually have origins inside the political system, reflecting the coming together of a complex array of decisions made by political actors. However these events frequently transpire because of external factors or contingencies that could not be foreseen. They are therefore not the inevitable outcome of the usual, more predictable pattern of policymaking and politics. Such events may be considered electoral shocks. In contrast, where events or decisions are within the normal gamut of party politics we should not consider it a shock. This also helps explain why we define shocks as abrupt changes to the status quo. Because their origins are at least partly exogenous it is possible to determine when they occurred: there is a discrete point in time at which a shock takes place, and whilst the effects of an electoral shock are likely to be prolonged, they will also be immediate.

2.   *Electoral shocks are manifest over prolonged time periods and are highly salient: they have the potential to be noticed and recognized even by people who do not have much interest in politics, and by people who might otherwise select into information that fits their partisan beliefs and preconceptions. Electoral shocks are very difficult for voters and politicians to ignore.*

Most political ups and downs are little recognized by the public. As hard as it may be to believe for people who are fascinated by politics, most people do not know the outcomes of major political negotiations, who is in the cabinet, and many do not understand the major policy shifts of political parties, what parties stand for, or what parties are focusing on in their election campaigns. Some people may be able to recognize party leaders in only a superficial and cursory way, relying on rumours and the occasional story to form an impression. However, there are other moments in politics and in public life that are inescapable. They permeate public discourse and reach beyond the Westminster bubble. Such moments have the potential to shape public opinion, even fundamentally so. For something to effect a major change in the public, it has to be recognizable and more than a 'blip' in the public's consciousness. As a result of being both substantial and persistent, shocks reach large numbers of people and they have the potential to create significant shifts in electoral behaviour. That is to say, they register in public opinion. They are also impossible for parties to ignore. Under normal conditions, political actors can frequently choose which issues to emphasize and which to ignore, usually opting to draw attention the issues that they 'own' (Petrocik 1996). However, electoral shocks are sufficiently salient that political actors are forced to engage with them even if they are electorally disadvantageous (Mader and Schoen 2018). Electoral shocks are highly salient and noticeable, and have the potential to change partisan attachments, party support, and to cut through public discourse in a way that regular events do not.

3.   *Electoral shocks are politically relevant and have the potential to change how parties are perceived and therefore to (re)shape the party system.*

Something could happen in a country that is hugely significant, and also extremely salient, but it might not be political or relevant to party choice. However, for a shock to be relevant to a *party* system, it has to be party political in nature, or potentially party political in nature, enabling political parties to compete around it and for vote choices to be swayed on the basis of it. Electoral shocks must, then, be changes that have the potential to impact on the party system because they affect how voters evaluate or feel about different parties.

To see the need for these three requirements, consider the following events that lack each one of the three criteria, and which we would not therefore classify as electoral shocks.

We could have a situation where there was an event or change that represented a sharp change from the status quo and was political, but failed to become salient. The establishment of the UK Supreme Court might be such an example. This was an important and abrupt constitutional change that almost entirely failed to register with the general public and had no apparent party political impact. It became temporarily salient in the media in 2017 when the Supreme Court ruled that an Act of Parliament was required to authorize withdrawal from the European Union, but in 2017 it did not remain noticeably salient over a sustained period or cut through public inattention to politics. In this period the Supreme Court did not penetrate the public consciousness and consequently its establishment was not an electoral shock.

We could also have a situation where a political event or change was highly salient but does not represent a sharp change in the status quo. Such events reflect the normal in-and-outs of regular party politics and do not fundamentally alter how parties are perceived in terms of what they stand for and how competent they are. For example, Theresa May's ill-considered 2017 manifesto commitment concerning the funding of social care which was labelled a 'dementia tax' falls into this category. It could also apply to popular policies such as new commitments to increasing NHS funding, to changes in party leaders, and to election campaigns. In each, the event or development is political and salient but does not represent a sharp change to the status quo. There are other examples that might be more borderline in terms of definition. While the choice of party leaders reflect changes within a political party, and often bring shifts in party policy, they can usually be considered a direct consequence of everyday party politics. The rise and fall of Margaret Thatcher were highly salient and politically relevant, and marked a clear change in policy direction. However, it is arguable whether Thatcher brought about—as opposed to reflected—fundamental changes in the nature of British politics. Similarly, the election of Jeremey Corbyn to Labour's leadership in 2015 had substantial effect on electoral politics in Britain. While the unusual circumstances of his election[1] mean that this might plausibly be considered a shock, the circumstances which enabled his victory originated from within the Labour Party. His election to the leadership should therefore be considered part and parcel of normal party politics and of the regular shifts in policy and political representation that entails. A change in leader or policy might have very large effects on electoral outcomes, but these are better understood through existing frames of analysis such as spatial and valence politics. This highlights that the abrupt change criteria does not merely mean that an event or decision changes something, but that the change is atypical and does not arise from the normal course of politics.

---

[1] Corbyn was elected leader in 2015 by a large majority of the membership vote. However, he had struggled to muster up the thirty-five nominations he required from the Parliamentary Party following Ed Miliband's resignation. Contemporary reports suggest he managed to secure sufficient nominations with the support of some who wished to ensure a contest that represented the full spectrum of voices in the party but did not expect him to win.

A third example would be a situation where an event was highly salient and represented a sharp change in the status quo but does not link to party politics. A clear-cut example of such an event would be if England (eventually!) won the World Cup. Such an event would be unavoidably salient and, at least in terms of national self-image, might be a large change from the status quo. But no party's fortunes are highly linked to the England team's performance, so it would not be an electoral shock.[2] A more borderline example would be the death of a monarch. This would again be hugely salient and represent a large change in the status quo for the national experience. However, while there is an obvious political element to the monarchy, the current party system and state of public opinion provides no immediate way for the death of the monarch to translate into electoral consequences. The death of a monarch is a political event but not a party political event.

In reality, of course, the three components of shocks are usually overlapping. Furthermore, the archetypal shock clearly and unambiguously fulfils all three criteria, but shocks can vary in their size and significance. Change becomes salient because it is so significant; the larger and more consequential the change, the more it becomes worthy of media attention and public attention. Public salience provides an imperative for political parties to compete on something that matters to large groups of voters, with the potential to become party political. Shocks may arise because of political decisions—or at least be painted as the responsibility of politicians—being, therefore, inherently party political in nature. However, events should not be considered shocks unless they exhibit all three characteristics; each are necessary conditions but none are sufficient on their own.

Our definition of shocks requires a higher threshold of change than has been used in the existing political science literature. Researchers of presidential and prime ministerial approval have used the term 'shock' to denote a wide range of events that leads to an interruption to a time-series, with simple and direct subsequent effects at the ballot box (Mueller 1970, e.g.; Kernell 1978; Ostrom and Simon 1985; Nadeau et al. 1999). In the US, Kernell (1978) demonstrated the effects of the Korean War, the Vietnam War, the economy, Watergate, and international 'rally' events on presidential approval. In the UK, the Falklands War, the poll tax, the Exchange Rate Mechanism (ERM) currency crisis, Major's reselection as Conservative prime minister, the Iraq War, have all been defined as shocks (Clarke and Lebo 2003; Green and Jennings 2017; Green and Jennings 2012). It is certainly true that some shocks in the existing literature would qualify as electoral shocks under our definition, for example, major economic crises and recessions, and the Watergate crisis.

---

[2] Some studies have claimed spillover competence effects of seemingly unrelated issues such as shark attacks and sporting outcomes (Achen and Bartels 2016; Healy, Malhotra, and Mo 2010). However, these results have not been replicated in subsequent studies (Fowler and Hall 2018; Fowler and Montagnes 2015) and are not likely to be major drivers of electoral outcomes.

It is important to reiterate that shocks are not defined by their electoral outcomes. Even if a shock moves voters, it may not affect aggregate outcomes depending on what other flows happen in that election, which could counteract the aggregate level outcome of shocks. A shock may be responded to successfully by the parties in the system, political entrepreneurs may fail to mobilize effectively in response to the shock, or voters may be too attached to their current parties to be moved by the shock. We expand on the contingent nature of shocks in section 3.6 of this chapter. But first, we illustrate the concept of electoral shocks with the five examples of the electoral shocks which shaped the outcomes and voting behaviour in the 2015 and 2017 British general elections. We discussed, above, the properties of shocks, and some cases that we would *not* categorize as shocks. Here we summarize five shocks in recent British politics that *do* possess the properties of electoral shocks.

3.3 Five electoral shocks in recent British politics

The following examples illustrate considerable variation in their nature but each meets our definition. We will demonstrate in later chapters (5, 6, 7, 8, and 9) how each of the following shocks has fundamentally reshaped the outcomes of the recent 2015 and 2017 British General Elections, the ways in which they have done so, and also how the underlying trends in destabilization have combined with these electoral shocks to create dramatic outcomes.

1. The EU immigration shock

The first shock we consider is the rapid rise and sustained level of immigration to the UK, particularly following the 2004 accession of ten new EU member states whose citizens suddenly enjoyed freedom of movement to the UK. EU migration reflected a sharp change from the status quo because it very substantially increased the flow of migration into Britain, representing a step-change in immigration policy. It also disrupted the traditional pattern of thermostatic policy-making and public opinion that had previously characterized UK immigration policy (Jennings 2009). When public concerns about immigration had been high in the past, governments tended to tighten immigration rules to bring numbers down. Despite Conservative promises to do so again, however, freedom of movement within the EU prevented any meaningful steps to reduce migration while remaining in the EU. In essence, the UK government was unable to control EU immigration or manage its speed, which became politicized in public and political debate. This *electoral shock* was highly salient due to the corresponding rise in media coverage of immigration, and in turn immigration routinely topped the list of most important issues stated by the public. Immigration from the EU was party political in nature due to: 1) the existing party competition over immigration and the willingness of the Conservative Party to use the issue against the Labour government; 2) the linkage of immigration to the long politicized issue of EU membership which had spawned two new challenger parties in the 1990s (UKIP, and formerly the Referendum Party) and; 3) the political campaigning of a charismatic radical right leader, Nigel Farage, who was well placed to capitalize on the EU immigration issue at the head of the already ascending party of UKIP.

2. The Global Financial Crisis

The second shock that reshaped British politics was the 2007–8 Global Financial Crisis, and the subsequent Great Recession. An economic crisis inevitably involves a change in the status quo as it directly affects the lived experience of the population in significant and far-reaching ways. It also led to a sharp, long-lasting, and important shift in policy—austerity—which was justified on the grounds of reducing the level of national debt and the government's budget deficit. The Global Financial Crisis and Great Recession were hugely salient, both through media coverage at the time, the strong sense of outrage over the failure of banks, the unaccountability of financial institutions that were 'too big to fail', and their direct effects on the economic well-being of British citizens. These concerns were also salient politically, providing the backdrop and justifications for political competition, blame attribution, and policy shifts. An economic crisis is inevitably linked to party politics because the economy is one of the most important ways that an incumbent government is judged, and also because of the ways in which all parties responded. The crisis was clearly an electoral shock in the 2010 election, but its impact persisted through to 2015, as we demonstrate in Chapter 6.

3. The Conservative and Liberal Democrat coalition

The third shock that shaped British politics was the Conservative and Liberal Democrat coalition formed in the wake of the 2010 election that delivered a hung Parliament. The coalition represented a sharp departure from the type of government most British voters had ever experienced, and a major disruption in the image of the Liberal Democrats, and hence to the nature of party choices available to voters. The Liberal Democrats had primarily been seen as an anti-Conservative, centre-left party, with the majority of its supporters falling attitudinally closer to Labour than the Conservatives (Russell and Fieldhouse 2005). Most people who expected a coalition would have expected the Liberal Democrats to govern more naturally with the Labour Party. In the space of one week, the Liberal Democrats abandoned this position, enabling a government led by a party that the majority of its supporters strongly opposed. The coalition also fulfils the salience and party political elements of the shock definition. A coalition government was not hugely unexpected in 2010. A coalition formed of the Conservatives and the Liberal Democrats, however, was a surprise. It was a huge news story, announced with great fanfare and sustained for five years of media attention. By virtue of being unusual and a different type of government to what people were accustomed to, it was certainly noticeable to the general public, and Nick Clegg, the Liberal Democrat leader, was a high-profile deputy prime minister. In short, if you knew one thing about the Liberal Democrats during this time period, it was likely to be that they had entered into a coalition with the Conservatives.

4. The Scottish Independence Referendum

The fourth shock that shaped British politics happened in Scotland. Since the advent of devolution in 1999, the SNP had been making inroads with Scottish voters in their campaign for Scottish independence. This culminated in a referendum on independence in September 2014. On the face of it, the outcome of the referendum was not a major change: the pro-independence 'Yes' side achieved 45 per cent of the vote, lost the referendum, and Scotland remained part of the UK. However, the referendum itself was a major departure from normal Scottish politics. It united the two major parties, Labour and the Conservatives, behind a common cause (the Union); it placed a high-stakes electoral choice into a binary decision, and in so doing demonstrated and deepened an existing schism in the Scottish electorate. It was unquestionably salient and unavoidable in Scotland, as well as throughout the UK (to a lesser extent). It permeated political and cultural life in Scotland for a prolonged and intense period, and it culminated in an exceptionally high level of participation, with an 84.6 per cent turnout. Finally, the independence referendum was clearly a party political issue given that the parties all took positions on independence on one side or the other, making it easy for voters to link their positions on independence to party politics.

5. The Brexit referendum and outcome

The final shock should come as no surprise: the 2016 EU referendum and the vote for Brexit. As with the Scottish independence referendum, the EU referendum exposed and accentuated visceral divides. The EU referendum was clearly a party political event: the referendum was called by the Conservatives to head off internal dissent and compete against UKIP, although the referendum campaign did not fall along party lines. The vast majority of Conservative, Labour, and

Liberal Democrat leadership opposed Brexit (although Labour's leader, Jeremy Corbyn, was naturally more Eurosceptic), as did the bulk of their MPs. Similarly, most of the smaller parties—the SNP, Plaid Cymru, and the Greens—lined up on the pro-Remain side. Only UKIP was united as a party behind the Leave campaign. There were, however, significant divisions *within* the two main parties: the official Leave campaign was headed by prominent Conservatives MPs, including Boris Johnson, and a small number of vocal Labour MPs launched a 'Labour Leave' campaign.

The referendum campaign was divisive and highly salient, but so was the aftermath of the referendum. The Conservatives, with a new leader who had supported Remain (Theresa May), almost universally threw themselves whole-heartedly behind Brexit (with some notable but more peripheral exceptions). Labour maintained a position of studied ambiguity, adopting a softer, more critical version of Brexit, following a brief period of infighting between Corbyn and the Parliamentary Labour Party which was resolved in Corbyn's favour. The Liberal Democrats, the SNP, and the Greens continued their opposition to Brexit. Suddenly, finding itself without a clear purpose, UKIP was engulfed in internal conflict. Since the outcome of the referendum, the trials and tribulations of the government's negotiations with the EU dominated the news cycle. The EU referendum and its aftermath are inescapable, enduring, and very high in salience. Brexit is perhaps the most vivid and stark example there is of an electoral shock.

Each of these examples is of special interest to us because of their proximity to the election outcomes in 2015 and 2017. However, this does not mean that earlier shocks did not have any impact on previous elections, or that shocks have not always been important drivers of volatility and election outcomes. What is particularly important now, as we discuss presently, is that shocks are taking place within an electorate that also exhibits a greater propensity for volatility and sensitivity to shocks. That combination of underlying volatility and shocks is necessary to understand the outcomes of recent elections, the increasing level of switching and system volatility, and the vulnerability of the British party system to future disruption.

3.4 How electoral shocks work

We identify three mechanisms through which shocks drive electoral behaviour. This is not to say that the way in which shocks shape electoral behaviour can be easily divided into separate categories. They typically work through a combination of multiple interacting mechanisms. However, these categories help us theorize more clearly about the combinations of ways in which shocks can shape election outcomes.

Salience

Parties and voters have policy positions, or potential positions, on a wide range of issues, but only a few of these are crucial in any particular electoral choice. However, a shock can change which of these issues a voter attaches weight to and how clearly they perceive the positions of the parties on the issue. The 'non-ignorability' of shocks makes them cut through other concerns and attachments, changing voters' views of what is important in politics. Any major high-profile disruption to politics has the potential to alter the relative importance of issues (or issue dimensions) to electoral choice.

The effects of salience on the factors that voters prioritize in their vote choice are well established on a wide range of issues. When issues become more salient voters tend to become better informed about those issues and about the parties' positions on them (RePass 1971). As a result, those issues are given greater weight in a voter's calculus (Green and Hobolt 2008). Voters have a wide variety of views on issues that make it hard for any party to simultaneously satisfy their preferences on all fronts. Parties therefore find it advantageous to downplay certain issues or maintain constructive ambiguity over what their position is (Somer-Topcu 2015). When an issue is highly salient, however, this ambiguity is harder to maintain: voters will make greater efforts to obtain information about the issues they see as most important. The media will also make greater efforts to pin down a party's position on a salient issue and communicate this to voters, while opposing parties may take the opportunity to convey negative information about their competitor's position on the issue. Ambiguity is a harder strategy to follow when an issue is highly salient, although as we discuss in Chapter 9, this is arguably the strategy adopted by Labour in 2017 with respect to Brexit. Consequently, when an issue is salient, parties are more likely to adopt the priorities of the electorate (Budge and Farlie 1983) and manage policy positions and campaigns accordingly.

Several of our shocks work through salience to an important degree. The sustained high levels of media coverage about immigration acted as a salience shock which increased the weight of immigration attitudes in the vote calculus. The shock had further reverberations, of course, when the Conservative Party responded to the rise of UKIP by promising to call a referendum on EU membership if they won the 2015 election (which they then did). The Scottish independence referendum was a salience shock insofar as it increased the weight that voters placed on their views on Scottish independence in their vote choice in 2015 and, to a lesser extent, in 2017. However, as noted above, salience shocks also affect the clarity of positions taken by parties: by making the position of parties clearer on the issue of independence, where some—most notably Labour—might have preferred to have maintained ambiguity to avoid splitting their base over the issue. As with the Scottish independence referendum, the EU referendum represented a salience boost to the issue of EU membership and the result of a vote to leave the EU guaranteed that this salience would remain high and hugely politically significant for years to come.

Party image

Shocks may fundamentally alter the image of a political party regarding who and what it represents, altering the effective choices available in the party system. We discussed above how voters may seek and gain greater clarity on party positions when shocks make issues and evaluations more salient. Shocks can also reshape the way a party is perceived with respect to what it stands for and which groups' interests it represents. This can happen via a number of different routes, each of which causes a sudden and fundamental change to a party's image and its purpose to voters. First, by revealing or emphasizing a new or previously obscured position on an issue, a shock may alter *what* a party is perceived to stands for with respect to issues and ideology. Second, and relatedly, any such change may lead to a change in *who* a party represents with respect to the social and demographic interest groups it favours. A party image shock can therefore involve a shift in either the social identity of a party or the political identity (or both). For example, Green et al. (2002) described how the enfranchisement of black Americans through the Voter Rights Act of 1965 led to their incorporation into the Democrat Party, bringing about a change in the social imagery of both the Republicans and the Democrats that ultimately led to realignment (Carmines and Stimson 1989). Third, a shock may shift the position of voters on issues independently of (or prior to) any change in the position of political parties, changing the issue distance between different groups of voters and the political parties. A major event, such as the Fukushima nuclear plan disaster, can lead to a change in public opinion on that issue which may in turn lead to a change in the position of political parties (Meyer and Schoen 2017).[3] The extent to which parties respond strategically to such a shift will determine the extent to which such an event affects party support (Mader and Schoen 2018).

In the case of Britain, we can draw on two examples detailed later in this book. First, the choice of a Conservative-led coalition shifted the image of the Liberal Democrats as a vehicle for preventing Conservative rule, and linked the Liberal Democrats to a Conservative-defined agenda. The coalition therefore acted as a party image shock to the Liberal Democrats. It was specifically the coalition with the Conservatives that made the change so dramatic: a coalition with

---

[3] Attitudes of the electorate tend to move quite slowly, whereas parties can change positions quite abruptly, especially in face of a shock. The analyses of shocks presented in this book suggest that shocks are more likely to affect how attitudes and values are aligned with party choice rather than by instigating a change in attitudes.

Labour would not have been as sharp a break with the status quo because it would not have changed the way that the Liberal Democrats were widely perceived. The coalition therefore changed many voters' perceptions of what the party represented. Second, the Scottish independence referendum changed the image of the Labour Party in Scotland. As noted above, while Labour had previously been widely regarded as a primarily working-class, left-wing party, the independence campaign highlighted their identity as a party of the Union, alongside the Conservatives. Many voters, especially those who favoured independence, began to redefine Labour in these terms, leading—as we show in Chapter 8—to mass switching to the SNP.

Competence

Electoral shocks can affect parties' reputations for sound judgement and management. Green and Jennings (2017) outline three consequences of 'competence shocks' for public opinion and electoral choice: competence shocks contribute to the loss of long-standing party reputations on issues, or their 'issue ownership' (Petrocik 1996), parties can suffer a deterioration in their perception of competence overall, and competence can become more electorally relevant. Competence shocks cut through otherwise stable party reputations on issues, causing the public to evaluate the ability of parties to handle and deliver on different issues, including their traditional issues. This is consistent with the ways in which the immigration shock worked (as described in Chapter 5) and the Global Financial Crisis (Chapter 6). The rise in immigration acted as a competence shock against the Labour government—and then the Conservative government—when both were unable to fulfil their promise to reduce net migration to the 'tens of thousands' once they took office. The outcome of the EU referendum had a supplemental effect of removing a lever for Conservative competence on immigration because freedom of movement within the EU meant that they previously had very limited policy tools to reduce EU immigration. The Global Financial Crisis took place under the Labour government and was widely seen as an indictment of Gordon Brown's economic management and Labour's economic policy more generally, particularly—and interestingly—after the 2010 General Election. The damage to Labour's reputation persisted under Ed Miliband, placed Labour in a strategic bind over economic policy in 2015, and created competition over blame for the deficit that went on to damage Labour's performance in the 2015 General Election.

Shocks provide a change in the relevance of different criteria by which voters might make their decisions. Simply, competence shocks make competence more salient to political choice, differentiating parties, making competence a more urgent criterion for voters, and by providing political opportunities to compete around handling and competence. Concerns around immigration—and the handling of immigration—became more salient to electoral choice following the immigration shock, providing UKIP, and latterly the Conservatives, with votes following the Brexit referendum. The effects of Labour's competence on the economy were also enhanced as the parties competed around this problem—and the necessity of different policy responses—throughout the period between 2010 and 2015.

3.5 Shocks as political opportunities

The impacts of electoral shocks depend not only on how they affect voters but also on the responses of political actors. In other words, they are a function of political supply and demand. This means that the outcomes of shocks are not determined solely by the shock, but also by the different ways in which political actors respond to them. Shocks can also have an effect by constraining the policy options open to a party. For instance, a terrorist attack might force a party to change foreign policy in a way it may have preferred to avoid, or a currency crisis might require a government to interfere with financial flows in a way that angers key supporters.

Shocks provide an imperative for parties to compete around newly salient issues. Not only are shocks impossible for voters to ignore, they are also impossible for parties to ignore. However, shocks do not simply create a burden that parties must bear: they also create new opportunities for strategic actors to alter their electoral fortunes. Consider the way in which the EU referendum affected the outcome of the 2017 General Election because the Conservatives—despite choosing the Remain-supporting Theresa May as their next leader—pursued a policy of hard Brexit, promising to leave the single market, and thereby avoiding the commitment to the principle of freedom of movement. This response, combined with the Conservatives' increased perceived competence on immigration, changed the pattern of party choice in 2017, leading many 2015 UKIP voters to defect to the Conservatives.

Shocks affect party strategies and electoral behaviour in ways that are not anticipated, and they also create unpredictability and uncertainty among politicians about how to respond, leaving them struggling to understand why the rules of politics have shifted beneath them. In policymaking, a shock or a crisis creates a sense of urgency and unusually rapid responses, less reliance on experts and more on ideology, but also a high degree of uncertainty (see Fischer, 2015). Such events are often highly technical and complex, meaning the ramifications cannot always be understood, increasing the potential for mistakes (Grossman 2015). Shocks are, by definition, unusual, differentiating them from the normal events of politics for which there are precedents, providing political actors invaluable experience of how to best handle them. While shocks provide new strategic challenges to politicians, the increased demand to *do something* means a range of actions are deemed to be politically necessary. By way of example, Labour and the Conservative pledges to cut net migration can be viewed as actions that were politically necessary, but which backfired given their inability to meet them. Ed Miliband's policy difficulties around austerity were a response to a successful effort to blame Labour for the financial crisis, and especially the level of national debt, and the demand to respond in some way for Labour's previous period of government. Consider again the EU referendum and the Brexit outcome. It might have appeared, on the face of it, that all the Conservatives needed to do in 2016 was immediately get behind the Brexit project and win over the majority of UKIP voters to increase the party's majority under Theresa May. Yet under the surface, the churn in the electorate, Labour's strong performance, combined with the salience of Europe following the EU referendum, meant that a fundamental change happened in 2017 that was not widely foreseen. The outcome was, in part, a product of the Brexit effect (a rise in votes for the two major parties) but it also demonstrated the unanticipated consequences that come with shocks (the loss of the Conservative Party's majority).

If a new issue or dimension becomes salient as a result of a shock, and if parties provide new choices to voters when competing on that dimension, realignment of electoral choice on that issue or dimension could be the result. For this to come about, the impact of the shock must be sufficiently long-lasting and strong enough to overcome the inertial forces we described above. Electoral volatility means that any durable pattern of electoral choice may be unlikely. Without an electoral shock and without differentiated responses from political actors, elections may still produce patterns of support which deviate from normal alignments as a result of regular political competition (Evans and Norris 1999). However, it is also unlikely that an electoral realignment will occur in the absence of an electoral shock.

3.6 Shocks within a volatile system

Earlier in this chapter we highlighted the combination of two destabilizing electoral forces in British politics: the long-term and gradual increase in underlying volatility caused by party-dealignment and party system fragmentation, and the impact of electoral shocks which create additional election specific peaks in switching. Although the elections of 2015 and 2017 were almost certainly unusual in terms of the large number of electoral shocks that preceded them, it is not at all clear that shocks have become more frequent over time more generally. Even if shocks themselves are not more likely to occur now than in the past, there are a number of reasons to expect that the potential *impact* of shocks on election outcomes has grown over time as a result of the weakening of partisan attachments and party system fragmentation.

First, shocks determine which parties gain and which parties lose from vote-switching. Therefore, insofar as shocks favour some parties over others, as the underlying level of volatility increases, the parties profiting from a shock stand to gain more at the expense of the losing parties. Even if the overall level of volatility was unaffected by a shock, the impact might be expected to be greater when the baseline level of volatility (the amount of voter switching we would expect on the basis of long-term trends in partisanship and fragmentation) is higher. In other words, because shocks influence the direction of vote-switching, higher levels of volatility can produce larger electoral swings. Second, as the underlying level of volatility increases, the additional churn created by electoral shocks becomes more likely to lead to marked shifts in electoral outcomes in terms of seats, since parties have a smaller base of voters on which they can rely. In contrast, when the baseline level of volatility is low, any additional vote-switching caused by shocks is less likely to bring about dramatic political change. Third, because unattached voters and smaller party voters have a greater propensity to switch, under most electoral conditions shocks might be expected to affect voters who do not iden-tify with a party—or identify only weakly—more than those that have a strong attachment.[4] In other words, party identification may provide some insulation from electoral shocks. This is consistent with the theories of partisan identifica-tion which argue that party identifiers are less likely to be swayed by new infor-mation or more likely to interpret that information in a way favourable to their own party (Lodge and Taber 2013). An example of the insulating effect of party identification is illustrated in Chapter 9. EU referendum vote had a stronger effect on 2017 vote choice among those identifying strongly with a major party compared to weak or non-identifiers. As suggested above, this insulating effect of party identification may not always hold because some shocks can cut through the stabilizing effect of party identification leading voters to update their relevant attitudes, evaluations, and even partisanship (Green, Palmquist, and Schickler 2002). For example, whilst the collapse of Liberal Democrat support was greater among non-identifiers and weak identifiers, the desertion rate of strong identifiers relative to weak/non-identifiers was similar to that seen in pre-vious elections, but with both strong and weak identifiers defecting at a higher overall level (Chapter 7).

It is important to note that the argument that unattached voters and smaller party voters have a greater propensity to switch does not mean they switch randomly, or willy-nilly. It is only because of some other stimuli that cause them to change their party choice. In normal times this might be driven by changes in voters or parties, such as voter preferences, party offers, or party competence. When a political shock occurs, volatile voters are most likely to react.

---

[4] The direction of this effect is complex and depends on the baseline level of volatility, the size of the shock, and the strength of the effect of party identification on vote choice.

Certainly, there is sufficient academic evidence to conclude that a dealigned electorate will be more likely to respond to political stimuli, and therefore more likely to exhibit responsiveness and switching in response to shocks. As noted earlier, weaker identifiers are less likely to rationalize information, and less likely to exhibit bias in the way they deal with evaluating politics and party policy positions. As a result, weaker attachments to political parties have been found to increase the impact of economic voting when electorates exhibit. Strong partisans are less affected by the ups and downs of economic performance, whereas weak party identifiers are much more so (Kayser and Wlezien 2011) and weaker partisans are more influenced by both issue positions and issue competence (Weßels et al. 2014). As a result, unattached voters have a broader choice set of political parties that they are willing to consider voting for. Moreover, people who have switched parties previously have already demonstrated a greater willingness to consider different and diverse political messages, policy positions, leaders, and priorities. This shortens the cognitive leap required to vote for a rival party.

We described above how increasing returns to electoral success (or positive feedback effects) mean that established parties enjoy institutionalized advantages. Hence, party systems are normally expected to persist, according to the freezing hypothesis of Lipset and Rokkan (Lipset and Rokkan 1967). As Pierson (2000, 258) explained,

Key historical junctures produced major political cleavages. These political divisions became organized into political parties. Once they have surmounted initial start-up costs and fuelled processes of adaptive expectations, these parties are reproduced through time, which generates 'frozen' party systems.

These institutionalized advantages, not least the majoritarian electoral system, still have a powerful effect on bringing the party system back towards equilibrium. This is apparent through the fact that major parties still retain substantially higher proportions of their voters between elections compared to minor parties. Nevertheless, partisan dealignment and fragmentation have weakened the ability of the system to remain in a stable equilibrium in the face of electoral shocks. Electoral volatility in tandem with electoral shocks counters the forces that stabilize the party system. Depending on the balance of forces, rapid change may occur as a result of shocks, because of the underlying vulnerability of the wider system.

3.7 The future of volatility and electoral shocks

It might be tempting to think that volatility could increase inexorably if the fragmenting and dealignment processes that lead to volatility are path dependent, and if shocks inevitably lead to further dealignment and fragmentation. However, this is not what is in fact happening, as we will demonstrate in the remainder of this book. Certainly, an obvious outcome of fragmentation and dealignment is the weakening of the in-built advantages of major parties, and further partisan dealignment could be seen as an inevitable consequence of new cohorts entering the electorate without the partisan identification of their parents. Importantly, however, shocks can lead to disruptions to these processes, as well as the acceleration of existing processes. In other words, shocks have the capacity to reduce fragmentation and increase partisan attachments, as well as the reverse.

Consider the outcome of the 2017 General Election, which delivered the largest two-party vote since 1970 and an abrupt pause, stop, or reversal (we cannot yet know which) in the fragmentation that had taken place up to 2015. The 2017 General Election was still a very volatile election. The total level of switching was very high between 2015 and 2017, though not as high as between 2010 and 2015. However, the amount of switching between the Conservatives and Labour between 2015 and 2017 was the highest on record. The *defragmentation* of the party system between 2015 and 2017 was just as much the result of volatility as was the fragmentation of 2015.

There are good reasons to think that volatility might now drop somewhat in a future election, since mainstream parties are more likely to retain their voters—even if those voters are previous minor party voters—and if more people identify with parties. There was a small hint of such an increase in identification in 2017, but nothing of sufficient magnitude or strength to suggest a major stabilization of support. The period after 2017 was so fraught with political difficulties on all sides that it is also easy to see the trend in partisan dealignment continuing, and while fragmentation has reversed, the electorate still has far lower levels of partisanship than in earlier decades. This means that the impacts of future shocks could be particularly substantial. What we also know, of course, is that a future shock or multiple shocks could happen. Indeed, Brexit is very likely to continue to reshape the British party system, whatever its outcome. It is shaping up to be a very substantial electoral shock. We consider a number of different ways in which the future of British politics might become more stable or unstable in the concluding chapter of this book, considering the possibility of different political identities around Brexit and early evidence for volatility looking ahead.

For now, it is important to note that our explanation of volatility and shocks does not imply that the British party system is on a one-way journey to greater fragmentation. Volatility does not inevitably lead to fragmentation and the processes that have led to volatility are not necessarily irreversible. However, a destabilized party system and more volatile electorate brings with it considerable uncertainty about the future of British elections and politics. It will be particularly responsive—and therefore less predictable—in its response to future shocks. Those shocks seem an inevitable part of the future of British politics.

3.8 Conclusions

Election outcomes cannot be understood without an appreciation of the long-term context in which they take place, and without understanding the major events that precede them. Voters do not decide how to vote in a vacuum of major events and changes that alter the political and electoral calculus. The volatility of the 2015 and 2017 elections did not come completely out of the blue: these tumultuous elections followed a steady increase in vote-switching in British elections that has, until now, been unexplained. In this chapter we explained this volatility by the long-term processes of partisan dealignment and the increasing votes for 'other' parties up to 2015 (fragmentation), both of which we go on to describe in detail in Chapter 4.

Once we account for the long-term trend in volatility and the destabilization of the British party system that results from it, it was not preordained that the vote flows would look anything like the way they did in the elections in 2015 and 2017, or that they would be the size they were. We need an explanation that can account for sharp and sudden changes in electoral volatility and outcomes. In this chapter we set out our explanation combining long-term volatility in the British electorate with the importance and mechanisms of *electoral shocks*; the major, salient political changes to the status quo that may cause substantial shifts in electoral choice.

Shocks work via mechanisms of salience, changes to party images, and perceptions of competence. They provide political opportunities and create an imperative for parties and political actors to respond, meaning that the effects of shocks may be absorbed, or may also create major and long-lasting changes in the electorate, and to elections. They may even lead to 'critical elections', where the basis of electoral choice alters such that realignment takes place between parties and voters. However, our theory of electoral shocks departs from critical election theory (Key 1955; Burnham 1970). Most importantly we do not dichotomize elections into those which are critical and those which are not, nor do we assume that shocks only occur as a precursor to such critical elections. Electoral shocks have the potential to sharply change the patterns of support for political parties at any election, the magnitude of the effect being determined by the nature of the shock, the response of political parties, and the underlying volatility in the electorate.

As such, an explanation based on electoral shocks incorporates explanations based on the competence of political leaders, the functioning of the economy, party and voter positions on issues, the salience of particular issues, and the representation of social groups. A theory of electoral shocks does not make other theories of electoral behaviour redundant: it provides the context to understand why and when they matter. Our explanation of electoral behaviour is, then, very different to one that applies one theory or model to all elections. Not all elections are the same and not all elections can be explained by the same sets of factors.

Electoral shocks have the potential to cause dramatic electoral outcomes under some conditions more than others. We argue that the increasing underlying volatility in the party system in Britain has enabled shocks to become particularly important in the elections that we are studying. The ballast that once maintained a more stable party system has weakened, making the system more vulnerable to the impacts of electoral shocks. Volatility and shocks could lead to the fragmentation of the party system, and they could lead to the defragmentation of the party system. They help to explain the seemingly unpredictable and tumultuous nature of recent British politics and elections.

4

The Rise of the Volatile Voter

Politicians and journalists have long obsessed over identifying the pivotal voters in elections; the 'swing voters' who might actually change which party they vote for. Each party, it is said, must win the swing vote in an election to have a chance of winning a majority. Swing voters have been thought of as a narrow segment of the electorate, those who might be won over by different parties given particular circumstances. Election strategists form profiles of the kinds of people they believe to be swing voters, such as 'Essex Man', 'Worcester woman', or 'Mondeo Man'. They are often thought to be the small but moveable part of an otherwise loyal electorate; a small island of active switchers among an ocean of habitual supporters who parties can count on election after election.

When Butler and Stokes looked at panel data of vote choice in the 1960s, they observed that only around 13 per cent of those who voted in both elections switched their vote choices between elections (Butler and Stokes 1969). They concluded that differential turnout and cohort replacement were the major drivers of electoral change. Slightly over a decade later, Särlvik and Crewe (1983) saw sufficient change (21 per cent of voters switched) that they considered there to have been a 'decade of dealignment'. However, even the switching seen there seems modest when compared to the levels seen in 2015 (43 per cent) and 2017 (33 per cent). Across the four elections from 2005 to 2017, around 60 per cent of voters switched parties at least once.[1] Far from being the minority of the electorate, swing voters—defined as people who switch their support to different parties between elections—now comprise the *majority* of the modern British electorate.

In Chapter 3 we argued that the growth in the number of these 'volatile voters' has increased the potential for electoral shocks to have a significant impact. That is to say, the more voters are prepared to move to another party, the more unstable the party system becomes. In this chapter we focus on the long-term changes that have helped to generate this more volatile electorate. We identify several potential influences on levels of vote-switching between elections. Some of these cannot account for the long-term increase in volatility because they do not follow the same trend over time. One—the increasing ideological similarity between the

---

[1] We calculate this in two ways. First, by taking British Election Study Internet Panel (BESIP) panellists who took all four post-election surveys and voted each time. This gives a stable voters figure of 39 per cent but is based on a sample of just 562 voters. The alternate approach supplements the panel data with vote recall data obtained as soon after the election as possible. This gives a much larger sample of 19,189 voters and a stable voter figure of 45 per cent.

Electoral shocks. Edward Fieldhouse, Jane Green, Geoffrey Evans, Jonathan Mellon, Christopher Prosser, Hermann Schmitt, Cees van der Eijk, Oxford University Press (2020). © Fieldhouse, Green, Evans, Mellon, Prosser, Schmitt, and van der Eijk.
DOI: 10.1093/oso/9780198800583.001.0001

main parties—does help to account for increasing volatility, but only to a modest extent. There are, however, two processes that can account for the substantial increases in volatility over the long term: *partisan dealignment* and *party system fragmentation.*

High levels of partisanship—or party identification—are expected to create a stable basis for vote choice and therefore limit voter volatility (Campbell et al. 1960; Butler and Stokes 1969). Consistent with this idea, we show that long-term partisan dealignment—the weakening of the attachments between voters and political parties—has a very strong impact on the level of electoral volatility. Additionally, and for a variety of reasons (which include institutional advantages and the electoral system), the larger parties tend to retain a greater share of their supporters from one election to the next. This means that the increased fragmentation of the party system in recent years has resulted in more voters switching their vote choices between elections. The success of smaller parties at one election tends to lead to lower overall levels of vote retention at the next election, increasing the amount of switching between elections as the votes for minor parties have increased over time, until, that is, the 2017 General Election.

Partisan dealignment and party system fragmentation only go so far in explaining increases in voter volatility. There remain unexplained increases in volatility in recent elections that cannot be understood without also taking specific events—electoral shocks—into account. In subsequent chapters we therefore focus on the electoral shocks that have led to an increasingly volatile electorate changing its electoral choices to an even greater extent, contributing to further volatility and dramatically shaping the outcomes of the 2015 and 2017 General Elections.

4.1 Partisan dealignment

The British two-party party system was relatively stable in the post-war era, with high levels of partisan identification associated with processes of political socialization and the strong class-based links of the two main parties. This stable system existed with strong party loyalties leading to stable patterns of vote choice. However, one of the best documented trends in British politics has been the decline in the number of people identifying with a political party, and the decline in the proportion of identifiers who have a strong attachment (Särlvik and Crewe 1983; Crewe, Särlvik, and Alt 1977; Dalton 1984).

In the BES, party attachment is measured using questions that ask respondents to say which party they feel closest to, followed up with a question about how strong those feeling of attachment are. Table 4.1 shows the question wordings used in the BES and British Social Attitudes (BSA) surveys. Note that the partisan strength wording changed slightly between the earliest waves of the BES and later surveys. The two series complement each other. The BES surveys provide a

Table 4.1 Party identification question wordings in the British Election Study and British Social Attitudes surveys

BES (1964–70)	BES (1970–present)	BSA (1983–present)
[Q1] Generally speaking, do you usually think of yourself as Conservative, Labour, Liberal, or what?	[Q1] Generally speaking, do you think of yourself as Labour, Conservative, Liberal Democrat, (Scottish National/Plaid Cymru) [in Scotland/ Wales], or what? DO NOT PROMPT	[Q1] Generally speaking, do you think of yourself as a supporter of any one political party? • Yes • No
[Q2 if no at Q1] Well, do you generally feel a little closer to one of the parties than the others? • Yes • No	[Q2 if 'none' at Q1] Do you generally think of yourself as a little closer to one of the parties than the others? • Yes • No	[Q2 if no at Q1] Do you think of yourself as a little closer to one political party than to the others? • Yes • No
[Q3 if yes at Q2] Which party is that?	[Q3 if yes at Q2] Which party is that? DO NOT PROMPT	[Q3 if yes at Q1 or Q2] Which one? DO NOT PROMPT
[Q4 if party given at Q1 or Q3] Well how strongly [party] do you feel: very strong, fairly strong, or not very strongly: • Very strongly • Fairly strongly • Not very strongly	[Q4 if party given at Q1 or Q3] Would you call yourself very strong [party], fairly strong, or not very strong? • Very strong • Fairly strong • Not very strong	[Q4 if party given at Q3] Would you call yourself very strong [party], fairly strong, or not very strong? • Very strong [party] • Fairly strong • Not very strong

time-series covering each election back to 1964. The BSA surveys only started in 1983, but are conducted every year, allowing us to analyse change in the electorate's partisan attachments between elections. The BSA questions consistently receive lower levels of respondents reporting a partisan attachment than the BES questions, likely due to the filter question which invites respondents to state a lack of identity.

Figure 4.1 shows the trend in this strength of attachment among party identifiers since 1964, as well as the percentage with no party identification, using BES data.[2]

---

[2] The party identification strength question wording was changed following the first three BES post-election panels in 1964, 1966, and 1970 and the second set of panels covering 1970 and 1974. This gives us an approximate picture of how much difference the wording makes. Using the original wording, 1970 has strong party identification of 47 per cent, compared with 44 per cent in 1966 and 30 per cent in 1974. Using the revised wording, the 1970 strong party identification figure is 42 per cent. This means that the old wording somewhat overstates the 1970–74 drop in party identification, although

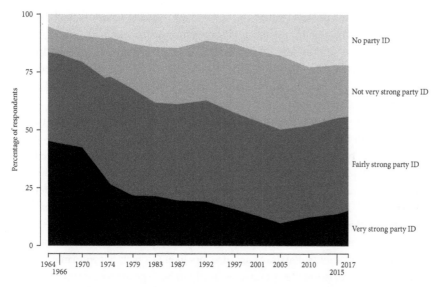

Figure 4.1 Declining levels of party identification and strength of identification

As can be seen in Figure 4.1, the combined size of the 'not very strong' and 'none' categories has increased steadily over the fifty years of British Election Studies. This long-term fall in party identity has mainly resulted from falls in levels of identification with the two major parties.[3] The proportion of the electorate reporting a very strong party identification has also plunged from 45 per cent in 1964 to only 10 per cent in 2005, with a particularly noticeable drop in strong identification in the 1970s.[4] On this measure, partisan identity had reached its nadir by the 2005 election and remained at a similar level since, with the two most recent general elections, 2015 and 2017, witnessing a small increase in partisan identification.

It is clear, then, that the linkage between the major parties and the electorate has weakened in Britain, as it has in many other advanced democracies (Dalton 1984; Dalton 2012b; Scarrow 2004; Clarke and Stewart 1998). If voters do

---

both wordings agree that the drop was large (17 percentage point versus 12 percentage points). We further conducted a survey experiment randomizing the two formulations and found lower levels (8 percentage points) of strong party identification using the post-1966 wording.

[3] Other parties have increased their levels of identification substantially in recent elections as their vote share has increased, but this accounts for a tiny share of all respondents.

[4] The extent of this sharp drop needs to be treated with caution. The strength of party identity was only asked of Labour and Conservative identifiers in the two 1974 elections, which will have had the effect of reducing the number of strong identifiers slightly. Miller, Tagg, and Britto (1986) find a less pronounced drop between 1970 and 1974 in their analysis of surveys conducted by the Conservative Party. In their study, very strong identifiers fell from 42 per cent in 1966 to 37 per cent in 1970, to 33 per cent in February 1974.

not identify with a political party, and if they lack a strong sense of attachment, it is much easier to switch support to another party or not to vote at all (Huddy 2013). It is not surprising, therefore, that partisan dealignment and vote-switching are closely connected phenomena (Blais et al. 2001; Dassonneville, Hooghe, and Vanhoutte 2012; Farrell, McAllister, and Broughton 1994; Johnston 1987; Dalton, McAllister, and Wattenberg 2000; Rattinger and Wiegand 2014).

The relationship between party identification and vote-switching can be understood through the ways in which party identification stabilizes a voter's loyalty to a political party. As we discussed in Chapter 3, partisanship can be viewed as a form of social identity that provides a lens through which voters evaluate politics—a 'perceptual screen' (Bartels 2002; Campbell et al. 1960; Huddy 2001; Butler and Stokes 1969).[5] Because the psychological motivations to maintain one's existing identity are very strong (Lodge and Taber 2013), partisans form judgements about political parties (and leaders, the economy, policy positions, etc.) in line with their prior attachments. Partisans are also less likely to seek out information that challenges their existing viewpoints, less likely to be exposed to contrary views in family and social networks, and less likely to accept information that is contrary to their existing preferences (Lodge and Taber 2013; Zaller 1992). Therefore, an electorate comprising fewer people holding strong partisan identities should lead to greater responsiveness to political events and competition. Not only are people less positively biased towards a preferred party, they are also less negatively biased against another. The result is a greater willingness to switch parties (Rattinger and Wiegand 2014).

Figure 4.2 demonstrates the level of vote-switching for respondents of different strengths of partisanship for each of twelve pairs of consecutive elections (labelled according to the second of each pair) starting with 1964–66 and ending with 2015–17. It replicates Figure 2.4 in Chapter 2, but for each level of partisan identification.

Figure 4.2 reveals three key relationships. First, across all of these pairs of elections, the more someone identifies with a political party, the less likely they are to switch their vote choice between elections. Second, the relationship between party identification strength and vote-switching—if we focus on the gap between the level of switching for each group—has remained broadly consistent over the past fifty years.[6] Third, and importantly, switching is higher in recent elections

---

[5] This view is not unchallenged even among scholars who agree that party identity is best characterized as a form of social identity. Green, Palmquist, and Schickler (2002) argue that apparent evidence for perceptual screens is better characterized as evidence for partisans holding genuinely different values in how they evaluate political events and strong priors about their preferences. Follow-up studies have tended to confirm the perceptual filter model (Bartels 2002; Druckman, Peterson, and Slothus 2013; Gaines et al. 2007; Lodge and Taber 2013), especially for low salience issues (Carsey and Layman 2006).
[6] Vote-switching between 2015 and 2017 was similar for strongly and fairly strong identifiers. This may be statistical variation or may reflect the cross-cutting importance of the EU in 2017 (see Chapter 9).

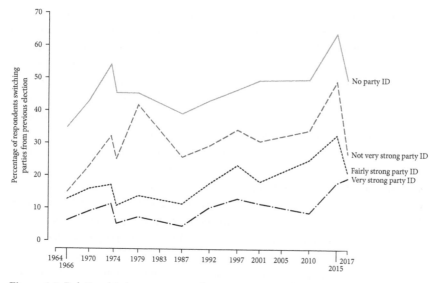

Figure 4.2 Relationship between party identity strength at election 1 and the probability that a voter switches parties at election 2 across different elections (labelled by second election)

within each category of party identification strength. The first two observations, in conjunction with the increase in non-identifiers and weak identifiers we reported earlier, suggest that partisan dealignment may account for at least part of the long-term rise in volatility. The third observation, however, suggests that increased volatility in recent elections cannot be explained by declining partisanship alone: partisan dealignment had, to a large degree, bottomed out by 2005, yet volatility continued to increase and did so even within the different levels of identification, at least until the most recent election in the data series in 2017.

How dealignment works: The role of generational replacement

The key process behind these changes is the replacement of older generations with strong party ties by younger generations with weak or no party ties. Party identification has been described as a long-term attribute of voters that is socialized at an early stage of development (Campbell et al. 1960; Butler and Stokes 1969). If the party identification of parents becomes weaker, so will that of their children, as parents cease to provide partisan cues (Martin and Mellon 2018; Dinas 2013). To put it another way, we would expect the children of the 1960s to be exposed to much more partisan socialization than the children of later decades, simply because the electorate in the 1960s had higher levels of party identification. There is, then, likely to be a 'ratchet effect' in partisan dealignment, with each generation being less likely to be socialized into partisanship than the one before.

To examine this process, we need to separate cohort replacement from within-cohort change.[7] For this we need data that are measured more often than once per election cycle. The British Social Attitudes Survey data provides a useful source, as it is conducted yearly, although the data only go back as far as 1983 rather than all the way to 1964. Using BSA data, Figure 4.3 shows that each new political generation (since those entering the electorate prior to 1964) has entered with lower levels of party identity than the political generation before. Most of these generations have maintained relatively stable levels of party identity once they have entered the electorate. The only exception to this stability is the most recent political generation: those who entered the electorate under the Conservative government since 2010 (we do not show them on the chart as they have only a handful of observed years). This newer generation displays unstable levels of partisanship that at times are higher than the preceding generation. This may be because these voters have been newly enthused by politics in the 2014–16 era, or it may simply be an artefact of the small sample size of voters in this age range.

The significance of generational replacement becomes clear when we decompose the change in party identity into *within-cohort change* and *cohort replacement*. In other words, we consider: what portion of change can be attributed to the

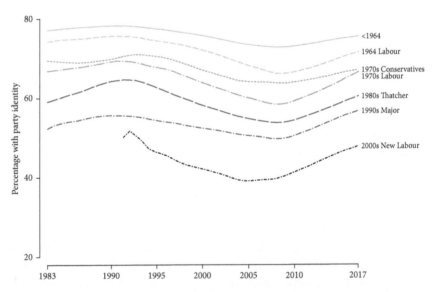

Figure 4.3 Percentage of respondents with any party identification over time for different cohorts (defined by the party in power when the voter reached voting age)

---

[7] By generational replacement we mean the change attributed to the differences in levels of partisan identification between cohorts leaving the electorate (dying off) and those entering as they come of age. Within-cohort change captures the extent to which the level of partisan identification of those in the electorate changes over time. We define a political generation according to the government in power when a person came of voting age.

differences between the average person entering and exiting the electorate, versus changes in the attitudes of people already in the electorate?[8] Figure 4.4 shows the trends in levels of party identity in the BSA, decomposed in this way. The total line (left-hand-side figure) shows the overall difference in party identification in the BSA compared to 1983, the first year the survey was conducted. The trend starts at zero, so the y-axis refers to the cumulative change that has taken place. Party identification declined by around 20 percentage points since 1983 up to 2009 followed by a partial recovery. By 2017, the total fall in party identification was only 9 percentage points compared with the first BSA survey in 1983.

The right hand panel of Figure 4.4 shows the percentage point change that can be attributed to within-cohort change and cohort replacement, respectively. The figure tells us that the increase in non-identification since 1983 has come almost entirely from cohort replacement—that is resulting from the difference between cohorts entering and leaving the electorate. Overall, the difference in partisanship

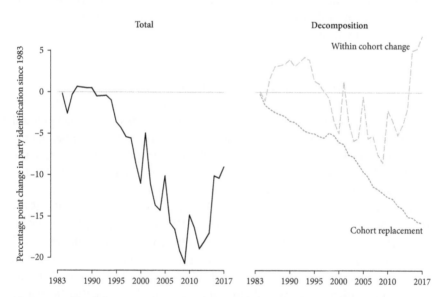

Figure 4.4 Total change in non-PID in BSA and decomposed into within-cohort change component and cohort-replacement component

---

[8] For detail of the equations we use to define within- versus between-cohort variation see the appendix to Chapter 4. Because we define the age cohorts narrowly (in single birth years) and we observe nearly all years sequentially in the BSA, this algebraic decomposition need only assume that there is no within-cohort change for the newest age cohort between the time when they entered the electorate and were interviewed. This approach is similar to that proposed by Firebaugh (1997; 1990). Firebaugh's approach has been criticized for not distinguishing age and period effects (Glenn 2005; Rodgers 1990) in its measure of cohort replacement. However, as Firebaugh (1997; 1990) argues, this critique conflates cohort replacement effects with cohort effects. Although our analysis is not an age-period-cohort (APC) analysis, APC models specified in line with Grasso et al. (2017) find large cohort effects in party identification.

between incoming and outgoing cohorts has contributed 15.8 percentage points towards dealignment since 1983.

From 2014 to 2017, the long-term decline in party identification driven by cohort replacement was somewhat offset by increasing levels of party identification within existing generations, but has so far been insufficient to reverse the overall trend. Within-cohort change shows large but not trending fluctuations year-to-year. In particular, we see large increases in rates of party identification in election years. This fits with the findings of Michelitch and Utych (2018) who found that, across eighty-six countries, levels of partisanship vary by 12 percentage points across the electoral cycle. Interestingly, the last four years of the available BSA data (2014–17) all show higher levels of party identity. This likely reflects the series of high-profile political events (2014 Scottish referendum, 2015 General Election, 2016 EU referendum, and 2017 General Election that took place in this time period). Nonetheless, given the higher partisanship of older cohorts, either existing cohorts will need to become much more partisan, or new cohorts entering the electorate will need to attain the far higher partisanship levels of their grandparents to maintain current levels of partisanship.

Why has partisan identification declined?

There is still the question of how this generational cascade of weakened political socialization was initiated. Previous researchers have suggested a number of possible causes, including the decline of class divisions in British party politics, the ideological convergence of parties, and the rise of a more informed and educated electorate. None of these provide convincing explanations of dealignment.

It has been claimed that class voting has declined since at least the 1970s (Crewe, Särlvik, and Alt 1977; Clark and Lipset 1991; Franklin and Mughan 1978), although this was disputed for many years on the basis that the claim conflated the absolute size of class-aligned voting with the relative propensity of classes to vote for Labour or the Conservatives (Heath, Jowell, and Curtice 1985; Evans 1999b). The evidence of class dealignment became much clearer after the rise of New Labour in the 1990s. Under Tony Blair's leadership, Labour shifted to the centre (Bara and Budge 2001) and focused less on appealing to the working class (Fairclough 2000; Evans and Tilley 2017, ch. 6). This was accompanied by a dramatic decline in MPs from working-class backgrounds (Heath 2015) and a similar fall in the extent to which Labour was perceived as a party that represents the working class. These changes were in turn accompanied by a large decline in differences between the working and middle classes in voting for Labour versus the Conservatives (Evans and Tilley 2017; Heath 2015). However, it is difficult to explain the decline in partisanship as a result of a decline in levels of class voting. A substantial amount of partisan dealignment preceded the onset of the most pronounced period of class dealignment, from 1997 onwards. Also, the partisan dealignment among the working class during the New Labour years does not explain a great deal of the more general downward trend in partisan identification.

Similarly, ideological convergence between the Conservative and Labour parties appears unlikely to explain the long-term decline of partisanship. Political polarization in Britain did not uniformly decline over the time period we are examining. In the late 1960s and 1970, Labour and the Conservatives appeared to be close together, in both their manifesto content and in the perceptions of voters.[9] Polarization then peaked in the 1980s before returning to levels similar to those in the 1960s. While the 2017 election saw a modest increase in the proportion of voters perceiving 'a great difference between the parties', the level has not returned to anywhere near that seen in the 1980s.[10] It is highly improbable that a curvilinear trend can explain a more or less linear decline.

Another influential explanation for the decline in voters' attachments to parties is the growth of a more educated, informed, and critical electorate. The theory of cognitive mobilization predicts that partisan cues should be more important for less educated citizens. Higher levels of education will therefore reduce partisanship because highly informed voters do not require the heuristic or shortcut of party labels (Dalton 1984). The average level of tertiary education has substantially grown among BES respondents since 1964, increasing from around 10 per cent to more than 35 per cent of the population in 2017, a trend which is certainly consistent with this idea. However, the evidence for cognitive mobilization as a cause of partisan dealignment is limited. Dassonneville et al. (2012) find that the aggregate patterns of education and partisan dealignment in Germany align closely, but the individual level relationship is absent or even reversed. Similarly, Berglund et al. (2005) find that the relationship between education and partisanship is not stable over time, and the relationship disappears in some cases once age is controlled for.

These factors do not explain a large portion of the over-time decline in party identity. This can be seen when we model the decline in party identity over the eleven elections between 1964 and 2017 using (pooled) post-election BES cross-sectional surveys. We estimate the impact of convergence (perceived difference between the major parties), cognitive mobilization (educational attainment), and

---

[9] Across this period, the perceptions of BES respondents on the differences between Labour and the Conservatives closely track left–right positioning measured by the Comparative Manifestos Project (Volkens et al. 2015).

[10] We should note, however, that despite the similarity in policy programmes in the 1960s, the two parties were seen as being very different in terms of whose interests they represented. The Labour Party was seen to clearly represent the working class and the Conservatives the middle class—the backbone of political competition at the time. After 1997, when the Labour Party abandoned its distinctive role in representing the working class, the electorate saw it as no longer representing the interests of the working class per se (Evans and Tilley 2017). The role of convergence with respect to social group representation—as opposed to ideology—in the decline of partisanship remains worthy of further investigation.

socialization (parental party identification) on whether a respondent has no party identification. We also control for other variables that, according to the literature, may be linked to party identification, including age, sex, marital status, class, religiosity, union membership, and region. A fixed-effect for each year is used to measure the trend in dealignment before and after adding the explanatory variables.[11] Our model shows that having no party identity is strongly predicted by perceiving Labour and the Conservatives to be similar, by lacking a religion, and by having a parent who lacked a party identity when the respondent was growing up. However, these factors explain relatively little of the over-time trend in partisan dealignment. The effect of education on non-identification is minimal at the individual level and explains none of the over-time trend in dealignment.

Figure 4.5 shows the increase in non-identification, compared with 1964, for each year before and after we account for differences in the explanatory variables. The solid line can be interpreted as the raw (unadjusted) increase in the proportions with no party identification compared to 1964. The dashed line is the remaining difference in each election year after differences in our explanatory variables are taken into account. Figure 4.5 shows that even after all of the potential influences described above are included, we can explain relatively little of the decline in party identity. In the 1980s, when parties were perceived as more

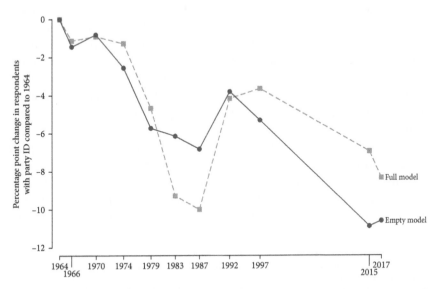

Figure 4.5 Percentage point decline in respondents with any party identity, compared with the level in 1964

[11] See Table A4.1 in the appendix for details of the model. The unexplained difference could be a combination of omitted variables and changes in the relationships between variables and dealignment.

polarized, voters were actually more dealigned than would be expected given the perceived levels of difference between the parties.

While our cohort analysis demonstrates that partisan dealignment has been driven primarily by generational replacement, the reason for this generational change is unclear. Even with the benefits of fifty years of BES data, and drawing on variables that represent the most plausible explanations of the decline in partisan dealignment, we cannot account for that trend. That is to say, we know that new cohorts are becoming less attached to political parties, but this is not explained empirically by party convergence, by cognitive mobilization, or by parental socialization. The cause of partisan dealignment, which is making the electorate more volatile and vulnerable to electoral shocks, is not something we can explain. We can, however, highlight its important consequences. Partisan dealignment is connected with volatility and also with a further source of increasing volatility, party system fragmentation, to which we now turn.

4.2 Fragmentation

In Chapter 2 we described how, alongside increased voter volatility, there has been a decline in the two-party vote share. The corollary of this has been a sharp rise in the share of smaller parties, and an increase in the effective number of electoral parties, calculated using Laakso and Taagepera's (1979) formulation. The two-party share of the vote has declined since the heyday of the two-party system in the 1950s and 1960s, with the lowest two-party shares recorded in 2010 and 2015. This was followed by a sharp reversal in 2017 and a drop in the effective number of electoral parties (see Figure 2.2).

Fragmentation is important for volatility because smaller parties do not typically retain voters to the extent that large parties do. A share of the vote for smaller parties in one election should increase the expected numbers of switchers in the following election. There are a number of reasons why we expect minor parties to struggle to hold onto their voters. They often campaign on a narrower set of issues than major parties, which means a voter may defect when they no longer see one of those issues as salient; their voters tend to have weaker partisan identification; and they often have fewer resources (campaign funding, quality candidates, media coverage, campaigners). While minor parties have been improving on these over time, they still have far less access to resources than major parties in the British system. Most importantly, in a majoritarian system such as that in the UK, there is the danger that minor party votes will be perceived as a wasted vote if the party fails to be competitive locally. There is also a subtle mathematical effect that makes it easier for major parties to retain voters. If we imagine an over-simplified model of voting where voters choose randomly, the larger parties would retain a higher proportion of their voters simply by chance. The Conservatives received 42.4 per cent of the vote in 2017, which means that they would only need to be twice as good at attracting their own previous voters as they are at attracting voters in general in order to reach 80 per cent retention. The Liberal Democrats, by contrast, received 7.4 per cent of the vote and would therefore need to be nearly eleven times better at attracting their own previous voters than voters in general, in order to maintain the same levels of retention.[12] To put it another way, the baseline likelihood that a voter does something common (voting Labour) two elections in a row is relatively high, compared to the probability that a voter does something rare (voting Green) two elections in a row. Insofar as *any* voters tend to make a new decision at each election (rather than sticking with their old vote choice by default and then deciding whether to defect), this will increase the observed retention rates for major parties and reduce the observed retention rates for minor parties.

What is the evidence that minor party voting contributes to electoral volatility? Figure 4.6 shows that the defection rate of Liberal Democrats and other minor party voters has been consistently higher than that of the major parties. Across our twelve election pairs, the Liberal Democrats lose an average of 44 per cent of their voters from the previous election, and 'other' parties have lost 50 per cent of their previous voters. Conservatives and Labour, by contrast, lose an average of 18 per cent and 17 per cent respectively (although this has increased somewhat over time).

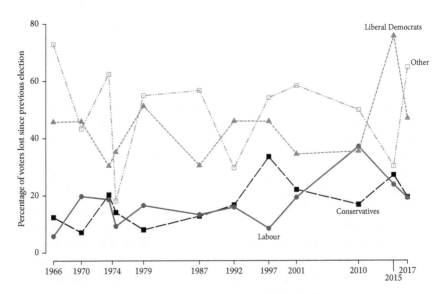

Figure 4.6 Proportion of a party's voters lost in the following election

---

[12] This follows the same logic as a pool effect in intermarriage rates. Blau, Blum, and Schwartz's (1982) study showed that much stronger preferences for in-group marriage are needed to maintain intermarriage in small social groups than large social groups.

Although minor parties are relatively more likely to rely on new recruits who have already shown a proclivity for switching, minor party volatility is not entirely driven by this. Looking across three sets of three elections, minor party voters who had voted for the same minor party in the two previous elections were still more likely to switch parties than major party voters who were voting for the major party for the first time.[13] Defection rates are even higher for new minor party voters, of whom at least three-quarters defected at the next election. This means that a strong minor party performance at the previous election greatly increases the expected level of volatility at the subsequent election. However, minor party voting is not independent of party identity, which is the other main driver of volatility. That is, minor party voters, on average, have considerably lower levels of party identity.

Sources of fragmentation

Fragmentation is linked to electoral volatility, but then we also need to ask the question of why has the party system become more fragmented?

The most obvious (tautological) answer is that major parties have failed to maintain their appeal to supporters. There are a number of reasons this may have occurred. First, political parties have long competed around economic issues since the emergence of the class cleavage following the industrial revolution (Lipset and Rokkan 1967). In Britain, party politics was organized around economic issues of left and right for many years (Heath, Jowell, and Curtice 1985; Evans, Heath, and Lalljee 1996). However, by the late 1990s and early 2000s, non-economic issues such as crime, immigration, and the environment have become more salient. The rise of a second ideological dimension was originally thought to be linked to increases in the prominence of 'post-material' values (Inglehart 1981), which focused on the increased importance of issues such as the environment. However, much of the rise in non-economic issues in Britain is the result of the increased salience of issues at the conservative end of the spectrum, such as crime and immigration (Green and Hobolt 2008). As we argued in Chapter 3, new issues can become salient not just though value change but as a result of a shock: we demonstrate this in Chapter 5 with respect to the increased importance of immigration and Europe.

Whatever the root cause, the rise of new issues is challenging for the major parties because it leads many voters to feel cross-pressured: that is, some voters will prefer one party on economic issues but another party on social or cultural issues. This trade-off is exacerbated by the fact that all British parties and their

---

[13] The three sets of triplets of elections with connected panel data we examine are February 1974–October 1974–1979; 2005–2010–2015; and 2010–2015–2017.

candidates show a strong correlation between their liberal–authoritarian and economic left–right views (r = 0.70) while there is no such correlation for voters (r = 0.04).[14] It is not just the major parties which fail to offer left–authoritarian or right–liberal choices to voters. Even UKIP, the Liberal Democrats, the SNP, and the Green party all offer either left-liberal or right-authoritarian positions. The difference with these smaller parties is that they downplay their economic message while emphasizing the second-dimension issues that are their focus. For example, immediately after the 2015 election, 46 per cent of BESIP respondents were unable to place UKIP on the economic redistribution scale, but only 25 per cent were unable to answer about UKIP's position on the EU integration scale. The rise of new issues has therefore opened up opportunities for new parties to compete around non-economic issues including the environment (the Greens), immigration and Europe (UKIP), and national self-determination (SNP and Plaid Cymru).

A second crucial factor in the failure of major parties to maintain their support is the decline of party identification that we discussed above. As we have already demonstrated, party identifiers are more likely to stay loyal in terms of their vote choices. British voters had strong attachments to Labour and the Conservatives in the 1960s and voted for them in high numbers. Consequently, the decline in partisanship has tended to hurt the major parties more than the smaller parties— simply because they started from a position of relative strength. As we saw in Figure 4.2, higher partisanship tends to reduce vote-switching at the subsequent election. In the 1960s, this protected the votes of Labour and the Conservatives, but subsequent dealignment weakened this protection. However, unlike some of the relationships we demonstrate in this chapter, the relationship between partisan dealignment and fragmentation is a contingent one. As Butler and Stokes (1969) observed, strong inherited partisanship tends to maintain existing electoral alignments. In the 1960s, strong partisanship protected the high vote shares of Labour and the Conservatives, but dealignment removed that protection. However, if smaller parties started with a base of strong partisans, dealignment could just as easily have led to the consolidation of the party system.

A third influence on fragmentation is likely to be the range of parties on offer to voters and how viable they are. The average number of parties standing in constituencies has been increasing, but it is not clear that the simple number of options is the most relevant measure. The mere presence of small parties does not meaningfully increase electoral choices if voters are not interested in them, do not know anything about them, or do not perceive them as having any chance of success. Electoral viability is likely to be crucial. To gain representation in a

---

[14] Correlations based on data from the British Candidate Survey 1992–2015 and BESIP 2014–2017. Left–right and liberal–authoritarian positions of candidates and voters measured using graded response item response theory (IRT) models to generate latent variables for each dimension.

first-part-the-post system like Britain's, new and smaller parties must overcome the fear of electors wasting their votes on parties which have little apparent chance of winning seats in Parliament (Duverger 1954; Franklin, Niemi, and Whitten 1994). In other words, small parties suffer because their supporters strategically vote for larger parties (Ferland 2014). One way that small parties can overcome this is by demonstrating viability by performing well in second-order elections. The Liberal Democrats in Britain have used local elections to demonstrate their electoral viability in particular areas (Russell and Fieldhouse 2005). Similarly, more permissive electoral rules at European Parliament elections lower the cost of electoral coordination, enabling smaller parties to overcome some perceived problems of viability (Prosser 2016b). European Parliament elections have been described as serving as 'midwives' to the birth of new parties in Europe, which subsequently start to play a significant role in first-order elections (Curtice 1989; Ysmal and Cayrol 1996). Examples of this include the French *Front National* who caused a major surprise when they won 11 per cent of the vote at the 1984 European Parliament election and then went on to win 9.6 per cent of the vote and their first seats in the National Assembly in 1986 (Ysmal and Cayrol 1996); and the German Greens (Muller-Rommel 1993) who gained representation in the European Parliament of 1983 (with 5.6 per cent of the vote) and on that basis, one year later, were able to enter the German federal parliament with 8.2 per cent of the vote.

The increasing number of second-order elections in Britain—in particular for devolved institutions and European Parliament—have provided additional opportunities for small parties to establish an electoral foothold, leading to increased small party vote share and fragmentation. The most dramatic example is undoubtedly UKIP's success in 2015 following their first-placed finish in the UK's European Parliament elections, but SNP and Plaid Cymru success was also built on strong performances in devolved elections; and Green success in 2015 was built on the back of strong European performances in 2009 and 2014.

A further important aspect of whether a party can be considered to be genuinely cognitively available to a voter is whether the party is regularly mentioned in the media (Hopmann et al. 2010). We collected mentions of ten parties[15] in nine national newspapers[16] to create an effective number of media parties measure, which is calculated in an equivalent way to the effective number of electoral parties measure (Laakso and Taagepera 1979), substituting shares of media mentions for shares of total votes cast. Figure 4.7 shows that the effective number of media parties has been steadily increasing over this whole time period, indicating

---

[15] Conservatives, Labour, Liberal Democrats, Plaid Cymru, Scottish National Party, UKIP, Green Party, Referendum Party, British National Party, and Respect. For details of the search terms used, see Table A4.3 in the appendix.

[16] *The Mail, Express, Telegraph, Times, Sun, Mirror, Guardian, Independent,* and *Star*.

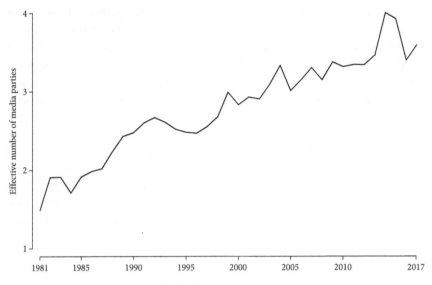

Figure 4.7 Effective number of media parties

that the electorate's media diet includes significant coverage of parties other than Labour and the Conservatives. It is worth noting, however, that while minor parties are receiving more coverage in total, the media attention that *each* minor party receives is still well below that received by each of the major parties. An upward trend does not prove that supply has an effect at the individual level, but the trend is at least consistent with supply having some role in increasing fragmentation.

4.3 Explaining volatility

We have considered how we can explain partisan dealignment and the fragmentation of the party system. We now show how each of these—partisan dealignment and fragmentation—have contributed to the over-time increase in electoral volatility in British elections.

To understand how much of the increased level of switching can be explained through the trends we described, we model the predictors of switching in the British Election Study inter-election panels over the previous five decades. We run a pooled logistic regression model of switching across the eleven inter-election panels for which we have the relevant variables, and include a dummy variable for each election pair.[17] As well as variables testing the impact of our two key factors,

---

[17] We weight each panel to contribute the equivalent of 1,000 cases, so that the larger recent panels do not overly influence the pooled effects. We cluster the standard errors at the election-pair level,

we include a measure of the ideological convergence of the major parties and a number of controls including education, sex, and marital status. To reflect the complex interplay between our key factors we include a number of interactions between these variables which are discussed below.

First, consider dealignment. Based on the evidence above, we expect an increase in the number of people who do not identify with a party (or identify only weakly) to account for some of the increase in vote-switching. However, we would not expect this mechanism to work for people who have a different party identity from the party they voted for at the previous election. In that case, a strong party identity will be pushing people away from their vote choice rather than attracting them to it. There has consistently been around 10 per cent of the British electorate who vote for one party but have an attachment to a different party, so it is important to interact the effects of party identity with an indicator of whether the voter identified with the same party they voted for previously (to avoid dampening the effect of party identity). To assess the impact of dealignment on volatility, we therefore include strength of party identification, whether or not a person voted for the same party as their party identification, and the interaction of these.

Figure 4.8 shows the relationship between party identity strength and vote volatility, by consistency of party identity and vote choice in the prior election (controlling for other factors). Voters who have no party identity at the first election have an average 35 per cent chance of switching to another party by the second election. Among consistent voters, switching falls to just 13 per cent for those with a strong party identification. In contrast, cross-pressured voters, those who voted for a party other than the one they were attached to, are more likely to switch their vote choice if their party identity is stronger (although that difference is not significant). In other words, the impact of partisan dealignment is conditional on consistency of vote and party identification.

To capture the effect of fragmentation, we include a dummy variable representing whether a respondent was a major party voter (Conservative or Labour) in the previous election. Our model tells us that even after accounting for party identification and other predictors of vote-switching, a voter who voted for another party in the first election was 23 percentage points more likely to switch parties in the subsequent election, compared to a major party voter.[18] The fact that people have increasingly voted for parties other than Conservative and Labour is therefore a substantial contributor to overall volatility. To illustrate this, take

but this either hardly affects the standard errors or in some cases shrinks them. This is promising, given that a substantial inflation of clustered standard errors compared with unclustered can indicate model misspecification (King and Roberts 2015). For the full regression tables of these models see Table A4.2 in the appendix.

[18] This figure is based on the marginal effect of voting for a minor party at election 1 on voting for a different party at election 2, accounting for all the other effects in our model.

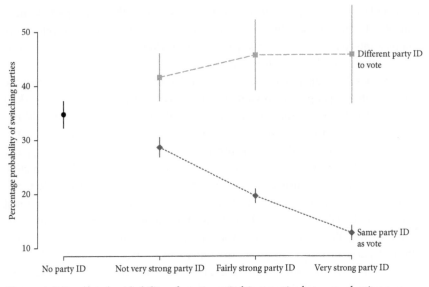

Figure 4.8 Predicted probability of a voter switching parties between elections depending on 1) whether their party identity and vote choice at the first election were the same and 2) the strength of their party identity at the first election. Predicted probabilities derived from logistic regression model fitted to twelve election pairs

two hypothetical elections where the major and minor party retention rates are 83 per cent and 50 per cent, respectively (the average values across all elections). In the first election, the major party share of the vote is 90 per cent (typical in the 1960s) and in the second it is 65 per cent (close to the level in 2010 and 2015). Based on just the different two-party vote shares, we would expect the first election to see 20 per cent of all voters switch parties and the second election to see 29 per cent of voters switch. In other words, a large proportion of the difference in individual-level volatility between the 1960s and 2010s can be attributed to the size of the minor party vote share.

We might expect that ideological convergence has some direct effect on voter volatility for two reasons. First, a reduced distance between two parties reduces the space that a voter has to jump from one to the other, and may therefore allow them to choose between the parties on other grounds than ideological position, such as performance (Green 2007). Second, a reduced distance between the two major parties increases the likelihood that a voter sees neither party as adequately representing their preferences and therefore switches to a minor party. Both of these mechanisms are explanations for why major party voters would be more likely to switch in the presence of convergence. However, neither mechanism would apply to non-major party voters, so we include an interaction of convergence with major party voting, so as not to obscure its effect among major party voters. To explore this we included a variable measuring the perceived difference between the major parties, and interacted this with whether or not the respondent voted for Labour or the Conservatives.[19] We find that while a perception of clear difference between the major parties reduces the likelihood of vote-switching, the effect is absent or even reversed for people who voted for other parties. A Conservative or Labour voter who perceives a great deal of difference between the parties is 9.9 percentage points less likely to switch parties at the next election than a Conservative or Labour party voter who perceived not much difference between the parties (Figure 4.9). However, if the voter supported another party at the first election, then seeing a great deal of difference between Labour and the Conservatives is associated with a 4.9 percentage points *higher* likelihood of switching parties at the next election.[20] In other words, convergence increases volatility for major party voters but has no effect, or perhaps even an opposite effect, among smaller party voters.[21] This makes sense spatially, as major party convergence leaves more space at the extremes for minor parties to compete. However, this means that as the level of support for minor parties has increased,

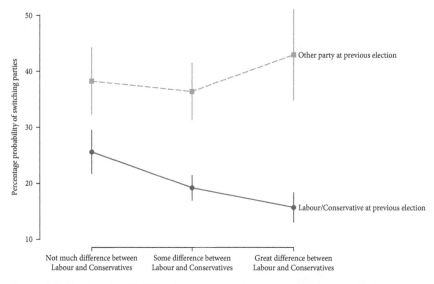

Figure 4.9 Predicted probability that a voter switches parties between elections depending on whether they voted for a major party and the amount of difference they perceive between Labour and Conservatives (pooled model of eleven election pairs 1964–2017)

---

[19] The pooled model predicting vote-switching therefore contains the main effects of having voted for a minor party at time 1, perceptions of major party convergence at time 2, and the interaction of those two effects.

[20] Note that this difference is not statistically significant.

[21] It is not possible to conclusively say whether this is a causal effect or instead reverse causation where identifiers are strongly motivated to see differences between 'their' party and their rivals.

the total effect of convergence on vote-switching has become weaker, dampening the negative effect of convergence on volatility.

We have seen that, over this period, fragmentation and dealignment in combination with party convergence affect the chance of voters switching allegiance between elections. But how far do these factors account for the sharp rise in volatility we documented in Chapter 2? To test this, we use a pooled model predicting party switching across the eleven pairs of elections we model between 1964 and 2017. This model simultaneously accounts for all the factors we have discussed: party system fragmentation, partisan identity, convergence, occupational class, education, and other demographics. We also include separate dummy variables for each election, so that we can estimate how much extra switching we see compared with the base category of the 1964–66 election pair. We then compare this residual level of switching to the actual level of switching that took place. If our model has explained the time trend then this residual level of switching should be substantially lower than the observed increase in switching. Figure 4.10 shows the time trend in vote-switching (measured as the percentage point increase in vote-switching compared with the 1964–66 elections) before and after modelling the variation.[22] The dark line shows the actual increase in switching since 1964 and 1966 and the lighter dashed line shows the residual increase in switching not explained by the model. We can clearly see that the variables included in the

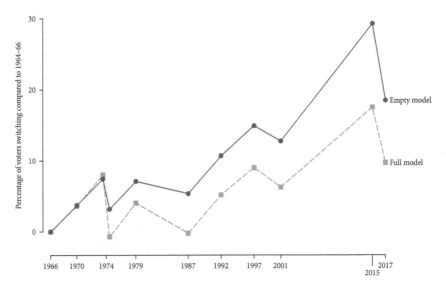

Figure 4.10 Percentage point increase in individual-level voter volatility, compared with the level seen between 1964 and 1966

---

[22] 2005–2010 vote-switching is not included in these models because the difference between Labour and Conservatives question was not asked as part of the online panel in 2010.

model explain a substantial portion of the increase in vote-switching since 1964–66. For instance, in 2015 the level of vote-switching was 29 percentage points higher than the level of switching between 1964 and 1966. However, once we account for how the predictors of vote-switching changed between the two elections, the residual increase in vote-switching falls to 17 percentage points. This means that we have explained around 40 per cent of the difference in vote-switching that was observed in 1964–66 and 2010–15. Thus, the dramatic result seen in 2015 can be partially explained by the long-term trends that have driven British politics, but we also need to look to election-specific factors or shocks to explain the extremely high level of volatility seen in that election.

To see how much each of the separate factors explains the trend over time shown in Figure 4.10 we calculate the percentage reduction in the mean of the marginal effect of all of the election year dummy variables compared to 1964–66, for a series of models. Each bar in Figure 4.11 represents the reduction in the mean marginal effect of the election dummy variables for models which include each factor separately. In other words, it shows what percentage of the area under the solid line in Figure 4.10 that can be explained by each factor. In the full model (model 4), we reduce the average increase in volatility by 43 per cent.[23] Figure 4.11 show that dealignment and fragmentation are the key factors in explaining

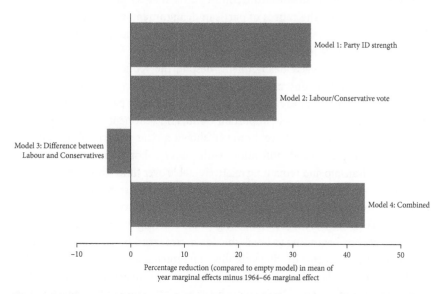

Figure 4.11 Percent of the increase in year marginal effects since 1964–66 explained by different sets of factors in the switching model

[23] As with the dealignment models, the remaining unexplained variation could be some combination of omitted variables and changes in the relationship between independent variables and vote-switching.

the increase in volatility, with convergence actually making the increase more anomalous.[24] Despite the importance of partisan dealignment and party system fragmentation, however, we clearly see several elections (1974, 1997, 2017, and especially 2015) that have large unexplained increases in volatility. As we show throughout the rest of the book in 2015 and 2017, these spikes in volatility, which are not explained by secular trends, are largely attributable to specific electoral shocks.

4.4 Conclusion

In the last fifty years, we have seen important long-term trends that have made voters more likely to switch parties between elections. In this chapter we have shown how the twin processes of partisan dealignment and party system fragmentation have underpinned this increase in volatility.

Whilst we have found a strong and consistent relationship between a voter's level of partisanship and the likelihood of them switching parties at the next election, and that this accounts for a substantial proportion of the trend in volatility, it is less clear why partisan identification has itself declined. We offered tests of the most plausible explanations of partisan dealignment and found that it is difficult to explain the downward trend in partisan attachments. Beyond generational replacement, the causes of partisan dealignment are somewhat elusive. We find little support for the cognitive mobilization theory that partisanship has declined because more educated voters have less need for partisan cues; and only a weak link to class dealignment, despite the reduction in class voting. Moreover, we do find substantial effects of party convergence on levels of party identification, but this does not account for the decline in partisanship. Partisan dealignment remains a hugely important trend, and yet one it is not yet possible to explain empirically. We have, however, shown a clear pattern of generational replacement in partisan identification; with newer cohorts entering with lower levels of partisanship and remaining relatively stable over time. This is important as it implies that voter volatility it is likely to stay with us for some time, as younger cohorts of voters with lower levels of party identification move through their voting lives. However, there are signs that young voters entering the electorate in the last few years may be beginning to break the downward trend in party identification.

The other main factor driving volatility is fragmentation. We have shown that smaller parties (other than Labour and the Conservatives) consistently lose a much higher proportion of their voters between elections than the major parties. This means that a higher share for these minor parties increases volatility.

---

[24] Interacting fragmentation with convergence also reduces the proportion of the time trend explained by fragmentation even though the overall model fit improves.

Fragmentation is explained by the rise of cross-cutting issues and, relatedly, the supply of viable choices.

Nonetheless, despite the strong relationship between fragmentation, dealignment, and voter volatility, these factors do not fully explain the upward trend in volatility. The factors included in our model accounted for some of the rise in the number of 'swing voters', but we saw that, even adjusting for all these factors, there are still large unexplained election-specific spikes, most notably in 2015. To understand these we must return to the implications of the theory we set out in the third chapter of this book: voter volatility is a product not only of long-term secular trends but is the result of unanticipated and unexplained electoral shocks which act as a catalyst for vote-switching, especially among an electorate who, for the reasons explored in this chapter, have become less fixed in their voting habits.

5

EU Accession Immigration
and the Rise of UKIP

Britain's relationship with the EU was at the root of two shocks that shaped the
2010, 2015, and 2017 British elections. The Brexit vote itself was the major shock in
2017, which we address in Chapter 9. This chapter examines the earlier shock of
EU immigration, which rose dramatically following the accession of ten new EU
member states in 2004. This shock had three key outcomes: first, the EU and
immigration became inexorably linked as political issues; second, this fusion of
these two issues led to the rise of UKIP by increasing the salience of immigration
and destroying the perceived competence of first Labour, and then the Conservatives,
on that issue; and third, the Conservative response to the UKIP threat led to the
calling of the EU referendum.

The rise of UKIP is one of the most significant shifts in party support in
Britain's recent history. UKIP was founded in 1991 (as the Anti-Federalist League),
but was initially eclipsed by its better-resourced Eurosceptic rival the Referendum
Party. Following the collapse of the Referendum Party, UKIP's fortunes slowly
began to turn. In the 1999 European Parliament Elections (the first held using a
system of proportional representation), UKIP won 6.5 per cent of the vote and
three MEPs (including Nigel Farage), giving them an important bridgehead into
the political arena. At the 2004 European Parliament Elections—buoyed by the
presence of well-known celebrity candidate Robert Kilroy-Silk—UKIP nearly
quadrupled its number of votes and pushed the Liberal Democrats into fourth
place. In 2009 UKIP performed similarly well at the European Parliament Elections,
finishing in second place thanks to a poor Labour performance. However, these
triumphs failed to translate into success in other electoral arenas, with the UKIP
vote plummeting back to earth at the general elections that followed.

The tide began to turn in 2012 as UKIP support ticked up in the polls: by 2013,
15 per cent of the electorate said they intended to vote for the party at the next
general election. Strong polling translated into electoral success when the party
made significant gains at the 2013 local elections, which heralded further success
in both the 2014 EU Parliamentary Election, in which they won 27 per cent of
votes and the most seats, and in the 2015 General Election, in which they won
13 per cent of the vote (but only one seat). UKIP's influence far exceeded their
representation at Westminster. The presence of a credible Eurosceptic challenger

Electoral shocks. Edward Fieldhouse, Jane Green, Geoffrey Evans, Jonathan Mellon, Christopher Prosser,
Hermann Schmitt, Cees van der Eijk, Oxford University Press (2020). © Fieldhouse, Green, Evans, Mellon,
Prosser, Schmitt, and van der Eijk.
DOI: 10.1093/oso/9780198800583.001.0001

prompted David Cameron to promise that a Conservative government would hold a referendum on EU membership—a promise that has profoundly affected British politics, as we discuss in Chapter 9.[1]

How and why did this happen? To answer that question we need to consider the conditions that may have led to UKIP's rapid rise in support. UKIP is often thought of as a radical right-wing 'challenger party'. Such parties are typically linked with positions on liberal-authoritarian issues such as European integration and immigration that have not received representation via mainstream parties. Some challenger parties have achieved electoral success and in doing so have opened new dimensions of competition, or extended and polarized existing ones (Adams et al. 2006; Meguid 2008; Hino 2012; Wagner 2012; van de Wardt 2014; Jensen and Spoon 2010).[1]

Challenger parties have long played a role in many European party-systems (see, for example: Kitschelt 1988; Kitschelt 1995). Historically, levels of support for challenger parties have been low (less than 5 per cent of the vote on average across Europe), but their levels of support have more than doubled in the last decade (Hobolt and Tilley 2016). Many explanations of this rise have often focused on the consequences of the Euro crisis. For Hobolt and Tilley (2016, 971), for example: voters 'choose challenger parties because they offer a rejection of, and an alternative to, the mainstream response to the crisis'. In some countries, however, these parties achieved notable earlier success in times of relative prosperity: for example, the *Front National* in France during the 1990s and the Dutch *Lijst Pim Fortuyn* in 2002. These parties point to another issue being key in understanding the rise of radical right parties: immigration. In Britain too, as we shall see, immigration played a key role in explaining the rise of UKIP, and the conditions were being put in place for immigration to emerge as a defining issue well before the arrival of the financial crisis.

The most influential explanations of UKIP's popularity have emphasized its appeal to the 'left-behind' losers of globalization. For Ford and Goodwin (2014, 270), UKIP is 'a working-class phenomenon. Its support is heavily concentrated among older, blue-collar workers, with little education and few skills.' However, others have found that the self-employed, traditionally the most right-wing of the social classes, are as solidly pro-UKIP as the working class themselves (Evans and Mellon 2016b). Additionally, UKIP's success could never have been achieved without substantial support from within the professional and managerial middle classes—the contemporary working class is simply too small (Evans and Mellon 2016b). Comparative research likewise finds that the self-employed and small employers such as shop owners, generally appear to provide important sources of radical right party support (Kitschelt 1995; Lubbers, Gijsberts, and Scheepers 2002; Ignazi 2003; Ivarsflaten 2005; Arzheimer and Carter 2006). More generally, this

---

[1] They are also referred to as 'niche parties' (e.g. Meguid 2008), but we will stick to the term challenger parties for sake of economy and clarity.

sort of interpretation has difficulty explaining the *timing* of UKIP's emergence from being a marginal party to one that represented one pole of arguably the key political issue dimension of the current era. The left-behind are not a new phenomenon in post-industrial societies (Evans and Tilley 2017).

In contrast to this focus on major social transformations, our thesis is that the primary catalyst for the increasing importance of immigration and the EU in British politics, which led to the rise of UKIP, was political: the decision taken in 2004 to open Britain's borders to EU accession countries. This decision set in train a process that raised the salience of immigration and led to the entanglement of the EU and immigration issues. A key issue was the inability of the government—*any* government—to respond to rising public concern. Although British immigration policy had previously responded to public opinion by restricting levels of immigration (Jennings 2009), controlling EU immigration was not possible because free movement between member states continued to be a fundamental EU principle. The lack of an effective policy mechanism to respond to this public concern resulted in attitudes towards the EU becoming increasingly aligned with concern about immigration.

In this chapter we first consider how Britain's relationship with the EU featured previously in electoral politics and why its impact on the dimensionality of political competition was muted until party decisions provided the conditions for the increased importance of immigration. We then examine the 2004 accession decision and how it acted as an electoral shock which helped shape the ensuing social and political context, leading to the emergence of UKIP, the reshaping of political allegiances, and, ultimately, Brexit.

5.1 Party competition and European integration

Across member states, party positions towards the EEC during the early phase of European integration—which was primarily concerned with market harmonization—were generally characterized by their economic left–right position. Parties on the right saw European integration as an opportunity to expand market competition, while those on the left saw it as a threat to protected national industries. As European integration broadened in scope, this alignment began to change, with party positions becoming more structured by the social and cultural dimension (often referred to as liberal–authoritarianism). Socially liberal parties began to see European integration as a way of fostering international cooperation, while for socially conservative parties, the EU was a threat to national autonomy and tradition (Hooghe, Marks, and Wilson 2002; Prosser 2016d).

For many years the EU was the dog that didn't bark in British electoral politics. Labour itself was somewhat hostile to joining the European Economic Community

(EEC) before and after the 1975 referendum, but Harold Wilson, the leader of the party in government, successfully obtained strong support for staying in the EEC (Saunders 2016). Despite Enoch Powell's infamous 'rivers of blood' speech in 1968 and the social unrest in the 1970s associated with far right groups (Billig 1978; Fielding 1981) concern about immigration only briefly and modestly affected vote choice (Studlar 1978).[2] In general, there was little sign of a new electoral alignment along the liberal–authoritarian dimension of political competition (Heath et al. 1990).

Divisions within Labour over Europe had helped catalyse the SDP split in 1981 (Crewe and King 1995) but the modernization of the party under Neil Kinnock, together with the European Economic Community's (EEC) move towards 'Social Europe' under the Delors Commission, meant that Labour's position on European integration began to soften. Conversely, the Conservative Party, which had led Britain into Europe, began to cool towards Europe as the scope of integration deepened. This transition was exemplified by Margaret Thatcher, who had been a driving force behind the adoption of the Single European Act (1986) but only two years later in her famous Bruges speech declared: 'we have not successfully rolled back the frontiers of the state in Britain only to see them re-imposed at a European level.' As Clements and Bartle (2009) note, these differences are even more appreciable in 1997, 2001, and 2005. By the 2001 Election, analyses of the party manifestos indicated that Europe was a 'major point of party contention' (Bara and Budge 2001). The systematic evidence of the manifesto project also corresponded with scholarly analyses of the shifting positions of the parties (Nairn 1972; Denman 1995; Turner 2000; Forster 2002).

As long as Labour maintained a Eurosceptic position, mirroring that of many of its traditional working-class supporters, the opportunity for Europe to become a new cross-cutting issue had been muted. Once they abandoned that position, the seeds of realignment were sown. This policy reversal was given sharpest emphasis following the emergence of Tony Blair as party leader in 1994 and prime minister in 1997 and Labour's rebranding as 'New Labour'.[3] This period saw the traditionally Labour-voting and Eurosceptic working class start to lose their allegiance to Labour (Evans 1999b). Between the landslide of 1997 and the sweeping Labour victory of 2001 the only noticeable defection away from Labour to the Conservatives was by voters who did not like Europe (Evans 2002).

---

[2] Analyses of the impact of responses to the question of have 'too many immigrants have been let into this country' in the 1960s and 1970s show an increase in its effect in 1970 following that speech. People who agreed were slightly more likely to vote Conservative and they perceived a much larger difference between Labour and Conservatives on immigration in 1970 than they had done in 1964 or 1966 (Butler and Stokes 1974), but it did not last (Heath et al. 1990).

[3] The same 1997 Election saw James Goldsmith's Referendum Party attempt and fail to force the Conservatives to agree to a referendum on membership of the union (Heath et al. 1998).

But they were small in number. The EU still did not have the power to reshape political alignments.[4]

5.2 The catalyst

Why did this change? Our contention is that a key shock that led to the rising importance and closer linkage of attitudes towards the EU and immigration was the Labour government's decision to implement immediate open borders with the ten 2004 EU accession states rather than imposing transitional controls on immigration. Nearly all other existing EU members (the other exceptions were Ireland and Sweden) applied these controls, which concentrated the migrant flows towards Britain, Ireland, and Sweden (Europa.eu 2011).

How did this decision come about? While UKIP has claimed that Labour followed an intentional policy of encouraging mass migration in order to boost the city of London and future ethnic minority voters (UK Independence Party 2016), the evidence suggests that the policy may have come from an incorrect assessment of the likely number of migrants.

One key piece of evidence the Labour government relied on when deciding whether to impose a transition period on free movement was a now infamous Home Office report that concluded that 'net immigration from the AC-10 to the UK after the current enlargement of the EU will be relatively small, at between 5,000 and 13,000 immigrants per year' (Dustmann et al. 2003). In fact, the rate of increase in workers born in post-2004 accession countries has been closer to 127,000 per year (Vargas-Silva and Markaki 2015).[5]

The Home Office report does state that 'If Germany imposes a transition period for the free movement of workers...we would not think that more than one in three immigrants who had intended to migrate to work in Germany would instead migrate to the UK' (Dustmann et al. 2003, 57). However what the paper does not explicitly state anywhere is that this 'small fraction' could constitute more than six and a half times as many immigrants from accession countries as the stated forecast.[6] The paper was not technically incorrect, but did a poor job of

---

[4] It might have done so had Gordon Brown not prevented Britain from joining the Euro, but his efforts in this respect diffused what could have become a basis of mobilization given the public's opposition (Evans 2003).

[5] It should be noted that these figures differ somewhat from estimates using the International Passenger Survey. However, all studies agree that the number of immigrants from the AC-10 countries to the UK exceeded the Home Office estimates by many multiples.

[6] The highest forecast of annual net immigration to Germany in the paper is 209,651 (Table 6.4). The highest numerical forecast that the paper shows for the UK is 12,568. Therefore the multiple of additional immigrants can be calculated as: ((209651/3) + 12568)/12568 = 6.56. This calculation is never conducted or hinted at in the Home Office paper. See Nicholas Watt and Patrick Wintour, 'How immigration came to haunt Labour: the inside story', The Guardian, 24 March 2015. Available at: https://www.theguardian.com/news/2015/mar/24/how-immigration-came-to-haunt-labour-inside-story

communicating the importance of Germany's choice to impose transitional controls. The UK government's decision not to impose transitional controls therefore appears to be a relatively non-strategic decision based on incorrect expectations that the effects would be minor—and was belatedly recognized as such by its primary proponent.[7]

5.3 The 'transmission belt' of concern

The impact of immigration from the accession countries on UK immigration levels were substantial. It maintained the already high levels of immigration that had occurred since the late 1990s (Figure 5.1). Most significantly, however, it changed the composition of immigration into the UK, at times displacing Commonwealth immigration as the largest source of foreign immigration (Figure 5.2).

Voters then reacted to the increase in EU immigration. Monthly Ipsos MORI data on what issue voters think is the most important (Figure 5.3) show that

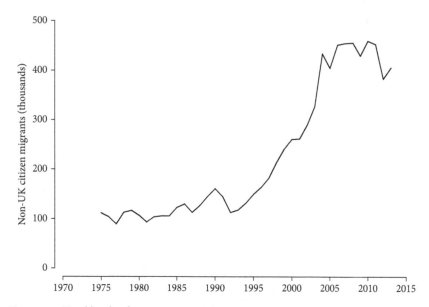

Figure 5.1 Total levels of immigration of non-UK citizens to the UK by year (thousands of immigrants)

---

[7] See Laura Hughes, 'Tony Blair admits he did not realise how many migrants would come to the UK after EU expanded', *The Telegraph*, 19 March 2017. Available at: http://www.telegraph.co.uk/news/2017/03/19/tony-blair-admits-did-not-realise-many-migrants-would-come-uk/?WT.mc_id=tmgliveapp_androidshare_AnjSzsdxpSsP

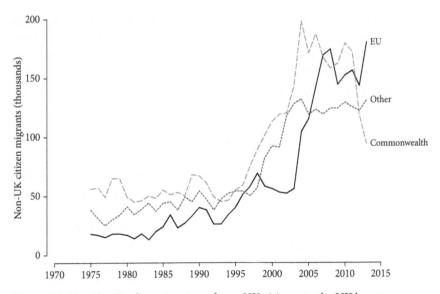

Figure 5.2 Total levels of immigration of non-UK citizens to the UK by year (thousands of immigrants) broken down by EU, Commonwealth, and other sources of origin

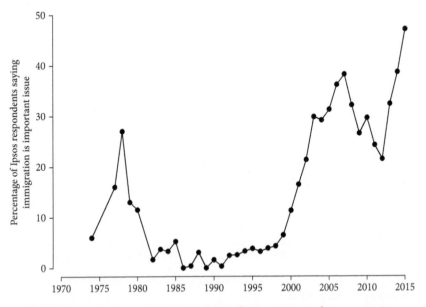

Figure 5.3 Ipsos MORI trends (1974–2015) on what percentage of voters mention immigration as an important. (Source: Ipsos MORI: 'What would you say is the most important issue facing Britain today?' 'What do you see as other important issues facing Britain today?' Concern is averaged for each year over all surveys fielded in that year)

immigration concern peaked in the mid-2000s just after accession migration started. Concern inevitably fell away at the height of the economic crisis of 2008/2009 as the economy dislodged it as the most important issue facing the country, only to elevate rapidly in the following years.

While it is clear that public concern tracks actual levels of immigration, the mechanism that connects the two is not necessarily straightforward. After all, people cannot observe national immigration rates directly, so people must either learn about immigration through their own local experience or through the media.

There is some evidence for a weak effect of local experience. Recent research has looked at the question of whether anti-immigrant attitudes are related to the level of immigration to an area (Kawalerowicz 2016). Kawalerowicz's research (following earlier work in the United States (Newman 2013)) concludes that only 6 per cent of total variance in attitudes towards immigrants is attributable to differences across constituencies, with the remaining 94 per cent varying at the individual level. In line with other research (e.g. Kaufmann 2017) Kawalerowicz finds that immigration *rates* were predictive of anti-immigrant attitudes while the absolute *level* of people born overseas was not. Furthermore, Kawalerowicz finds that immigration rates are less predictive of anti-immigrant sentiment where there is a larger existing foreign-born population.[8]

We find that these patterns also hold for the salience of immigration (just 4.7 per cent of variance in the salience of immigration is at the local authority level), with the exception that the levels of the foreign-born population are also predictive of anti-immigrant attitudes after controlling for individual covariates (see Appendix Tables A5.1 and A5.2).[9] Although there is clearly some role for local experience, the available evidence suggests that local experiences of immigration account for only a small proportion of the variation in either attitudes towards immigration or its salience.

In general terms, there is strong evidence that the media play a key role in shaping public opinion (Bartels 1993; Kellstedt 2003; King, Schneer, and White 2017). More specifically, studies in other European countries have found that the media shapes levels of concern about, and attitudes towards, immigration (Boomgaarden and Vliegenthart 2007; Boomgaarden and Vliegenthart 2009; Van Klingeren et al. 2015; Thesen 2018). Likewise, in Britain, media reporting of immigration appears to feed public concern. This can be seen by comparing Figure 5.3 and Figure 5.4, which show how closely mass readership newspaper coverage

---

[8] This relationship may be better explained by a non-linear relationship between immigrant levels and sentiment, but the wider point stands that any specification explains only a small proportion of the variance in attitudes.

[9] The marginal effect of moving from the lowest to highest immigration rates is around 3 percentage points for people in areas with the lowest levels of prior immigration, so the effect is modest even at its greatest extent.

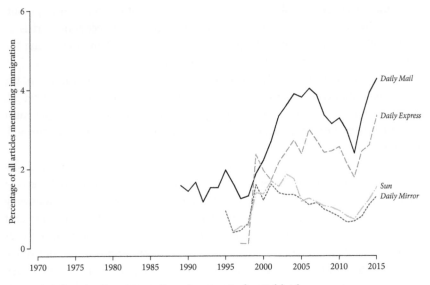

Figure 5.4 Levels of coverage of immigration in four tabloid newspapers

Table 5.1 Correlations of immigration importance (Ipsos MORI), coverage of immigration in the *Daily Mail* and *Daily Express*, and total immigration levels (International Passenger Survey)

	Immigration importance	*Daily Mail*	*Daily Express*	*The Sun*	*Daily Mirror*	Immigration levels
Immigration importance	1.00					
Daily Mail	0.97	1.00				
Daily Express	0.83	0.91	1.00			
The Sun	0.43	0.68	0.66	1.00		
Daily Mirror	0.30	0.55	0.58	0.93	1.00	
Immigration levels	0.86	0.89	0.76	0.19	0.10	1.00

corresponds with both immigration levels and levels of concern about immigration. The correlations between immigration level, newspaper coverage, and public concern are shown in Table 5.1. The strongest correlation is between public concern and the *Daily Mail*'s coverage (r = 0.97), followed by public concern's relationship with immigration levels and the *Daily Express*'s coverage. The relationship between immigration concern and coverage of immigration in the *Sun* and the *Daily Mirror* is considerably lower. This fits with other analyses which have found that the *Mail* and *Express* have consistently higher negative portrayals of immigration and immigrants (Gerard 2016). Once we model immigration concern as a function of coverage in the *Daily Mail* and immigration rates simultaneously, as shown in Appendix Table A5.3, there is no remaining effect of actual immigration levels on public concern about immigration.[10] This suggests that the vast bulk of concern over immigration is mediated by media coverage and is not the result of direct observation by voters.[11] While there is no direct effect of immigration rates, the *Daily Mail*'s coverage is sufficiently strongly correlated with actual immigration ($r = 0.89$) that public concern tracks the actual rate of immigration closely.[12]

The links between immigration, media coverage, and public concern are impressively close, but immigration still need not have evolved into a powerful political issue. As we argued in Chapter 3, the impact of shocks is conditional on the response of political actors. To understand why EU immigration had such an impact, we need to consider how parties typically deal with issue concerns via their policy responses. In this respect, policy is often conceptualized as following a thermostatic model (Wlezien 1995), where a policy output such as redistribution is reduced when it gets too far above the level that public opinion prefers, and that public opinion responds in turn to the effects of these policy changes. As a result, in the long run, policy and public opinion remain in step, although they are subject to over-corrections in the short term.

British immigration policy previously responded to public opinion in a fairly thermostatic manner, with governments strengthening asylum policy and border controls in response to public concern over immigration (Jennings 2009). However, the rapid growth of EU immigration changed this relationship, with both concern and levels of immigration rising over an extended period. The fact that immigration was defined as a fundamental freedom within the EU seriously limited the ability of any government to adopt policies that would limit it. In fact, we can see evidence of attempts at a response by the government in Figure 5.2, which shows that Commonwealth migration plummeted a few years after increased EU accession migration began. However, while the voters have responded to rising immigration by becoming more concerned, the usual thermostatic response of more restrictive controls was absent. As a result, immigration continued to be high and public concern rose yet further. This further reinforces our argument that EU accession migration represented a sharp change in the status quo of British politics. In such circumstances new political issues can become sufficiently salient to begin driving vote choices in what is normally a unidimensional system of party competition.

---

[10] We should be careful about over-interpreting this null relationship as it is based on only twenty-five years of data. The *Daily Mail* is the only newspaper that entirely eliminates the relationship between immigration rates and immigration concern.

[11] As well as driving the salience of immigration, UKIP also benefited more directly from media attention. Murphy and Devine (2018) find strong evidence that media attention to UKIP drove increasing support for UKIP in the poll.

[12] The close link between immigration and media coverage could result from a number of processes: deliberate attempts to influence policy; a reflection of the principal agent relationship between voters who dislike immigration and the media who try to find stories their readers are interested in; or the paper's coverage may itself reflect the level of immigration and the supply of available stories to cover.

5.4 The changing relationship between EU and immigration attitudes

Given how strongly entwined they have become in contemporary politics, one would be forgiven for thinking that immigration and the EU would always have been tightly linked issues. However, just as there have been significant shifts between party ideology and positions on European integration, so too have there been large changes among the general public (van Elsas and van der Brug 2015; Eichenberg and Dalton 2007). As European integration progressed, opposition based on economic left-wing concerns about market integration gave way to concerns driven by liberal–authoritarian issues like immigration and cultural threat (McLaren 2002; McLaren 2006; Tillman 2013).

We can see the stark nature of this change by examining the relationship between immigration attitudes and European integration preferences in the 1975 EEC referendum and at the 2015 General Election. In Figure 5.5 we compare EU preferences among people who think there are too many immigrants using evidence from the 1975 EEC referendum (Crewe, Robertson, and Sarlvik 1975) and the 2015 BES post-election face-to-face survey.

In 2015, a respondent's attitude towards immigration was an extremely strong predictor of their EU attitudes, with 51 per cent of respondents who believe there are too many immigrants supporting leave, compared with just 11 per cent of those who did not think there were too many immigrants. In the 1975

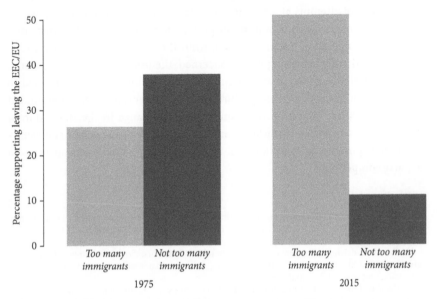

Figure 5.5 The relationship between believing there are too many immigrants and support for leaving the EU in 1975 and 2015

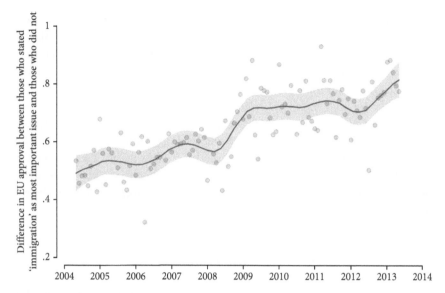

Figure 5.6 The growing link between responses to 'How much do you approve of Britain's membership of the EU?' and 'what is the most important issue facing the country?'

EU referendum, by contrast, the difference was far smaller (12 percentage points) and in the *opposite* direction.

However, we can also examine the extent to which voters' attitudes towards the EU and immigration are linked over time in a more granular way and using more contemporary data by examining the BES Continuous Monitoring Survey (Sanders and Whiteley 2014b). This survey is carried out every month and asks separately about which political issue is currently most important to respondents and their level of approval of the EU.[13]

Figure 5.6 shows the difference between the average support for the EU among respondents who said that immigration was the most important issue facing the country and respondents who said another issue was the most important. The results show that even in early 2004 there was a positive relationship between concern about immigration and disapproval of the EU. However, the relationship clearly strengthens substantially over time, with the gap in EU perceptions between people who worry about immigration and those who do not almost doubling between 2004 and 2013.[14]

We also know anti-EU attitudes rose over this same time period. After initial ambivalence towards Britain's membership of the EEC in the 1970s, public

---

[13] Wording: Overall, do you strongly approve, approve, disapprove, or strongly disapprove of Britain's membership in the European Union?

[14] The data for the Continuous Monitoring Survey is not available publicly after 2013.

support had increased steadily through the 1980s before it peaked in 1991, when 57 per cent of those surveyed said Britain's membership of the Common Market was 'a good thing' and only 14 per cent said it was a 'bad thing'.[15] From that peak however, support for integration steadily eroded throughout the 90s, before stabilizing in the mid-2000s. However, anti-EU sentiment increased at the same time as immigration and the EU were becoming linked issues and the Eurozone crisis was reaching its peak. Anti-EU sentiment ran very high during this period, but initially this did not translate into political opposition. In the CMS data, disapproval of Britain's membership of the EU peaked in late 2011—*before* the rise of UKIP—and declined steadily thereafter. Only when the potent combination of the EU and immigration came together did the European issue achieve a political breakthrough.

5.5 The political consequences

The link between immigration and the EU provided the perfect opportunity for a radical right party to prosper electorally. Immigration was initially integrated within traditional two-party left–right competition. The Conservatives took a harder line on the issue, promising to reduce net migration to the tens of thousands. This appeal was relatively successful in the 2005–10 election cycle when the Conservatives were not in government, so that by 2009–10 substantial numbers of voters were defecting from Labour because of the government's handling of immigration (Evans and Chzhen 2013). This was particularly striking given the country was then also in the midst of a major financial crisis. In the 2010–15 electoral cycle, however, the impact of immigration and the EU moved decisively from favouring the Conservatives who, once in government were powerless to implement effective reduction of EU immigration, to favouring UKIP. This was aided by UKIP's emphasis on a more typical radical right agenda, making anti-immigrant policies a central and vocal part of its agenda along with its existing anti-EU agenda (Ford and Goodwin 2014). Indeed, many of the voters that the Conservatives won from Labour and the Liberal Democrats in 2010 by campaigning on immigration subsequently moved onwards to UKIP in 2015 (Evans and Mellon 2016b).

The reasons for this reversal are not difficult to ascertain, given that the Conservative-led coalition government continued to promise to reduce net immigration to less than 100,000, and did reduce non-EU immigration, but could do nothing about immigration from the EU. Consequently, EU nationals now formed, for the first time, the plurality of immigrants. As a result, EU immigration was

---

[15] https://ec.europa.eu/commfrontoffice/publicopinion/index.cfm/Chart/getChart/chartType/lineChart//themeKy/3/groupKy/3/savFile/10000

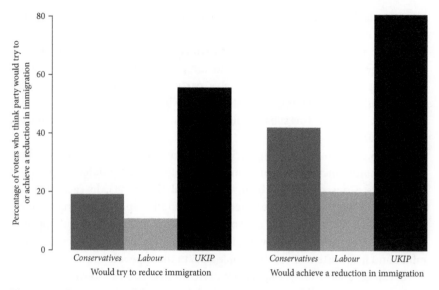

Figure 5.7 Perceptions of the parties' desire to reduce immigration and their ability to do so

even more salient and the government's impotence became even more apparent. As can be seen from answers to a question in the 2015 BES survey shown in Figure 5.7, all parties were seen to have aspirations that outstripped their ability to reduce immigration, but UKIP was believed to be by far and away the party most likely to do so if they were in government. Given the growing importance of immigration to the electorate, this gives a basis for expecting substantial levels of immigration-related vote-switching to UKIP.

The EU, Immigration, and Vote-Switching 2010–15

To assess the importance of the EU and immigration to political choice, we model the 2015 vote choice of various groups of 2010 voters looking at how EU and immigration attitudes (as measured in 2010) predicts the flows in the merged 2010 and 2015 BES internet panels.

In the 2010 BES pre-election panel wave, respondents were asked to describe their feelings about immigration[16]—whether they had felt a series of emotions about immigration. We run an IRT model on indicator variables of whether respondents' felt angry, disgusted, uneasy, or afraid about immigration, and a

---

[16] Which, if any, of the following words describe your feelings about immigration (Please tick up to FOUR): Angry, Happy, Disgusted, Hopeful, Uneasy, Confident, Afraid, Proud, No feelings, Don't know.

binary variable measuring whether respondents said immigration was the most important issue.[17]

Because we run separate models for each 2010 party origin, we also include people who have a different identity to the party they voted for in the non-identifying category on the basis that a party identification with a different party is unlikely to be an impediment to them switching in future (as we demonstrated in Chapter 4). This substantially increases the proportion of non-affiliated voters in each year.

Figure 5.8, Figure 5.9, and Figure 5.10 show predicted probabilities from three separate multinomial models predicting 2015 vote choice for different groups of 2010 voters: Conservatives, Labour, and Liberal Democrats. In each case, the latent immigration variable (measured in 2010) and EU approval strongly predict switching to UKIP in 2015. The only other variable that has a consistent impact is having a strong party identity, which inhibits switching. Demographics have only minor and inconsistent effects (see Table A5.5 in the appendix).

We can get a sense of the importance of EU/immigration concern by considering two counterfactual scenarios where respondents did not express any of the negative emotions about immigration or cite it as the most important issue (15 per cent of respondents fell into this category). In the first scenario we just look at the direct effect that this reduction in immigration concern would have

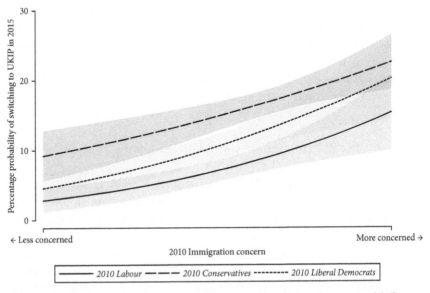

Figure 5.8 Predicted probabilities of switching to UKIP in 2015 for voters of different 2010 party origins with different levels of 2010 immigration concern

---

[17]   Table A5.4 in the appendix shows the results of the IRT model.

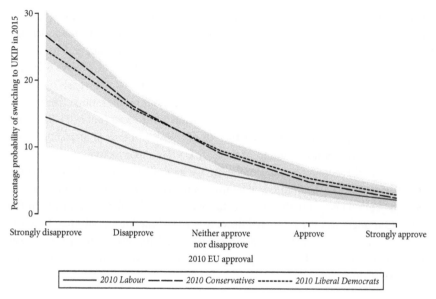

Figure 5.9 Predicted probabilities of switching to UKIP in 2015 for voters of different 2010 party origins with different levels of EU approval in 2010

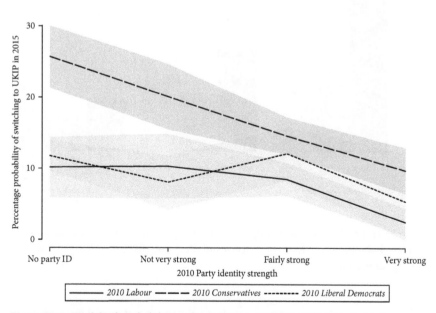

Figure 5.10 Predicted probabilities of switching to UKIP in 2015 for voters of different 2010 party origins by 2010 party ID strength

had on the UKIP vote. In the second scenario, because immigration is so closely linked with the EU, we also impute (predict the values based on the model) the levels of EU approval that respondents would have had had they not been concerned about immigration (using the regression model in Table A5.6 in the appendix). This model predicts levels of support for Europe on the basis of several factors including a respondent's level of concern about immigration. This imputation of EU approval moves the mean score from 2.81 to 3.38 (out of 5). This predicted level of anti-Europeanness is then used along with the counterfactual level of concern about immigration to predict the UKIP counterfactual.[18]

Based on this counterfactual simulation, we estimate that the levels of switching to UKIP would have been drastically lower in the absence of a salient immigration issue in 2015. Figure 5.11 shows the actual flows to UKIP for respondents in the 2010–15 models and the estimated flows to UKIP if the immigration and the EU had been less salient. If immigration concern had not been widespread, fewer than 5 per cent of the three main parties' supporters in 2010 would have switched to UKIP in 2015.[19]

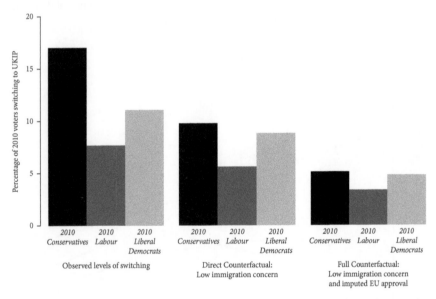

Figure 5.11 Levels of vote switching to UKIP among respondents in the multinomial models under the actual levels of concern and the counterfactual scenario of low immigration concern

[18] Note that we only examine voters in England and Wales given the very different patterns of response in the Scottish party system, where UKIP never achieved prominence.
[19] As we cannot rule out selection effects or reverse causation completely on the basis of this analysis, the true counterfactual figure likely falls between the direct and full counterfactuals.

UKIP and Brexit: the spillover

Although UKIP performed very well in 2015 by the standards of minor parties in British politics, their most important impact on British politics was indirect: by activating the EU as a salient political issue, UKIP helped bring about the 2016 EU referendum. The 12.9 per cent of the vote that UKIP won in 2015 substantially underestimates the potential of their appeal in the electorate. Not only had UKIP won half a million more votes at the European Parliament election the year before, the relative aggregate stability in the polls belies considerable volatility. Among respondents who took the six waves of the BES internet panel fielded between February 2014 and May 2015, 23 per cent voted for UKIP in at least one (European Parliament, local, or general) election, and a further 7 per cent said they intended to vote UKIP at least once. The popularity of a distinctly Eurosceptic challenger party posed an obvious threat to the main British parties, especially the Conservatives.

Although the 2016 EU referendum was unique in being an in/out referendum, the strategic use of holding (or at least, saying you are going to hold) referendums on the EU to avoid electoral competition over European integration is well established in the EU (Oppermann 2013; Prosser 2016a). The logic of this strategy is that by holding a referendum on the EU, governing parties provide an electoral outlet for Eurosceptic voters and, in doing so, minimize the extent to which EU attitudes influence vote choice in general elections. In Britain, this strategy was first adopted by Labour under Blair (Oppermann 2008). Faced with a potential backlash over its preferred European policy, Blair offered (but avoided holding) referendums on first Britain joining the Euro, and second the ratification of the proposed 2004 Constitutional Treaty.

The same strategy lay behind the Conservative's decision to hold a referendum on EU membership. UKIP's surge and the continuing salience of immigration were key drives behind the decision to hold a referendum (Shipman 2016). It is no coincidence that, following a year in which UKIP's support in the polls had jumped by about ten points, in January 2013 David Cameron announced that there would be an in/out referendum on Britain's membership of the EU.

5.6 Conclusion and discussion

We have argued that the 2004 decision on open immigration from EU accession countries appears to have unintentionally unlocked potent issues in British politics. This decision was highly salient (as we can see from public concern and media coverage), a large change from the status quo (because the government was unable to formulate a policy response), and clearly highly relevant to party politics, as the series of election results from 2010 to 2017 have shown. In Chapter 3 we identified three main ways that a shock can affect electoral politics. The EU accession shock worked primarily through two of these mechanisms. The first was through increasing *salience*: concern about immigration, specifically EU immigration, can be traced to an increase in EU accession migration resulting directly from this decision. Our evidence is consistent with the media functioning as an information transmission belt to which the electorate responded. The second effect of the EU accession shock was through its effect on *competence* evaluations. The inability of any government to respond thermostatically to this growing concern—illustrated clearly by the coalition's government's year-on-year failure to reduce or even flatten off EU immigration rates—provided the opportunity for a challenger party, UKIP, to fill that representation gap. Thus a spiral of interconnected immigration fears and Euroscepticism emerged, resulting in a dramatic upsurge in support for UKIP, the only occupant of the anti-EU, anti-immigration space that was perceived to be competent on the issue and which provided representation for more socially conservative voters.

While not denying that challenger parties need to seize the opportunities provided by mainstream party decisions, much as the literature on the role of opportunity structures (e.g. Kitschelt 1995) would predict, our analysis shifts the focus to the actions of the governing party in providing the catalyst for a swift and dramatic surge in immigration concern. Evidence that political decisions of this sort can act as salience shocks that elevate immigration concerns and facilitate the swift emergence of radical right challenger parties has also been seen recently in Germany, where Chancellor Merkel's decision to welcome immigration from outside the EU in 2016 in response to the Syrian crisis transformed the fortunes of Germany's own radical right challenger party, the AfD (Alternative für Deutschland). Arzheimer and Berning (2017) track the change in the AfD's fortunes during this period when they reorientated themselves to become an immigration-focused party rather than just an anti-EU party. Immigration gave their EU message far more mobilizing power.

As a final point, we should note that the impact of EU immigration appears to be unrelated to any increase in intolerance in the electorate. In other words, rising concern about rising levels of immigration does not indicate that xenophobia per se is on the rise. This should not surprise us: the electorate is now substantially more highly educated than in previous decades and higher education is more strongly associated with tolerance and social liberalism than just about any social attribute (Evans, Heath, and Lalljee 1996; Evans 2002; Tilley 2005). If anything, therefore, attitudes towards immigrants have become less negative over time as the population has become increasingly more socially liberal (Harding 2017). This can be seen from responses to a BES question on the belief that 'there are too many immigrants' asked at various points over the last forty or so years (see Figure 5.12). These confirm that people were, if anything, a little less likely to believe there are too many immigrants in Britain in 2015 than they were in previous decades and

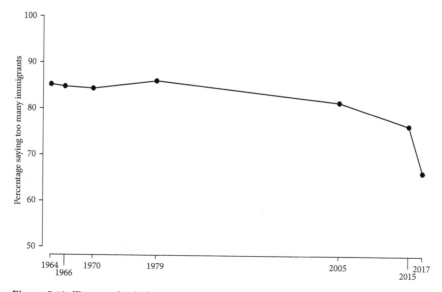

Figure 5.12 'Do you think that too many immigrants have been let into this country, or not?'

had become much less likely to believe there are too many immigrants by the time of the 2017 Election. Growing intolerance does not appear to lie behind recent responses to immigration or the rise of UKIP.[20]

That the electorate is not getting more intolerant does not mean, however, that dislike of immigration is not present. As we can see from Figure 5.12, there has always been a substantial anti-immigrant bloc of voters who could be mobilized if the issue became (and stayed) politically salient. The decision to allow unfettered EU immigration ahead of all other major recipient countries provides the ideal shock for this political mobilization.

We examine the impact of Brexit as an electoral shock in Chapter 9, which examines how the EU has moved from being a predictor of UKIP support to being almost as important a predictor of Conservative voting as economic right-wing attitudes. While UKIP largely vanished in 2017, their *raison d'etre* has only grown in importance.

---

[20] The role of challenger parties in promoting as well as seizing upon new issues has been highlighted by, among others, de Vries and Hobolt (2012). However, the rise in concern about immigration is unlikely to be simply a consequence of UKIP's presence: as our over-time data shows, immigration became salient in the public and media agendas before UKIP became an electorally viable party. This is consistent with the findings of extensive cross-country over-time comparisons conducted by Bohman and Hjerm (2016) who find no effect of a radical right, challenger party presence on anti-immigration attitudes.

6

The Global Financial Crisis

The word shock suggests something short and sharp. This does not mean that shocks only have short-term effects. A major shock is—by our definition—persistent and impossible to ignore. Shocks have the potential to reshape politics for a prolonged period of time, as happened in the case of the Global Financial Crisis.

The Global Financial Crisis, which began in 2007–8, was the most significant financial crisis since the Great Depression of the 1930s. The financial crisis was a major policy shock, causing substantial disruption to the economy and unprecedented financial support to the banking sector by the British government. The financial crisis resulted in a major competence shock for Labour, as voters began to see them as less trustworthy on the economy. In the subsequent 2010 General Election, Labour lost power after thirteen years of government and the Conservatives formed a coalition government with the Liberal Democrats. However, the 2010 General Election did not mark the end of the political impact of the Global Financial Crisis. The crisis dominated British politics between 2010 and 2015. We show in this chapter how it played a role in the outcome of the 2015 General Election, seven years after the escalation of the financial crisis in Britain.

Focusing on the shock of the Global Financial Crisis offers several novel insights into economic voting, the outcome of the 2015 General Election, and the ways in which shocks have electoral effects. The economic vote is usually thought of as a short-term mechanism: a reward or punishment for the incumbent depending on recent economic conditions (see Lewis-Beck and Stegmaier 2000 for a review). Voters are thought to be 'myopic', focusing only on the recent or immediate state of the economy. The short-term economic vote is certainly part of the economic voting story in 2015: the Conservatives did better among people who thought the economy was improving in the run-up to the 2015 General Election, and Labour did worse. However, we show that the economic vote can have a much longer time horizon. We demonstrate one way in which it does so: voters can continue to blame parties for past economic performance and carry over those memories and evaluations into future elections.

The Global Financial Crisis impacted directly on perceptions of Labour's economic competence, but it also created a political opportunity for the Conservatives. The Conservatives won votes in 2015 by successfully piling blame for the aftermath of the financial crisis onto the previous Labour government. The Conservatives achieved this by attributing responsibility for the level of UK debt to Labour and

Electoral shocks. Edward Fieldhouse, Jane Green, Geoffrey Evans, Jonathan Mellon, Christopher Prosser, Hermann Schmitt, Cees van der Eijk, Oxford University Press (2020). © Fieldhouse, Green, Evans, Mellon, Prosser, Schmitt, and van der Eijk.
DOI: 10.1093/oso/9780198800583.001.0001

by winning electoral support on the basis of the widely perceived need for austerity measures: reductions in public spending to reduce the national debt and the size of the budget deficit. This shows how politicians can capitalize on old shocks to score new political points by persuading voters to attribute new blame for past policies and their effects. The nature of shocks means they can provide political opportunities well into the future.

6.1 The shock of the Global Financial Crisis

The Global Financial Crisis was a profound economic shock with wide-reaching consequences for the economy and financial institutions in the UK and internationally. The crisis began with the collapse of the US subprime mortgage market, which precipitated an international banking crisis. The US bank Lehman Brothers was forced to file for bankruptcy in September 2018, and others in the US were expected to follow. Despite the US Federal Government providing significant financial support to the US banking sector, banks continued to face severe difficulties borrowing money, and house prices dropped sharply. These problems spilled over to British banks in the autumn of 2018, leading to the nationalization of Northern Rock, a major high street mortgage lender. To stave off a larger banking crisis, the British government underwrote UK banks in the form of loans and guarantees ('the bailout of British banks') to the tune of £500 billion. The rescue package was designed to shore up economic and public confidence in the banking system and achieve, in Chancellor Alastair Darling's words, nothing less than the prevention of panic and social disorder.[1] The bailout package resulted in the government—and the UK taxpayer—becoming a major shareholder in Lloyds Bank and in RBS. The EU followed the UK government's initiative of investing vast amounts to maintain confidence in their national banking systems, with international coordination by seven central banks to lower interest rates to calm the crisis.

Despite substantial government intervention in the crisis, a period of widespread recession followed: a global economic downturn, a debt crisis in the Eurozone, and a period dubbed 'The Great Recession' (see Bermeo and Pontusson 2012 for a review). The Great Recession 'was a once-in-a-century event which disrupted the economies of most of the world's advanced democracies' (Clarke et al. 2016, 30). British GDP saw its largest drops in 2008,[2] but the question of when Britain would enjoy an economic recovery—and in particular a drop in the rising costs of fuel and other goods—ran well into the period after the 2010 General Election. Inflation only began to decline perceptibly in 2013.[3]

---

[1] uk.businessinsider.com/alistair-darling-uk-breakdown-of-law-and-order-financial-crisis-2018–5
[2] https://www.ons.gov.uk/economy/grossdomesticproductgdp/timeseries/ihyq/qna
[3] https://www.ons.gov.uk/economy/inflationandpriceindices/timeseries/l55o/mm23

One political outcome of the Global Financial Crisis was a period of 'austerity' in British public policy: substantial reductions in public spending, resulting in—among other things—a prolonged wage-increase freeze for public sector workers. The incoming Conservative–Liberal Democrat coalition committed to reducing the size of the national debt and the budget deficit. The degree to which the Conservative–Liberal Democrat coalition sustained this policy is contested (as was its necessity) but the 'age of austerity' was to dominate the politics of the period after the 2010 General Election. Austerity only declined in political focus due to the subsequent political preoccupation with Brexit. It was only in October 2018—a full ten years after the start of the financial crisis—that Prime Minister Theresa May declared, somewhat controversially, 'the end of austerity'[4] in her speech to the Conservative Party Conference, and the October 2018 budget promised public spending increases.

The penalty to the Labour Party: long-term perceptions and political opportunities

On the face of it, the Labour government might have been expected to avoid a substantial electoral penalty for its handling of the financial crisis. The Labour government's handling of the crisis—in particular the banking bailout—was not without praise, and Labour reminded voters that this was an international banking crisis, caused by failures made by international financial institutions. After all, the counterfactual of what might have happened had Labour *not* intervened so decisively could have been extremely severe. However, the Conservatives pointed to Labour's public spending as part of the problem, arguing that the size of the national debt and budget deficit were exacerbating Britain's economic problems and compounding the impact of the crisis. The decision to use £500 billion, with the justification that the banks were 'too big to fail', was a very difficult pill to swallow for voters, likely to be especially difficult for those in the most demanding economic circumstances. Moreover, presiding over a significant recession—regardless of actual levels of responsibility—is not good news for any government. The 2010 General Election saw a five-point swing from Labour to the Conservatives, with the economy an important influence on electoral choice (Whiteley et al. 2013; Johnston and Pattie 2011; Chzhen, Evans, and Pickup 2014). If voters thought the economy had worsened prior to 2010—and 59 per cent did—they were less likely to vote for Labour in 2010. This electoral penalty was likely to have been particularly pronounced for people and households who saw a decline in their income due to the crisis, or who were affected in other direct ways

[4] https://www.bbc.co.uk/news/av/uk-politics-45733093/theresa-may-s-full-speech-to-2018-conservative-conference

(Singer 2018). The shock meets our definition for being highly salient: an unmissable event that was noticeable and unavoidable for British voters, and which remained especially salient in the long-term for those people most affected.

One reason the shock of the crisis continued into 2015 is that the financial crisis had a long-term impact on Labour's reputation for economic competence. From thereon, the Conservatives became more trusted on the economy, reversing Labour's lead on the economy that the party had enjoyed since the early 1990s. The question of Labour's competence on the economy had dogged Labour before the 1990s. It was only following the Exchange Rate Mechanism crisis (in 1992) which badly damaged the Conservatives' reputation for economic competence, that Labour had a commanding lead over the Conservatives on economic competence. This lead continued until the Global Financial Crisis of 2008. Much also changed *between* 2010 and 2015: the Conservatives gained an increased lead on the economy as the economy began to improve in 2013 and subsequently, and that lead widened further as the parties approached the 2015 General Election. While we can only speculate about what a different Labour strategy during this period might have achieved, it is highly unlikely that the lead the Conservatives gained in 2010 could have been reversed between 2010 and 2015 in the absence of another major economic shock. Shocks tend to substantially alter party reputations for competence, and are unlikely to be fundamentally reversed in the course of 'normal' politics (Green and Jennings 2017). The impact of the crisis continued to damage Labour's chances as Labour went into the 2015 Election. Below we show that pre-2010 economic evaluations carried forward to shape vote choices in 2015, and one mechanism through which this happened was via Labour's competence on the economy. In line with conventional theories of economic voting, the main beneficiary of Labour's troubles on the economy was the main alternative party of government, the Conservatives. More unusually, however, from an economic voting perspective, a smaller party—UKIP—also benefited from Labour's economic difficulties. Like the Conservatives, UKIP picked up voters who thought the economy was struggling before 2010. What distinguished UKIP voters from Conservatives on the economy in 2015 was that UKIP voters did not see the economy getting any better.

Another reason the crisis continued to damage Labour, a full seven years later, is that the crisis dominated the competition between the major parties between 2010 and 2015. The shock of the financial crisis provided a significant political opportunity which the Conservatives took advantage of. It is important to note that, had the financial crisis not been such a salient and important economic and political shock, the potential for parties to mobilize public opinion and competition around it would have been lower.

Labour was increasingly blamed for the consequences of the financial crisis *after* the 2010 General Election—in particular for the level of UK debt. The crisis was used as justification for spending cuts aimed at reducing the size of the national debt and cutting the budget deficit. This served to benefit the Conservatives, helping them stave off some electoral blame for the negative consequences of austerity, and it also placed Labour in a difficult strategic position. Labour could either admit that spending had been too high prior to 2010 and commit to the reduction of the deficit (thereby appearing economically responsible but supportive of the policies of austerity), or deny that the deficit was too high and argue against the necessity of austerity. Blaming Labour for the size of the national debt had a substantial impact on Labour's electoral support in 2015, even once we take into account Labour's earlier blame for the crisis. Furthermore, support for the Conservatives was greater among those who thought that austerity was necessary. We demonstrate below how both explanations provide a mechanism through which the long-term effects of pre-2010 economic evaluations influenced vote choices in 2015.

6.2 Estimating the long-term and short-term economic vote in 2015

To assess whether ratings of the economy *prior to 2010* (the evaluations closest in our dataset to the financial crisis) also had an impact on the 2015 General Election, we need to compare the effects of the 2015 economy on vote choice in 2015 (the short-term economic vote) with evaluations of the economy in 2010 on vote choice in 2015 (the long-term economic vote). Furthermore, in order to explain the long-term effects of pre-2010 evaluations, we need to assess the degree to which these effects run through the competence ratings of the Labour Party in 2015, blame for Labour's responsibility of the crisis in 2010 and Labour's responsibility for the level of UK debt in 2015, and the impact of voters' assessments of the necessity of austerity.

We use a dataset that follows respondents across both the 2010 BES internet panel and the 2015 internet panel to examine the long-term impact of voters' evaluations of the economy. The model we estimate is a multinomial logit model of 2015 vote choice among English voters.[5] The model estimates the likelihood of voting for each of the Conservatives, Labour, Liberal Democrats, UKIP, and the Green Party[6] as a function of retrospective socio-tropic (how well the national economy is doing) economic evaluations measured in 2010 and 2015.[7] We control

---

[5] For reasons of comparability we exclude voters in Scotland and Wales.

[6] For reasons of space we do not report the results for the Green Party, which were generally not substantially related to economic perceptions.

[7] The question asks 'How do you think the general economic situation in this country has changed over the last 12 months? Has it:' 1) Got a lot worse, 2) Got a little worse, 3) Stayed the same, 4) Got a little better, 5) Got a lot better. Answers are taken from the pre-campaign wave of the 2010 BES Internet panel and wave 4 (also the pre-campaign wave) of the 2014–15 BES Internet panel.

for respondent age, gender, income, education, economic left–right and liberal–authoritarian values (measured with IRT models, see Tables A6.1 and A6.2 in the appendix), 2010 immigration attitudes (Table A5.4 in the appendix), and 2010 and 2015 party identity strength, specified as alternate-specific predictors.[8]

The nature of the data means our analysis has some limitations. Variables that we would ideally have measured before the financial crisis, such as political values, are not measured until 2014–15 because these questions were not asked as part of the 2010 panel. Likewise, we include controls for partisanship measured in 2010 and 2015. The downside of this is that they could themselves be affected by the crisis. Economic values might change in response to the economic crisis (Gonthier 2017) and some voters might update their partisanship in response to political performance (Fiorina 1981). The inclusion of 'downstream' variables biases statistical estimates of effect size (Rosenbaum 1984). This is likely to lead us to *underestimate* the effect of economic evaluations. We cannot simply ignore these controls, however. The overwhelming weight of evidence shows that economic perceptions are highly coloured by partisanship (Wlezien, Franklin, and Twiggs 1997; Bartels 2002; Evans and Andersen 2006; van der Eijk et al. 2007; Evans and Pickup 2010; Pickup and Evans 2013; Healy et al. 2017).[9] Excluding these controls is likely to lead to a substantial *over*estimate of the effect of economic evaluations. We report the results from our models (see Table A6.3 in the appendix) with our most stringent set of control variables, and expect the results to represent the lower bound of the substantive size of effects.

Figure 6.1 shows the estimated relationship between 2015 vote choice and economic evaluations measured before the 2010 General Election, in the immediate aftermath of the crisis (left-hand side of Figure 6.1)—and economic evaluations measured before the 2015 election (right-hand side of Figure 6.1). The right panel shows a strong effect of 2015 economic perceptions that fits with a classic economic voting story: the Conservatives were rewarded for the perception of an improving economy, and punished if the economy was perceived as getting worse. Note also that, consistent with other research on coalition governments and economic voting (Duch and Stevenson 2013; Duch, Przepiorka, and Stevenson 2015), the Liberal Democrats get very little reward for an improving economy (see also Chapter 7). Conversely, we see the inverse relationship for the opposition parties. Voters who thought the economy had got worse were more likely to vote Labour. We also see

---

[8] By 'alternate-specific predictors' we mean that the party identity part of the model is specified such that a specific party identity only *directly* impacts on the probability of voting for that party (though it will still have an indirect effect on voting for other parties). For example, we estimate the effect of Labour Party identity strength on voting Labour rather than Conservative, but not on voting UKIP rather than Conservative.

[9] There is also some evidence that it is not just answers to survey questions that are coloured by partisanship but actual economic behaviour (Gerber and Huber 2009), although the veracity of this finding has been disputed (McGrath 2017).

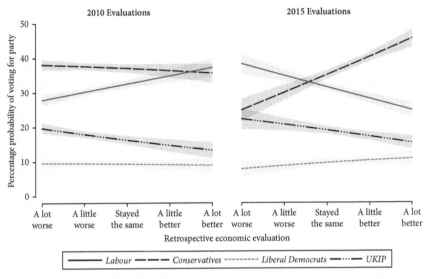

Figure 6.1 Predicted probability of 2015 vote choice by 2010 and 2015 economic evaluation

a similar slope—albeit at a lower absolute level—in the relationship between economic perceptions and voting UKIP.

Moving to the left panel, to the effects of pre-2010 economic evaluations, we see that economic evaluations measured *five years earlier* are still substantially related to 2015 vote choice. British voters in 2015 were not simply myopically voting on short-term economic changes that took place in the run-up to the 2015 election. Voters who thought the economy was doing badly in 2010 continued to punish Labour in 2015. What is perhaps most interesting, however, is that 2010 economic evaluations exert little influence on whether someone is likely to be a Conservative or Liberal Democrat voter. There is a relationship, however, between 2010 economic evaluations and the probability of voting Labour and the probability of voting UKIP. This pattern distinguishes the long-term economic vote we see here from the classic economic vote which sees economic voting as occurring between the two major alternative parties of government. The long-term economic vote benefited UKIP in the 2015 General Election.

The combined effect of both 2010 and 2015 economic evaluations is that Labour fared worst among those who thought the economy was doing badly in 2010 *and* who thought it was doing well in 2015. The Conservatives did best among those who thought the economy was doing well in 2015. The Liberal Democrats fared badly across the range of economic perceptions in both years. UKIP did best among those with the most pessimistic evaluations—those who thought the economy was doing badly in both 2010 *and* 2015.

It is also important to remember that it is not just the slopes of regression models that are important but also the distribution of the underlying variables.

In 2015 the British economy had begun to recover from recession, as inflation and unemployment both declined. At the same time, concerns over the economy abated (measured by the percentage of people listing the economy as the most important issue) and there was increasing economic optimism (Clarke et al. 2016). According to the BES panel data we are using here, the proportion of people thinking the national economy was getting better before the 2010 General Election was 23 per cent, whereas this figure was 46 per cent before the 2015 General Election.

How can we account for the persistence of this long-term economic effect in 2015? We identify three ways in which the shock of the economic crisis persisted into 2015—its effect on evaluations of Labour's competence, attributions of responsibility for government debt, and attitudes towards the necessity of austerity.

6.3 The crisis as a competence shock

Public perceptions of governing competence are prone to change over the long-term in response to external shocks (Green and Jennings 2017). Figure 6.2 shows the percentage of people rating Labour and the Conservatives as 'best' on the economy, between 1990 and 2018. The Conservatives had been dominant on economic competence under Margaret Thatcher and John Major until Britain crashed out of the Exchange Rate Mechanism in September 1992 ('Black Wednesday'), which acted as a major competence shock. The ERM crisis was followed by a period of division and damaging stories of sleaze for the Conservatives, and Labour's reputation on the economy overtook that of the

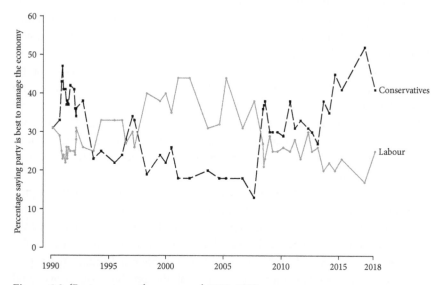

Figure 6.2 'Best party on the economy', 1990–2018

Conservatives'. Under Tony Blair, and initially under Gordon Brown, Labour had a commanding lead over the Conservatives on the economy—a lead that lasted for around fifteen years and three general elections. Labour lost its lead in 2009 in the wake of the financial crisis and the subsequent Great Recession. However, the Conservatives' economic lead was not commanding until shortly before the 2015 Election (and then subsequently reached its maximum around the 2017 General Election).

The loss of Labour's reputation on the economy around 2009 was in some senses inevitable. As we argued above, Labour was bound to take some reputational damage simply by being in government during a profound economic crisis. Voters tend to punish incumbents irrespective of that government's actual ability to control a particular outcome (Achen and Bartels 2016). The Labour government's approach to the financial crisis was dramatic and—in some quarters at least—unpopular. Many found it difficult to understand how a government could afford to spend £500 billion on the financial sector that had just acted so irresponsibly. Furthermore, Labour had adopted a 'light touch' attitude towards regulation of the financial sector prior to the financial crisis. New Labour saw the City as an engine of economic growth which could be harnessed to benefit society as a whole—perhaps epitomised by Peter Mandelson's infamous remark that New Labour was 'intensely relaxed about people getting filthy rich as long as they pay their taxes'. Furthermore, Labour was being blamed for the crash by political opponents. Indeed, it 'proved to be a very potent message in the 2010 General Election, so much so that echoes of it were still being heard in 2015' (Clarke et al. 2016, 39). That is to say, the claim that Labour was to blame for the crisis was powerful in 2010 and it was still being made effectively in 2015.

To demonstrate the effect of competence as a mediating mechanism for the long-term effect of the economic vote in 2015, we add respondents' ratings of how well Labour would handle the economy in 2015 to our model of 2015 vote choice. Figure 6.3 reports the predicted probabilities of voting for each party in 2015 across the range of Labour's economic handling evaluations in 2015. We see a similar pattern to Figure 6.1: Labour was most likely to win votes from people who thought Labour would handle the economy well, whilst the Conservative and UKIP picked up votes from those who thought Labour would handle the economy badly. Adding the mechanism of competence to the model also substantially reduces the apparent effect of long-term 2010 economic perceptions on 2015 Labour vote choice.

Again, it is not just the slope of these lines that is important but the underlying distribution of responses. Figure 6.2, earlier, showed a stark change in how people felt about Labour's economic competence before and after the financial crisis. We can see just how important a difference this made to Labour's vote share in 2015 by showing the predicted probabilities of voting Labour at Labour's mean pre-crash economic handling rating, (measured at the pre-2005 BES wave) and Labour's mean economic handling in 2015 (from the pre-election wave in 2015).

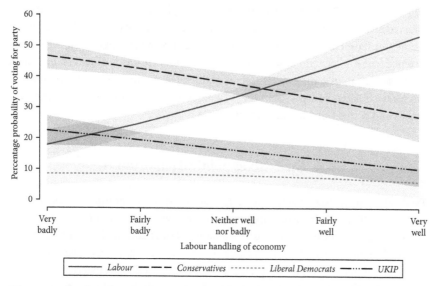

Figure 6.3 Predicted probability of vote choice by 2015 Labour economic handling

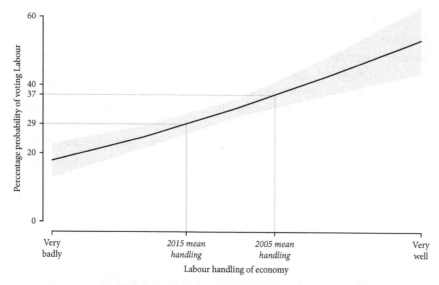

Figure 6.4 Predicted probability of voting Labour in 2015 by perceptions of Labour's handling of the economy, showing the 2005 and 2015 mean perceptions

This is shown in Figure 6.4. The predicted likelihood of voting Labour in 2015 is 8 percentage points higher at pre-crash values for economic competence than if we hold Labour's competence at post-crash values—a substantial difference.

We should be cautious in putting too much weight on this sort of counterfactual. We are not saying that Labour would definitely have tied the vote with the

Conservatives in 2015, or even beaten them outright, had its competence not been affected much earlier by the financial crisis. We can surmise that the Conservatives would not have emphasized competence as a campaign strategy if Labour's competence had not lagged behind the Conservatives'. The bases of voters' decisions are to some extent endogenous to party strategies: competence matters more in electoral choice when the question of competence is made salient by political events and actors (Green and Jennings 2017).

6.4 The crisis as political opportunity

Political competition around the crisis dominated the politics of the period between 2010 and 2015. The Conservatives took two very clear positions: (i) that there was an urgent need to reduce the national debt and the budget deficit (the cost of borrowing for the level of public expenditure) and this meant that the government needed to pursue a range of difficult and painful austerity measures, and (ii) that these policies were necessary because Labour had been profligate in office, sustaining a dangerous level of spending, worsening the impact of the financial crisis on the British economy, and making austerity necessary. These political messages were not an inevitable outcome of the financial crisis and recession that occurred before 2010. They were a clear political strategy to increase the extent to which Labour was blamed for the level of UK debt, to harness the relative Conservative competence on the economy, and to rule out alternatives to austerity as a means of creating prosperity (Clarke et al. 2016). George Osborne (then Conservative Chancellor of the Exchequer) seized upon the political opportunity that had been created by the crisis. After Labour's 2010 defeat, Liam Byrne, Chief Secretary to the Treasury under Brown, left a note to his incoming successor in which he lamented: 'I'm afraid there is no money'. It had been intended as a light-hearted and friendly gesture (Byrne 2015) but the letter was repeatedly brandished by Conservative politicians during the 2015 Election campaign to underline their argument about Labour's profligacy in office. The Conservative campaign message as the parties approached the 2015 General Election was that the choice was one of 'competence versus chaos': competence under the Conservatives or chaos under Ed Miliband's Labour Party. A recurring theme was Labour's—and Ed Miliband's—unsuitability to govern given their previous handling of the economy.

The politics of austerity placed Ed Miliband in a bind. He could either distance Labour from the spending decisions made by Gordon Brown and concede that the level of UK debt was too high (and by implication that it contributed to the size of the economic crisis in Britain), or defend the spending decisions of the Labour government to argue against austerity but run the risk of accepting blame for the level of UK debt. The Conservatives were able to capitalize on those difficulties.

The blame game and austerity

Voters blamed a range of actors for the financial crisis itself. In 2010, 52 per cent of BES respondents thought international financiers were responsible, and 73 per cent chose to blame British banks. Relatively few people thought Labour was responsible for the crisis: only 39 per cent mentioned the Labour government and 36 per cent mentioned Gordon Brown specifically.[10] By 2015, however, Labour was widely seen as being responsible for the aftermath, with 55 per cent of BES survey respondents saying Labour was responsible for the level of UK debt.

We examine the effect of apportioning blame to Labour by adding these variables to our model of 2015 vote choice. Figure 6.5 shows the marginal effects of blaming Labour for the crisis in 2010 and blaming Labour for the level of debt in 2015 on the probability of voting for each party in 2015. The left panel shows that there is no statistically significant effect of blaming Labour for the crisis. The right panel shows, however, that there was a statistically significant and large effect of blaming Labour for the level of debt. This operated to the detriment of Labour and the benefit of the Conservatives.

The perception that Labour were responsible for high levels of debt was a problem for Labour, but the politics of austerity were more complex than this simple story. As Figure 6.6 below shows, the vast majority of both 2010 Labour and 2010

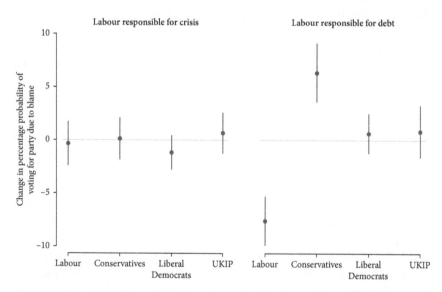

Figure 6.5 Marginal effects of blaming Labour for the financial crisis in 2010 and blaming Labour for the level of debt in 2015 on the probability of voting for each party in 2015

[10] Note that these figures represent the chance to 'tick all that apply', so respondents could say multiple actors were responsible.

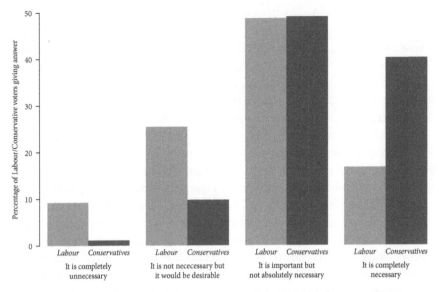

Figure 6.6 Necessity and desirability of reducing the national deficit among 2010 labour and Conservative voters

Conservative voters (and respondents overall) thought that eliminating the deficit was important. Even among 2010 Labour voters, very few (9 per cent) thought that eliminating the deficit was completely unnecessary.

In order to assess the effect of views about austerity, we combine answers to a number of questions about the necessity and method of cutting the deficit, and whether cuts to public spending, local services, and the NHS had gone too far using an IRT model (shown in Table A6.4 in the appendix).

We add this combined variable to our model of 2015 vote choice, again assessing the degree to which this explanation accounts for the long-term effect on the economy. Figure 6.7 shows the predicted probabilities of voting for each of the four largest parties across the combined measure. The more pro-austerity a respondent was, the greater the probability that they voted Conservative (and the more likely they were to vote UKIP), whereas Labour vote choice in 2015 was stronger among respondents who were more anti-austerity, even controlling—as we do—for left–right political values. This graph demonstrates the importance for the Conservatives of justifying their policy of austerity. Voters who were persuaded of the need of austerity were more likely to support the Conservative Party in 2015, an effect that had the potential to shift 2010 Labour voters as well as former Conservatives. Both of the effects we report here—for blaming Labour for the level of UK debt, and agreeing that austerity is necessary—are also significant in models only analysing 2010 Labour voters. That is to say, Labour's support among those who voted for the party in 2010 was also reduced because of the message that Labour was responsible for the deficit, and because of

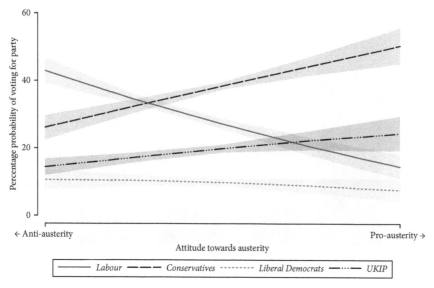

Figure 6.7 Predicted probability of vote choices by austerity attitudes

the belief that austerity was a necessary policy response. Both models suggest that these were additional effects resulting from the political competition around the crisis, changes in evaluation that took place between 2010 and 2015.

6.5 The Global Financial Crisis in a context of partisan dealignment

We note that the impact of the Global Financial Crisis was large and sustained because the shock was large and sustained. However, it also happened within a context of a more volatile electorate, less rooted to parties via strong partisan attachments. A simple illustration can serve to highlight this point.

Our story about long-term economic voting effects, of pre-2010 election economic evaluations on 2015 vote choice, is based, in part, on the long-lasting reputational damage of the crisis on Labour's economic competence. Figure 6.8 shows the relationship between party identity strength among 2005 Labour voters and evaluations of Labour's economic competence, in 2010. The weaker the identification in 2005, the less positive Labour's competence rating. If we imagine that more people fall into the right-hand side of Figure 6.8, it follows that Labour's economic competence would not have fallen back to the same levels as it did after 2010, and the Conservatives, on the flip side, would not have been as positive.

To summarize, if there were more party identifiers in the electorate, and more strongly identifying people among them, we can conclude that there would have

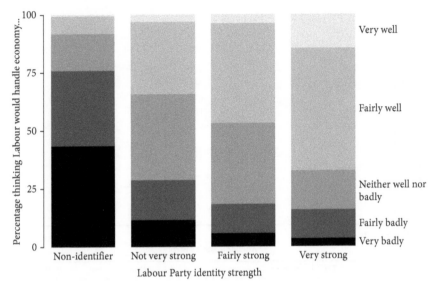

Figure 6.8 2010 Labour Party identity strength and Labour's economic competence, 2015

been greater stability in economic evaluations and greater stability, therefore, in the response to the economic conditions that were precipitated by the Global Financial Crisis and great recession, and the subsequent political competition in response to them.

6.6 What about the 2017 General Election?

Only two years later, the importance of the Global Financial Crisis at the 2017 Election could not have been more different. As Figure 6.2 clearly showed earlier, Labour's perceived competence on the economy continued to flounder. Indeed, the 2017 Conservative competence lead over Labour was even greater than it was in 2015. Despite this, Labour increased its vote share considerably in 2017. The key to understanding the 2017 Election is, as we discuss in more detail in Chapter 9, Brexit. Without pre-empting our discussion of the direct impact of the EU referendum on the 2017 here, it is important to understand how the aftermath of the referendum affected the ongoing influence of the financial crisis on vote choice.

The most obvious effect of the EU referendum is that Brexit rapidly displaced austerity as the key object of political contention. This happened in two ways. First, and most obviously, discussion about Brexit itself took centre stage as the country grappled with how it would leave the EU. Second, one early consequence of the vote to Leave was a loosening of austerity as the new Chancellor, Philip Hammond, dropped the target of putting the budget into surplus by 2020.

Meanwhile, under new leader Jeremy Corbyn, Labour took up active opposition to austerity, and with public support for austerity faltering, the Conservatives seemed reluctant to push the austerity issue in the 2017 Election campaign.

Brexit also affected the politics of the economy in 2017 indirectly. As we have already discussed, partisanship influences the way in which people perceive the political and economic world. As Figure 6.9 shows, after the referendum, whether someone voted Leave or Remain played a similar role. For the two years prior to the referendum, there is little to distinguish the mean retrospective economic evaluations of Leave and Remain voters; in the aftermath of the referendum, however, Remain voters became slightly more pessimistic about how the economy had *already changed.*

Together, these effects resulted in the rapid evaporation of the effects of the financial crisis on vote choice. Building on our previous model of vote choice, we now model the 2017 vote, adding 2017 economic evaluations to our model, and additionally controlling for 2017 party identity and the EU referendum vote (see Table A6.5 in the appendix). Figure 6.10 shows the predicted probability of voting for each party according to 2010, 2015, and 2017 economic evaluations. The right-hand panel shows that economic evaluations were still an important predictor of vote choice in 2017. However, the left and centre panels show that earlier economic evaluations were no longer significant predictors of vote choice in 2017.

Together, the different elections demonstrate that economic voting is not a static phenomenon that always has equal effects—or the same kinds of effects—in every election, nor is it necessarily a simple reward–punishment phenomenon

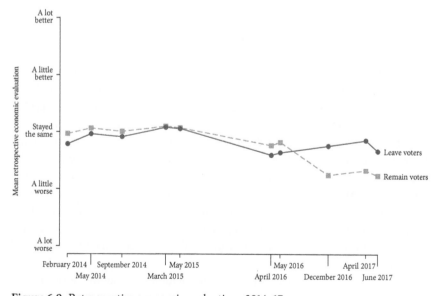

Figure 6.9 Retrospective economic evaluations 2014–17

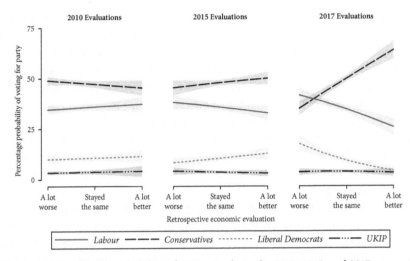

Figure 6.10 Predicted probability of 2017 vote choice by 2010, 2015, and 2017 retrospective economic evaluations

that responds to short-term economic considerations and political choices only in the context of one election. Shocks—and economic shocks—can have long-lasting electoral consequences, they can be magnified and accentuated by political competition, but they can also cause different considerations to be overwhelmed by new factors. This further points to a contextual understanding of political behaviour, and to the importance of better understanding the varied consequences of electoral shocks.

6.7 Conclusions

Shocks, if they shape elections, do not necessarily only have consequences in the immediate election following the shock. In this chapter we demonstrated that the Global Financial Crisis left a long-lasting mark on the way voters decided how to choose between political parties in a subsequent election: in 2015. Such was the size, magnitude, and salience of the financial crisis that voters carried forward their previous evaluations of the economy into their vote choice in 2015. Furthermore, because of the way in which shocks create political opportunities, Labour was further harmed in 2015 because voters blamed Labour for the size of the national debt and the necessity of austerity. The Conservatives were able to compete around the crisis, attributing blame towards Labour as well as benefiting from a short-term upturn in the economy that happened prior to the general election in 2015.

The implications of this chapter are important for understanding the economic basis of the outcome of the 2015 Election. It is not sufficient just to look to the short-term nature of the economy to understand electoral choice in this election (or perhaps, in many other elections). While the improving economic conditions benefited the Conservatives in 2015, this has to be seen in the much larger economic context that continued to overshadow British politics and the memories of British voters. We also showed that the Global Financial Crisis, and its aftermath, was not only relevant to the votes for the two largest parties in 2015: Labour and the Conservatives. Our explanation also accounts for some of UKIP's success in 2015. UKIP benefited in 2015 from long-term economic evaluations prior to 2010, and from perceptions of Labour's economic (in)competence. That is to say, we find an effect of long-term economics on UKIP's vote share in 2015. In a system in which multiple parties compete for votes, not all 'performance'-based assessments will see vote-switching between the government and the main party of opposition, as traditional models of economic voting commonly assume. Minor parties can be outlets for dissatisfaction about economic performance, as UKIP was in 2015.

Our analysis, then, brings new insights to bear on the literature on economic voting. One such insight is how economics and economic performance can be a source of support for populist parties, such as UKIP. Another is how voters' economic assessments might have much longer consequences than has previously been assumed. The majority of the economic voting literature sees the economic vote as a short-term effect of recent economic evaluations on the outcome of an election.[11] However, emerging evidence for the nature of a longer-term economic vote (see Hellwig and Marinova 2015; Wlezien 2015) suggests that electorates can blame governments long into the future. One way this happens is via long-term disruptions to reputations for party competence (Green and Jennings 2017). A reputation, once lost, is very hard to recover, such that past governments can suffer an electoral penalty long after they have lost office. In this chapter we demonstrated the way in which political blame can accentuate, prolong, and even add new blame to parties that have previously been in government. The 'blame game' does not need to be understood as something that takes place at the time of a shock or a crisis. In the example of the Global Financial Crisis, the blame over the level of UK debt happened after the election in which Labour lost office (2010), and helped win the Conservatives the election in 2015.

Electoral shocks shape electoral behaviour in important, and potentially long-lasting ways. This chapter has demonstrated how shocks can remain relevant in public opinion and electoral choice long after they occurred. If a shock is sufficiently memorable and parties still compete around its legacy, then there is no reason to assume that voters will only blame a party or a government in one election. A large shock will not be easily forgotten—or forgiven. This might well be relevant

---

[11] A range of examples include: Kramer (1971); Tufte (1978); Lewis-Beck (1990); Campbell (1992); Alesina, Londregan, and Rosenthal (1993); Lewis-Beck and Stegmaier (2000); Duch and Stevenson (2008); Kayser and Wlezien (2011); and Achen and Bartels (2016).

for some of the other shocks that we document in this book, and in shocks that have yet to take place. If Britain leaves the European Union in such a way that there is a deeply felt economic cost, and if one party's reputation for competence is badly damaged, there is no reason to think that will not impact on the electoral behaviour of British voters for multiple elections. That is just one of the lessons we can draw from the long-lasting electoral impact of the Global Financial Crisis.

7

Reward, Blame, and Guilt by Association?

The Electoral Collapse
of the Liberal Democrats

In 2010, the Liberal Democrats recorded their highest general election vote share since 1983 (as the SDP-Liberal Alliance) and their largest number of seats since 1929 (as the Liberal Party). In 2015 they won only 8.1 per cent of the vote, only a third of what they managed five years earlier, making it their worst performance since 1970. As a result, they faced almost complete electoral wipe-out, winning only eight seats, losing forty-nine of the fifty-seven they had won in 2010. The fall in the Liberal Democrat vote was the largest single election drop in support for any party in Britain since 1931, when the Liberals had been similarly annihilated in the aftermath of a coalition.

Two years later, in 2017, some hoped that the Liberal Democrats—as Britain's most consistently pro-EU party—might ride an anti-Brexit wave to recovery. Instead, the Liberal Democrats only made a net gain of four seats and lost a further half point of vote share.

In this chapter we explore the reasons behind the 2015 collapse and failure to recover in 2017. Part of this story is well known—left-leaning Liberal Democrat voters deserted in droves (cf. Cutts and Russell 2015)—but the full picture is more complex. In many countries, junior partners do badly in elections following coalition participation (Buelens and Hino 2008). Parties in coalition governments always face a trade-off between the unity of the coalition government and the distinctiveness of their party image. Some argued that this dilemma was particularly acute in an adversarial political system such as Britain's (McEnhill 2015). As we will show though, it was not the nature of British politics that sunk the Liberal Democrats in 2015, but the nature of the Liberal Democrats' support. The Liberal Democrats were particularly poorly suited to withstand the potential electoral backlash of coalition because they had few partisan voters and relied heavily on tactical support. These problems were compounded by perceptions of viability—the more unpopular the Liberal Democrats became, the less likely it seemed they would be able to win seats. The less likely they were to win seats, the less point there was in lending the Liberal Democrats a tactical vote.

Electoral shocks. Edward Fieldhouse, Jane Green, Geoffrey Evans, Jonathan Mellon, Christopher Prosser, Hermann Schmitt, Cees van der Eijk, Oxford University Press (2020). © Fieldhouse, Green, Evans, Mellon, Prosser, Schmitt, and van der Eijk.
DOI: 10.1093/oso/9780198800583.001.0001

These problems continued in 2017 with little sign of recovery. What the similarity in the 2015 and 2017 Liberal Democrat vote share conceals, however, is that there was considerable turnover beneath the surface. Less than a fifth of those who voted for them in 2017 had voted for them in 2010 before the coalition was formed. Moreover they only retained 50 per cent of those that supported them in 2015.

7.1 The 2010–15 coalition

The hung Parliament following the 2010 Election was, in part, the result of the long-term trend of declining support for the two major parties and the rise of the political fortunes of 'other' parties, particularly the Liberal Democrats (Chapter 2). The 2010–15 Conservative–Liberal Democrat coalition government was the first peacetime coalition in Britain since the 1930s and was most British voters' first experience of coalition government. In this chapter we consider how the hung Parliament and the subsequent experience of coalition government acted as a shock to the British political system. Although, unlike the other shocks in this book, it was entirely a product of electoral politics, we can consider it an electoral shock for several reasons. First, it was not an inevitable outcome of the normal electoral process. The hung Parliament was contingent on a number of factors, including the closeness of the Conservative and Labour vote share and a strong performance of the Liberal Democrats, together with a long-term decline in the number of marginal seats which has reduced the tendency of the first-past-the-post system to deliver large majorities for the leading party (Curtice 2010). Indeed it was not just a hung Parliament that was contingent but a hung Parliament with a particular configuration of seats that meant the Liberal Democrats could only form a viable coalition with the Conservatives (Cowley and Kavanagh 2015). Even very small shifts in party support could have opened up a different set of post-election possibilities.

Second, the coalition was hard for voters to ignore: the Westminster Parliament had been considered *the* model of single-party majority rule (Webb 2000), yet the 2010 Government was clearly and unambiguously a coalition with Nick Clegg, the Liberal Democrat leader, taking a high-profile position as deputy prime minister. Third and perhaps most crucially, it had the potential for enormous electoral consequences. For most of the period since their formation in 1988, the Liberal Democrats had carefully navigated a path of 'equidistance' between the major parties to avoid alienating voters from either side of the political spectrum (Russell and Fieldhouse 2005). However, in more recent elections the Liberal Democrats had positioned themselves as part of a 'progressive alliance', and were regarded by many as being more left-wing than Labour (Russell and Fieldhouse 2005). Prior to 2015, many Liberal Democrat voters were Labour supporters voting tactically, and Liberal Democrat voters were generally more sympathetic to Labour than to the Conservatives (Russell, Fieldhouse, and MacAllister 2002). By entering a coalition

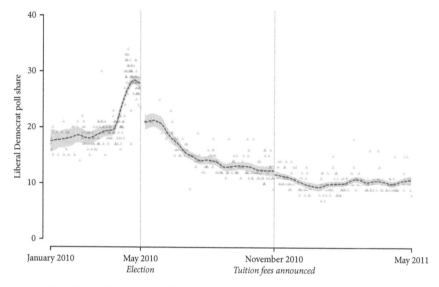

Figure 7.1 Liberal Democrat polling share in the run-up to and aftermath of the 2010 election

with the Conservatives there was a clear danger they risked upsetting the carefully constructed appeal they had spent many years building.

From the beginning of the Conservative–Liberal Democrat coalition, many observers believed it would not end well (Bale 2012). As the Victorian Prime Minister Benjamin Disraeli—once remarked, 'England does not love coalitions.'

At first glance this appears to be true. Together, the coalition parties lost 14.4 per cent of the vote at the 2015 Election, the largest swing against a British government since the expansion of the franchise in 1918 (Green and Prosser 2016). Of course, however, this punishment was not equally shared between the Conservatives and the Liberal Democrats. It would be fairer to say Britain does not love junior coalition partners. Figure 7.1 show the Liberal Democrat's polling performance in the run-up to and immediate aftermath of the 2010 Election. Public support for the Liberal Democrats plummeted almost as soon as they joined the coalition. By July 2010 the Liberal Democrats were polling at 16 per cent, 7 percentage points lower than their performance at the 2010 Election. By the end of August they had reached 12 per cent. By the end of 2010 they had polled below 10 per cent for the first time. The rapid fall of the Liberal Democrats in the polls— which occurred largely *before* the publication of the Browne Review of Higher Education Funding—belies the commonly held view that the Liberal Democrats were seriously damaged by the abandonment of their pledge to abolish tuition fees.[1] At the 2015 Election the Liberal Democrats lost two-thirds of their vote and

---

[1] Although the tuition fees issue became a stick that was used to beat the Liberal Democrats, its prominence in explanations of the collapse in Liberal Democrat support far outstrips the evidence

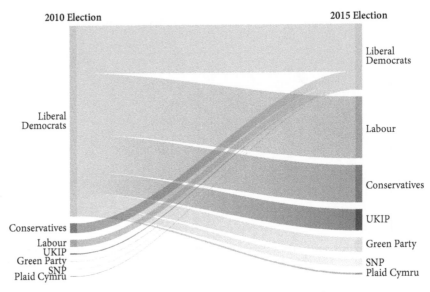

Figure 7.2 2010 and 2015 vote choice of 2010 and 2015 Liberal Democrats voters

forty-nine of their fifty-seven MPs. The Conservatives seemed to avoid punishment altogether and increased their vote share by 0.8 per cent, winning twenty-four more seats than they did in 2010.

In this chapter we show that the damage to the junior coalition partner was not simply the consequence of accountability in coalition government or dislike of coalition in general, but rather the consequence of this *specific* coalition. The most obvious consequence of going into coalition with the Conservatives is that the Liberal Democrats were punished by their left-wing supporters. However, this is only part of the story. Figure 7.2 shows the size of the flow of votes to and from the Liberal Democrats between 2010 and 2015. It shows that in 2015 the Liberal Democrats not only lost votes to Labour and the other progressive parties, but that a large chunk (20 per cent) of 2010 Liberal Democrat support actually went to their coalition partners, the Conservatives, and a not inconsiderable proportion (11 per cent) ended up voting UKIP—perhaps the ideological polar opposite of the Liberal Democrats in the British party system. These losses were compounded by the failure to recruit new voters. Figure 7.2 also shows that the Liberal

that it had a large effect on Liberal Democrat support. As well as the fact that Liberal Democrat support collapsed before the tuition fees announcement, other pieces of evidence suggest that, at most, tuition fees had a small impact on Liberal Democrat votes. In incumbent Liberal Democrat seats where they had won over 28 per cent of the vote in 2010, they lost only slightly more votes in seats with relatively large numbers of students (23.9 points) compared to seats with relatively few students (21 points) (Curtice, Fisher, and Ford 2016). Additionally, less than 1 per cent of lost Liberal Democrat supporters mentioned education (including tuition fees) in their most important issue responses.

Democrats gained a small number of voters from other parties in 2015. But for every vote they gained, the Liberal Democrats lost eight.

The Liberal Democrat to Conservative flow and the electoral geography of Liberal Democrat MPs are key to understanding how the Conservatives managed to win a majority at the 2015 Election. It is clear that Labour were the main beneficiaries of defecting Liberal Democrat voters. In terms of seats, however, the Conservatives won twenty-seven former Liberal Democrat seats to Labour's twelve. The explanation of this apparent discrepancy was the nature of party competition in Liberal Democrat seats. In most (thirty-eight) Liberal Democrat seats the Conservatives were the second largest party at the 2010 Election, while Labour was second in only seventeen. Competition in Liberal Democrat–Conservative seats was also much closer than Liberal Democrat–Labour seats. At the 2010 Election, the Conservatives had twice as many votes as Labour on average in Liberal Democrat-held seats. Consequently, although on average the Labour vote went up in Liberal Democrat seats and the Conservative vote went down, the Conservatives were better positioned to benefit from the collapse in Liberal Democrat support.

The small increase in the Conservative share of the vote in 2015 conceals large changes under the surface. Although the Liberal Democrats lost 15.1 percentage points of the vote, Labour and the Conservatives only increased their vote share by a combined 2.1 percentage points. At the individual level, the Conservatives lost large numbers of voters at the 2015 Election and were particularly damaged by the rise of UKIP, as we discussed in Chapter 5. However, the defection of voters from the junior coalition partner to the senior helped cover those losses.

In this chapter we show how the Liberal Democrats' choice to join the coalition and the backlash of their left-of-centre base not only had disastrous consequences in 2015 but also continued to damage their chances of recovery in 2017. We find that the Liberal Democrats faced a problem common to other junior coalition partners: the difficulty in claiming credit for government achievements. Ultimately, however, the electoral impact of these problems was minimal. Most of the Liberal Democrat collapse can be attributed to the nature of Liberal Democrat voters.

7.2 The nature of the Liberal Democrat vote

After their formation in 1988, the Liberal Democrats maintained a policy of 'equidistance' between the Conservatives and Labour. However, under the leadership of Paddy Ashdown and later Charles Kennedy, the Liberal Democrats repositioned themselves as part of a broader anti-Conservative alliance. During this period, centre-left voters were actively encouraged to switch tactically between Labour and the Liberal Democrats depending on the local electoral context (Russell and Fieldhouse 2005). Building on local viability and carefully targeted campaigning, they increased their number of seats to forty-six in 1997, peaking at sixty-two in 2005, aided by the convergence of the Conservative and Labour parties (Green 2015) and dissatisfaction with Labour over the Iraq War (Fieldhouse, Cutts, and Russell 2006).

That the electoral fortunes of the Liberal Democrats went hand in hand with their adoption of an anti-Conservative position means that it is unsurprising that many Liberal Democrat voters were angry and disappointed that their vote for the Liberal Democrats resulted in a Conservative-led coalition government. Moreover, compared to Labour and Conservative voters, Liberal Democrat support has been different in two regards. First the Liberal Democrat vote has historically been 'soft', with much lower levels of partisanship and a high reliance on tactical support. This lack of a strong partisan core meant that many Liberal Democrat voters viewed the Liberal Democrat participation in government unfiltered by a Liberal Democrat partisan screen, whilst some viewed it through the lens of Labour partisanship. Second it has been particularly reliant on local campaigning and support from tactical voters, which dried up in the wake of the coalition.

A weak partisan base

Compared to the major parties, the Liberal Democrats have always suffered from a lack of strong attachment to the party. The proportion of Liberal Democrat voters who say they have a Liberal Democrat party identity has historically been much lower than that of the two major parties (Russell and Fieldhouse 2005). Liberal Democrat identifiers have also historically been less likely than other partisans to vote for their natural party (Crewe 1985; Norris 1997). Moreover, Liberal Democrat voters have also been the most likely to switch parties between elections (Crewe 1985; Russell and Fieldhouse 2005).

This was still the case in 2010 when they entered coalition. Figure 7.3 shows that, according to the BESIP, the proportion of Liberal Democrat voters in 2010 who identified with the party was substantially lower than the Conservatives or Labour, particularly those who identified strongly with the party. Also notable is the number of Liberal Democrat voters who identified with no party—indeed the Liberal Democrats won most of its votes among those who did not have a party identity in 2010—and those who identified with another party. In total, only half of 2010 Liberal Democrat voters identified with the party, and only one in ten of those saw themselves as very strongly Liberal Democrat, with 44 per cent of identifiers seeing themselves as not very strong Liberal Democrat. A fifth of 2010 Liberal Democrat voters had a Labour Party identity and 5 per cent had a Conservative Party identity.

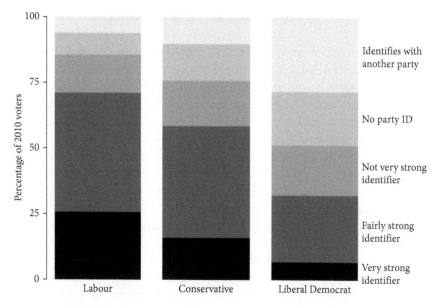

Figure 7.3 Party identity of Conservative, Labour, Liberal Democrat 2010 voters

The absence of a large partisan core to the Liberal Democrat vote meant that the problems faced by junior coalition partners were likely to land particularly heavily on the Liberal Democrats.

As we will see, Liberal Democrat partisans were more likely to give the party credit for positive changes during the coalition government. Previous research shows that partisanship 'raises a perceptual screen through which the individual tends to see what is favourable to his partisan orientation (see Chapter 4). The stronger the party bond, the more exaggerated the process of selection and perceptual distortion will be' (Campbell et al. 1960, 133). Partisan voters are more likely to receive favourable information about their party because they pay attention to information relevant to their own party, receive communications from the party, and have more interactions with party activists (Adams, Ezrow, and Somer-Topcu 2014). Partisans are also more likely to engage in motivated reasoning—political cognition is an affectively driven cognitive process and partisan voters are likely to process political information in ways which maintain their existing partisanship (Lodge and Taber 2005; Lodge and Taber 2013; Redlawsk 2002; Erisen, Lodge, and Taber 2014). This helps explain why partisan voters are likely to see their party as being more influential in a coalition (Meyer and Strobl 2016).

If the Liberal Democrats had started with a stronger partisan base in 2010 it is likely that their role in the coalition would have been seen favourably by a larger number of people and that more of their voters would have weathered the storms of coalition partnership.

Tactical voting and local campaigning

The second aspect of the nature of the Liberal Democrat vote that may have affected its electoral fortunes in coalition government is the importance of local campaigning (Cutts 2014; Johnson 2014; Russell and Fieldhouse 2005) and support from those who tactically vote Liberal Democrat to keep out their least preferred of the Conservatives and Labour (Fieldhouse, Shryane, and Pickles 2007). Figure 7.4 shows the self-reported reasons for voting Conservative, Labour, or Liberal Democrat in the 2010 British Election Study. Compared to the Conservatives and Labour, fewer voters supported the Liberal Democrats because they thought they had the best policies or the best leader, and a much higher proportion said they voted Liberal Democrat when they really preferred another party or for tactical reasons. This made them vulnerable to desertion as a result of being seen to have taken sides by joining the coalition.

The majority (56 per cent) of those who loaned their vote to the Liberal Democrats when they really preferred another party were Labour supporters. As suggested above, those who voted Liberal Democrat to keep out the Conservatives were unlikely to be happy with the Liberal Democrats going into coalition with the Conservatives and this is likely to have led to a 'tactical unwind' (Fisher and Curtice 2006), with Labour supporters seeing no reason to lend the Liberal Democrats their vote.

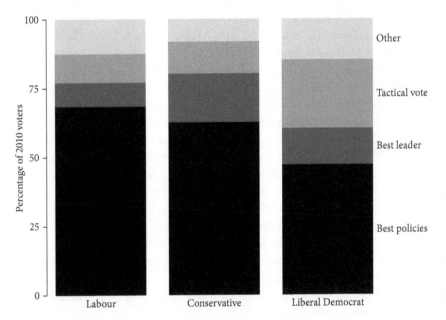

Figure 7.4 Stated reason for voting for party in 2010 by party voted for

However, this tactical unwind may have extended beyond Labour supporters (and other supporters of other progressive parties like the Green Party) who were angered by the Liberal Democrats going into coalition with the Conservatives. The main challenge faced by third parties in the UK is overcoming the 'credibility gap' they face because of the first-past-the-post electoral system (Russell and Fieldhouse 2005). Historically, the Liberal Democrats have used local elections to demonstrate their electoral viability in particular areas (MacAllister, Fieldhouse, and Russell 2002; Cutts 2014; Russell and Fieldhouse 2005). Governing parties generally lose votes in British local elections (Prosser 2016c) and the Liberal Democrats were no different, and indeed they fared particularly badly, averaging 14.5 per cent of the projected national share of the vote at local elections between 2011 and 2014—just over half the 28 per cent they recorded in 2009.[2] Combined with their poor showing in the national polls, this is likely to have severely harmed perceptions of the local viability of Liberal Democrat candidates. As well as left-leaning tactical voters abandoning the Liberal Democrats out of anger at their participation in a Conservative-led government, the resulting collapse in the viability of Liberal Democrat candidates is likely to have led tactical voters to desert the Liberal Democrats more generally.

7.3 The effects of coalition participation

The central dilemma of coalition government is managing the trade-off between the compromises necessary for stable government while retaining a distinctive partisan profile (Martin and Vanberg 2008). Previous analysis of the coalition agreement suggests that the Liberal Democrats were successful at negotiating the compromise necessary for stable government, but less successful at maintaining a distinctive party profile. A comparison of the Conservatives and Liberal Democrat 2010 electoral manifestos and the coalition agreement shows that in some respects the Liberal Democrats got a good deal. About 75 per cent of Liberal Democrat manifesto pledges made it into coalition agreement, compared to about 60 per cent of Conservative pledges (Hazell and Yong 2012), and the overall policy position of the coalition agreement was closer to the Liberal Democrat manifesto than the Conservatives (Quinn, Bara, and Bartle 2011). However, not all manifesto promises are viewed with equal importance by voters (Mellon, Prosser, et al. 2018). Many of the Liberal Democrat 'wins' in the coalition agreement were on relatively unimportant or low-salience issues (Bale 2012) and several flagship Liberal Democrat policies—the proposed constitutional reforms like the AV referendum and a

---

[2] British local elections are held in a rotating combination of different councils and no official national results are reported. The 'projected national share of the vote' is the national vote estimated and reported by the BBC.

wholly or mainly elected House of Lords—ultimately proved disastrous (Hazell and Yong 2012). Overall, 'the Liberal Democrats' focus on "minor" policies blinded them to the far more important issue of how to manage the economy, a matter which they agreed with—or conceded to—the Conservatives' (Hazell and Yong 2012, p. 40).

Similarly, although the Liberal Democrats secured a greater proportion of ministerial and cabinet posts than their share of government MPs, these largely took the form of junior ministers spread across departments and all the 'great offices of state' were held by Conservatives. The Liberal Democrats' tactics in both the coalition agreement and their ministerial appointments was to try to sell the idea of coalition government to the British public and show that it could be just as effective and efficient as single-party government.

The experience of coalition in other countries suggests that, as coalitions continue, parties of government will seek to differentiate themselves in order to win votes (Martin and Vanberg 2008). This can be seen in the Conservative–Liberal Democrat coalition. Once the government was settled and the Liberal Democrats realized they were facing an enormous electoral backlash, they sought to claim credit for particular government policies and for blocking Conservative proposals (Cutts and Russell 2015). However the lack of key portfolios made it difficult to sell the contribution of the Liberal Democrats to the government (Russell 2010; McEnhill 2015; Cutts and Russell 2015).

Research from other countries suggests that junior partners are generally not given much credit for the government's achievements (Anderson 2000; Duch and Stevenson 2008; Fisher and Hobolt 2010), and the experience of Liberal Democrats proved to be no different. Many voters do not follow day-to-day policymaking and instead use heuristics to aid their political decision-making (Lau and Redlawsk 2001). In coalition government, the prime minister's party is seen to be in control of the agenda and so receives the credit and blame for the government's actions.

In order to examine attributions of responsibility for policy changes during the coalition government we use a set of questions about change and responsibility in six policy areas from the pre-election wave of the 2015 BES internet panel: the economy, cost of living, the National Health Service, schools, immigration, and crime.[3]

---

[3] For each policy area, respondents were asked either 'Do you think that each of the following are getting better, getting worse or staying about the same?' (the economy, NHS, and schools) or 'Do you think that each of the following are getting higher, getting lower or staying about the same?' (cost of living, immigration, and crime). Answers were giving on a five-point scale. Respondents were then asked 'Thinking about the changes you just described, who do you think these are the result of?' The answer options were not mutually exclusive, and here we make use of whether or not respondents thought the 'Conservatives in UK government' and/or the 'Liberal Democrats in UK Government' (coded as a binary variable, 1 = party responsible for change in policy area). The other answer options were 'the last Labour UK government', 'the Scottish government' (if the respondent was in Scotland), 'the Welsh government' (if the respondent was in Wales), and 'none of these'.

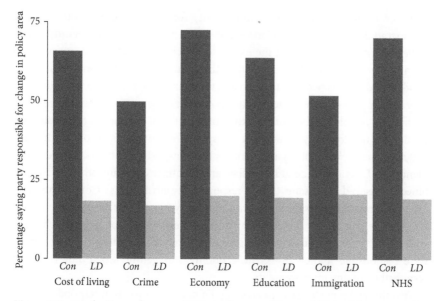

Figure 7.5 Attributions of responsibility to Conservatives and Liberal Democrats for change in six policy areas during 2010–15 coalition

Figure 7.5 shows that, as we would expect from the comparative literature, the Conservatives receive considerably greater attributions of responsibility than the Liberal Democrats. Between 50 per cent and 73 per cent of respondents said the Conservatives were responsible for changes in each policy area, while only 17 per cent to 21 per cent say the same thing about the Liberal Democrats.

Previous research has also suggested that partisan identifiers are more likely to give their own party credit for achievements in coalition (Meyer and Strobl 2016). If this was true in 2015 then, among Liberal Democrat identifiers at least, the party might get some credit for coalition. To test this we modelled whether each coalition partner was held responsible for a range of policy areas as a function of their pre-coalition (2010) party identification.[4] The results show a number of consistent patterns across the six policy areas. First, respondents were consistently less likely to attribute responsibility for policy changes to the Liberal Democrats. With the exception of two of the policy areas, even Liberal Democrat partisans were less likely to attribute policy success to the achievements of their own party rather than the Conservatives. Only for the NHS and education do Liberal

[4] We specify a series of logistic regression models, with separate models for the Conservatives and Liberal Democrats in each policy area. The dependent variable is a binary variable where 1 = the party responsible for change in policy area. The independent variables are perceived change in the policy area, the respondent's 2010 party identification (none, Conservative, Liberal Democrat, any other party), and self-reported levels of political attention (0: No attention–10: A great deal of attention). Full results are shown in Table A7.1 in the appendix.

Democrat partisans attribute responsibility for policy success to the Liberal Democrats at the same rate as Conservative partisans do to the Conservative Party.

Perhaps more importantly, the extent to which each partner was given credit for a policy area depended on whether the change in that area was regarded as good or bad. This is best illustrated using the example of the economy, although a very similar pattern is found across each policy area. Figure 7.6 shows the predicted probability of holding the Conservatives or the Liberal Democrats responsible for changes to the economy by whether a respondent thought the economy had got better or worse. We plot separate graphs for non-party identifiers, Conservative identifiers, Liberal Democrat identifiers, and identifiers with any other party combined (measured at the same time as responsibility attributions). Conservative and Liberal Democrat partisans are much more likely to say their party is responsible for positive changes in the economy and not responsible for negative changes, while partisans from other parties are more likely to say the governing parties were responsible if they think the economy was getting worse but were not responsible for any improvements.

Two things are particularly interesting. First, the non-partisan respondents generally act somewhere in between partisan groups when attributing responsibility to the Conservatives, being less likely to attribute success to the Conservatives than Conservative partisans, but also less likely to attribute failure to the Conservatives than other partisans. However non-partisans act almost exactly the same as other partisans when attributing responsibility to the Liberal Democrats, only attributing responsibility to them for negative changes (but still at a much lower rate than for the Conservatives).

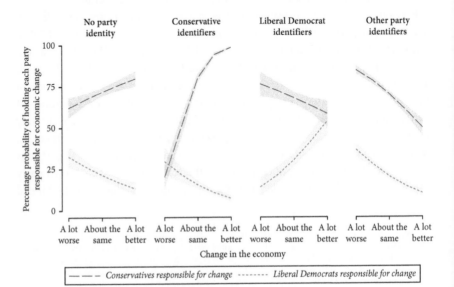

Figure 7.6 Attribution of responsibility for change in the economy

Second, Liberal Democrat partisans act like other partisans when attributing responsibility to the Conservatives, holding the Conservatives relatively more responsible when they thought the economy had got worse. Like Conservative identifiers, they are also relatively more likely to credit their own party if they thought the economy was getting better. Notwithstanding this, in absolute terms, Liberal Democrat partisans were equally likely to credit the Conservatives as their own party when they thought the economy had got a lot better.

There was little reciprocal generosity from Conservative partisans, who were less likely than non-partisans and partisans of other parties to attribute responsibility to the Liberal Democrats for any changes to the economy, except when they thought the economy had got a lot worse. An exception to this general pattern occurs for the NHS and education, where Conservatives give a tiny bit more credit to the Liberal Democrats than other- and non-partisans do.

These results make it clear that the Liberal Democrats suffered from the same problem faced by other junior coalition partners—they were not held responsible by most voters for the actions of government, and so were unlikely to be rewarded for any government successes.

7.4 Explaining the 2015 collapse

We have considered some of the reasons for the Liberal Democrat collapse in 2015, including the reliance on tactical votes coupled with the desertion of left-leaning voters; the lack of credit they received for achievements in government; the reduced viability resulting from their poor poll showing; and the low level of partisan identification. To evaluate how important a role each of these factors played, we model the 2015 votes of English respondents who voted Liberal Democrat in 2010 in the combined BES 2010–15 panel data.[5]

We restrict this model to 2010 Liberal Democrat voters because we are primarily interested in the desertion of 2010 Liberal Democrat voters, which contributed so heavily to their poor performance in 2015. The loyalty rates of 2010 Liberal Democrats was around one in four (as we saw in Figure 7.2), compared to the average retention rate between 1964 and 2010 for the Liberal Democrats of three in five and of around four in five for Labour and the Conservatives. Of course, retention is only half the story—the Liberal Democrats also failed to recruit new

---

[5] We estimate a multinomial logistic regression restricted to voters in England because the existence of nationalist parties in Scotland and Wales means those voters have a different choice set. We model vote choice in 2015 as a function of variables measured in wave 4 of the BES 2015 panel: feelings towards the political parties, the perceived relative chances of the Liberal Democrats winning the respondent's constituency compared to the Conservatives and Labour, perceptions of changes to the economy and whether the Liberal Democrats were responsible for those changes, and feelings towards Nick Clegg. The results of this model are shown in Table A7.2 in the appendix.

voters to replace those they had lost. However, trying to estimate who might have been recruited to the Liberal Democrats had circumstances been different would push the logic of our counterfactual approach beyond what it is capable of showing. We therefore focus here on why previous supporters abandoned the Liberal Democrats.

Using the model, we then estimate what proportion of 2010 Liberal Democrats would have voted Liberal Democrat in 2015 under a series of counterfactual conditions and compare them to the proportion that actually did in reality: 28 per cent. These are illustrated in Figure 7.7.

The first counterfactual examines the role of attribution of responsibility for changes to the economy. We estimate this counterfactual to test the extent to which the Liberal Democrats fell victim to the problem of attribution common to junior coalition partners. To do so, we model what the Liberal Democrat vote share would have been if *everyone* held the Liberal Democrats responsible for changes to the economy. This represents a ceiling for what the level of attribution of responsibility might be, but, as Figure 7.7 shows, this does next to nothing to the estimated Liberal Democrat retention rate. Indeed, if anything it *reduces* the Liberal Democrat vote slightly, though this difference is not statistically significant. The lack of change here is likely to be because in the counterfactual there are more people who think the economy got *worse* holding the Liberal Democrats responsible for this negative change. The Liberal Democrats may have faced difficulty getting credit for the achievements of the coalition government, but they also avoided some of the blame.

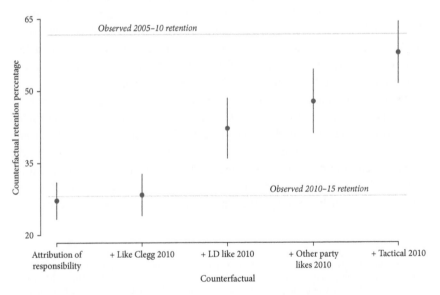

Figure 7.7 Estimates of the proportion of 2010 Liberal Democrat voters voting Liberal Democrat in 2015 under different counterfactual conditions

We estimate the other counterfactuals by substituting the values of the variables used in the model with the answers the same respondents gave to the same questions before the 2010 Election. Doing so enables us to answer the question of what would have happened in 2015 if respondents still had similar perceptions of the Liberal Democrats as they did before they entered the coalition with the Conservatives. First, we estimate the effect of feelings towards Nick Clegg. The Clegg counterfactual suggests that even if Nick Clegg had been as popular as he was at the height of 'Cleggmania', on its own this would have made no difference to Liberal Democrat losses.

Next, we estimate the effect of changing feelings about the Liberal Democrats as a party. The answer, unsurprisingly, is that the Liberal Democrats would have retained more of their voters, and would have kept around 42 per cent of those who voted Liberal Democrat in 2010, fourteen points more than they did in reality. Although this is a large change, it is important to note that even if people still liked the Liberal Democrats to the same degree as they did in 2010, the model estimates they *still* would have lost nearly six in ten of their previous voters (considerably higher than typical Liberal Democrat losses).

In part this is due to how voters felt about the other parties. It is not just the absolute levels of how voters feel about political parties that determines their vote but rather how much they like each party *relative* to the other parties. If feelings towards all the parties had stayed the same as their 2010 levels the Liberal Democrats would have kept 48 per cent of their vote, an additional 6 points higher than the effect of feelings towards the Liberal Democrats alone.

However, even if feelings towards all parties had stayed at the same levels as 2010 the Liberal Democrats still would have retained substantially fewer voters than their usual levels of retention. The final counterfactual points to one reason for this—as the perennial third party in British politics, the Liberal Democrats have long faced a 'credibility gap'—whereby people who might otherwise have voted Liberal Democrat voted for a different party because they thought they stood no chance of winning their constituency. With the collapse of the Liberal Democrats in the opinion polls and local elections, it would not be surprising if the credibility gap exacerbated the Liberal Democrats collapse. The counterfactual analysis supports this idea—if respondents' perceptions of the relative chances of the Liberal Democrats compared to Labour and the Conservatives were the same as their 2010 perceptions, the Liberal Democrats would have kept 58 per cent of their vote, which is statistically indistinguishable from their 2005–10 levels of retention (and in line with their historical retention rates).

These counterfactuals raise the question of why people's feelings about the Liberal Democrats changed between 2010 and 2015. We are also interested in the changes in feelings towards the Liberal Democrats among those who did not vote Liberal Democrat in 2010, as these formed the pool of potential recruits. To investigate these questions, we model the change in feelings about the Liberal Democrats

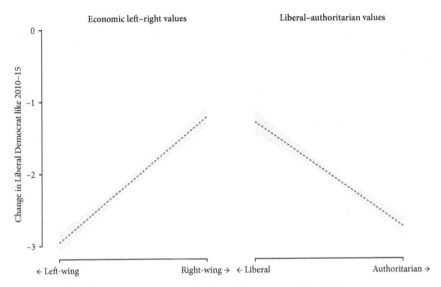

Figure 7.8 Change in feelings towards Liberal Democrats 2010–15 by economic left–right and liberal–authoritarian values

between 2010 and 2015 using a linear regression model, controlling for how they felt about the Liberal Democrats at the outset (see Table A7.3 in the appendix). We focus on a combination of 2010 and 2015 predictors: respondents' positions on the economic left–right and liberal–authoritarian values scales, and whether, and how strongly, they identified with the Liberal Democrats before the coalition.

Figure 7.8 shows strong effects for both left–right and liberal–authoritarian values. Perhaps unsurprisingly given the widespread perception that the Liberal Democrats were an anti-Conservative progressive party, the feeling scores of those on the left dropped by about twice as much as those on the right. Conversely however, the relationship with liberal–authoritarian values runs in the opposite direction—with more authoritarian voters becoming more hostile to the Liberal Democrats than liberal voters. In other words, following coalition, the Liberal Democrats became more unpopular among more left-wing voters while maintaining popularity among their traditional core support: voters with liberal social values.

Figure 7.9 shows that changes in feelings towards the Liberal Democrats depended strongly on prior partisanship, reported before the 2010 Election. Conditional on their political values, the largest decrease in liking the Liberal Democrats was among those voters who did not identify with the party or only identified weakly (who also tended to start from a lower level to begin with). By contrast, very strong Liberal Democrat identifiers, on average, liked the party as much in 2015 as they had in 2010. This suggests that, had they had a stronger partisan core, the Liberal Democrats would have experienced a much less dramatic collapse in their vote.

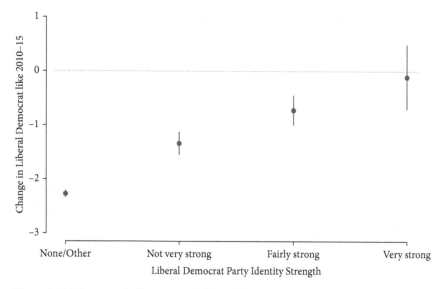

Figure 7.9 Change in feelings towards Liberal Democrats 2010–15 by strength of Liberal Democrat identity in 2010

Among 2010 Liberal Democrats, we also find that changes in feelings about the Liberal Democrats depend on why they voted Liberal Democrat in the first place. Those who voted for the Liberal Democrats because they thought they had the best policies were the most stable in their feelings about the party (though even these dropped by nearly two points), while those who voted Liberal Democrat because they liked Nick Clegg, and particularly those who voted tactically for the party, experienced the largest drops in support.

7.5 2015–17: The recovery that never happened

After their electoral disaster in 2015, Nick Clegg resigned as leader and was replaced with Tim Farron. However, a new leader seemed to do little to repair the damage that had been done by the coalition, and the Liberal Democrats continued to flounder in the polls. Following the EU referendum in 2016 (which we discuss in Chapter 9), the Liberal Democrats set out an unambiguously pro-European position and called for a second referendum on the terms of Brexit. Glimmers of a possible recovery appeared in late 2016 when the Liberal Democrats won the Richmond Park by-election, and they began to nudge ever so slightly upwards in the polls.

These first shoots of a recovery came to a crashing halt with the announcement that there would be an early election in 2017. The Liberal Democrats found themselves outside the media spotlight during the campaign and many wavering

Labour voters—perhaps seeing no other viable option—began to flood back to Labour (Mellon et al. 2018a). The most media attention the Liberal Democrats received during the campaign was not of the sort they wanted, as Farron, an Evangelical Christian, faced repeated questions about whether he thought gay sex was a sin.

The 2017 Election results were a mixed bag for the Liberal Democrats. In terms of votes, the 2017 Election saw the further erosion of Liberal Democrat support with a decrease in their share by half a percentage point. In terms of seats, the result was more positive, as they finished the election with a net gain of four seats. However this result hides considerable turnover in Liberal Democrat MPs. Half of the 2015 Liberal Democrat seats were lost—including the seat of former leader Nick Clegg—as was their recently won by-election seat of Richmond Park. These losses were offset by regaining seven seats they had lost in 2015 and one they had lost in 2010.

The churn in Liberal Democrat seats is the first clue that there was more switching to and from the Liberal Democrats beneath the surface than their similar votes shares in 2015 and 2017 would suggest. What the stability in overall vote share conceals is that on some measures, the Liberal Democrats experienced a partial recovery between 2015 and 2017, but this was offset by further losses. We can see this in Figure 7.10, which shows the outflow of Liberal Democrat 2015 voters and the origins of their 2017 voters. The key difference between this figure and the equivalent plot for 2010–15 (Figure 7.2) is that although the Liberal Democrats lost many voters (their 2015–17 loyalty rate was only 50 per cent), these were offset

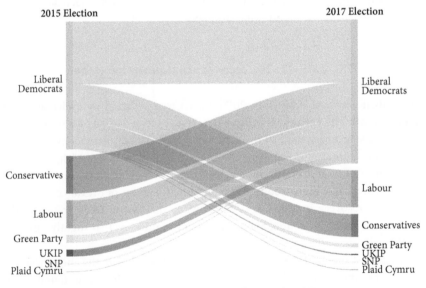

Figure 7.10 2015 and 2017 vote choice of 2015 and 2017 Liberal Democrats voters

by similar gains from other parties. Relatively speaking, in 2017 the Liberal Democrats continued to lose votes to Labour more heavily than to the Conservatives, with 29 per cent of their 2015 voters defecting to Labour and 18 per cent to the Conservatives. By contrast, in 2017 they recruited more voters from the Conservatives (26 per cent of their 2017 vote previously voted Conservative) than from Labour (19 per cent).

While Figure 7.10 demonstrates that the Liberal Democrats electoral performance stabilized in 2017 it does not suggest any hint of return to the pre-coalition situation. Our data also indicate (not shown in Figure 7.10) that there was little sign of the Liberal Democrats recovering a substantial proportion of those supporters who deserted after the coalition. Only 19 per cent of their 2010 supporters voted for them again in 2017, making up around half (52 per cent) of their 2017 support. These included 32 per cent who had stayed with them in 2015 and a further 20 per cent who returned in 2017 having not voted Liberal Democrat in 2015. However, these returners represented only 10 per cent of all those who had deserted the Liberal Democrats in 2015. In other words, the damage done by the 2010 coalition shock to Liberal Democrat support persisted in 2017.

When we examined the 2015 collapse of the Liberal Democrats, our counterfactuals suggested that two factors were particularly important in explaining the collapse in the Liberal Democrat vote in 2015: how people felt about the party and how well people expected the Liberal Democrats to do in their constituency. We examine how each of these factors changed in 2017 in turn.

First, we examine how feelings towards the Liberal Democrats changed between 2015 and 2017 using the same model we used to examine changes between 2010 and 2015 (see Table A7.3 in the appendix). Figure 7.11 shows the predicted level of change in feelings towards the Liberal Democrats by economic left–right and liberal–authoritarian values. For left–right values, there is a gentle slope indicating that economically left-wing people increased their liking of the Liberal Democrats slightly more than right-wing people. The most important aspect of this relationship, though, is its relative flatness—people across the economic dimension were likely to feel more positively about the Liberal Democrats in 2017 than they did in 2015. By contrast, there is a much steeper relationship between feelings towards the Liberal Democrat and liberal–authoritarian values, as liberals became more favourably disposed towards the Liberal Democrats in the two years after the 2015 Election while social conservatives stayed more or less where they were.

We also know authoritarians became much more negative about the Liberal Democrats from 2010 to 2015 (as shown earlier in Figure 7.8). Together these changes mean that Liberal Democrat support was much more closely aligned with political values than it had been before they entered the coalition (Figure 7.12). In 2010, on the economic left–right dimension, feelings towards the Liberal Democrats were relatively even across the left and centre of the scale before dropping off on the right-hand side of the scale. Following the coalition with the Conservatives,

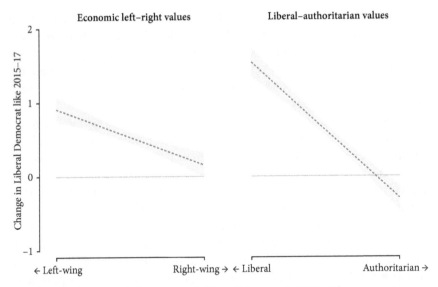

Figure 7.11 Change in feelings towards Liberal Democrats 2015–17 by economic left–right and liberal–authoritarian values

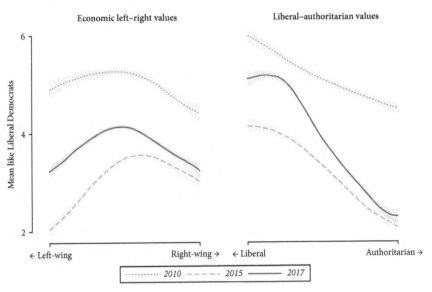

Figure 7.12 Relationship between economic left–right and liberal–authoritarian values and feelings towards the Liberal Democrats in 2010, 2015, and 2017

in 2015 there was a much greater drop in pro-Liberal Democrat feelings on the left-hand side of the scale than on the right (as shown earlier in Figure 7.8). In 2017 there was an uneven recovery (Figure 7.11) as feelings towards the Liberal Democrats recovered on the left, leaving a peak in the centre of the distribution and falling away towards both extremes. This uneven recovery resulted in a pattern similar to that seen in 2010 but at a considerably lower level of favourability. On the liberal–authoritarian dimension, the Liberal Democrats have always been more popular on the liberal end of the scale, but with a larger fall among social conservatives in 2015 (Figure 7.8) and a stronger recovery among social liberals in 2017 (Figure 7.11), feelings towards the Liberal Democrats were much more closely aligned with liberal–authoritarian values than they had been previously. This suggests the Liberal Democrat party post-coalition was much more reliant on a traditional liberal support base rather than on the anti-Conservative centre-left voters that had driven its support before 2010. Undoubtedly this uneven recovery was partly driven by attitudes towards Brexit which, as we show in Chapter 9, are strongly related to liberal–authoritarian values.

Earlier we showed that a lack of Liberal Democrat Party identification made the party more vulnerable to decline in 2015. But how did their soft base affect their recovery in 2017? We can investigate this by looking at how feelings changed among pre-coalition Liberal Democrat identifiers (Figure 7.13). This shows a mirror image of the 2010–15 relationship (Figure 7.9), with the least change among none and other party identifiers and increasing positive changes as Liberal Democrat identity gets stronger. This suggests that their weak partisan base may also have contributed to the failure to recover in 2017.

Even though the Liberal Democrat recovery was lopsided, overall, they were more popular in 2017 than 2015, with mean likes scores increasing from 3.4 to 3.8. How then, can we explain why their vote share actually went *down* in 2017? The answer is largely due to the fact that, in most seats, the Liberal Democrats were not seen as viable and were therefore perceived as a wasted vote. When we examine

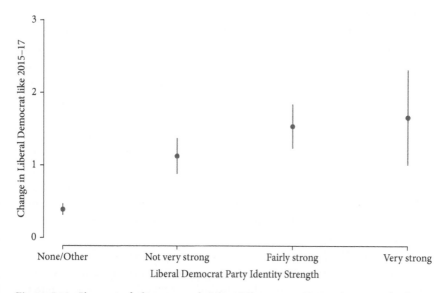

Figure 7.13 Change in feelings towards Liberal Democrats 2015–17 by strength of Liberal Democrat identity in 2010

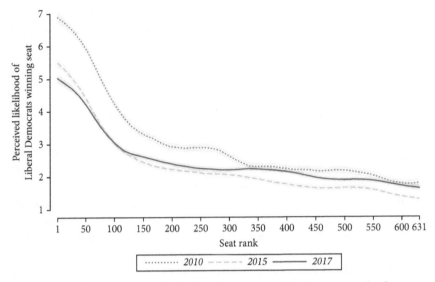

Figure 7.14 Perceived likelihood of Liberal Democrats winning a respondent's constituency in 2010, 2015, and 2017 by rank of Liberal Democrat vote share at previous election

expectations of how well they would do in respondents' constituencies in 2010, 2015, and 2017, we can see that the Liberal Democrats' 'expectation gap' problem got worse between elections. Figure 7.14 plots the perceived likelihood of the Liberal Democrats winning a respondent's constituency against the rank ordering of Liberal Democrat vote share in that seat at the previous election. Between 2010 and 2015 there was a sharp drop in how well voters thought the Liberal Democrats would do in their constituencies across the board. Between 2015 and 2017 we see a curious pattern. In places where the Liberal Democrats had no chance of winning, expectations recovered slightly (we might think of this improvement as going from 'no chance' to 'next to no chance'). In the seats where the Liberal Democrats had the best chance of winning (based on previous performance), their perceived likelihood of winning actually fell even further.

As we discussed earlier, overcoming the expectations gap has been a perennial problem for the Liberal Democrats. Participation in coalition not only destroyed their good standing with many of their potential supporters, it also damaged their credibility as a viable electoral force. Some of the electorate seemed at least partially willing to forgive the Liberal Democrats by 2017, and they had been gaining steady ground in local and parliamentary by-elections, but perhaps the election came too early for them.

We can put all of these factors together by running a model of Liberal Democrat vote choice in 2017 (see Table A7.4 in the appendix) and estimating a series of counterfactuals, as we did earlier, by substituting 2010 values of variables into the

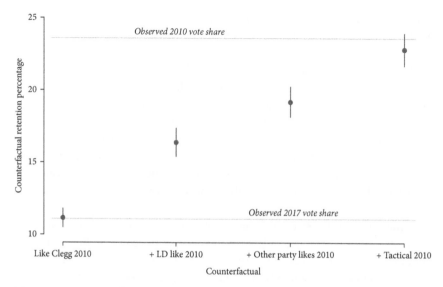

Figure 7.15 Estimated proportion voting Liberal Democrat in 2017 under different counterfactual conditions

model. Because of the different context of the 2017 Election, unlike the earlier model, here we include both defections and recruitment to see the overall effect of the change in attitudes towards the Liberal Democrats. These counterfactuals are shown in Figure 7.15, and show clearly that we cannot explain the failure of the Liberal Democrats to perform better by any single factor. Instead, it was the combination of feelings towards the Liberal Democrats, feelings towards other parties, and perceptions of Liberal Democrat viability.

The counterfactuals estimate that, on their own, feelings towards the Liberal Democrat leader would have made no difference to Liberal Democrat performance. If feelings towards the Liberal Democrats had recovered to 2010 levels, the Liberal Democrats would have gained an additional 5.2 percentage points of the vote. Combined with feelings towards other parties, this would have increased by an additional 2.8 points, and with perceptions of viability adding a further 3.6 points. Taken together, this would have meant a doubling of the Liberal Democrat vote share, putting them roughly back on par with their 2010 performance.

7.6 Conclusion

After five years of coalition government, the 2015 Election saw the dramatic collapse of the Liberal Democrat vote—seeming to confirm Disraeli's adage that Britain 'does not love coalitions'. However, a more nuanced examination of what happened between 2010 and 2015 suggests that the collapse of the Liberal Democrats was due to the nature of this *specific* coalition, and not because Britain in general is somehow unsuited to coalition government.

Our analysis shows that the Liberal Democrats faced a problem common to junior coalition partners in other countries—the difficulty of claiming credit for government success. Voters were much more likely to hold the Conservatives responsible for both positive and negative changes in multiple policy areas.

Going into coalition government was particularly damaging to the Liberal Democrats because of the nature of their support base—characterized by low levels of partisanship, a centre-left and socially liberal bias in political values, and a heavy reliance on tactical support. This made the Liberal Democrats unsuited to withstand the electoral costs of coalition participation, especially coalition with the Conservatives.

Perhaps the most noticeable symptom of this was an uneven drop in support, with economically left-wing voters turning against the party in 2015. Added to this, low levels of partisanship meant that many Liberal Democrat voters viewed the compromises and trade-offs inherent in coalition government unfiltered by a favourable 'partisan screen'. Perhaps even more problematically for the Liberal Democrats, a large proportion of their voters saw their participation in coalition through the lens of Labour partisanship—something unlikely to result in a favourable view of the Liberal Democrats in coalition with the Conservatives, regardless of their achievements in government.

The nature of the pre-coalition Liberal Democrat support base also acted as a brake on their recovery after 2015. Strong Liberal Democrat partisans were relatively quick to forgive the Liberal Democrats, with their feelings towards them returning to pre-coalition levels by the time of the 2017 Election. However there were very few of these voters, and non-partisan and tactical supporters were much less forgiving. The nature of politics in the aftermath of the EU referendum— which we will discuss in detail in Chapter 9—also contributed to the uneven nature of the Liberal Democrat recovery. Feelings towards the Liberal Democrats recovered substantially among social liberals, who saw eye to eye with the Liberal Democrats on Brexit. More socially conservative voters, many of whom had given the Liberal Democrats tactical support in the past (an aspect of the Liberal Democrat vote that has perhaps been poorly understood), were much less forgiving.

Absolution was not the only challenge faced by the Liberal Democrats in 2015 and 2017. The collapse of support for the Liberal Democrats in the polls and their losses in local elections over the 2010–15 Parliament created a vicious cycle for the Liberal Democrats, first in 2015 and continuing into 2017. As their support plummeted, the Liberal Democrats looked a less good bet for tactical voters hoping to block a rival party from winning seats. We showed that perceptions of the likelihood of the Liberal Democrats winning local constituencies had a significant impact on whether 2010 Liberal Democrats chose to vote for the Liberal Democrats again in 2015, regardless of changes in voters' feelings towards them. The same was true in 2017. Although there were glimmers of a recovery in late 2016, they were not enough to overcome perceptions that the Liberal Democrats were unlikely to win in most seats.

Looking at the bigger picture, the electoral fortunes of the Liberal Democrats are closely tied with the rise—and sudden collapse—of party system fragmentation in British elections. The rising vote share for 'other' parties since 1970 was in large part due to increasing support for the Liberal Democrats. The collapse of the Liberal Democrats had two seemingly contradictory effects on party system fragmentation. In 2015, former Liberal Democrat voters helped to prop up support for Labour and the Conservatives, but also boosted the shares of the other small parties—UKIP, the Greens, and the SNP.

In 2017, when these other small parties faced challenges of their own, the absence of a viable third party option in the Liberal Democrats meant that many voters had nowhere to turn but to the Conservatives or Labour. It was not immediately obvious, but the collapse of the Liberal Democrats was the first step in the sudden contraction of the British party system that took place in 2017.

8

Scotland

A Tale of Two Referendums

One of the most significant factors behind the fragmentation of party support at the 2015 General Election was the success of the SNP and the collapse of Scottish Labour. The 2015 Election was Labour's worst performance in Scotland in terms of vote share since 1918 and the best ever achieved by the SNP. By 2017, although the SNP gains had receded from the high of 2015, the picture in Scotland had changed fundamentally. The Conservatives, who had held no more than a single Scottish seat since 1992, pushed Labour into third place. Scotland has seen unique levels of volatility in recent general elections and these changes, and their explanation, are an essential part of understanding GB-wide change.

The SNP's share of the nationwide vote increased from 1.6 per cent in 2010 to 4.7 per cent in 2015, making a large contribution to the rise in challenger-party voting at the national level. However, the local picture was even more dramatic. In 2010, Labour won forty-one of fifty-nine seats in Scotland with over 40 per cent of the Scottish vote, while the SNP won only six seats with 20 per cent of the vote. In 2015, Labour could muster only 24 per cent of the popular vote and a single Westminster seat, while the SNP won 50 per cent of the vote and all but three of the fifty-nine Scottish seats. The SNP landslide made them the third largest party in the Westminster Parliament. Much of this success persisted into the 2017 General Election but the SNP's vote share fell by thirteen percentage points between 2015 and 2017 to 37 per cent and the party lost twenty-one of their fifty-six seats. The main beneficiaries were the Scottish Conservatives, whose vote doubled to 29 per cent and who gained thirteen seats. Scottish Labour's vote recovered slightly to 27 per cent, but they won only seven seats, making them only the third largest party.

What precipitated these dramatic changes in electoral fortunes? In this chapter, we consider how an electoral shock—the Scottish independence referendum—altered the basis of political alignments in Scotland. We demonstrate that the referendum brought about a shift in the underlying structure of political allegiances through widespread changes to political identities and the nature of their relationship to party support. We show how the referendum acted as a catalyst for Labour's collapse in Scotland in 2015, leading to a realignment of voters and parties according to whether they supported Scottish independence. This realignment occurred primarily because the referendum aligned attitudes towards

Electoral shocks. Edward Fieldhouse, Jane Green, Geoffrey Evans, Jonathan Mellon, Christopher Prosser, Hermann Schmitt, Cees van der Eijk, Oxford University Press (2020). © Fieldhouse, Green, Evans, Mellon, Prosser, Schmitt, and van der Eijk.
DOI: 10.1093/oso/9780198800583.001.0001

independence and party choice more closely rather than because it substantially increased support for independence. Having voted in favour of Scottish independence, Yes supporters appeared unable to reconcile themselves with supporting a unionist political party.

Scottish electoral politics was further disrupted by the EU referendum in 2016, which cut across both traditional party lines and the emergent independence divide. This second shock led to a largely unexpected Conservative revival at the 2017 General Election. As in the rest of Britain, the EU referendum drew voters back to the main parties, reversing the fragmentation of 2015 (see Chapter 9) but maintaining high levels of electoral volatility.

This, then, is the tale of how two referendums—and two electoral shocks—can help explain dramatic political changes in the 2015 and 2017 General Elections, as they unfolded in Scotland.

This first part of the chapter examines the impact of the Scottish referendum on voting in the 2015 General Election. We then consider how the EU referendum brought about a Conservative resurgence in Scotland in 2017.

8.1 The independence referendum: An electoral shock

The Scottish independence referendum took place on 18 September 2014 and was the result of a long-running campaign for independence led by the SNP since their formation in 1934. The Scottish government announced the decision to hold the referendum following the SNP victory in the Scottish Parliamentary Elections of 2011. It required the agreement of the UK Parliament, which the coalition government in Westminster formally provided in the 2012 Edinburgh agreement.

Formally, both campaigns were non-partisan, but the major Westminster parties (and their Scottish counterparts) all lined up to back the *Better Together* campaign, while the SNP dominated the *Yes Scotland* campaign, although *Yes Scotland* did involve members of other parties including the Scottish Greens and Labour for Independence. The result of the referendum saw the pro-Union ('*Better Together*') side winning by a margin of 55 per cent to 45 per cent, despite a dramatic narrowing of their lead in the polls in the run-up to referendum day. The referendum followed a hard-fought campaign and the turnout rate of 85 per cent—the highest ever recorded for a vote in Scotland—underlined the high level of engagement across the electorate.

Many of Labour's electoral problems were brewing well before the referendum was announced. Although Labour had won the majority of Scottish seats in every general election since 1959, they had come second to the SNP in the Scottish Parliamentary elections in 2007 and 2011. Notwithstanding this, Labour had enjoyed a comfortable lead in the opinion polls (for Westminster elections) in Scotland throughout the period from the 2011 Scottish Parliament Election through

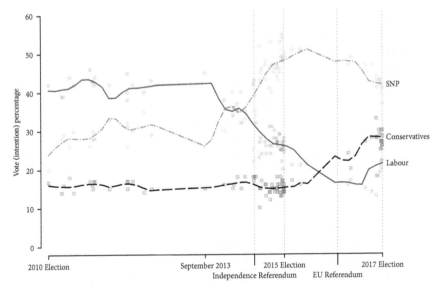

Figure 8.1 SNP, Labour, and The Conservatives in the polls: Westminster voting intention, March 2011–June 2017

to April 2014, when the referendum campaign was in full swing (Figure 8.1). However, from then on the picture changed dramatically. The referendum campaign seemed to damage Labour's popularity, which continued to erode right through to the 2015 General Election, which delivered Labour's worst defeat in Scotland since 1918. There was very little sign of recovery for Labour in 2017 when they fell into third place behind the Conservatives. The most dramatic period of decline for Labour immediately followed the referendum, which reflected a strengthening of the alignment between independence referendum voting and party choice in the immediate post-referendum period.

8.2 Labour's decline, 2014–15

The decline in Labour's popularity was not spread evenly across the population. Data from the BES internet panel and the Scottish Referendum Study (SRS) (Henderson et al. 2014) reveal that the referendum had little impact on the voting intentions of Scots who voted against independence (Figure 8.2). Rather, the shifts in Scottish voting behaviour occurred primarily among those who supported independence: large numbers of whom deserted Labour and switched their allegiance to the SNP.

Figure 8.2 shows that while around two-thirds of Yes voters intended to vote for the SNP before the independence referendum (February–March 2014),

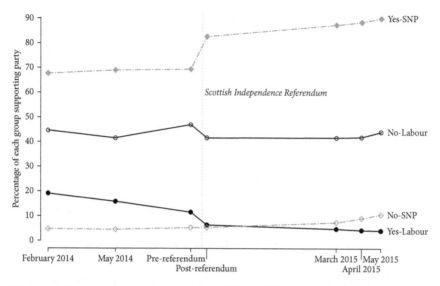

Figure 8.2 General election vote intention of Yes and No voters, 2014–15

approximately 20 per cent still intended to vote Labour. Despite the SNP lead among pro-independence voters, Labour's comfortable lead among unionists meant that Labour was still ahead in the opinion polls at the start of 2014. The picture changed very little in May following the European Parliamentary Elections, in which the SNP won the most votes in Scotland by a margin over Labour of 29 per cent to 25 per cent: a narrower victory than in the 2009 European elections. After the independence referendum in September 2014, however, a dramatic change occurred: 83 per cent of Yes voters now intended to vote SNP (an increase of 13 points compared to the immediately pre-referendum wave) compared to only 6 per cent who intended to vote Labour (a decrease of 5 points from the pre-referendum wave). By the time of the General Election in 2015 90 per cent of Yes voters reported voting for the SNP.

8.3 From referendum voting to party choice

In Chapter 3, we set out how major political events can act as shocks that alter the structure of political alignments. In this chapter, we explore the mechanisms by which one such event—the Scottish independence referendum—had precisely this effect. By choosing sides in the referendum, many voters faced potentially conflicting political loyalties, and were therefore forced to reconsider both their partisan allegiances and their political values. For example, could Labour identifiers who were Yes voters reconcile supporting a SNP-backed Yes campaign and opposing the Labour backed 'No' campaign, with continuing to support Labour? In short, the answer appears to be 'no'.

The most common understanding of electoral behaviour is that people cast votes that reflect their political preferences and party attachments. Previous research has shown that the reverse causal ordering can also be true: the act of casting a vote for a party may lead to changes in voters' attachments to parties (Markus and Converse 1979; Dinas 2014). This is one way in which second-order elections—where the 'costs' of voting for different parties are lower—provide opportunities for small parties to gain support and increase their perceived viability in subsequent first-order elections (Farrer 2015; Prosser 2016b; MacAllister, Fieldhouse, and Russell 2002).

Referendums present a rather different set of circumstances and opportunities, but they have the potential for influencing first-order elections in a similar fashion. The main difference is that a referendum is not a straightforward competition between parties. In this sense, we might expect the potential for spillover to be reduced. For example, if parties are not in direct competition with each other, the result cannot act as a guide to voters about electoral viability and hence strategic voting. However, if a referendum is structured by party competition—that is, the political parties are openly campaigning on one side of the debate or the other—then a referendum campaign might expose previously latent issues in party choice, raising the salience of a potentially cross-cutting political cleavage. For example, the Parti Quebecois enjoyed an increase in both vote share and seats in the 1981 Quebec provincial elections (Clarke 1983) that followed the unsuccessful 1976 referendum campaign.

Insights from political and social psychology help explain why attitudes and attachments might shift as a result of political behaviour. Voters engage in motivated reasoning in order to reconcile new political information with their pre-existing views and behaviours (Lodge and Taber 2013). Motivated reasoning tends to increase the *stability* of political attitudes and alignments, and the act of voting can buttress voters' affective orientations towards a pre-existing attitude or affiliation. For example, partisanship can be reinforced by voting because voting provides signals about group identity, which in turn strengthens partisan ties (Dinas 2014). However, the same process can lead to a *change* in political attitudes and alignments in the event of one-off or idiosyncratic political behaviours. For example, Bølstad et al. (2013) find a positive effect of tactical voting on preferences for the party voted for, attributing this to the reduction of cognitive dissonance: having voted for a party it is harder to dislike that party and it is easier to like it.

In political psychology, partisan identification has been likened to social identity (Greene 1999; Huddy 2001; Greene 2004; Huddy, Mason, and Aarøe 2015; Huddy 2013). Social Identity Theory (Tajfel and Turner 1979; Tajfel 1981) suggests that a person's perceptions of other members of a group can affect their attitudes and norms through a process of self-categorization and meta-contrast whereby group members maximize inter-group differentiation and minimize within-group differentiation (Turner et al. 1987). Self-categorization may therefore lead a person to more strongly differentiate between their own party and its opponents (Duck, Hogg, and Terry 1995; Greene 2004). Moreover, an individual's behaviour may reinforce their group identification (if the behaviour is aligned with their identity), especially when that behaviour is public.

If political partisanship can form the basis of social identity and self-categorization, it seems plausible that other salient political divisions might also act as a basis for social identities. In the case of the Scottish referendum, the campaign and the position that citizens adopted was highly salient and socially significant. The referendum therefore had the potential to make Yes-voting Labour supporters regard Labour as part of an out-group ('unionists'), and the SNP as an in-group ('nationalists'). Competing social identities could lead to a switch or weakening of party identification among Labour supporters who voted Yes. Certainly, such a shift would reduce the cognitive dissonance of combining pro-Labour and pro-independence identities. This dissonance (and its resolution) is nicely summed up by a quotation from a Yes voter on whatscotlandthinks.org: 'I am a trade unionist and coming from a Labour supporting background I should be red through and through but I could never vote for such a bunch of lying toe rags.'

By shifting the basis of voter identity from being defined by a party to an alternative form of self-categorization (nationalist versus unionist), the referendum weakened the salience of traditional partisanship. Moreover, an increase in the salience of a new group identity (e.g. 'nationalists' or 'Yes voters') can override the attitudes and norms associated with other groups the person identifies with (Mullen, Brown, and Smith 1992; Eifert, Miguel, and Posner 2010). In other words, citizens moved their attitudes and norms into line with those of their new identity. In the case of Yes voting, these attitudes and norms would be feeling more Scottish, more pro-independence, and less favourably inclined towards those on the unionist side—including the Labour Party.

While it is possible for citizens to hold multiple political identities, it seems likely that identifying with the Yes campaign (or as a nationalist-separatist) might supplant existing party identities because these identities came into direct conflict with Labour identification. This is particularly the case given the high salience of Scottish independence and the strong identity-basis of the Scottish independence campaign.

8.4 Labour's dwindling base

The crucial shift we wish to explain in this chapter is the exodus of Labour voters between spring 2014 and May 2015. Comparing wave 1 (February 2014) and wave 6 (May 2015) of the internet panel, we find that one third of all those who supported Labour in early 2014 shifted to the SNP by the time of the 2015 General Election, and these made up 12 per cent of all Scottish voters. This is not to say that there was no important change prior to 2014, but the 2015 BES panel data (which started in February 2014) is still able to capture a substantial proportion of the shift from Labour to the SNP. Because of our interest in the collapse of Labour voting in 2015, in the following analysis, we focus on Scots who intended to vote Labour when we first interviewed them in 2014. Figure 8.3 provides an illustration of how Yes voters in this group intended to vote in Westminster elections at two key moments (immediately prior to the referendum, and immediately after the referendum), and how they actually voted at the 2015 Election. The thickness of each block is proportional to the size of the group, with the darker blocks indicating those intending to vote Labour and the lighter blocks indicating those intending to vote SNP (and actually doing so in the final time point).

Immediately before the referendum, about two-thirds of previously Labour-supporting Yes voters were still intending to vote Labour, a proportion which dropped to less than half in the immediate aftermath of the referendum. By the time of the 2015 Election, Labour only hung onto a small minority of its previous supporters on the Yes side: around four in five Yes voters who had intended to vote Labour fifteen months earlier voted for the SNP in 2015.

As we discussed in Chapter 4, the independence referendum took place in the context of weak partisan identification. Stronger identities provide more

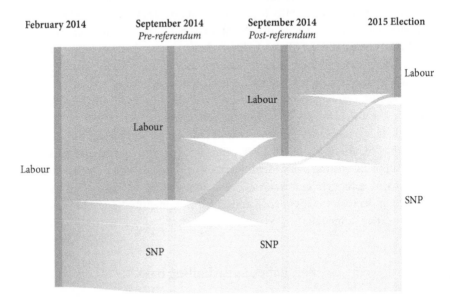

Figure 8.3 Flow of votes between Labour and SNP for initially Labour-supporting Yes voters between key periods in the run-up and aftermath of the Scottish independence referendum

Table 8.1 Proportion of Labour/Yes voters switching to the
SNP by pre-referendum Labour party identity strength

Labour Identity Strength	% Voting SNP in 2015
None/Other party	83
Not very strong	80
Fairly strong	79
Very strong	61

motivation to resolve conflicting demands in ways which maintain existing identities and so we would expect fewer strong Labour identifiers to defect to the SNP after the referendum, which is what we see in Table 8.1. However, such was the importance of the referendum that even a majority of very strong Labour identifiers in February 2014 who voted Yes switched to the SNP (but did so at a rate more than 20 points lower than non-identifiers).

For 'No' supporters, we would not expect a conflict between their political identities—voting No was perfectly compatible with continued support for the unionist Labour and Conservative parties—and so we would expect less switching between parties following the referendum.

The preceding analyses have shown how voting for independence was closely related to shifts in attitudes and party support in the run-up to and after the referendum. We are interested in whether the referendum as a shock had an effect on vote choice, and if so, whether this was due to a change in people's attitudes and identities, or a change in the relationship between those attitudes and identities and vote choice. To investigate this, we turn to multivariate longitudinal models to provide evidence of the most likely direction of causal effects. These models allow us to estimate the effects of variables we are interested in on referendum vote choice as well as the reverse, so we are able to get a good picture of any two-way relationship.[1] In other words, we can show how attitudes, evaluations, and identities informed referendum vote choice, and in turn how these were affected by that vote choice.

8.5 The independence referendum effect

Our key objective is to measure the effect of Independence Referendum voting intention and referendum vote on switching to the SNP, while controlling for those

---

[1] Although we cannot completely isolate the causal effect due to the possibility of reciprocal causality, our cross-lagged models minimize this problem by measuring the explanatory variables in the preceding time point and by allowing us to control for lagged versions of the dependent variable. A simplified illustration of the structure of these models is shown in Figure A8.1 in the appendix.

factors (measured in the previous wave) that affected referendum vote, as well as other factors that might have precipitated switching.

Before examining the impact of the referendum on the outcomes of interest, we should note that many of the factors that influenced general election vote choice also influenced referendum voting. Explaining referendum vote choice is not the main aim of this chapter, but it is worth noting that, controlling for prior referendum vote intention, the main influences on referendum vote in May 2014 were devolution preferences[2] and feelings towards the party leaders (see Table A8.2 in the appendix for the full results of the cross-lagged model). Prior to the referendum, approval of the Scottish government and hypothetical economic expectations also played a role in predicting referendum vote intention. Referendum vote was also influenced by devolution preferences, satisfaction with UK democracy, and expectations about the Scottish economy if Scotland became independent.

Our models also account for vote intention at the previous wave, vote at the 2010 Westminster and 2011 Holyrood elections, British and Scottish national identity, approval of Scottish government performance, party leader like scores, devolution preferences, and satisfaction with democracy in the UK. Given these very comprehensive controls, it is perhaps not surprising that referendum vote intention has no significant impact on general election vote intention in the first wave, and is only marginally significant in the second wave. However after the referendum had taken place, referendum voting has a statistically significant and substantively large effect in every subsequent wave. We illustrate the impact of referendum vote (intention in pre-referendum waves) on switching to the SNP if the respondent did not intend to vote SNP in the previous wave in Figure 8.4. The plot shows a large increase in the effect of referendum vote between the pre-referendum and post-referendum waves. This suggests that voting in the referendum—nailing one's colours to the mast in that election—had a greater effect on party choice than intention alone. More specifically, voting Yes directly led to an increase in the probability of voting SNP in the 2015 General Election among erstwhile Labour supporters. Referendum vote continues to predict switching in the further post-referendum waves, but the effect has a declining magnitude as the election approaches. The size of the effect declines before May 2015, reflecting the fact that, by that point, all but a handful of Yes voters had already switched to the SNP (as shown in Figure 8.2).

---

[2] These were measured on a latent scale estimated with an IRT model, using respondent preferences for whether the Scottish government should have control of different policy areas (Welfare, the NHS, Defence, Tax, and Policing), see Table A8.1 in the appendix.

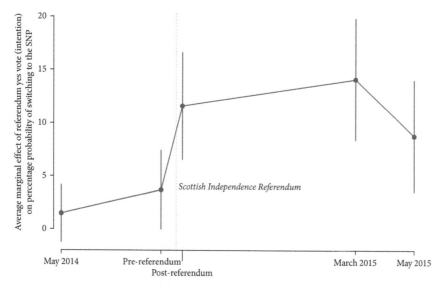

Figure 8.4 The average marginal effect of referendum Yes vote (intention) on switching to the SNP if not intending to vote SNP in the previous wave

8.6 Changing identities?

In February 2014, 89 per cent of our cohort of Labour supporters identified with the party, but this fell to 75 per cent by March 2015 and 65 per cent by May 2015 (post-election). However, this fall occurred mainly within those who voted Yes in September 2014: Labour identity among Yes voters in this group fell from 84 per cent in February 2014 to 37 per cent in May 2015. Although Labour identification also fell among No voters, the equivalent drop was much smaller, from 90 per cent to 77 per cent.

To reveal the extent to which these shifts in identity result from referendum voting or from some other change in attitudes or evaluations we look to our model. Figure 8.5 shows the impact of referendum vote on identifying with Labour and the SNP, allowing for the same control variables as the vote choice models. The pattern is very similar to that seen for the effect of the referendum on switching to the SNP: before the referendum there is no clear and consistent effect of referendum vote intention on identifying with Labour. However, following the referendum, those who voted Yes were less likely to continue to identify with Labour in every subsequent wave.

We cannot model SNP identity before the referendum vote for the simple reason that there are so few SNP identifiers among our cohort of Labour supporters. Following the referendum, however, referendum vote strongly predicts identifying

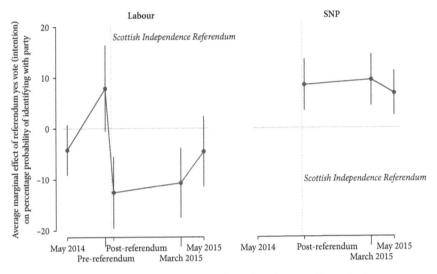

Figure 8.5 The average marginal effect of referendum Yes vote (intention) on identifying with Labour and the SNP

with the SNP. Nearly half (45 per cent) of this group (all of whom had intended to vote Labour in February 2014) who voted for independence identified with the SNP by the time of the General Election in May 2015. Thus, the referendum also had an *indirect* effect on party choice at the general election through its influence on party identification. Indeed, it is worth noting that in the 2015 post-election wave, SNP party identity was a very strong predictor of switching to the SNP for the first time.

8.7 Changing evaluations and attitudes

Changes in party support and identification do not occur in isolation from political attitudes and evaluations. Table 8.2 shows the aggregate change in various attitudes among our cohort of Labour supporters between the start of our study in February 2014 and March 2015 (pre-election). There are large changes in the approval of the Scottish government, feelings towards the party leaders, and party identity, especially among those intending to vote for independence. Just over half (55 per cent) of the Yes-voting respondents approved of the Scottish government in February 2014, and this increased to nearly three-quarters (74 per cent) in March 2015. Yes voters became more negative in their feelings about Ed Miliband after the referendum, while No voters were stable in their opinions. The largest changes are how Yes and No voters felt about the SNP leaders. Before the referendum, there was already a clear divide in how future Yes and No voters felt

Table 8.2 Aggregate changes in attitudes by wave (Labour t1 supporters)

Variable	All		Yes Voters		No Voters	
	Feb 2014	March 2015	Feb 2014	March 2015	Feb 2014	March 2015
Scottishness (1–7)	5.4	5.5	6	6.1	5.2	5.3
Britishness (1–7)	5.4	5.5	4.4	4.3	5.8	5.9
Devolution preferences (z score)	−0.2	−0.2	0.3	0.4	−0.4	−0.4
Approve of Scottish government (%)	25.4	35.9	55	74.4	13.3	21
Satisfied with UK democracy (1–4)	2.4	2.3	2	1.9	2.5	2.4
Like Miliband (0–10)	5.9	5.6	5.6	4.7	6	6
Like Salmond/Sturgeon (0–10)	2.6	4	4.8	7.5	1.7	2.7
Identify with Labour (%)	88.6	75.2	84	50	90.3	84.7
Identify with SNP (%)	2.3	10.7	6.7	35.3	0.6	1.5

about Alex Salmond, with Yes voters on average liking Salmond by 3.1 points more than No voters. Before the 2015 Election, Yes voters on average liked Sturgeon by 4.8 points more than No voters.[3] Although there were only small net changes in Scottishness, Britishness, and satisfaction with UK democracy, changes in Britishness and satisfaction with UK democracy moved in opposite directions for Yes and No voters, with Yes voters becoming more Scottish and No voters more British. Scottishness, on the other hand, increased slightly among both Yes and No voters. It is also worth noting that the percentage of these who intended to vote Yes among February 2014 Labour supporters was only 17 per cent, but 28 per cent reported voting Yes in September 2014.

Together these findings suggest that referendum voting precipitated a change in attitudes towards devolution, evaluations of Scottish government performance, satisfaction with UK democracy, Scottish and British identities, ratings of political leaders, as well as *directly* affecting vote choice and partisan identification. To test this more thoroughly, we modelled these variables as dependent variables in the same modelling framework (Table A8.2).[4] What we find is that all the explanatory variables from our vote choice model were predicted by referendum vote choice

---

[3] In part these changes also reflect the fact that, on average, people liked Nicola Sturgeon more than Alex Salmond. Measured in the post-referendum wave (the only time point we have ratings for both leaders), Yes voters had a mean rating for Sturgeon of 5.9 and Salmond of 5.5 and No voters rated Sturgeon 2.1 and Salmond 1.4. Interestingly, No voters also liked Nicola Sturgeon more after the referendum than before it, though their overwhelming feeling was still negative.

[4] The explanatory variables include the lagged version of the dependent variable, party identification, referendum vote choice/intention, and the same range of controls as previously.

throughout the period, with the exception of Scottish national identity, which was only significantly affected by referendum vote in the immediate aftermath of the referendum. In other words, through Yes voting, the referendum helped shift attitudes in favour of the SNP by leading to a reduction in British identity, increased approval of the Scottish government, preference for a more radical devolution of powers, and a reduction in satisfaction with UK democracy. One example of how attitudes were influenced by referendum voting over the period is illustrated in Figure 8.6 which shows how referendum voting was associated with a decrease in feelings of Britishness (and to a lesser extent an increase in Scottishness), especially immediately after the referendum.

Social Identity Theory suggests that feelings towards leaders are strongly influenced by their position as in-group members (Hogg 2001; Haslam, Reicher, and Platow 2010). Figure 8.7 illustrates the effect of referendum Yes vote (intention) on how voters felt about Ed Miliband and the leader of the SNP (Salmond before and immediately after the referendum, Sturgeon before the 2015 Election). Referendum vote (intention) is a strong influence on how voters felt about party leaders, particularly the leaders of the Yes side and the SNP. An almost identical pattern is found for approval of the Scottish government (not shown), the effect of which also peaked in the immediate run-up to the referendum.

In the following section we explore how, by altering the distribution and alignment of political attitudes and evaluations, referendum voting *indirectly* led to an increase in SNP voting in the general election among erstwhile Labour voters.

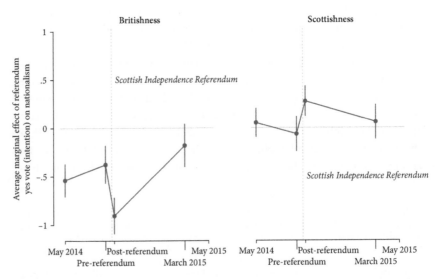

Figure 8.6 Average marginal effect of referendum Yes vote (intention) on national identity (1–7 scale)

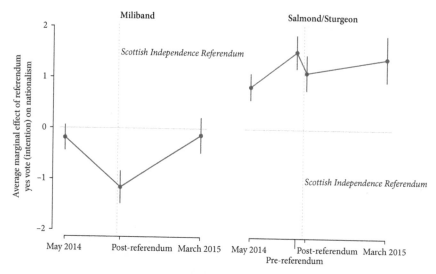

Figure 8.7 Average marginal effect of referendum Yes vote (intention) on feelings towards Labour and SNP party leaders (0–10 scale)

8.8 What if the referendum never happened?

Did people switch to the SNP because the referendum led to changes in the underlying attitudes that underpinned their vote choice, or were their attitudes relatively stable while the relationship between attitudes and vote choice changed? In order to further illuminate *how* the referendum affected the 2015 General Election voting, we decompose the shift in party support as a result of the referendum into (i) changes in the *distribution* of attitudes, evaluations, and identities and (ii) changes in the *alignment* of attitudes and party choice.

We estimate the predicted share of the vote the SNP might have achieved under a series of counterfactual conditions, where post-referendum data about the attitudes and preferences shown in Table 8.2 are substituted for the same respondents' pre-referendum data in a (pre-referendum) model of SNP vote intention (see Table A8.3 in the appendix for the results of this model). From this, we can see how much change in voters' attitudes, evaluations, and identities contributes to the increase in SNP support, as opposed to any change in how those attitudes align with vote choice.

Figure 8.8 shows the predicted proportion of 2010 Labour voters voting SNP in the pre- and post-referendum models. The proportion intending to vote SNP in the pre-referendum model (May 2014) was 13 per cent while the proportion who actually voted SNP was 33 per cent. The first two counterfactuals—holding referendum vote and political attitudes at pre-referendum levels—both show negligible effects on the proportion predicted to vote SNP (predicted proportions of

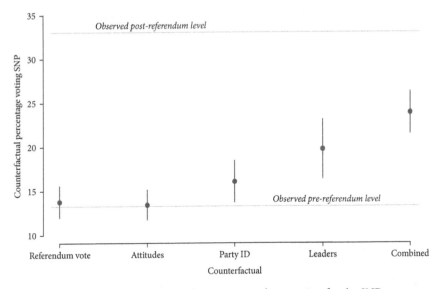

Figure 8.8 Counterfactual effect of change in attitude on voting for the SNP among 2010 Labour voters

13.8 per cent and 13.4 per cent respectively, neither of which is statistically significantly different to the actual pre-referendum proportion). The counterfactuals indicate that party identity and leader ratings account for part of the increase in SNP support: the predicted proportions were 16 per cent and 20 per cent respectively, both of which are statistically significantly different to the baseline. Combining all the counterfactual conditions together gives a predicted proportion of 23.9 per cent—an increase of 10.3 percentage points—just over half of the actual 20 percentage point change.

It is clear from this counterfactual analysis that changes to underlying attitudes— such as national identity, preferences for devolution, satisfaction with British democracy, and approval of the Scottish government—play only a small part in explaining the sudden rise of the SNP after the referendum. Instead, changes in variables relating to political identity—partisanship and feelings towards political leaders—can explain about half the shift of Labour voters to the SNP after the referendum.

What also changed after the referendum is how attitudes, evaluations, and identities *aligned* with party choice. Examining the differences in coefficients between the pre- and post-referendum models tells us that there were several important changes to how attitudes, evaluations, and identities predict SNP voting (see Table A8.3 in the appendix). While Britishness has a similar coefficient between models, Scottishness does not predict SNP voting before the referendum but does post-referendum. Similarly, approval of the Scottish government and devolution preferences do not predict SNP voting pre-referendum but do post-referendum. Interestingly, although there are considerable changes to the distribution of leader ratings after the referendum, the coefficients for both SNP leaders and Miliband are much smaller after the referendum. This indicates that although feelings about leaders changed substantially, the effect of these feelings actually diminished, suggesting that changes in feelings about leaders largely result from other changes in political identities and alignments, rather than being a major contributing factor in and of themselves. Finally, the magnitude of the coefficient for referendum vote increases by 70 per cent, supporting the claim that it was the act of actually casting a vote in the referendum, and not simply the intention, that is important for understanding the post-referendum realignment.

In summary, we have shown that voting for independence in the referendum had a strong effect on switching vote intention (and ultimately actual vote) from Labour to the SNP. This was mainly because of a crystallization of support for the SNP among Yes voters and, more generally, among those with pro-independence attitudes, rather than a large-scale shift in support for independence. We now turn to the General Election of 2017 in which the wheels came off the SNP bandwagon.

8.9 The EU referendum and 2017 General Election

Although the SNP remained the largest party in Scotland at the 2017 Election, they lost over a quarter of their vote share and twenty-one of the fifty-six seats they had won in 2015. However, Labour was not the prime beneficiary of this reversal. Instead, the Scottish Conservatives nearly doubled their vote share from 15 per cent in 2015 to 29 per cent in 2017, picking up twelve seats, and became the second largest party in Scotland (the first time they beat Labour at a General Election in Scotland since 1959). Labour only modestly improved their vote share by 2.8 percentage points and picked up six seats, while the Liberal Democrats managed to gain three seats despite a slight decrease in their share of the vote.

What explains these sudden changes in electoral fortunes?

On the one hand, Labour won over 15 per cent of 2015 SNP voters compared to only 8 per cent for the Conservatives (Table 8.3). Many of these were voters returning home, with 39 per cent having voted Labour in 2010 compared to only 14 per cent SNP and 20 per cent Liberal Democrat. Crucially, however, almost a quarter of 2015 Labour supporters defected to the Conservatives in 2017, compared to only 7 per cent in the opposite direction. So what lay behind this unusually high level of switching between the major parties? We have already seen how the 2014 independence referendum led to the rise of the SNP in 2015 at the expense of Labour, and we have shown how the political divisions created by a referendum counteracted traditional party loyalties. In this section,

Table 8.3 2015–17 vote flow, Scotland

2015 Vote	2017 Vote			
	Con	Lab	LD	SNP
Conservative	86.1	6.5	3.5	3.9
Labour	24.2	61.5	6.1	6.5
Liberal Democrat	36.2	14.8	44.3	4.6
SNP	8.1	15.2	1.8	74.0

we explore how a second shock to the Scottish party system—the 2016 EU referendum—interacted with the earlier shock of the independence referendum. In Chapter 9, we examine the impact of the EU referendum on electoral politics in more detail, and show how it exposed cross-cutting political divisions. Here we explore the impact of the EU referendum in Scotland, and more specifically how, in combination with the Scottish independence referendum, it brought about the surprising result we saw in 2017.

As we have already seen, the Scottish independence referendum created clear divisions in Scottish politics. The SNP, the cheerleaders for independence, were unambiguously in favour of staying in the EU, and, following the vote to leave, tried to leverage Brexit to force a second independence referendum with the aim of keeping Scotland in the EU (McHarg and Mitchell 2017). The Scottish Conservatives, united against independence, were divided over Brexit during the EU referendum campaign, but took a clear stance in favour of Brexit following the referendum result, albeit one that is generally seen as more soft-Brexit supporting than their English counterparts (McEwen 2018). Scottish Labour, also against Scottish independence, tried to carve out a position on the EU somewhere between the SNP and the Conservatives.

The EU referendum clearly cut across the divisions over Scottish independence, with around 60 per cent of both Yes and No voters in the 2014 referendum voting to remain in the EU. Using data from the BES internet panel on how people voted in both the 2014 independence and 2016 EU referendums produces four categories of respondents (excluding respondents who did not vote in one or both referendums). The two largest groups were those that voted No in 2014 and Remain in 2016 (34 per cent of voters in 2017) and Yes/Remain voters (28 per cent), followed by No/Leave voters (22 per cent), and finally Yes/Leave voters (16 per cent). We look at how each of these groups voted in the 2015 and 2017 elections.

Figure 8.9 shows that those who voted for independence in 2014 and for Remain in the EU referendum voted heavily in favour of the SNP at both elections. These are the voters whose position was in line with SNP policy. As we saw above, the vast majority of Yes voters supported the SNP following the independence

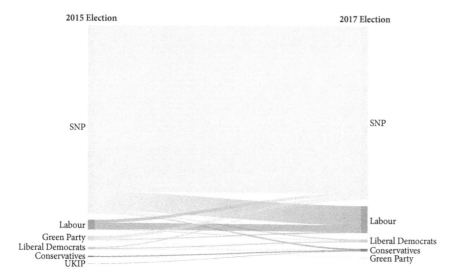

2015 Election

2017 Election

SNP

SNP

Labour

Labour

Green Party

Liberal Democrats

Liberal Democrats

Conservatives

Conservatives

Green Party

UKIP

Figure 8.9 2015 and 2017 vote choice for Scottish independence Yes and EU referendum Remain voters

referendum, and, notwithstanding the normal impact of SNP performance and everyday politics, those that agreed with the party on Brexit had no reason to desert it in 2017. The vast majority (92 per cent) of Yes/Remain voters voted SNP in 2015 and this level of support only declined slightly (84 per cent) in 2017.

The importance of the EU referendum in restructuring voting in Scotland is illustrated quite dramatically by the change among Yes/Leave voters, 89 per cent of whom voted for the SNP in 2015 compared to only 57 per cent in 2017 (Figure 8.10). More than four in ten respondents in this group switched to another party in 2017, with similar proportions going to the Conservatives and to Labour. Given the Conservatives' low base in this group in 2015, their success in attracting one in five of Yes/Leave voters in 2017 highlights the importance of the EU referendum. Just as Labour's position on the independence referendum cost Labour votes in 2015, in 2017 many SNP voters were driven away by the party's strong pro-Remain stance.

Those that both voted against independence and to Remain in the EU made up the largest share of the four groups in the Scottish electorate. Figure 8.11 shows that, despite its poor performance overall, Labour dominated this group in 2015, winning around half of these voters. In 2017, however, Labour lost about one in five of these voters to the Conservatives, with a smaller share going to the Liberal Democrats. Smaller numbers of 2015 Conservatives and Liberal Democrats also shifted to Labour, cancelling out some of these losses. Altogether, Labour only won about four out of ten of No/Remain voters in 2017. As a result of picking up a

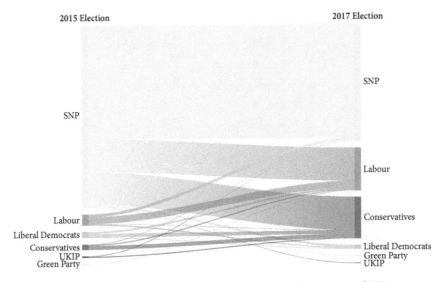

Figure 8.10 2015 and 2017 vote choice for Scottish independence Yes and EU referendum Leave voters

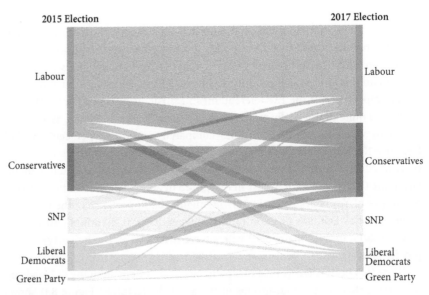

Figure 8.11 2015 and 2017 vote choice for Scottish independence No and EU referendum Remain voters

large number of Labour voters and around one in three 2015 Liberal Democrat voters, the Conservatives increased their share of this group from 21 to 33 per cent between 2015 and 2017. Although the Conservatives were more clearly associated nationally with a hard Brexit, the softer approach from the Scottish Conservatives, together with a strong position against a second independence referendum clearly resonated with this group.

Perhaps more crucial to the Scottish Conservatives' success were the No/Leave voters, whose referendum votes were most in line with the Conservative positions on independence and Brexit. Figure 8.12 shows that this group split almost evenly between the Conservatives and Labour in 2015, but that, in 2017, the Conservatives won almost three times as many of these voters as Labour (65 per cent versus 23 per cent). A closer inspection of the flow of votes among this group reveals that the Conservatives picked up nearly half of 2015 Labour voters, six in ten 2015 Liberal Democrats, and the vast majority of 2015 UKIP voters (Figure 8.12). The SNP also lost over three-quarters of their support among this group, 96 per cent of whom opposed a second independence referendum. The effect of these changes was to nearly double the Conservative share of the vote in this group to 65 per cent, helping them become the second largest party in Scotland.

As we saw earlier in this chapter, pro-independence voters rapidly shifted to the SNP in 2015, virtually wiping Labour off the electoral map. In 2017, Yes/Remain voters mainly stayed loyal to the SNP, but the SNP suffered heavy losses to the major unionist parties among Yes/Leave voters. The relative success of the Conservatives in attracting a substantial minority of No/Remain voters—despite the national party's hard-line position on Brexit—also significantly contributed to their increased vote share. By contrast, Labour performed relatively poorly among the No/Leave group, losing a large proportion of these voters to the Conservatives. The ability of the Conservatives to capture No/Remain voters as well as a clear majority of No/Leave voters clearly reflects the importance of the two referendums in defining Scottish voters' political identities.

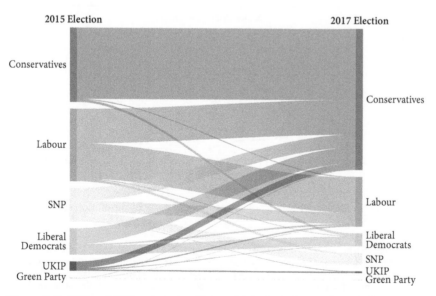

Figure 8.12 2015 and 2017 vote choice for Scottish independence No and EU referendum Leave voters

The relative strength of the new political identities forged in the heat of two referendum campaigns shaped the outcome of the 2017 General Election in Scotland, opening the way for a Conservative recovery based on a strong unionist and Brexit message. We asked a battery of questions about identification with the Yes/No side in the Scottish referendum (in April 2017) and with the Leave/Remain side in the EU referendum (based on similar questions relating to social identities) and found that a large proportion of No/Remain voters more closely identified with 'No' than with 'Remain' (39 per cent). Among this group, the Conservatives led Labour by 45 per cent to 34 per cent. Among those who identified more strongly as 'Remain' than 'No' (36 per cent), Labour led the Conservatives 53 per cent to 20 per cent.

The emergence of the Brexit dimension and how it cut across the independence referendum is illustrated in Figure 8.13 and Figure 8.14, which show how devolution and European integration preferences aligned with vote choice in 2015 and 2017.[5] As explained earlier in this chapter, devolution preference was a strong predictor of referendum vote in 2014 and, through that, 2015 General Election vote. This is illustrated in the top panel of Figure 8.13, which shows how SNP

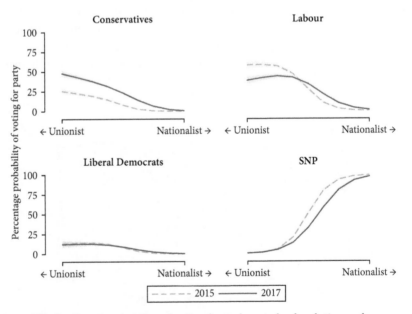

Figure 8.13 Predicted probability of voting for each party by devolution scale

[5] The dependent variable is reported vote in 2015 and 2017. Independent variables are stable value/ attitudinal positions measured as latent variables generated from IRT models (results shown in the appendix) using responses to (i) economic left–right (Table A6.1) and (ii) authoritarian–liberal (Table A6.2) values batteries, (iii) devolution preferences (Table A8.4), and (iv) EU scale (Table A8.5). The results of the vote choice model are shown in Table A8.6 in the appendix.

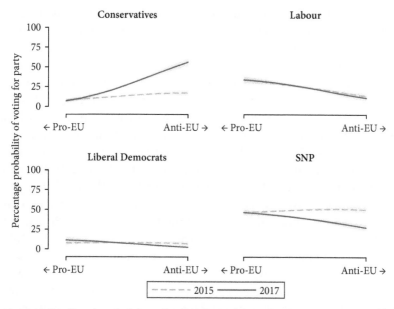

Figure 8.14 Predicted probability of voting for each party by EU scale

voting rises steeply as voters move towards the nationalist end of the scale, while controlling for liberal–authoritarian, left–right, EU, and immigration attitudes. However, in 2017, while this effect is still strong, it is somewhat more muted than it was in 2015. This is mirrored by a weakening of the relationship between Labour voting and devolution preferences. This suggests that that there may have been a slight weakening of the impact of the independence referendum by 2017 as Labour regained support among nationalists at the expense of the SNP. By contrast, Conservative voting rose across virtually the full range of devolution preferences, although the increase was greatest among unionists. Although slightly weakened compared to 2015, the independence cleavage was still of paramount importance in structuring party support in Scotland. We can gauge this by comparing indicators originally designed to measure the strength of class alignment. The Thomsen index (also known as log odds measure of class voting—a measure of relative class voting) calculated for the SNP versus other parties for Yes and No voters was 3.4 in 2015, falling to 3.2 in 2015.[6] These are both extremely high values if we benchmark them against the height of British class voting during the post-war era

[6] The log odds is calculated as the natural log of (% Yes-voting SNP/%Yes-voting other): (% No-voting SNP/% No-voting other). The simple odds (not logged) dropped more dramatically from 29.8 to 24.2. An alternate measure is the Alford index (measured here as % Yes-voting SNP—% No-voting SNP) which dropped from 69 in 2015 to 64 in 2017. For reference, the Alford index of class voting from 1945 to 1960 in Britain was 37.3 (Nieuwbeerta and De Graaf 1999). All measures suggest that independence voting dropped in 2017, but the level was still extremely high compared to measures of class voting in Britain.

(1945–60) when the Thomsen index of class voting was 1.64 (Nieuwbeerta and De Graaf 1999). The independence cleavage was weakened by the EU referendum, but not by a vast amount.

Figure 8.14 reveals how the cross-cutting impact of Europe (defined by attitudes towards integration with the European Union) became much stronger in 2017, partly explaining the weaker pull of devolution preferences. The figure shows that having anti-European attitudes was a much stronger predictor of Conservative voting in 2017 than in 2015.[7] This is mirrored in the weakening of support for the SNP among anti-EU voters. In short, the rise of the European dimension accounts for the rise of the Conservatives at the expense of the SNP in 2017. In contrast, the net effect of EU attitudes on the Labour vote barely changed between 2015 and 2017. Although we saw above that Labour lost a large number of Leave supporters to the Conservatives, they also lost substantial numbers of Remain voters (also to the Conservatives) and gained some Leave supporters from the SNP.

We can also examine the effects of the two referendums on SNP partisanship. The interaction of the two referendums is a clear illustration of the capacity for a new shock to disrupt the effects of an earlier one. Figure 8.15 shows trends in the strength of SNP partisanship among those who voted Yes in the independence

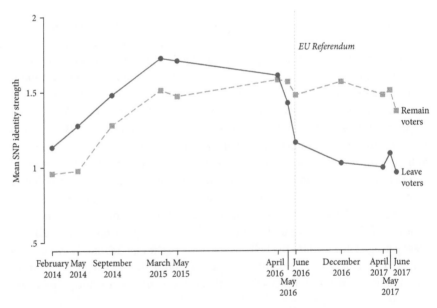

Figure 8.15 Strength of SNP identity among 2014 Scottish independence referendum Yes voters who voted Remain and Leave in the 2016 EU referendum, on a scale where 0 = no/other party id, 1 = not very strong Conservative id, 2 = farily strong Conservative id, 3 = Very strong Conservative id

---

[7] This is also the case in England and Wales, as shown in Chapter 9.

referendum and later voted Remain or Leave in the 2016 EU referendum. Leave-voting independence supporters started with slightly stronger SNP identities, but both Leavers and Remainers moved in parallel in the run-up to, and aftermath of, the Scottish independence referendum. Once we reach the EU referendum, however, there is a divergence in trends. Remainers felt slightly more strongly SNP compared to the year before, while Leavers had begun to waiver, though they still felt fairly strongly SNP. In the wake of the EU referendum there was an immediate and sharp drop in the strength of SNP identity among Leavers which did not recover by the 2017 election.

Overall, the 2017 General Election outcome in Scotland reflected the impact of two electoral shocks. First, the consequences of the independence referendum were still being felt, allowing the SNP to remain dominant over Labour (albeit to a lesser degree than in 2015). Overlaid on this was the impact of the EU referendum, which contributed to the resurgence of the Scottish Conservatives.

8.10 Conclusions

The 2015 General Election was disastrous for Labour, not least because of their collapse in Scotland. The reduction in Labour's Scottish vote and the rise of the SNP contributed significantly to the overall fragmentation of party support in the 2015 General Election. The Scottish independence referendum acted as a shock to a system that was already unstable due to the long-term weakening of party identities and the decline of Labour's traditional class-based appeal. In this chapter, we have shown how the independence referendum precipitated a shift in allegiances of those backing independence—to the extent that 90 per cent of Yes voters voted for the SNP, including most of those who had still intended to vote Labour early in 2014. Overall, Labour lost one-third of its supporters to the SNP between early 2014 and the 2015 General Election (and nearly half since 2010), the vast majority of whom voted for independence. To put it simply, Yes voters could not reconcile a Labour vote with the position they had taken on the referendum.

This shift occurred in two phases. First, there was a gradual drift to the SNP before the referendum, when there was considerable crossover between party support and positions on independence. This process continued between the referendum and the 2015 General Election, when party alignments crystallized along the independence cleavage. The peak effect of the referendum on changes to party identity, attitudes, and vote choice was in September 2014—immediately after the referendum—but it continued to have an effect on each wave through to election day. Moreover, these changes to vote choice in 2015 were linked to changing partisan identities. Yes voting increased the likelihood of identifying with the SNP and reduced identification with Labour. Changes in party identification were driven primarily by referendum vote choice, especially in the period following the referendum, with Yes voters much less likely to continue identifying with Labour and more likely to identify with the SNP. Only 30 per cent of those supporting Labour in February 2014, and who ended up voting SNP, identified with Labour in May 2015 (compared to 80 per cent at the outset). In other words, shifts in voting were associated with shifts in party identification.

Voting Yes also led to a change in political attitudes in a direction consistent with and more favourable to the SNP and less favourable to Labour. Through this effect on attitudes, voting Yes indirectly led to an increase in the probability of voting SNP in the 2015 General Election. However, we demonstrated that only a fraction of Labour's loss of 2010 voters to the SNP was attributable to changes in attitudinal positions. The impact of the referendum on political attitudes was less about changing people's minds (to become more Scottish-minded or more pro-devolution), than it was about a strengthening of the alignment between these attitudes and party support. After the referendum had taken place those who had voted Yes in 2014 were no longer prepared to lend Labour their support. In this sense, in terms of our theory of electoral shocks, the independence referendum acted as a shock to the salience of nationalism, devolution, and independence. Voters' position on independence simply mattered more after the independence referendum than they had before. However, the post-referendum strengthening of the relationship between independence attitudes and party identification and voting in the independence referendum may also have acted as a shock to the image of the Labour Party in Scotland, causing voters to see it primarily as a party of the union rather than as a party of the left. The data available and models presented here do not allow us to differentiate between the impact of the changing salience of the independence issue and the changing image of the parties.

We have shown that the Scottish independence referendum had a profound realigning effect on party support in Scotland, cementing the link between SNP voting and pro-independence attitudes, and contributing to the fragmentation of party support across Britain as a whole, in 2015. However, the SNP could not rest on their laurels: by 2017 the Scottish electorate had contributed to a reversal in party fragmentation and the rise of the two-party national vote. A second electoral shock in the form of the EU referendum disrupted the new political equilibrium in Scotland. While the SNP remained the largest Scottish party in the UK Parliament, they lost considerable ground to both the Conservatives and Labour, who won over a substantial proportion of pro-independence Leave voters. Meanwhile, among anti-independence Leave voters, the Conservatives became the favoured party. In the space of three general elections, the Scottish party system was completely transformed. The SNP moved from third place in 2010 to first in 2015 and 2017; Labour fell from first to third; and the Conservatives rose from fourth to second. These dramatic changes were the result of two major electoral shocks in the shape of two referendums less than three years apart. In the following chapter, we discuss the wider impact of the Brexit shock across Britain as a whole.

9

Brexit and the Reshaping of British Electoral Politics

In April 2017 Prime Minister Teresa May announced an early general election in the expectation of achieving an increased majority to strengthen her hand in Brexit negotiations, and to provide a mandate for the government's Brexit strategy. The outcome was quite the opposite, with the Conservatives losing their overall majority (despite winning 42.4 per cent of the vote) and relying on a confidence and supply arrangement with the DUP in order to govern. Labour's revival under Jeremy Corbyn, which deprived the Conservatives of their anticipated majority, helped produce the highest two-party share since 1970. Moreover, not only did we see a return to 'two-party politics', but a restructuring of the basis of this two-party support. To give just two examples: in 2017 Kensington—the most affluent constituency in the country and one of the most cosmopolitan—fell to Labour for the first time ever; while Stoke-on-Trent South, a poor working-class area in a struggling former industrial city, went from Labour to the Conservatives—again for the first time ever. Within two years of the 2015 Election we had seen the political map of Britain redrawn.

In this chapter we show that the shock that led to these changes was the outcome of the 2016 referendum on Britain's membership of the EU. The EU referendum resulted in strategic decisions by political parties that brought about substantial changes in the alignment of party voting. Electoral competition between the two main parties, dominated ideologically since the Second World War by concerns relating to redistribution, taxation, and the free market versus social protection, now also focused on the EU, immigration, and liberal–authoritarian values. For the first time in modern history, economic left–right competition between Labour and the Conservatives was accompanied by a commensurate emphasis on a second cultural, or social, dimension of politics.

As a consequence of this transition in the links between voters' attitudes and their choice between Labour and the Conservatives, we also saw the rising importance of two key social bases of politics: education and age. This saw Labour become the party of the younger and more highly educated voter, and Conservatives the party of older voters and those without such qualifications.

Electoral shocks. Edward Fieldhouse, Jane Green, Geoffrey Evans, Jonathan Mellon, Christopher Prosser, Hermann Schmitt, Cees van der Eijk, Oxford University Press (2020). © Fieldhouse, Green, Evans, Mellon, Prosser, Schmitt, and van der Eijk.
DOI: 10.1093/oso/9780198800583.001.0001

9.1 The evolving EU divide

As we discussed in Chapter 5, in recent decades, party positions towards the EU have become increasingly structured along the cultural dimension (Prosser 2016d). In the early days of Britain's membership of the EEC, party divisions over Europe fitted relatively neatly into Britain's traditional economic left–right axis of political competition. The single market was seen as a predominately capitalist enterprise on the left—among its most pronounced antagonists being the iconic left-wing figure Tony Benn—and was opposed by the Labour Party in the 1980s, while being favoured by pro-market Conservatives. However, as European integration progressed and parties switched their positions. Labour became increasingly pro-EU following their 1989 policy review and subsequent endorsement of the EU project by Tony Blair. At the same time, there was increasingly open Euroscepticism among the Conservatives in the 1990s. Together, these changes broke the link between economic left–right positions and the EU at the party level (Evans and Butt 2007; Evans 1999a). Likewise, as European integration changed, so too did the nature of voter attitudes towards European integration, which shifted from economic left-wing concerns about market integration to liberal–authoritarian issues like immigration and cultural threat (van Elsas and van der Brug 2015; Eichenberg and Dalton 2007; McLaren 2002; McLaren 2006; Tillman 2013).

Following the realignments of the 1990s, European integration had become in effect a cross-cutting political cleavage with the potential to be a vote loser for both the divided Conservatives (Evans 1998) and for a Labour Party that was moving away from the values of its core working-class base (Evans 2002; Evans 1999a). Nonetheless, these cross-cutting effects were of only minor political significance. A more fundamental shock was necessary for them to transform politics.[1] As one of us remarked at the time: 'Europe now cross-cuts the left–right basis of voting...at present this impact remains small. Yet it may become more important as integration proceeds and new and possibly more contentious questions than even monetary union arrive inescapably on the political agenda' (Evans 1999a). As we saw in Chapter 5, before the growth of immigration from the 2004 and 2007 accession countries, the EU question did not have the salience to transform politics. The increasing salience of immigration and the emergence of UKIP as an attractive destination for Conservative defectors (whether MPs or voters) was an obvious motive for Cameron's strategy of promising a referendum on the EU. By promising a vote on the EU, Cameron hoped Eurosceptic MPs and voters would not defect to UKIP, who were obviously advocating such a policy (Evans and Menon 2017; Prosser 2016a). The limited public salience of the EU twenty years

---

[1] Monetary Union may have exercised Tony Blair, the prime minister of the time, but it had little impact on the electorate because his Chancellor, Gordon Brown, removed it from the agenda (Evans 2003).

ago—even though there was even then intensive in-house fighting among the Conservative elite—is indicated by the failure of James Goldsmith's Referendum Party to obtain much support in the 1997 General Election when running on, in effect, a similar platform to that advocated later by UKIP (Heath et al. 1998).

As we saw in Chapter 5, the public salience of the EU increased over the years following the 2004 accession of primarily Eastern European countries from which there were high rates of immigration. Even then, however, concern about Britain's relationship with the EU itself was still muted. People were more concerned about immigration. Following the 2016 referendum, however, the salience of the EU itself increased substantially. In every wave of the BES panel study we asked about the most important issue (MII) facing the country. Even in 2015, Europe was only mentioned as the most important issue by 3 per cent of respondents. By 2017 it had become the most cited issue, named by no less than 36 per cent (it reached this point in the pre-EU referendum wave of the BESIP).[2] Brexit had arrived as a focal concern of the British public. To understand how Brexit then affected vote choice in 2017, we need first to understand the Brexit vote itself.

9.2 Social divisions, values, and Brexit

While the underlying causes of support for Brexit are complex, previous research has shown that voting to leave the EU was strongly associated with a number of social characteristics and political values (Hobolt 2016; Goodwin and Milazzo 2017). In particular, Brexit supporters were more likely to be older, male, less well-off, and far less likely to have higher educational qualifications than Remain supporters. Leave voters were also much more likely to oppose immigration and hold authoritarian attitudes.

Figure 9.1 shows how voting for Brexit varied by values and attitudes in the BES internet panel. Brexit voting was strongest among people with more socially conservative views, as indicated by responses on the liberal–authoritarian scale, and anti-immigration attitudes, while economic left–right values had no relationship with Brexit voting. This confirms findings elsewhere (Evans and Menon 2017; Kaufmann 2016): Brexit was about differences in social and cultural preferences, not economic inequality. It also helps to explain the social divisions that underpinned Brexit.

As has been known for some time, economic and liberal–authoritarian values are differentially distributed across the population: left–right economic values tend to be

---

[2] Despite this, Brexit was barely discussed as an issue by key figures during the campaign. As noted in Chapter 2, the discussion focused on a wide variety of other policy issues including social care, fox hunting, responses to terrorist attacks, and austerity. In the minds of many of the voters however, the most important factor at stake in the election was Brexit, see Prosser (2017).

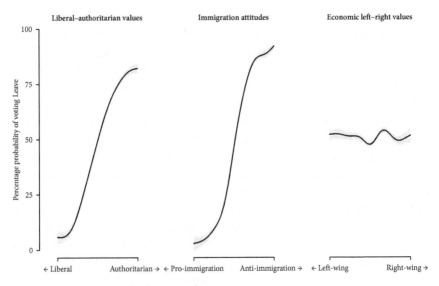

Figure 9.1 Brexit voting by key attitudes

influenced by economic circumstances such as income, while liberal–authoritarian ones are more closely connected with education and age (Heath, Evans, and Martin 1994; Evans, Heath, and Lalljee 1996). These patterns are also reproduced in our surveys. Figure 9.2 shows the mean scores on the left–right scale (where higher is more right-wing) and on the liberal–authoritarian scale (where higher is more liberal). The young, the highly educated, and those with very high levels of income are distinctively more liberal in their responses on the liberal–authoritarianism scale, although the relationship with income is not linear (as the poorest are also more liberal than those in the middle income range).[3] On the left–right scale the more educated and those with higher incomes are more economically right-wing, whilst the relationship with age is curvilinear (the youngest and oldest being most left-wing).

We would therefore expect these sources of social division to be expressed similarly when it came to voting in the referendum. Given the relationship between demographics and attitudes, we would expect demographic voting patterns to align with their attitudinal correlates: income should follow a similar pattern to left–right economic values, and age and education to liberal–authoritarian values. This is exactly what we see in Figure 9.3: pronounced differences by age and education—with younger and more highly educated people being far more likely to vote to remain in the EU. The effects of income are noticeably weaker than the gradients for age and education, although they are still present, with high-income respondents more likely to vote to remain. This income gradient is primarily a

---

[3] The curvilinear income effect is likely to be a result of the confounding effect of age, which as well as being related to liberal values (middle panel) is also related to income.

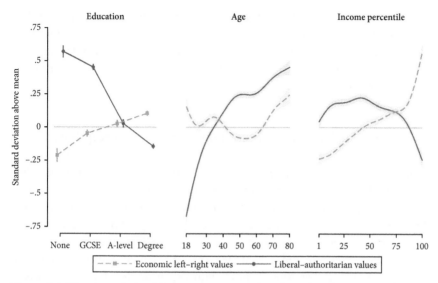

Figure 9.2 Bivariate relationship between economic right and authoritarian values, and education, age, and income

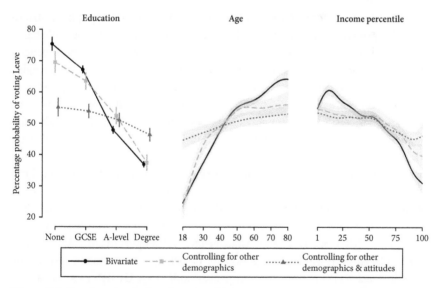

Figure 9.3 Brexit voting by key demographics

result of the link between higher education and higher income. Once education and age are controlled for, the effects of income are much reduced. The effects of education and age are largely removed by the inclusion of attitudes (left–right, liberal–authoritarianism, and immigration), indicating that the differences between young and old and between more and less educated are largely driven by their values and attitudes.

The issue of Leave versus Remain clearly cut across the traditional values dimension of British politics—economic left–right. However, it was not inevitable that this cross-cutting issue would disrupt vote choice in 2017. To understand why it did, we need to consider how the parties reacted to the strategic opportunities provided by the Brexit vote.

9.3 Post-Brexit Party strategy and voters' perceptions

In the run-up to the referendum, the parties—especially the Conservatives—had been split. Importantly though, most of the leadership of the party—and the official government position—was in favour of Remain. Following the EU referendum, however, Theresa May staked a claim for being *the* party of Brexit ('Brexit means Brexit' as she repeated on numerous occasions), and the vast majority of the Conservative Party followed suit. At the Conservative Party annual conference in Birmingham in October 2016 the prime minister made clear that the UK would control immigration, make its own laws, and strike trade deals with third countries with an overt rejection of a 'Norway' or 'Switzerland' model: Brexit meant 'hard Brexit'.

The motivations for this are easy to understand given the geographic distribution of Brexit votes and the rise of UKIP on the Conservatives' Eurosceptic flank. The Leave versus Remain divide cut across Labour and Conservative constituencies in various ways. Traditionally Conservative areas in Lincolnshire, East Anglia, and Kent had already seen UKIP garner significant support in 2015, and they formed the rural heartland of the Brexit vote in 2016 (Boston topped the chart with 75.6 per cent voting Leave). Various Conservative coastal towns with older populations had also seen substantial levels of UKIP voting in 2015, and likewise witnessed Leave victories.

Alongside these rural and coastal constituencies, smaller cities and northern towns—traditional Labour heartlands—also disproportionately voted to Leave. Stoke-on-Trent, dubbed 'Brexit central' during its February 2017 by-election, had a Leave vote of 69.4 per cent, while Hartlepool saw 69.4 per cent vote similarly. In both places, UKIP had received reasonable levels of support in 2015. A pro-Brexit stance placed both Midlands and northern working-class Labour Leave-voting seats in reach and held out the prospect of killing off UKIP.[4] This was a goal assisted by the implosion of UKIP, who in the aftermath of the referendum lost both their main reason for existing and their charismatic leader, Nigel Farage.

---

[4] Of course, the risk from this strategy was losing support in certain large cities. Labour strongholds such as Manchester (60.4 per cent) and London (59.9 per cent) were pro-Remain. Presumably, however, the apparently enfeebled pro-Remain parties—Labour under a very unpopular Corbyn and the discredited Liberal Democrats—were assumed to have been unlikely to make yet substantial further gains in areas where they were already strong.

A key part of the Conservative Party positioning itself as the party of Brexit was the pledge to end freedom of movement. As we discussed in Chapter 5, the Conservatives had long promised to reduce net migration but in practice had achieved very little. In part this was due to the inability to end EU freedom of movement (though non-EU immigration also remained high under the Cameron government). Leaving the EU gave the Conservatives considerably greater scope to control Britain's immigration policy. Figure 9.4 shows that there was a remarkable increase in the number of people who thought the Conservatives would be able to reduce immigration after the EU referendum. This perception was closely related to UKIP–Conservative flows, with 2015 UKIP voters who perceived the Conservatives as being able to handle immigration in 2017 almost twice as likely to defect as those who still perceived the Conservatives as unable to control immigration.

However, it was not just on immigration that the Conservatives appealed to Brexiteers. Figure 9.5 shows changing perceptions of party positions on the EU among Leave and Remain voters. It shows that, post-referendum, the Conservative Party successfully redefined themselves as the more hard-line party on Europe among Leave voters—precisely the voters the Conservatives sought to attract. Remainers had long seen the Conservatives as Eurosceptic and saw them as even more so after the referendum, but the shift among Leavers was far more dramatic. Leave voters on average moved from regarding the Conservatives as being in favour of further EU integration before the referendum to seeing them as very strongly against EU integration by the time of the 2017 General Election.

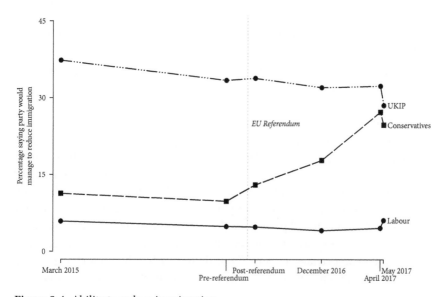

Figure 9.4 Ability to reduce immigration

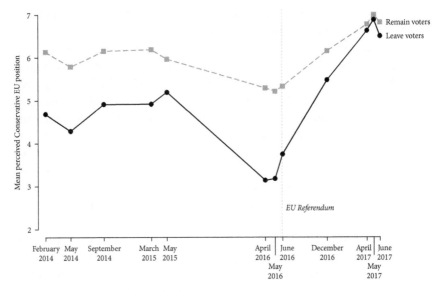

Figure 9.5 Perceived Conservative position on EU integration

As Figure 9.6 shows, no such changes occurred for Labour who, in contrast to the Conservatives, had been equivocal about their Brexit position, criticizing the government's handling of the negotiations while maintaining that they too supported leaving the EU. Despite some ambiguity over what Labour's actual position on Brexit was, it was widely perceived to be softer than the Conservatives. The two parties were now clearly demarcated on the key issues of EU immigration and Brexit.

To further explore the effects of these changes, we estimated the counterfactual difference in 2017 vote share if the perceptions of party positions had not changed from their pre-referendum level to their pre-2017 election level. We estimated this as a conditional logit model with alternative specific coefficients for self and party distance on three policy scales: left–right, EU, and immigration, and a binary variable for each party measuring their perceived likelihood of successfully reducing the level of immigration if they were in government, and controlling for which party the respondent voted for in 2015. We estimate the vote choice model using pre-election values for the distance and immigration competence variables (see Table A9.1 in the appendix for the results). The counterfactual is then estimated by substituting the same respondents' pre-referendum values for the observed 2017 values for all parties simultaneously. The counterfactual shows that two changes were important—Conservative EU distance, and the Conservative's immigration competence (Figure 9.7). If these variables had not changed from their pre-referendum values, the counterfactual estimates that the Conservative

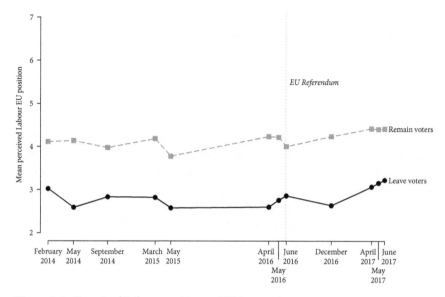

Figure 9.6. Perceived Labour position on EU integration

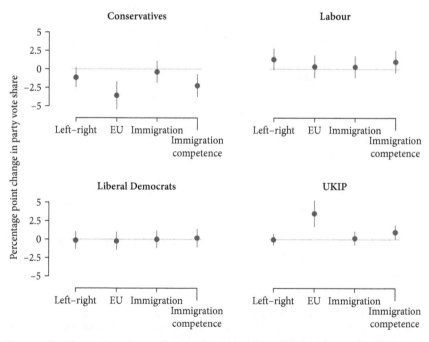

Figure 9.7. Change in 2017 vote share under counterfactual observations of voter–party left–right, EU, immigration distance, and perceptions of immigration competence

vote share would have been 3 to 4 percentage points lower than it actually was, with UKIP's vote share correspondingly higher.[5]

9.4 Brexit, values, and realignment

To see the effect of the referendum on the way attitudes towards EU integration mapped onto major party competition we can compare how support for the major parties changed among pro- and anti-EU people between 2015 and 2017. The changing alignment of vote choice between 2015 and 2017 is illustrated in Figure 9.8 which shows the percentage point change in the vote share of the Conservatives and Labour by EU attitudes, liberal–authoritarian values, attitudes towards immigration, and economic left–right values.[6] In 2015, the Conservatives

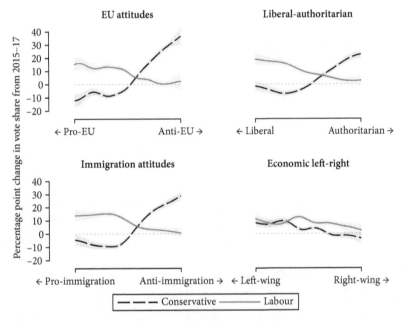

Figure 9.8 Bivariate relationship between liberal–authoritarianism, economic left–right, anti-immigrant attitudes and anti-EU attitudes, and change in the Conservative and Labour vote share 2015 to 2017

[5] The counterfactual UKIP vote for EU distance would have been higher because of the drop in vote share won by the Conservatives under the pre-referendum perception of Conservative EU distance (rather than a change in the perceived position of UKIP).

[6] Because we are interested in change between 2015 and 2017, rather than use votes in a referendum that took place a year after the 2015 election, we operationalize EU attitudes in the same way as our other scales, by pooling answers to questions in multiple waves of our panel (for more detail see Table A8.5 in the appendix). As well as allowing us to examine the relationship between EU attitudes and

already enjoyed a considerable advantage over Labour at the anti-EU side of the scale, but in 2017, this advantage increase sharply. While Labour made gains on the pro-EU side, the change in Labour vote was less strongly related to EU attitudes than the Conservative vote.

When we look at liberal–authoritarian values and attitudes towards immigration (which are both highly correlated with support for Brexit), we see a similar, albeit slightly less pronounced, shift in party support. The Conservatives took an increased share of socially conservative voters between 2015 and 2017, while Labour took a higher share of socially liberal voters. The same pattern is even more noticeable for attitudes towards immigration: those opposed to immigration became substantially more likely to vote Conservative, whilst those more favourably disposed to immigration were increasingly more likely to vote Labour. The Conservatives' increased share of anti-EU, anti-immigration, and authoritarian voters reflected their recruitment of a large proportion of 2015 UKIP voters. In contrast, when we look at change along left–right lines—a values dimension which we saw above (Figure 9.1) is uncorrelated with Brexit voting—change in both Labour and Conservative support was almost completely unrelated to voters left–right position despite Labour's leftward shift in policy, which was widely recognized by the electorate.[7]

So far, we have looked at the issues that tap into the cultural dimension of politics separately. However, we know that the issues of the EU and immigration are closely entwined with one another, and with liberal–authoritarian values. We also know these issues were already important in 2015 (see Chapter 5). To assess the combined impact of the cultural dimension on competition between the two major parties, and how it changed between 2015 and 2017, we estimate a series of vote choice models using BES Internet Panel respondents who voted in 2015 and 2017. Because of our interest in the competition between the major parties in our initial models, we restrict our analysis to English respondents who voted for Labour or Conservative in either election. Below we extend the analyses to voters for all parties and to Scotland and Wales.[8] The first model estimates the role of the

---

vote choice prior to the referendum, this approach gives us the additional advantage of being able to differentiate between strong and weak supporters of either side. This is important because strong Remain/Leave supporters were much more likely to change their political behaviour as a result of Brexit than people who did not care much either way. This measure of EU attitudes scale is a very strong predictor of Brexit vote, a bivariate logit model predicting EU referendum vote correctly classifies 90 per cent of respondents. We measure the other variables using the same approach: liberal–authoritarian values (Table A6.2), immigration attitudes (Table A9.2), and economic left–right values (Table A6.1).

---

[7] Voters perceived the change in Labour position on economic issues moving from a mean of 3.6 in 2015 to 2.9 in 2017 on the redistribution scale (where low is pro-redistribution) and from 3.1 to 2.6 on the left–right scale (where low is left).

[8] Our Conservative vs. Labour model excludes Scotland and Wales because the party choice set is different in those countries making the Conservative–Labour contrast non-comparable due to infringement of the assumption of independence of irrelevant alternatives.

economic dimension, using left–right values and attitudes towards redistribution (measured, like the other variables, as a derived variable from an IRT model, see Table A9.3 in the appendix). The second model estimates the role of the cultural dimension, using liberal–authoritarian values, the EU integration scale, and the immigration scale. The third model combines all of these variables to estimate the overall impact of the two dimensions. The results of these models are shown in Table A9.4 in the appendix.

We are not interested here in the predicted probability of voting for the Conservatives or Labour. Rather, we are interested in how much of the overall pattern of voting in each election is explained by each dimension. We assess this using a measure of overall model fit, McFadden's pseudo R-squared.[9] Figure 9.9 shows this statistic for each of our three models in 2015 and 2017. As we saw in Figure 9.8, the relationship between vote choice and the left–right and cultural dimensions did change between 2015 and 2017. This is confirmed in Figure 9.9, which shows little change in the overall explanatory power of the political values but marked changes in the relative contribution of the economic and cultural

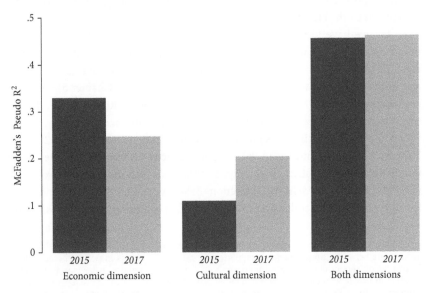

Figure 9.9 Goodness-of-fit of three logit models of Conservative–Labour vote choice in England in 2015 and 2017

[9] Unlike the R-squared statistic in an OLS regression, McFadden's pseudo R-squared cannot be interpreted in terms of proportion of variance explained. A well-fitting model will give substantially lower values than an equally well-fitting OLS model. McFadden suggests that a pseudo R-squared of between 0.2 and 0.4 represents an 'excellent' fit (McFadden 1979). Although by this measure, our combined models do provide an excellent fit of the data, we are more interested in the *relative* fit of the models between elections.

dimensions. More specifically, there is a large drop in the importance of the economic dimension between 2015 and 2017 and a corresponding rise in the importance of the cultural dimension. We do need to be cautious about running a variable race over which dimension is the more important at each election as the pseudo R-squared for each model is affected by how well each dimension is measured as well as how important that dimension is for vote choice. Nevertheless, the changes are sufficiently large that we can reasonably draw the conclusion that the economic dimension was more important than the cultural dimension in explaining Conservative–Labour vote choice in 2015. However, following the EU referendum, the cultural dimension became a better predictor of Conservative versus Labour voting, meaning that in 2017 the importance of both dimensions was roughly equal. This represents perhaps the most notable shift in the value basis of major party competition in recent history.

Whilst Figure 9.9 shows a clear increase in the importance of the cultural dimension in Conservative versus Labour competition, we show below that switching from smaller parties played an important part in the restructuring of major party voting around Brexit. In particular, the Conservatives gained a large number of Leave voters who are more socially conservative from UKIP, whilst Labour made more gains amongst more liberal Remain voters, especially from the Greens and the Liberal Democrats. So was the cultural dimension better at explaining party choice overall in 2017 than in 2015 or was it that competition on this dimension simply became better at differentiating Conservative and Labour voters? To address this question we estimated equivalent multinomial vote choice models for everyone who voted in 2015 and 2017.We fitted separate models for England, Scotland, and Wales to reflect the different choice sets available (the results are shown in Tables A9.5, A9.6, and A9.7 in the appendix respectively). The results for England, shown in Figure 9.10, suggest that there was very little change in the predictive power of the two dimensions when we consider vote choice across all parties. The importance of the economic dimension did decline very slightly in 2017 relative to 2015. Conversely, the importance of the cultural dimension increased very slightly in 2017 relative to 2015. Combining both dimensions together substantially improves the fit of the model, and again it fits the data slightly better in 2017 than it does in 2015. However, while there were small changes between these two elections, the relative importance of each dimension changed very little between 2015 and 2017. The models for Scotland and Wales also include IRT scales representing respondents' views on devolution and independence (see appendix Table A8.4 for Scotland and Table A9.8 for Wales). Taking these into account, in Scotland there is almost no change in the explanatory power of the economic dimension and an increase in the importance of the cultural dimension. However, in both years these were dwarfed by the importance of the devolution dimension. The picture in Wales was similar to that in England, with a small drop in the explanatory power of the economic dimension and an increase in the cultural

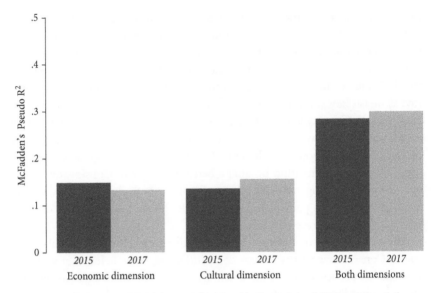

Figure 9.10 Goodness-of-fit of three multinomial logit models of Conservative, Labour, Liberal Democrat, UKIP, and Green Party vote choice in England in 2015 and 2017

dimension, while the devolution dimension was much less important than in Scotland, and relatively less important than the economic or cultural dimensions.

In summary, while the cultural dimension became a much stronger predictor of Conservative versus Labour vote choice in England in 2017, in terms of overall party competition, both dimensions remained important to understanding the vote, and the overall picture is one of stability (Surridge 2018).

To show how the EU referendum triggered these changes we can examine when the changes in relative levels of support for different parties among Leave and Remain voters took place. Figure 9.11 shows the voting intention for each party in each wave of the BES 2014–17 panel survey. There is a very clear jump in Conservative support among Leave voters immediately after the referendum. The trend in UKIP support mirrored that of the Tories, but the decline occurred mainly between November 2016 and the General Election in 2017, after Nigel Farage resigned his leadership of the party.[10] Labour support had increased among Remainers between the 2015 General Election and the referendum. However, these gains were reversed immediately following the referendum when tensions within the Labour Party came to a head. Labour support only recovered during the 2017 Election campaign, among voters from both sides of the EU divide, suggesting that Labour's 2017 campaign performance was attributable more to Corbyn's election campaign than to Brexit (Mellon et al. 2018a).

---

[10] Wave 11 of the BES panel survey was undertaken in November 2017 and wave 12 in April 2017.

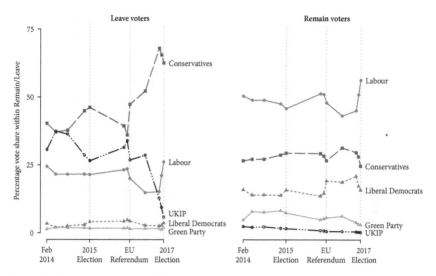

Figure 9.11 Party support by EU vote 2014–17

In order to demonstrate show how these Brexit-related changes led to vote-switching between the parties, we can examine the flow of the vote between 2015 and 2017. Figure 9.12 shows how Leave voters who started at different 2015 party origins cast their vote at the 2017 election. Most notably, the UKIP vote collapsed, with by far the largest portion switching to the Tories. More than half of UKIP's 2015 voters who voted again in 2017 switched to the Conservatives, compared with only 18 per cent to Labour and a further 18 per cent who stayed loyal to UKIP. Labour picked up some Leave voters from UKIP, but lost even more to the Conservatives.

The pattern for Remain voters is slightly more complex. As befitting their stance on Brexit, the Conservatives lost Remain voters to the Liberal Democrats and Labour (Figure 9.13). Despite having the clearest pro-EU position and a promise of a second referendum, the Liberal Democrats failed to pick up many more Remain voters than they lost. Instead, Labour, who were already the most popular party in 2015 among voters who voted Remain in 2016, won the lion's share. Despite an ambiguous position on the single market, Labour was seen as the best bet for those wanting to keep closer ties with our European neighbours. Not only did they win over a large number of Remainers from the Conservatives, but also from the pro-EU Greens and Lib Dems. Nearly two-thirds of 2015 Greens went to Labour as well as around a quarter of Liberal Democrats. However, the Green defection does not seem to be primarily driven by the EU issue. Most of the Green voters defected to Labour before the EU referendum had taken place. Instead, the Green defection appears to be driven by Labour's changing leadership under Jeremy Corbyn (who was personally very popular with those who voted Green in 2015 and was ideologically much closer to them than previous Labour leaders)

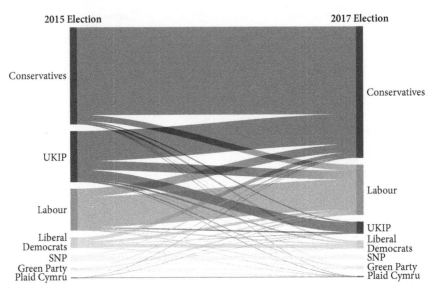

Figure 9.12 Where the Leave vote went

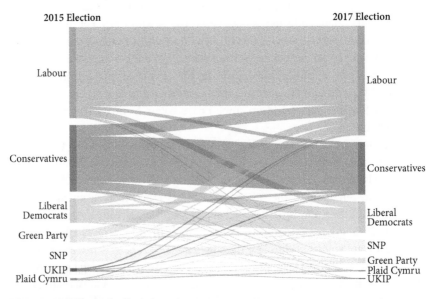

Figure 9.13 Where the Remain vote went

and their dislike of New Labour.[11] In fact, Corbyn was substantially more popular among 2015 Green voters (with a mean of 6.4 out of 10 on April 2016 like scores) than he was among 2015 Labour voters (with a mean of 5.7 out of 10). Importantly,

---

[11] In a model of switching from the Greens, attitudes to Tony Blair negatively predicted choosing Green over Labour in 2015, controlling for overall perceptions of the Labour Party.

the bulk of this switching took place prior to the EU referendum, with 40 per cent of 2015 Green voters (of those who stated a preference) in the pre-referendum wave already intending to vote Labour. Ultimately 60 per cent of 2015 Green voters defected to Labour.

The cumulative effect of Brexit on party choice is clear from the relationship between vote choice in 2015 and 2017 and EU referendum vote (Table 9.1). In 2015, Labour already had a 14 percentage point lead over the Conservatives among voters who later voted to Remain in the EU referendum. This lead increased to 29 percentage points in 2017. There was even greater polarization on the Leave side, where the Conservatives went from a 20 percentage point lead over Labour in 2015, to a 36 percentage point lead in 2017. In 2017, it seems clear that the Conservatives had become the party of Brexit, winning 63 per cent of the Leave vote, with Leave voters making up 71 per cent of Conservative support. In contrast, Labour won over half the Remain vote, relying heavily on Remain support which made up two-thirds (67 per cent) of their voters in 2017. The Liberal Democrats failed to make headway among Remainers despite a clear commitment to backing a second referendum, and experienced an unusually high volatility in their support with more than half of their 2017 voters recruited since 2015. The vast majority (79 per cent) of these new voters supported Remain. However, this recruitment did not translate into increased vote share at the aggregate level because they lost half of their 2015 voters with a higher rate of loss (65 per cent) among the 27 per cent of their 2015 voters who supported Leave.[12] In Chapter 7

Table 9.1 Vote share by EU referendum vote, 2015 and 2017

	2015		2017	
	Remain	Leave	Remain	Leave
Conservative	30	44	25	63
Labour	44	24	54	27
Lib Dem	11	5	13	3
SNP	4	2	4	1
Plaid Cymru	1	0	1	0
UKIP	1	22	0	3
Green Party	7	2	2	1
n	7,033	7,186	7,217	7,056

Source: BESIP wave 6 and wave 13 wt_new_w6w13

---

[12] Although the Liberal Democrats have long been a pro-EU party, they nevertheless attracted a large contingent of anti-EU voters in elections prior to 2017 (Russell and Fieldhouse 2005). The considerable churn in their vote in 2017 is also reflected in the Liberal Democrat seats. The Liberal Democrats finished the election with a net gain of four seats, but this hides considerable turnover. Half of the 2015 Liberal Democrat seats were lost—including the seat of former leader Nick Clegg—as was their recently won by-election seat of Richmond Park. These losses were offset by regaining seven seats they had lost in 2015 and one they had lost in 2010.

we showed how the Liberal Democrats failed to recover in 2017 because of the lasting impact of the coalition shock on their core support, together with the damage to their electoral viability that entailed. As a result, they improved on their average 2015 level of support only among pro-European voters.

Other significant changes were also correlated with Brexit: the Greens lost more than four out of five of their 2015 supporters, the vast majority of whom had voted to Remain in the EU. As noted above, this shift largely took place before the EU referendum campaign, yet was still an important part of how Labour's 2017 vote became dominated by Remainers. Meanwhile, UKIP's 2015 vote, almost entirely made up of Leave supporters, was devastated.

These patterns of switching suggest a fundamental shift in British politics. In total, 32 per cent of respondents voted for a different party in 2015 and 2017, a slightly lower percentage than switched between 2010 and 2015, although 2010, 2015, and 2017 are the three highest recorded levels of volatility across all elections covered by BES panels between 1964 and 2017 (see Chapter 2). More importantly, however, despite spanning only a two-year period, 2015–17 saw the highest recorded level of combined Labour–Conservative switching as a percentage of Labour and Conservative voters at the previous election (in either direction) in any BES inter-election panel (the full series is shown in Chapter 2).[13] Other elections that saw high levels of switching between Labour and the Conservatives took place during periods of convergence between the parties, which may have made it easier to jump the 'gap' between the two major parties. The fact that 12 per cent of 2015 Conservative voters switched to voting for a Corbyn-led Labour Party indicates a major change in the political landscape.

We have shown in earlier chapters that party identification acts as a constraint on volatility, but did it offer any protection against the Brexit shock? Figure 9.14 shows the retention rates for the Conservatives and Labour on each referendum side and for party identifiers and non-identifiers. Both the Conservatives and Labour retained high proportions of their 2015 voters who shared the same referendum side as the party majority (Leave for Conservatives and Remain for Labour) among both party identifiers and non-identifiers (at the time of the 2015 election). However, among those who voted against the majority position of their 2015 party in the referendum, there are very different retention rates for identifiers and non-identifiers. The Conservatives lost nearly half of their non-identifying 2015 voters who voted Remain. By contrast, the Conservatives only lost around a fifth of Conservative-identifying Remain voters. We see a parallel picture on the Labour side among Leavers. Party identification cushioned the effect of the Brexit shock. Had levels of party identification been higher, Brexit—as with other shocks—would have had a smaller impact on the outcome of the election.

---

[13] These figures are for Britain as a whole for comparability across the whole series.

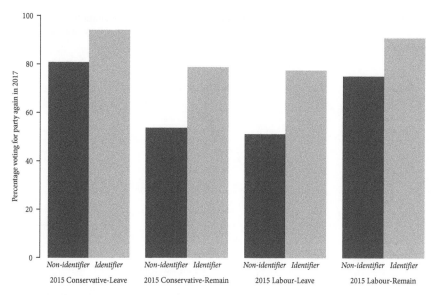

Figure 9.14 Loyalty rates 2015–17

We saw earlier how values and social characteristics were related to one another, and to support for Brexit. We also know that these intertwined values and social characteristics are related to party preferences. However, the degree to which any one of them is important for someone's vote will be influenced by the extent to which the parties differ over the issues at stake. The EU referendum made opinions on issues such as immigration and Brexit more relevant to party choice than they had been in 2015. We would therefore expect to see the Conservatives become more popular among older, less educated, and more socially conservative voters in 2017 compared to 2015, whilst Labour should have become more popular among younger, more highly educated, and more liberal voters. When we examine these changes, this is indeed what we see.

Figure 9.15 shows the relationship between age and vote in 2015 and 2017. There is a clear shift between the elections that is correlated with the demographics of Brexit. In 2015, older voters were more likely to be Conservative and younger voters more likely to be Labour. In 2017, this trend was exaggerated even further, with a sharp increase in the age gradient of vote choice. This reflected the success of the Conservatives among the older Leave vote, many of whom defected from UKIP, and the success of Labour among the more pro-Remain younger voters. Thus, although there was no 'Youthquake' in voter turnout (which among the 18–24 year-old group was under 50 per cent in both 2015 and 2017), there certainly was a dramatic change in the electoral choices of younger voters (Prosser et al. 2018). The changing age relationship does not seem to be driven primarily by education or income, as controlling for these does little to attenuate the change

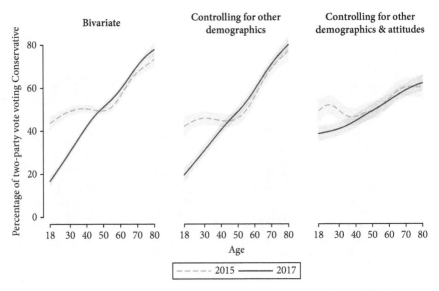

Figure 9.15 Bivariate relationship between age and Conservative share of the Labour/Conservative vote in 2015 and 2017

in the relationship. However, controlling for values and attitudes (including immigration and EU attitudes) does greatly reduce both the age gradient and the change between the two elections. This suggests that the changing age relationship is driven to some degree by the stronger role that the issues of immigration and the EU played in Conservative versus Labour vote choice in 2017.

Similarly, when we look at education (Figure 9.16) there are large changes that are again correlated with the pattern of Brexit support. From one election to the next, we see large increases in Conservative support among those with the lowest levels of education and a rise in Labour support among those with the highest levels of education. Much of the changing relationship seems to be driven by the changing age and income relationships we saw in the previous figure, as educated respondents tend to be younger and more affluent than less educated respondents. Consequently, controlling for income reduces the Conservatives' advantage among degree holders in 2015 and controlling for age reduces Labour's advantage among degree holders in 2017. Controlling for attitudes further flattens the relationship between Conservative–Labour vote choice and education, indicating that the relationship is partly accounted for by the more anti-EU and anti-immigration attitudes of less highly educated voters.

There were also changes in the relationship between household income and vote choice between 2015 and 2017, as shown in Figure 9.17. Labour increased its share of the two-party vote in the richer half of the income distribution, especially in the upper-middle income range. The net effect of these changes was that the income gradient on Conservative and Labour voting flattened in 2017, except for

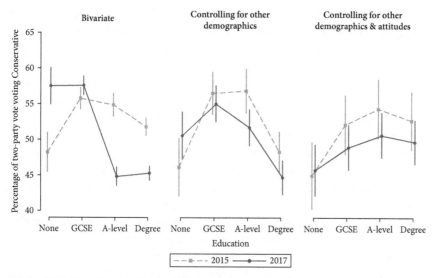

Figure 9.16 Bivariate relationship between education and Conservative share of the Conservative/Labour vote in 2015 and 2017

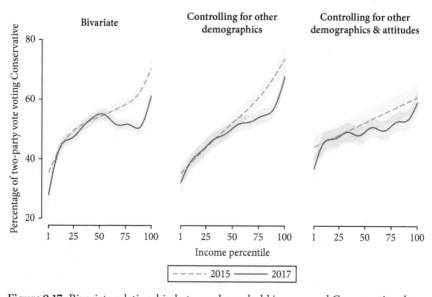

Figure 9.17 Bivariate relationship between household income and Conservative share of the Conservative/Labour vote in 2015 and 2017

the poorest groups, who swung towards Labour.[14] This is also reflected in class voting (measured on the 2015 and 2017 face-to-face BES and BSA surveys). They show Labour's lead remaining constant among working-class voters but narrowing the Conservative's lead among middle-class voters.[15] Again, these income changes seem to partially reflect the changing age and education gradients as the relationship looks much more similar across the years after controlling for the other demographics and flattens further after controlling for values and issue preferences.

To summarize what we have shown here, the shock of the EU referendum greatly increased the link between attitudes towards the EU and Conservative versus Labour voting. This change propagated a series of other demographic and attitudinal realignments. First, because immigration attitudes and the EU are closely linked (see Chapter 5), 2017 also saw a strengthening of the link between immigration attitudes and Conservative versus Labour voting. Next, because immigration is also closely linked to authoritarian values, 2017 witnessed an increased link between authoritarian values and Conservative versus Labour voting. Finally, the increased salience of issues linked to the cultural dimension also strengthened the link between Conservative versus Labour voting and various demographic correlates of that dimension. Most notably, because education is associated with more liberal values, higher levels of education switched from predicting Conservative voting in 2015 to predicting Labour voting in 2017. Similarly because older voters are much more anti-EU, anti-immigrant, and authoritarian, the age gradient steepened in 2017. However, these new cleavages cut across existing cleavages such as income (lower income is associated with authoritarian/economically left-wing attitudes).

9.5 Conclusions

The Brexit referendum was the biggest shock to British politics in decades and affected the 2017 General Election via each of the three mechanisms we described in Chapter 3. The Brexit vote fractured party competition in Britain. In 2015,

---

[14] The relationship between social characteristics, values, policy preferences, and vote choice changed substantially between 2015 and 2017. Inevitably however, these variables and their patterns of change are not independent of each other. Social characteristics predict values, which in turn predict policy preferences. To unravel the interdependence of these variables and to understand how Brexit changed the alignment of social characteristics, values, and party choice we have also estimated a series of SEM models. The patterns shown in the figures in the text all proved to be robust in these multivariate analyses.

[15] The BES and BSA face-to-face surveys tell somewhat different stories about the changes in class voting between 2015 and 2017, but the most accurate analysis is probably to combine both surveys. When we do that, the Conservatives held a 13 percentage point lead over Labour among middle-class (higher managerial and professional plus lower professional) voters in 2015 which fell to 7 percentage points in 2017. Labour led by 9 percentage points among working-class (routine and semi-routine) voters in 2015 which increased to 10 percentage points in 2017.

social and cultural issues such as the EU and immigration had previously driven voters *away* from the major parties. In the aftermath of Brexit, these issues drove the choice between the Conservatives and Labour. This was a manifestation of the increased salience of the issues of EU and immigration in the wake of the vote to leave the EU. The increased salience of these issues was also reflected in the number of voters who identified Europe and immigration as the most important issues during the 2017 campaign. Salience alone, however, does not fully explain the dramatic shifts seen in 2017. The shift to major party voting in line with attitudes towards Europe and immigration was also a product of changes in voters' evaluations of competence that followed the Brexit vote. After the referendum, the Conservatives' unambiguously pro-Leave stance and their opposition to immigration were seen as more credible once the EU was no longer seen as a constraint on their actions. We saw how, following the EU referendum, the Conservatives' perceived willingness to reduce immigration rose sharply, helping them win over Leave voters, especially from UKIP. This was made all the easier by UKIP's loss of their charismatic leader, and the internal disputes and financial chaos that rendered the party ineffective.

Moreover the outcome also depended heavily on the political response to the Brexit vote and the resultant shifts in the *image* of parties. Most notable was the Conservative Party's strategic decision to get firmly behind Brexit—promising to ensure that Brexit really meant Brexit, and to put an end to freedom of movement of labour from the EU. Consequently, the aftermath of the referendum changed Leave voters' perceptions of where the Conservatives stood on Europe, giving voters a clear choice and transforming the image of the Conservatives on Europe.

Labour's consolidation of the Remain vote was perhaps less the product of their position on Brexit—which was more ambiguous—and as much to do with traditional left–right economic divisions. Labour's move to the left under Corbyn, and away from any remaining association with New Labour, drained the Green Party of support even before the EU referendum took place. This left the Liberal Democrats and Labour as the only Remain-leaning parties in contention in England, while the choice for Remainers also included the nationalist parties in Scotland and Wales.[16] The Liberal Democrats did not meaningfully recover from the collapse in electoral viability that contributed to their 2015 losses (as identified in Chapter 7), and their unambiguously pro-European stance alienated many of their remaining Eurosceptic supporters. As a result, Labour were the only viable option for many English voters wishing to support a Remain-leaning party.

However, the EU referendum positions of the major parties was not all that mattered, but also what kind of Brexit the parties would seek to achieve in the negotiations that lay ahead. Labour was supported by those favouring continued economic

---

[16] Among Welsh BESIP respondents, Plaid Cymru won 13 per cent of Remain voters and 9 per cent of Leave voters.

integration while allowing freedom of movement, whereas the Conservatives were strongly favoured by those who wanted to control immigration. By providing a stark choice on such a crucial national issue, the EU referendum resulted in a reversal of the fragmentation of support we saw in 2015, and the unprecedented surge in the combined two-party vote. Although Brexit was not the only explanation for this change it was certainly important. Not only did it help bring about the collapse of UKIP, boosting the Conservative vote in England and Wales, but, as we saw in Chapter 8, it assisted the Conservative revival in Scotland at the expense of the SNP. On the Remain side, outside Scotland, Labour benefited from being the only viable party for those wanting a 'soft' Brexit.

The effects of Brexit on electoral alignments are not limited to values. The relationship between these values and social and demographic characteristics means that existing social cleavages have been disrupted. While social cleavages are typically thought of as long-standing rifts in society that change only slowly, our analysis shows that moving from an economic basis of major party competition to a two-dimensional one can bring about a rapid realignment of social groups. Brexit has realigned voters and parties with regard to age, education, and income as well as along the lines of social values.

A key theme of this book is that the British electorate is now capable of very high levels of volatility. The gains for the major parties are by no means secure. Neither are the transformational changes in the ideological and value bases of their support, nor are the new social cleavage of education and the demise of the traditionally role of income and class. As we saw in Chapter 4, the fundamental conditions of declining party identification and high levels of voter volatility mean that if parties change their positions, then different voters will vote for them. The new support base for the Conservatives has to a large degree been taken from UKIP, but if the Conservatives are seen to have failed to deliver on Brexit, especially on control over immigration, then it is unlikely that these supporters will stick with them. Newly recruited party supporters are even less loyal than the average voters in our generally volatile electorate.

In the longer term, the outcome of the Brexit process can be expected to affect the electoral relevance of Britain's relationship with the EU. If freedom of movement is finally ended, concern about immigration is likely to decline, making it less likely to provide a driver of support for the Conservatives, or indeed any other party. If immigration and Britain's relationship with the EU become less salient then we are likely to see domestic economic issues and social divisions based on inequality re-emerge as the primary basis of electoral competition. Should freedom of movement continue, however, or non-EU immigration increase markedly, then it seems likely that parties will continue to compete on this issue.

As the ramifications of Brexit play out, the longer-term impact of the Brexit shock remains to be seen. What is clear is that the dramatic changes between the 2015 and 2017 General Elections were not determined primarily by traditional economic issues, although these continued to be important. Nor were the changes the result of social change—a two-year time span is a blink of an eye in that respect. The shifts can only be understood by reference to the biggest political shock that Britain has experienced for many years.

10

Conclusions

V. O. Key (1955, 18) finished his essay on critical elections by posing the question:

what characteristics of an electorate or what conditions permit sharp and decisive changes in the power structure from time to time?

In the ensuing decades, a great deal of research has considered this question. Lipset and Rokkan (1967) famously documented how party systems became frozen, and Pierson (2000) described how positive feedback effects (or increasing returns on electoral success) help reproduce existing patterns of party dominance. However, in recent decades electoral alignments have been weakening in industrial democracies, and party systems have experienced increased fragmentation and electoral volatility (Dalton, Flanagan, and Beck 1985). But why do stable patterns of party support break down? Critical elections theory sets out the conditions under which realignments are likely to take place, including institutional, ideological, and social change (Evans and Norris 1999; Mayhew 2000). We have found that part of the explanation for recent sharp and decisive changes does indeed lie in such long-term developments. However, we show that this is only part of the story. This book reveals how the party system has become increasingly unstable in Britain and how this has made it more vulnerable to the impact of electoral shocks. These shocks shape election outcomes whether they be realigning or otherwise, and have led to the dramatic election outcomes experienced in 2015 and 2017.

We identified two important trends that have created instability and volatility in the British party system. The first is partisan dealignment, which is driven by the replacement of more partisan generations with new cohorts of citizens lacking partisan identities. The second is the gradual decline in the vote share of the two major parties, and corresponding increase in support for smaller parties, at least until 2017 ('party system fragmentation'). This was made possible by the rise of new issues outside the traditional economic left–right agenda on which new and smaller parties are better able to compete, and an increase in the supply of those parties facilitated by the expanding range of elections (especially European and devolved elections) in which smaller parties have been able to prove themselves to be viable competitors. The result of these changes is a more volatile electorate, characterized by an increase in the rate of voters switching parties between elections over time. The majority of British voters are now switchers, with around 60 per cent

Electoral shocks. Edward Fieldhouse, Jane Green, Geoffrey Evans, Jonathan Mellon, Christopher Prosser, Hermann Schmitt, Cees van der Eijk, Oxford University Press (2020). © Fieldhouse, Green, Evans, Mellon, Prosser, Schmitt, and van der Eijk.
DOI: 10.1093/oso/9780198800583.001.0001

switching their votes at least once over three elections. In this way, our analysis took us full circle to the very first volume produced using the BES: *Political Change in Britain* (Butler and Stokes 1969b), which observed the degree to which electoral volatility existed in the early 1960s, and the importance of this 'short-term conversion' in the context of a relatively stable and aligned electorate. That book is broadly remembered for addressing the question of stability in electoral behaviour as a result of strong class and partisan-based voting in British elections. In fact, it also set the stage for the importance of volatility, and provided the benchmark against which we can see the very substantial increase in switching in the British electorate, bringing us to the events of the present day.

These gradual, long-term changes to the electorate and party system, however, do not explain the uneven and volatile nature of recent elections on their own. Nor do they explain the destination of increased vote-switching: that is, which parties gain and lose most from volatility in any given election, and whether the vote-switching causes further fragmentation of the party system (as in 2015) or de-fragmentation of the party system (as in 2017). To understand these changes, another element is crucial—electoral shocks. We use the term 'shocks' to describe major political events or developments that have the potential to alter the political system and cut through the normal ebbs and flows of regular party politics.

We defined electoral shocks by three criteria:

1. *Electoral shocks are an abrupt change to the status quo. They are not necessarily exogenous to the party system, but they are more than simply the outcomes of normal everyday politics. They represent a significant and often unanticipated change.*

2. *Electoral shocks are manifest over prolonged time periods and are highly salient: they have the potential to be noticed and recognized even by people who do not have much interest in politics, and by people who might otherwise select information that fits their partisan beliefs and preconceptions. Electoral shocks are, therefore, very difficult for voters and politicians to ignore.*

3. *Electoral shocks are politically relevant and they have the potential to change how parties are perceived and therefore to reshape the party system.*

We presented evidence of five electoral shocks, each fulfilling these three criteria, and each leading to substantial changes in vote choice among the British electorate. Unlike existing approaches to understanding voting behaviour, our approach puts shocks at the centre of the explanation for understanding political change, rather than treating them as nuisance factors which interfere with 'normal' patterns of electoral behaviour. The effects of the different shocks we examined, however, vary considerably, both in terms of the voters and the parties that were affected, and also in terms of the mechanisms by which each shock mattered.

Some electoral shocks, such as the economic crisis and Brexit, are relevant to most, or all, of the electorate, but not all shocks affect all voters. For example, the immigration shock had a much greater effect among opponents of immigration, who were much more likely to switch to UKIP in 2015. We also saw how the formation of the 2010–15 coalition hugely affected 2010 Liberal Democrat voters, but was less relevant to people who supported other parties. However, the haemorrhaging of the Liberal Democrat vote inevitably meant a larger pool of voters for other parties to compete for. Similarly, the Scottish independence referendum only directly affected voters in Scotland, but the SNP's success had spillover consequences for party competition in the rest of the UK. The prospect of Labour losing many of its Scottish seats undermined their chances of winning an outright majority and contributed to speculation about potential coalition partnerships.

The mechanisms by which these electoral shocks led to vote-switching vary from case to case. We identified three ways in which shocks can affect vote-switching: via changing perceptions of competence; changes to the salience of particular issues and dimensions; and changes to the social and political image of a party. We also pointed to the importance of shocks as political opportunities that increase uncertainty but at the same time create a strong pressure on political parties to respond in some way. Shocks can change the ways parties compete for and win votes, making their consequences unpredictable and contingent on political strategies and the politicization of shocks in public and media discourse.

Looking first at shocks to competence, in Chapter 4, we demonstrated how the global financial crisis damaged Labour's reputation for economic management, with long-run consequences. Our analysis showed that voters who judged the economy as performing badly before 2010 were still punishing Labour—and rewarding the Conservatives and UKIP—in 2015. This is a much longer-term economic voting effect than has been assumed in the economic voting literature. It suggests that voters are able to attribute responsibility for past performance and—under certain circumstances—continue to punish the party perceived to be responsible for economic downturns over prolonged time periods. This blame was, of course, politically contested. Labour was blamed for the national debt *after* 2010 because the Conservatives successfully made Labour's alleged fiscal irresponsibility part of political discourse. This discourse contributed to the Conservative Party's arguments that the austerity measures adopted by the coalition government were necessary. This demonstrates how shocks can create political opportunities that can continue to shape political competition for an extended period of time.

Chapter 5 provided evidence for another shock that affected the perceived competence of parties: the surge in immigration following the UK government's decision not to delay free movement of people from EU Accession countries. The inability of successive governments to respond to growing concerns about immigration severely damaged the perceived competence of Labour on the issue, and then the Conservatives. This provided the opportunity for an anti-immigration party to fill that gap, leading to a dramatic upsurge in anti-European attitudes and support for UKIP.

The immigration shock did not only work through competence. The rise in EU immigration also increased the salience of immigration among the electorate. Immigration routinely featured as one of the most important issues in BES surveys in the run-up to the 2015 General Election, and was one of the two issues most cited by Leave voters to explain their choice in the EU referendum. Similarly, an increase in the salience of Scottish nationalism was a crucial aspect of the Scottish independence referendum shock, insofar as Westminster vote choice became very closely aligned with attitudes towards independence. As a result of the referendum campaign, the emphasis on issues beyond the dominant left and right economic dimension provided a basis for vote-switching in Scotland. Most notably, those that favoured independence deserted Labour in large numbers and voted for the SNP in 2015. In both these cases, the issues that underpinned voters' own views on the shock—immigration and Scottish independence respectively—became more important in determining electoral choices.

The impact of the independence referendum was not only about the salience of Scottish independence and devolution. In Chapter 3, we described how a shock may alter the social and political image of parties by forcing parties to respond to an issue that may have been of little importance to vote choice, and to clarify their position which previously may have been obscure. Although it is difficult to differentiate between the effect of the independence referendum shock on the salience of independence and its impact on the political image of Labour, it seems likely that both played an important role in the strengthening of the association between Yes voting and SNP voting in 2015. Whereas before the independence referendum voters could view Labour primarily through the lens of the economic left–right dimension, after the referendum campaign—in which Labour campaigned alongside the Conservatives to stay in the UK—voters also viewed Labour through the prism of the battle over independence. As a result of the shock to both salience and party images, the referendum precipitated a shift in allegiances of those backing independence to such a degree that 90 per cent of Yes voters voted for the SNP, including most of those who had previously voted Labour. Labour lost nearly half of its 2010 voters to the SNP at the 2015 General Election, the vast majority of whom had voted for independence the previous year.

Perhaps a more straightforward example of a shock to the image of a political party was described in Chapter 7. The main reason that the Liberal Democrat vote collapsed after the formation of the 2010 coalition was not primarily about responsibility for unpopular policies. Rather, it was a change in what its supporters perceived the party stood for once it had sided with the Conservatives—the 'old enemy' of many Liberal Democrat voters. It was the very nature of the Liberal Democrat support base that meant that the coalition with the Conservatives damaged their popularity so much. Not only was that support base predominantly on the economic centre-left with a social liberal bias in political values, but many Liberal Democrat voters were natural Labour supporters lending the Liberal Democrats tactical support to keep out Conservative candidates. The coalition therefore affected the image of the Liberal Democrats as a plausible alternative for moderate centre-left voters. Their more left-wing supporters were much more likely to grow to dislike the party after coalition than those on the right, leading them to desert in large numbers 2015.

As we have already noted, electoral shocks need not work through a single mechanism. Perhaps the biggest electoral shock of all (at least in the period in which we primarily focus: between 2008 and 2017) was the 2016 referendum on EU membership. The impact of the referendum acted through all three of the mechanisms we have described. First, it was a shock to salience. The EU referendum raised the importance of the issue of Europe in vote choice, such that support for the major parties coalesced around how people voted in the referendum, and strengthened the link between immigration and major party vote choice. The increased salience of the cultural dimension was reflected in the number of voters who identified Europe and immigration as their most important issues. Second, we showed how, following the EU referendum, the Conservatives' perceived competence to reduce immigration rose sharply, helping them win over people who had voted for UKIP in 2015. Third, the referendum altered the image of the Conservatives, such that they were now seen as *the* party of Brexit following the EU referendum. By the time of the 2017 General Election, both Leavers and Remainers were in firm agreement about where the Conservatives stood on Europe. We showed in Chapter 9 how the strategic decision to get firmly behind Brexit helped the Conservatives sharply increase their vote share, underling the importance of shocks as political opportunities. Of course, this might only have had a short-term electoral pay-off in 2017, and might be the root of a longer-term penalty depending on the outcome of Brexit.

These electoral shocks—and the political responses to them—shaped the elections of 2015 and 2017, increasing volatility and dramatically affecting the political winners and losers. In 2015, the net beneficiaries were the smaller parties, although both Labour and the Conservatives were able to capitalize on the collapse of the Liberal Democratic vote. In contrast, in 2017, the clear beneficiaries of volatility were the two major parties, leading to the largest two-party vote share since 1970. The record levels of switching were possible, in part, because of the long-term weakening of attachment of voters to political parties and the increase in voter volatility we described in Chapter 4. Indeed, each of the shocks we examined had a greater impact on vote-switching among weak or non-party identifiers, as party identification acts as a buffer against vote-switching.

10.1 Future shocks

As we write, British politics continues to stumble through a period of seemingly interminable crisis. The obvious question is what will happen in future elections? Will levels of individual volatility remain high or will we see an increase in partisan loyalty? Does the abrupt shift towards two-party politics at the 2017 Election mark the beginning of a new era of Conservative and Labour dominance, or will 2017 turn out to be a blip on an otherwise continued trend toward party system fragmentation? Will Scottish electoral politics continue to be defined by the nationalist–unionist dimension or will Westminster politics return to pre-eminence? Will issues connected to the liberal–authoritarian dimension continue to increase their importance or shall we see a return to the politics of left and right?

The short answer—and this will hopefully not come as a surprise at the end of a book about political shocks—is that *it depends what happens next.*

The electoral shocks we have discussed in this book were largely unanticipated and their consequences unforeseen. Even the effects of anticipated shocks are unknowable. At the time we are putting the finishing touches on this book, we still do not know whether Brexit will definitely happen, and, if it does, what Brexit will actually look like, let alone what its economic and social and political consequences will be. If Brexit goes well and the economy quickly recovers, or booms, would divisions over Brexit be quickly forgotten? Or, given that the main drivers of attitudes towards Brexit, such as authoritarianism, have little to do with economic preferences, would voting be increasingly defined by the social dimension? Recent elections have clearly shown that campaigning on second-dimension issues can be a successful strategy, and it is unlikely that future political entrepreneurs will forget this lesson. If Brexit goes badly and the economy crashes, however, might future elections be driven by Brexit blame, incompetence, and recrimination? An economic crash could result in the perennial issues of redistribution, austerity, and economic competence reasserting themselves.

We might not be able to predict with any certainty how future shocks will affect the fortunes of specific political parties. However, just as we have situated shocks in the context of long-term trends in British politics, we can point to features of the British electorate and institutions that might encourage or impede future volatility and fragmentation. In other words, while we might not be able to anticipate future shocks, we are able to identify the conditions that will be likely to shape their impact.

Our analysis points to two long-term factors that predict voter volatility: the level of partisanship and the size of the minor party vote. The size of the minor party vote shrunk in 2017 with Labour and the Conservatives both greatly increasing their vote shares. This strong two-party performance may be associated with lower levels of volatility at the next election, because major parties are better at retaining their voters than minor parties. We do have to be careful about this extrapolation, however. Chapter 9 showed that Labour and the Conservatives are now competing on both the economic and social dimensions. Because these dimensions are uncorrelated in the population,[1] this leaves large numbers of voters for each party cross-pressured, making it potentially harder than usual for the major parties to retain their 2017 support. Given the high degree of polarization of attitudes on Leave and Remain, a compromise Brexit that pleases neither side has the potential to harm both Labour and the Conservatives.

One important consideration that might point towards the possibility of a period of primarily two-party politics is that smaller parties are likely to find establishing viability even more challenging than they have in recent elections. The 2015 Election demonstrated for UKIP what 1983 did for the SDP: diffuse national support is very difficult to translate into seats under the British electoral system. In Chapter 7 we showed that the Liberal Democrats face a viability problem that will likely continue to impede their electoral rehabilitation. History shows that the Liberal Democrats know how to overcome those viability problems through targeted campaigning in by-elections and local elections (Russell and Fieldhouse 2005), but these strategies take time. Brexit will also result in an important electoral change for Britain's minor parties—the end of European Parliament elections. As we discussed in Chapter 4, European Parliament elections have provided a national platform for minor parties and have been an important stepping stone for later success in British elections. Via MEPs, European Parliament elections have provided an important source of funding and resources for smaller parties. Without this platform, minor parties will likely find getting their foot in the electoral door an even greater challenge.

The second factor influencing volatility is partisan dealignment. The level of partisanship no longer appears to be falling in Britain, but it does not appear to be increasing either. Our analysis shows that partisan dealignment has taken place mostly through a process of generational replacement. Therefore, any changes will tend to be slow, with a sudden surge in levels of partisanship seeming unlikely. Voters with no partisanship or low levels of party identity are much more likely to switch parties between elections, and so voters are still relatively unconstrained from switching parties. It therefore seems likely that partisan dealignment will continue to promote volatility at future elections. It would be a mistake, though, to assume that changes in partisanship can only move in one direction, or that partisanship must become less relevant to political decisions over time. Comparative research generally shows declines in partisanship across countries, but the size of these declines has varied substantially (Dalton 2012a; Dalton 2012b). Even where partisanship has declined, it does not necessarily translate into the kinds of volatile outcomes we have seen in Britain.

---

[1] In the BES Internet Panel the economic left–right and liberal–authoritarian scales have a correlation of 0.03.

The example of the United States is instructive. Overall levels of partisanship in America have declined but partisanship has become *more* important to vote choice over time (Bartels 2000; Brewer 2005). There is academic disagreement over whether this is because the American public has polarized (Abramowitz 2010) or merely sorted (Fiorina and Abrams 2008; Fiorina, Abrams, and Pope 2006) but the result is the same: Americans are less likely to switch away from 'their' party than in the past. The effect of polarization on volatility might be expected to counter the effects of partisan dealignment, making voters less willing to switch between parties. For example, in Chapter 4 we showed that major party voters who saw greater difference between the Conservatives and Labour less more likely to switch their votes between elections. However, since the early 1990s, not only have British voters become less aligned to parties, they have also become less polarized (Adams, Green, and Milazzo 2012), making the potential impact of shocks all the more powerful. Should the British electorate become *more* polarized (as recent evidence indicates they might) then we might expect the effects of future shocks to be dampened.

A further lesson from the American experience of polarization is that the nature of political issues under contention is very important. In the US, partisan sorting has been shown to be driven by 'culture wars'; issues such as race (Carmines and Stimson 1989), abortion (Adams 1997), gun control, and the environment (Lindaman and Haider-Markel 2002). These issues tend to be structured by authoritarianism (Hetherington and Weiler 2009), and as the salience of 'culture wars' issues has increased, American partisanship has in turn become increasingly structured by authoritarianism (Goren and Chapp 2017). Hetherington and Weiler (2009) argue that affective polarization has increased in the US because authoritarianism results in a fundamental clash of worldviews. People are now 'divided over things that conjure more visceral reactions than economic issues (Hetherington and Weiler 2009, 11).

Until recently, Britain had largely escaped political conflict over the sorts of issues that have defined the American culture wars, but Brexit has highlighted similar conflicts. As we showed in Chapter 9, the cultural dimension is a key structuring factor in voters' Brexit positions. We demonstrated the importance of Brexit for understanding voting in 2017, but what are the consequences for partisanship?

Figure 10.1 shows how the strength of Conservative Party identity among 2015 Conservative voters varied over the waves of the BES Internet Panel for those who voted Leave or Remain at the 2016 EU referendum. From early 2014 to the EU referendum in 2016, the strengths of Conservative Party identity among Remain and Leave voters moved in parallel (although Remainers started off with weaker Conservative Party identities). Following the EU referendum, however, we see a divergence. Among Leavers, Conservative identity strength increased. Among Remainers, it declined. In other words, the large-scale switching of

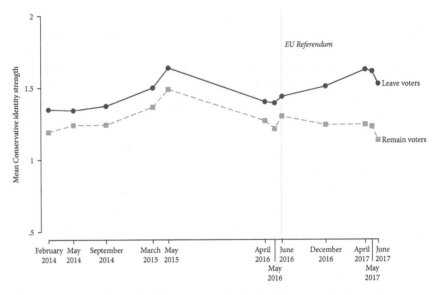

Figure 10.1 Mean strength of Conservative Party identity among Leave- and Remain-voting 2015 Conservative voters, on a scale where 0 = no/other party id, 1 = not very strong Conservative id, 2 = fairly strong Conservative id, 3 = very strong Conservative id

pro-Brexit voters to the Conservatives was not simply an example of 'short-term conversion' (Butler and Stokes 1974) but also marked an underlying shift in the structure of partisan alignment.

Brexit might play a more direct role in influencing political identification in Britain by acting as an identity in its own right. Hobolt, Leeper, and Tilley (2018) demonstrate the degree to which people have come to identify with Remain and Leave as a social identity, akin to partisan identities. Indeed, BES data shows that people express a stronger identification on average with one of the referendum sides than they do with any political party, not just in the EU referendum but also the Scottish independence referendum.

Figure 10.2 shows the strength of party identity captured through a battery of items designed to measure party identification as a social identity (Bankert, Huddy, and Rosema 2017), compared with equivalent identity scales for the EU and Scottish referendums (see appendix for details). In every case, voters report stronger identification with their side on the cross-cutting issue than they do with parties. Additionally, the proportion of people who report an identity on either side of the issue is higher for both referendums than for party identity. In other words, the decline of party identity may not necessarily reflect a decline in political identities more generally. Whether identification with the causes of leave or remain (or independence in Scotland) turns out to be sustained political *identities* remains to be seen.

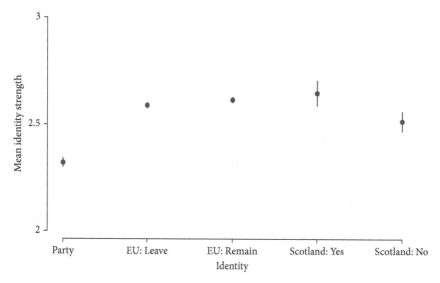

Figure 10.2 Strength of political identities measured using the seven-item social identity scales for party, EU referendum side, and Scottish referendum side

The American experience again provides some clues as to what the future effects of Brexit identities might look like. Mason (2015, 2016) argues that cross-cutting identities weaken the perceived distinctiveness of different groups and allow people to feel like they belong to a broader range of identities, undermining 'the cognitive and motivational bases of in-group bias and negative emotion' (Mason 2015, 131). Mason argues that racial, religious, cultural, and political identities have come into alignment in the US. As Americans have become increasingly socially sorted, affective polarization has followed. In Britain, as we demonstrated in Chapter 9, party choice has become more closely aligned with Brexit voting. The implications of that for polarization are explored in Figure 10.3. This shows the predicted scores (from a regression model, see Table A10.1 in the appendix) of how much respondents like the Conservative and Labour parties as a function of party strength and referendum identity immediately before the 2017 General Election.[2] The results show that when holding the strength of each identity constant, Conservative identifiers, who also identify as Leavers, feel more positively about the Conservatives and more negatively about Labour, compared to Conservatives who also identify as Remainers. Similarly, Labour identifiers who identify as Remainers feel more positively about Labour and less positively about the Conservatives than their Labour and Leave-identifying counterparts. This provides preliminary support for the expectation that any increasing alignment

---

[2] The strength of each identity is set to the overall mean strength of identity with each group (i.e. how strongly Conservatives identify as Conservative, how strongly Leavers identify as Leavers, etc.).

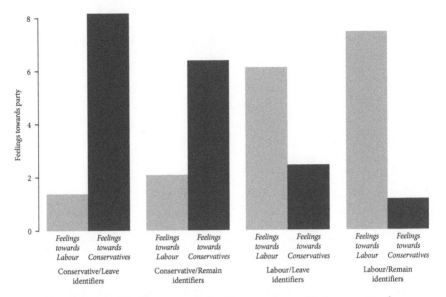

Figure 10.3 Predicted feelings towards the Conservative and Labour parties for aligned and unaligned party and Brexit identities of equal strength (wave 11 of the BES Internet Panel)

of competing political identities has some potential to fuel affective polarization in Britain.

Perhaps the most powerful factor that may counteract this is the continuing importance of social class in British politics (Evans and Tilley 2017; Evans and Mellon 2016a) which cuts across the party–Brexit alignment. Even in 2017, when Brexit heavily influenced voting decisions, social class still proved to be an important predictor of vote, albeit slightly weaker than in 2015. Labour, under Corbyn's leadership, pursued traditional left-wing polices which appealed to its traditional working-class base at the same time as its socially liberal policies increased its appeal among highly educated professionals. Cross-cutting political cleavages are likely to result in lower overall levels of affective polarization. How cultural and economic issues structure vote choice in the future—and influence political identities and affective polarization—will depend on both the nature of the parties' economic appeals and how they navigate the process and outcome of Brexit.

It is important not to underestimate the potential for future shocks to disrupt the effects of the Brexit shock. We do not have to look far for an example of one shock disrupting the effect of another. In Chapter 8 we showed how Scottish independence supporters flocked to the SNP in 2015, only for Brexit to peel Leave-supporting Yes voters away in 2017. In Chapter 6 we showed how the Brexit shock interrupted the effect of the global financial crisis.

The very nature of shocks means that it is impossible to predict the form that any future shocks will take. From major institutional reforms such as an elected

House of Lords, a split in one (or both) of the major parties, to military conflict, economic crisis, or a major environmental catastrophe—the list of possible future shocks with the potential to disrupt British politics is endless. With hindsight, it has been possible to identify the concatenation of trends, decisions, and events that resulted in the shocks we have examined in this book. Future researchers will likewise be able to identify the portents of future shocks in our current politics. Undoubtedly, the seeds of future disruption have already been sown.

Our aim in this book is not to foretell future events, but to understand the impact of such events and to provide a new way of approaching the study of elections. We have set out an approach to the study of elections which emphasizes the interplay between the slowly evolving social and political context and the impact of electoral shocks. Just like complex systems in other domains, party systems are susceptible to change, depending on the level of inertia and volatility in the system and the exposure to external shocks (Prindle 2012). The long-term decline in partisan alignment in Britain and the rise of smaller parties have weakened the forces which have helped maintain the status quo and left the party system more volatile and more vulnerable to the impact of electoral shocks. To understand electoral outcomes, we need to consider not only the reaction of voters to shocks but the behaviour of political parties and other political actors. Electoral shocks present an opportunity (or a threat) to which politicians and parties must respond. How they do so shapes whether they are the winners or the losers of voter volatility.

The mechanisms by which shocks matter to electoral outcomes complement rather than compete with existing theories of voter behaviour. The mechanisms that we identified each draws directly on established theories of voter choice. First, to understand the impact of shocks to salience we rely on positional (spatial) and salience theories of voter behaviour. Second, to understand how shocks to competence affect vote choices we must draw on performance and valence theories. Third, to understand the impact of shocks that change the social and political image of parties, we draw on sociological, psychological, and spatial theories of voter behaviour. Thus, we do not advocate abandoning any of these long-established theories, but rather we suggest that there is no one-size-fits-all model that explains voter behaviour and electoral outcomes across different geographic and historical contexts. Different theories explain voter choices in different electoral circumstances. As those circumstances change as a result of electoral shocks, the relevance of one theory or another is also liable to change. What matters in one election or one country might not matter so much in another. Although we have presented evidence relating to the UK elections of 2015 and 2017, our approach is applicable across different contexts, even though the nature of electoral shocks and the underlying conditions of stability or volatility will vary.

Appendix to Chapter 4

Table A4.1 Pooled no party identity fixed–effects model empty and full

	Empty	Full
(Intercept)	−2.638***	−1.357***
	(0.130)	(0.181)
Father no party ID		0.653***
		(0.045)
Union member		−0.076
		(0.051)
Age		−0.014***
		(0.001)
Male		−0.002
		(0.045)
White		−0.160
		(0.096)
Not married		0.026
		(0.046)
Degree		0.004
		(0.053)
No religion		0.297***
		(0.046)
Class (Base = Intermediate)		
Middle		−0.041
		(0.063)
Working		−0.104*
		(0.050)
Difference Conservative/Labour (Base = Not much difference)		
Some Difference		−0.566***
		(0.057)
Great difference		−1.087***
		(0.058)
Region (Base = London/South East)		
Midlands/Eastern		0.098
		(0.057)
North		−0.148*
		(0.058)
Scotland		−0.029
		(0.079)
South West		−0.206*
		(0.087)
Wales		−0.254*
		(0.107)

Continued

Table A4.1 Continued

	Empty	Full
Election effects (Base = 1964)		
1966	0.213	0.171
	(0.178)	(0.181)
1970	0.124	0.140
	(0.206)	(0.209)
1974 (Oct)	0.353*	0.192
	(0.152)	(0.155)
1979	0.683***	0.595***
	(0.154)	(0.158)
1983	0.721***	1.007***
	(0.140)	(0.145)
1987	0.781***	1.062***
	(0.139)	(0.145)
1992	0.494***	0.542***
	(0.145)	(0.149)
1997	0.645***	0.487***
	(0.143)	(0.147)
2015	1.092***	0.813***
	(0.141)	(0.147)
2017	1.072***	0.931***
	(0.144)	(0.151)
Elections	11	11
AIC	16284.715	15415.530
N	22276	22276

* $p<0.05$ ** $p<0.01$ *** $p<0.001$

Empty	Dealignment	Fragmentation	Convergence	Convergence + fragmentation	Other	Combined
Party ID at election 1 (Base = Not very strong)						
None/DK	−0.381***					−0.349***
	(0.0872)					(0.0927)
Fairly strong	0.273					0.210
	(0.161)					(0.165)
Very strong	0.192					0.226
	(0.171)					(0.212)
Difference between parties (Base = No difference)						
Some difference			−0.332***	−0.0703		−0.0875
			(0.0774)	(0.172)		(0.167)
Great difference			−0.643***	0.149		0.222
			(0.114)	(0.257)		(0.248)
Voted Con/Lab at election 1		−1.532***		−0.928***		−0.665**
		(0.134)		(0.218)		(0.236)
Party ID=Vote at election 1	−0.785***					−0.653***
	(0.0909)					(0.0830)
(Fairly strong PID) * (PID=Vote)	−0.953***					−0.749***
	(0.196)					(0.196)
(Very strong PID) * (PID = Vote)	−1.515***					−1.282***
	(0.190)					(0.223)
Con/Lab * Some difference				−0.345		−0.324
				(0.270)		(0.272)
Con/Lab * Great difference				−0.992*		−0.901*
				(0.416)		(0.401)
Degree					−0.0111	0.130
					(0.0744)	(0.0668)
Male					−0.0348	−0.0920*
					(0.0422)	(0.0396)
Not married					−0.0566	−0.0344
					(0.0766)	(0.0730)
Age					−0.0112***	−0.00889***
					(0.00186)	(0.00194)

Continued

Table A4.2 Continued

Empty	Dealignment	Fragmentation	Convergence	Convergence + fragmentation	Other	Combined
Election 2 (Base = 1966)						
1970	0.277***	0.325***	0.258***	0.282***	0.280***	0.266***
	(0.00355)	(0.00551)	(0.00602)	(0.00771)	(0.00377)	(0.00943)
1974	0.565***	0.611***	0.502***	0.564***	0.526***	0.552***
	(0.00533)	(0.0117)	(0.00532)	(0.0115)	(0.00655)	(0.0133)
1974.5	0.284*	0.0418	0.245***	0.0553**	0.249***	-0.0578*
	(0.118)	(0.0225)	(0.00186)	(0.0208)	(0.00329)	(0.0284)
1979	0.370***	0.381***	0.566***	0.425***	0.528***	0.324***
	(0.0110)	(0.0116)	(0.0107)	(0.0166)	(0.00335)	(0.0212)
1987	0.0945***	0.0761*	0.640***	0.213**	0.372***	-0.0305
	(0.0174)	(0.0336)	(0.0477)	(0.0665)	(0.00825)	(0.0656)
1992	0.426***	0.491***	0.845***	0.597***	0.695***	0.371***
	(0.0171)	(0.0205)	(0.0245)	(0.0295)	(0.00628)	(0.0350)
1997	0.991***	0.806***	0.947***	0.795***	0.938***	0.651***
	(0.114)	(0.00878)	(0.0245)	(0.0295)	(0.0104)	(0.0291)
2001	0.798***	0.649***	0.812***	0.647***	0.843***	0.479***
	(0.110)	(0.0142)	(0.0110)	(0.0173)	(0.0117)	(0.0256)
2015	1.517***	1.205***	1.617***	1.291***	1.601***	1.157***
	(0.0980)	(0.0260)	(0.0138)	(0.0256)	(0.0239)	(0.0465)
2017	1.080***	0.846***	1.240***	0.963***	1.147***	0.718***
	(0.0972)	(0.0202)	(0.0261)	(0.0295)	(0.0286)	(0.0529)
Constant	-1.911***	-0.611***	-1.514***	-0.721***	-1.328***	0.447**
	(0.0933)	(0.103)	(0.0607)	(0.141)	(0.103)	(0.168)
N	20361	20361	20361	20361	20361	20361

* p<0.05; ** p<0.01; *** p<0.001

Equation for within- and between-cohort variation

We define A_{ct} as the proportion of respondents at time t in age cohort c and N_{ct} as the proportion of age cohort c that does not identify with a political party at time t. Therefore for two periods (1 and 2) we define:

$$within\ cohort\ change = \sum_{c \in [18,19\ldots99,100)} (N_{c2} - N_{c1}) * A_{c1}$$

and

$$between\ cohort\ change = \sum_{c \in [18,19\ldots99,100)} (A_{c2} - A_{c1}) * N_{c1}$$

Table A4.3 Factiva Search terms used to calculate the effective number of media parties

Party	Search string
Conservative	(Conservative or Conservatives or Tory or Tories) AND party
Labour	(Labour) AND party
Liberal Democrats	(Liberal Democrat or Liberal Democrats or Lib Dem or Lib Dems or Lib-Dem or Lib-Dems) AND party
Green	(Green Party) AND party
Plaid Cymru	(Plaid Cymru) AND party
SNP	(SNP or Scottish National Party) AND party
UKIP	(UKIP or United Kingdom Independence Party) AND party
Respect	(Respect Party) AND party
BNP	(British National Party or BNP) AND party
Referendum	(Referendum Party) AND party
the (control)	the

Appendix to Chapter 5

Table A5.1 Multilevel logit predicting immigration being seen as the respondent's 'most important issue'

Log(Immigration change)	0.473*
	(0.188)
Log(Immigration level)	0.396***
	(0.089)
Log(Immigration change) * Log(Immigration level)	−0.122**
	(0.039)
Education level (Base = No qualifications)	
GCSE D–G	−0.163
	(0.101)
GCSE A*–C	−0.177*
	(0.073)
A level	−0.539***
	(0.079)
Undergraduate	−0.941***
	(0.078)
Postgraduate	−1.460***
	(0.119)
Age	0.073***
	(0.010)
Age^2	−0.001***
	(0.000)
Newspaper (Base = None)	
The Express	0.820***
	(0.123)
The Daily Mail	0.844***
	(0.062)
The Mirror	−0.239**
	(0.081)
The Daily Star	0.816***
	(0.194)
The Sun	0.865***
	(0.065)
The Daily Telegraph	0.111
	(0.100)
The Financial Times	−0.898
	(0.533)
The Guardian	−2.155***
	(0.222)
The Independent	−1.040***
	(0.246)
The Times	−0.608***
	(0.134)
The Scotsman	−0.292
	(0.366)

The Herald	−0.821*
	(0.356)
The Western Mail	−0.589
	(0.389)
Other local newspaper	−0.190
	(0.121)
Other Newspaper	−0.208*
	(0.096)
Constant	−4.639***
	(0.435)
N Respondents	14,584
N Regions	11
N Local Authorities	787

* p<0.05; ** p<0.01; *** p<0.001

Table A5.2 Interclass correlation coefficients from the multilevel logit model shown in Table A5.1

Level	Empty model	Full model
Region	0.021	0.012
	(0.010)	(0.006)
Local authority	0.047	0.024
	(0.010)	(0.008)

Table A5.3 OLS model predicting yearly proportion of respondents saying immigration is an important issue as a function of newspaper coverage of immigration (Newspaper coverage and immigration levels are standardized)

	Daily Mail	*Daily Express*	*The Sun*	*All*	*Daily Mail + polynomial*
Daily Mail	0.101***			0.148***	0.105***
	(0.015)			(0.026)	(0.017)
Daily Express		0.034		−0.004	
		(0.021)		(0.019)	
The Sun			0.027*	−0.022	
			(0.012)	(0.017)	
Immigration	0.029	0.116*	0.130***	−0.003	0.023
	(0.021)	(0.041175)	(0.031)	(0.033)	(0.035)
Year	0.004	−0.002	0.000	0.004	−0.011
	(0.002)	(0.005)	(0.004)	(0.003)	(0.080)
Year^2					0.001
					(0.003)
Year^3					0.000
					(0.000)
Constant	−7.609	3.14	−0.728	−8.099	20.988
	(3.864)	(9.208)	(8.803)	(5.037)	(159.143)
Adjusted R^2	0.967	0.81	0.86	0.955	0.965
N	25	17	18	17	25

Table A5.4 Two-parameter IRT model of
immigration concern in the 2010 BESIP

Most Important Issue is immigration	
Discrimination	1.382***
	−0.047
Difficulty	1.547***
	−0.038
Immigration emotions: angry	
Discrimination	3.415***
	−0.164
Difficulty	0.122***
	−0.011
Immigration emotions: disgust	
Discrimination	2.451***
	−0.073
Difficulty	0.250***
	−0.012
Immigration emotions: uneasy	
Discrimination	0.591***
	−0.023
Difficulty	−0.080**
	−0.029
Immigration emotions: afraid	
Discrimination	1.871***
	−0.049
Difficulty	0.755***
	−0.017

* $p < 0.05$ ** $p < 0.01$ *** $p < 0.001$

Table A5.5 Same vote in 2010 versus UKIP contrasts from multinomial logistic regression models of different groups of 2010 voters

	2010 Labour	2010 Conservative	Liberal Democrat
EU approval	−0.508***	−0.650***	−0.698
	(0.119)	(0.088)	(0.104)
Immigration concern	0.706***	0.394***	0.773
	(0.163)	(0.110)	(0.161)
Strength of ID with 2010 party (Base = No/different party ID)			
Not very strongly	−0.083	−0.480*	−0.880*
	(0.415)	(0.213)	(0.354)
Fairly strongly	−0.461	−0.979***	−0.615*
	(0.336)	(0.179)	(0.285)
Very strongly	−1.983***	−1.499***	−2.042**
	(0.517)	(0.241)	(0.773)
Education level (Base = No qualifications)			
GCSE D–G	−0.224	−0.454	−0.181
	(0.541)	(0.383)	(0.700)
GCSE A*–C	−0.162	−0.453	−0.747
	(0.390)	(0.255)	(0.495)
A level	−0.132	−0.321	−0.765
	(0.471)	(0.270)	(0.536)
Undergraduate	−0.546	−0.675*	−1.025*
	(0.463)	(0.273)	(0.492)
Postgrad	−14.501	−0.067	−0.850
	(707.056)	(0.369)	(0.626)
Other qualification	−0.517	−0.640*	−0.583
	(0.488)	(0.272)	(0.515)
Age	0.006	−0.014*	0.011
	(0.012)	(0.007)	(0.010)
Female	−0.467	−0.291	−0.136
	(0.262)	(0.148)	(0.236)
Constant	−0.249	1.750**	1.715*
	(0.945)	(0.543)	(0.826)
N origin voters	1,056	1,588	1,178
N UKIP switchers	81	270	130
Pseudo R^2	0.1381	0.1155	0.0923

* $p<0.05$ ** $p<0.01$ *** $p<0.001$

Table A5.6 OLS regression predicting approval of EU membership (five category dependent variable) used for imputation of EU approval under conditions of low anti-immigrant preferences

Immigration concern	−0.617***
	(0.020)
Education level (Base = No qualifications)	
GCSE D–G	0.054
	(0.083)
GCSE A*–C	0.152**
	(0.058)
A level	0.418***
	(0.062)
Undergraduate	0.554***
	(0.058)
Postgrad	0.802***
	(0.073)
Other qualification	0.387***
	(0.061)
Age	−0.002
	(0.001)
Female	−0.219***
	(0.029)
2010 General Election Vote (Base = Conservatives)	
Labour	0.715***
	(0.039)
Liberal Democrat	0.723***
	(0.038)
SNP	−0.952
	(1.071)
Plaid Cymru	0.508***
	(0.191)
UKIP	−0.534***
	(0.064)
Green Party	0.735***
	(0.142)
British National Party (BNP)	−0.260
	(0.133)
Other	0.155
	(0.112)
Constant	2.263***
	(0.096)
Adjusted R^2	0.390
N	5,501

Appendix to Chapter 6

Table A6.1 Graded response IRT model of economic left–right values

	Measured in wave:				
	1–5	6	7–9	10–12	13
Government should redistribute income from the better off to those who are less well off					
Discrimination	1.954***	2.139***	2.018***	1.961***	2.074***
	(0.0166)	(0.0198)	(0.0171)	(0.0183)	(0.0194)
Difficulty (base = Strongly disagree)					
≥Disagree	−2.141***	−1.860***	−2.138***	−2.042***	−1.868***
	(0.0173)	(0.0162)	(0.0173)	(0.0181)	(0.0165)
≥ Neither agree	−1.017***	−0.857***	−1.044***	−0.954***	−0.868***
nor disagree	(0.00968)	(0.00972)	(0.00978)	(0.0102)	(0.00986)
≥ Agree	−0.166***	−0.0595***	−0.149***	−0.0735***	−0.0414***
	(0.00754)	(0.00811)	(0.00755)	(0.00812)	(0.00818)
= Strongly agree	1.020***	1.099***	1.131***	1.254***	1.216***
	(0.0102)	(0.0113)	(0.0106)	(0.0123)	(0.0120)
Big business takes advantage of ordinary people					
Discrimination	2.147***	2.647***	2.278***	2.163***	2.438***
	(0.0189)	(0.0254)	(0.0200)	(0.0212)	(0.0235)
Difficulty (base = Strongly disagree)					
≥ Disagree	−2.863***	−2.613***	−3.013***	−3.046***	−2.719***
	(0.0268)	(0.0256)	(0.0303)	(0.0341)	(0.0278)
≥ Neither agree	−1.819***	−1.523***	−1.785***	−1.897***	−1.600***
nor disagree	(0.0140)	(0.0123)	(0.0137)	(0.0162)	(0.0133)
≥ Agree	−0.972***	−0.820***	−0.902***	−0.968***	−0.770***
	(0.00903)	(0.00862)	(0.00866)	(0.00978)	(0.00874)
= Strongly agree	0.548***	0.499***	0.663***	0.635***	0.687***
	(0.00813)	(0.00817)	(0.00836)	(0.00909)	(0.00893)
Ordinary working people do not get their fair share of the nation's wealth					
Discrimination	2.528***	3.033***	2.709***	2.516***	2.811***
	(0.0214)	(0.0285)	(0.0231)	(0.0236)	(0.0263)
Difficulty (base = Strongly disagree)					
≥ Disagree	−2.515***	−2.375***	−2.657***	−2.668***	−2.405***
	(0.0207)	(0.0209)	(0.0231)	(0.0261)	(0.0217)
≥ Neither agree	−1.484***	−1.284***	−1.509***	−1.566***	−1.342***
nor disagree	(0.0108)	(0.0102)	(0.0108)	(0.0124)	(0.0107)
≥ Agree	−0.742***	−0.571***	−0.718***	−0.703***	−0.539***
	(0.00760)	(0.00750)	(0.00745)	(0.00809)	(0.00759)
= Strongly agree	0.595***	0.610***	0.668***	0.753***	0.764***
	(0.00767)	(0.00797)	(0.00775)	(0.00881)	(0.00861)

Continued

Table A6.1 Continued

	Measured in wave:				
	1–5	6	7–9	10–12	13
There is one law for the rich and one for the poor					
Discrimination	2.513***	3.089***	2.743***	2.525***	2.672***
	(0.0213)	(0.0292)	(0.0237)	(0.0240)	(0.0251)
Difficulty (base = Strongly disagree)					
≥ *Disagree*	−2.334***	−2.083***	−2.444***	−2.504***	−2.260***
	(0.0181)	(0.0166)	(0.0196)	(0.0230)	(0.0195)
≥ *Neither agree*	−1.342***	−1.166***	−1.415***	−1.491***	−1.274***
nor disagree	(0.0100)	(0.00942)	(0.0102)	(0.0119)	(0.0106)
≥ *Agree*	−0.704***	−0.624***	−0.764***	−0.809***	−0.618***
	(0.00750)	(0.00750)	(0.00752)	(0.00838)	(0.00789)
= *Strongly agree*	0.502***	0.410***	0.452***	0.477***	0.586***
	(0.00747)	(0.00746)	(0.00722)	(0.00799)	(0.00826)
Management will always try to get the better of employees if it gets the chance					
Discrimination	1.560***	1.892***	1.714***	1.637***	1.792***
	(0.0146)	(0.0187)	(0.0157)	(0.0168)	(0.0180)
Difficulty (base = Strongly disagree)					
≥ *Disagree*	−3.212***	−2.865***	−3.287***	−3.303***	−2.987***
	(0.0333)	(0.0310)	(0.0351)	(0.0390)	(0.0334)
≥ *Neither agree*	−1.694***	−1.475***	−1.665***	−1.775***	−1.565***
nor disagree	(0.0155)	(0.0141)	(0.0147)	(0.0174)	(0.0152)
≥ *Agree*	−0.688***	−0.624***	−0.708***	−0.770***	−0.619***
	(0.00960)	(0.00952)	(0.00929)	(0.0105)	(0.00973)
= *Strongly agree*	0.916***	0.848***	0.957***	0.979***	0.990***
	(0.0111)	(0.0109)	(0.0109)	(0.0122)	(0.0118)

* p<0.05 ** p<0.01 *** p<0.001

Note: The direction of the predicted score is then reversed to give a scale that runs from left to right.

Table A6.2 Graded response IRT model of liberal–authoritarian values

	Measured in wave:				
	1–5	6	7–9	10–12	13

Young people today don't have enough respect for traditional British values

	1–5	6	7–9	10–12	13
Discrimination	2.216***	2.302***	2.365***	2.481***	2.443***
	(0.0188)	(0.0215)	(0.0199)	(0.0226)	(0.0225)
Difficulty (base = Strongly disagree)					
≥ *Disagree*	−2.409***	−2.268***	−2.269***	−2.116***	−2.019***
	(0.0188)	(0.0195)	(0.0176)	(0.0174)	(0.0169)
≥ *Neither agree*	−1.357***	−1.219***	−1.266***	−1.204***	−1.062***
nor disagree	(0.0109)	(0.0113)	(0.0104)	(0.0106)	(0.0104)
≥ *Agree*	−0.523***	−0.390***	−0.397***	−0.377***	−0.289***
	(0.00776)	(0.00830)	(0.00746)	(0.00769)	(0.00789)
= *Strongly agree*	0.726***	0.804***	0.839***	0.798***	0.837***
	(0.00825)	(0.00931)	(0.00838)	(0.00856)	(0.00898)

For some crimes, the death penalty is the most appropriate sentence

	1–5	6	7–9	10–12	13
Discrimination	2.249***	2.387***	2.342***	2.317***	2.432***
	(0.0200)	(0.0233)	(0.0207)	(0.0222)	(0.0237)
Difficulty (base = Strongly disagree)					
≥ *Disagree*	−0.933***	−0.771***	−0.816***	−0.839***	−0.794***
	(0.00924)	(0.00949)	(0.00885)	(0.00959)	(0.00957)
≥ *Neither agree*	−0.394***	−0.260***	−0.273***	−0.312***	−0.310***
nor disagree	(0.00749)	(0.00795)	(0.00728)	(0.00781)	(0.00797)
≥ *Agree*	−0.0518***	0.101***	0.106***	0.0809***	0.0701***
	(0.00704)	(0.00767)	(0.00699)	(0.00742)	(0.00755)
= *Strongly agree*	0.769***	0.903***	0.919***	0.912***	0.846***
	(0.00843)	(0.00968)	(0.00883)	(0.00942)	(0.00918)

Schools should teach children to obey authority

	1–5	6	7–9	10–12	13
Discrimination	1.981***	2.045***	2.060***	2.209***	2.212***
	(0.0172)	(0.0196)	(0.0177)	(0.0204)	(0.0207)
Difficulty (base = Strongly disagree)					
≥ *Disagree*	−2.669***	−2.517***	−2.434***	−2.319***	−2.322***
	(0.0223)	(0.0231)	(0.0200)	(0.0201)	(0.0206)
≥ *Neither agree*	−1.664***	−1.553***	−1.461***	−1.403***	−1.428***
nor disagree	(0.0132)	(0.0139)	(0.0121)	(0.0122)	(0.0128)
≥ *Agree*	−0.774***	−0.628***	−0.530***	−0.515***	−0.494***
	(0.00884)	(0.00934)	(0.00817)	(0.00834)	(0.00863)
= *Strongly agree*	0.795***	0.900***	0.974***	0.918***	0.932***
	(0.00893)	(0.0103)	(0.00947)	(0.00948)	(0.00977)

Censorship of films and magazines is necessary to uphold moral standards

	1–5	6	7–9	10–12	13
Discrimination	1.120***	1.159***	1.153***	1.251***	1.259***
	(0.0120)	(0.0138)	(0.0123)	(0.0140)	(0.0143)
Difficulty (base = Strongly disagree)					
≥ *Disagree*	−2.363***	−2.203***	−2.234***	−2.055***	−2.061***
	(0.0252)	(0.0264)	(0.0242)	(0.0233)	(0.0239)
≥ *Neither agree*	−0.967***	−0.835***	−0.825***	−0.793***	−0.790***
nor disagree	(0.0138)	(0.0146)	(0.0131)	(0.0132)	(0.0136)

Continued

Table A6.2 Continued

	Measured in wave:				
	1–5	6	7–9	10–12	13
≥ *Agree*	0.000659	0.140***	0.180***	0.163***	0.192***
	(0.0105)	(0.0119)	(0.0107)	(0.0107)	(0.0111)
= *Strongly agree*	1.967***	2.074***	2.203***	2.043***	2.026***
	(0.0218)	(0.0255)	(0.0239)	(0.0230)	(0.0232)
People who break the law should be given stiffer sentences					
Discrimination	2.351***	2.520***	2.555***	2.565***	2.554***
	(0.0201)	(0.0236)	(0.0216)	(0.0236)	(0.0239)
Difficulty (base = Strongly disagree)					
≥ *Disagree*	−2.742***	−2.567***	−2.541***	−2.484***	−2.532***
	(0.0227)	(0.0227)	(0.0204)	(0.0217)	(0.0230)
≥ *Neither agree*	−1.712***	−1.531***	−1.500***	−1.490***	−1.536***
nor disagree	(0.0126)	(0.0125)	(0.0113)	(0.0121)	(0.0128)
≥ *Agree*	−0.639***	−0.471***	−0.420***	−0.433***	−0.403***
	(0.00789)	(0.00818)	(0.00730)	(0.00774)	(0.00802)
= *Strongly agree*	0.635***	0.726***	0.792***	0.773***	0.774***
	(0.00775)	(0.00864)	(0.00795)	(0.00833)	(0.00856)

* $p<0.05$ ** $p<0.01$ *** $p<0.001$

Table A6.3 Multinomial logistic regression model of 2015 vote

Conservatives (base category = Labour)	Model 1	Model 2	Model 3	Model 4	Model 5
2010 Retrospective economic evaluation	−0.268*** (0.0629)	−0.237 (0.139)	−0.234*** (0.0642)	−0.227*** (0.0652)	−0.223 (0.146)
2015 Retrospective economic evaluation	0.669*** (0.0765)	0.179 (0.212)	0.479*** (0.0800)	0.570*** (0.0789)	0.108 (0.218)
Labour economic competence		−1.001*** (0.175)			−0.851*** (0.185)
Conservative economic competence		0.712*** (0.192)			0.580** (0.201)
Attitude towards austerity			0.929*** (0.100)		0.695** (0.237)
Labour responsible for Global Financial Crisis				0.0306 (0.146)	−0.600 (0.332)
Labour responsible for level of national debt				1.155*** (0.157)	0.616 (0.365)
Age	0.0315*** (0.00557)	0.0313** (0.0116)	0.0336*** (0.00569)	0.0324*** (0.00566)	0.0323** (0.0119)
Female	−0.263 (0.134)	−0.245 (0.294)	−0.135 (0.138)	−0.153 (0.137)	−0.173 (0.302)
Education level (Base = no qualifications)					
Below GCSE	0.588 (0.346)	0.434 (0.782)	0.517 (0.350)	0.621 (0.352)	0.491 (0.793)
GCSE	0.348 (0.255)	−0.134 (0.576)	0.333 (0.259)	0.339 (0.261)	−0.0322 (0.581)
A Level	0.530* (0.270)	−0.110 (0.606)	0.545* (0.275)	0.487 (0.277)	−0.0184 (0.617)
Undergraduate	0.370 (0.256)	−0.506 (0.576)	0.326 (0.261)	0.271 (0.262)	−0.478 (0.586)
Postgraduate	0.411 (0.342)	−0.548 (0.780)	0.313 (0.350)	0.244 (0.346)	−0.623 (0.787)
Other	−0.219 (0.431)	−1.225 (0.883)	−0.246 (0.438)	−0.252 (0.436)	−1.067 (0.905)
Income percentile	0.00723* (0.00286)	0.0126* (0.00630)	0.00662* (0.00292)	0.00694* (0.00291)	0.0132* (0.00645)
Missing income data dummy	−0.197 (0.229)	0.215 (0.499)	−0.206 (0.234)	−0.167 (0.230)	0.165 (0.503)
Economic left–right values	1.461*** (0.0974)	1.328*** (0.215)	1.163*** (0.103)	1.420*** (0.0990)	1.164*** (0.223)
Liberal–authoritarian values	0.902*** (0.0963)	0.799*** (0.210)	0.864*** (0.0985)	0.869*** (0.0977)	0.796*** (0.213)
Immigration attitudes	0.257** (0.0940)	0.184 (0.215)	0.248** (0.0955)	0.208* (0.0960)	0.249 (0.220)
2015 not very strong Conservative Party id	0.794*** (0.171)	0.179 (0.366)	0.751*** (0.174)	0.722*** (0.172)	0.0952 (0.372)
2015 fairly strong Conservative Party id	1.002*** (0.167)	0.506 (0.376)	0.914*** (0.170)	0.930*** (0.169)	0.418 (0.383)
2015 very strong Conservative Party id	1.513*** (0.293)	2.228* (1.094)	1.406*** (0.298)	1.463*** (0.294)	2.176* (1.104)

Continued

Table A6.3 Continued

Conservatives (base category = Labour)	Model 1	Model 2	Model 3	Model 4	Model 5
2015 not very strong Labour Party id	-1.366***	-0.518	-1.309***	-1.204***	-0.333
	(0.227)	(0.499)	(0.231)	(0.233)	(0.510)
2015 fairly strong Labour Party id	-2.645***	-0.764	-2.504***	-2.450***	-0.729
	(0.255)	(0.515)	(0.258)	(0.260)	(0.525)
2015 very strong Labour Party id	-4.145***	-2.626*	-3.932***	-3.874***	-2.447
	(0.675)	(1.245)	(0.695)	(0.685)	(1.338)
2010 not very strong Conservative Party id	0.392*	-0.240	0.393*	0.355*	-0.186
	(0.160)	(0.356)	(0.162)	(0.161)	(0.362)
2010 fairly strong Conservative Party id	0.830***	0.795*	0.853***	0.779***	0.792*
	(0.184)	(0.394)	(0.187)	(0.185)	(0.402)
2010 very strong Conservative Party id	0.562*	0.997	0.612*	0.501	1.065
	(0.274)	(0.657)	(0.279)	(0.274)	(0.684)
2010 not very strong Labour Party id	0.129	-0.0588	0.242	0.172	-0.0780
	(0.217)	(0.461)	(0.221)	(0.222)	(0.464)
2010 fairly strong Labour Party id	-0.0610	-0.555	0.0229	0.0474	-0.633
	(0.253)	(0.529)	(0.257)	(0.259)	(0.537)
2010 very strong Labour Party id	-0.520	-0.553	-0.529	-0.428	-0.727
	(0.515)	(1.033)	(0.531)	(0.519)	(1.057)
Constant	-3.567***	-1.542	-3.350***	-4.122***	-1.761
	(0.540)	(1.232)	(0.552)	(0.560)	(1.314)
N	4228	992	4218	4228	992

Liberal Democrats (base category = Labour)	Model 1	Model 2	Model 3	Model 4	Model 5
2010 Retrospective economic evaluation	-0.190**	-0.0375	-0.176*	-0.184**	-0.0288
	(0.0686)	(0.158)	(0.0689)	(0.0703)	(0.162)
2015 Retrospective economic evaluation	0.378***	0.540*	0.297***	0.327***	0.507*
	(0.0843)	(0.241)	(0.0880)	(0.0864)	(0.244)
Labour economic competence		-0.641**			-0.637**
		(0.201)			(0.208)
Conservative economic competence		-0.131			-0.127
		(0.202)			(0.216)
Attitude towards austerity			0.399***		-0.220
			(0.110)		(0.276)
Labour responsible for Global Financial Crisis				-0.153	-0.422
				(0.164)	(0.378)
Labour responsible for level of national debt				0.673***	0.580
				(0.160)	(0.393)
Age	0.0155*	0.0126	0.0168**	0.0161**	0.0132
	(0.00605)	(0.0130)	(0.00612)	(0.00610)	(0.0132)
Female	-0.261	0.144	-0.244	-0.190	0.0791
	(0.150)	(0.350)	(0.152)	(0.152)	(0.358)
Education level (Base = no qualifications)					
Below GCSE	0.394	0.523	0.386	0.405	0.646
	(0.435)	(1.210)	(0.437)	(0.436)	(1.215)
GCSE	0.420	1.150	0.421	0.382	1.256
	(0.323)	(0.884)	(0.325)	(0.326)	(0.888)
A Level	0.219	0.658	0.226	0.207	0.757
	(0.339)	(0.908)	(0.341)	(0.341)	(0.914)

Undergraduate	0.223	0.0935	0.218	0.137	0.134
	(0.317)	(0.884)	(0.320)	(0.320)	(0.891)
Postgraduate	−0.0307	−0.586	−0.0485	−0.169	−0.745
	(0.388)	(1.053)	(0.391)	(0.391)	(1.068)
Other	−0.0526	−1.707	−0.0469	−0.0859	−1.741
	(0.517)	(1.443)	(0.519)	(0.516)	(1.450)
Income percentile	0.00424	0.00310	0.00390	0.00438	0.00370
	(0.00310)	(0.00704)	(0.00312)	(0.00313)	(0.00715)
Missing income data dummy	−0.261	0.384	−0.281	−0.278	0.384
	(0.268)	(0.583)	(0.271)	(0.268)	(0.581)
Economic left–right values	0.699***	0.521*	0.557***	0.665***	0.586*
	(0.102)	(0.244)	(0.111)	(0.104)	(0.253)
Liberal–authoritarian values	−0.0417	−0.228	−0.103	−0.0647	−0.278
	(0.101)	(0.230)	(0.102)	(0.101)	(0.235)
Immigration attitudes	0.121	0.186	0.124	0.0999	0.181
	(0.110)	(0.265)	(0.110)	(0.111)	(0.270)
2015 not very strong Liberal Democrat Party id	1.348***	1.341**	1.357***	1.337***	1.464**
	(0.212)	(0.504)	(0.213)	(0.213)	(0.516)
2015 fairly strong Liberal Democrat Party id	1.897***	1.604**	1.872***	1.883***	1.584**
	(0.264)	(0.550)	(0.266)	(0.265)	(0.554)
2015 very strong Liberal Democrat Party id	3.621***	1.958	3.653***	3.644***	1.636
	(0.718)	(1.345)	(0.736)	(0.722)	(1.384)
2015 not very strong Liberal Democrat Party id	−0.787**	−1.092	−0.760**	−0.680**	−1.003
	(0.250)	(0.565)	(0.251)	(0.253)	(0.573)
2015 fairly strong Labour Party id	−1.579***	−1.855**	−1.511***	−1.477***	−1.770**
	(0.256)	(0.614)	(0.256)	(0.258)	(0.622)
2015 very strong Labour Party id	−3.062***	−16.42	−2.938***	−2.924***	−15.76
	(0.577)	(895.4)	(0.579)	(0.580)	(645.0)
2010 not very strong Liberal Democrat Party id	0.605**	0.762	0.591**	0.637**	0.667
	(0.200)	(0.481)	(0.201)	(0.202)	(0.490)
2010 fairly strong Liberal Democrat Party id	0.270	0.627	0.264	0.283	0.568
	(0.264)	(0.581)	(0.265)	(0.265)	(0.590)
2010 very strong Liberal Democrat Party id	0.752	1.050	0.743	0.730	0.914
	(0.495)	(1.121)	(0.496)	(0.494)	(1.095)
2010 not very strong Labour Party id	−0.152	0.515	−0.128	−0.118	0.343
	(0.262)	(0.562)	(0.263)	(0.264)	(0.565)
2010 fairly strong Labour Party id	−0.0137	0.637	−0.0116	0.0172	0.546
	(0.277)	(0.623)	(0.278)	(0.280)	(0.631)
2010 very strong Labour Party id	−0.115	0.0657	−0.0933	−0.0583	0.0224
	(0.453)	(1.204)	(0.455)	(0.456)	(1.209)
Constant	−2.415***	−1.721	−2.278***	−2.630***	−1.840
	(0.592)	(1.474)	(0.597)	(0.607)	(1.536)
N	4228	992	4218	4228	992

UKIP (base category = Labour)	Model 1	Model 2	Model 3	Model 4	Model 5
2010 Retrospective economic evaluation	−0.359***	−0.310*	−0.334***	−0.326***	−0.331*
	(0.0650)	(0.149)	(0.0659)	(0.0671)	(0.154)

Continued

Table A6.3 Continued

UKIP (base category = Labour)	Model 1	Model 2	Model 3	Model 4	Model 5
2015 Retrospective economic evaluation	0.212** (0.0716)	0.110 (0.209)	0.0527 (0.0758)	0.142 (0.0738)	0.0377 (0.214)
Labour economic competence		-0.947*** (0.181)			-0.868*** (0.193)
Conservative economic competence		0.0678 (0.185)			-0.0485 (0.193)
Attitude towards austerity			0.767*** (0.0979)		0.388 (0.236)
Labour responsible for Global Financial Crisis				0.0866 (0.148)	-0.811* (0.347)
Labour responsible for level of national debt				0.775*** (0.152)	0.565 (0.373)
Age	0.0265*** (0.00591)	0.0418** (0.0132)	0.0274*** (0.00599)	0.0276*** (0.00597)	0.0420** (0.0134)
Female	-0.594*** (0.137)	-0.547 (0.311)	-0.526*** (0.140)	-0.514*** (0.139)	-0.583 (0.319)
Education level (Base = no qualifications)					
Below GCSE	0.258 (0.320)	0.923 (0.793)	0.217 (0.324)	0.293 (0.323)	1.090 (0.805)
GCSE	0.373 (0.233)	0.481 (0.581)	0.351 (0.237)	0.369 (0.237)	0.601 (0.585)
A Level	0.261 (0.257)	0.109 (0.639)	0.298 (0.261)	0.241 (0.262)	0.243 (0.647)
Undergraduate	-0.171 (0.245)	-0.185 (0.602)	-0.209 (0.251)	-0.243 (0.250)	-0.115 (0.609)
Postgraduate	0.173 (0.355)	0.00454 (0.855)	0.103 (0.362)	0.0251 (0.358)	0.0137 (0.865)
Other	-0.0621 (0.425)	-0.483 (0.959)	-0.0750 (0.430)	-0.103 (0.429)	-0.293 (0.979)
Income percentile	0.00186 (0.00294)	0.0109 (0.00652)	0.00127 (0.00300)	0.00154 (0.00298)	0.0116 (0.00664)
Missing income data dummy	-0.0635 (0.232)	0.0459 (0.549)	-0.0731 (0.236)	-0.0462 (0.232)	-0.00686 (0.546)
Economic left–right values	0.723*** (0.0921)	0.730*** (0.216)	0.468*** (0.0990)	0.690*** (0.0938)	0.652** (0.228)
Liberal–authoritarian values	0.907*** (0.0942)	0.633** (0.213)	0.864*** (0.0962)	0.882*** (0.0951)	0.627** (0.215)
Immigration attitudes	0.626*** (0.0925)	0.803*** (0.213)	0.621*** (0.0939)	0.581*** (0.0939)	0.851*** (0.219)
2015 not very strong UKIP party id	0.658* (0.283)	0.985 (0.573)	0.669* (0.283)	0.702* (0.283)	1.015 (0.581)
2015 fairly strong UKIP party id	1.987*** (0.225)	2.306*** (0.463)	2.003*** (0.225)	1.994*** (0.225)	2.379*** (0.471)
2015 very strong UKIP party id	2.823*** (0.315)	2.899*** (0.622)	2.921*** (0.319)	2.864*** (0.317)	2.889*** (0.644)
2015 not very strong Labour Party id	-1.597*** (0.238)	-0.372 (0.511)	-1.558*** (0.242)	-1.414*** (0.242)	-0.275 (0.524)
2015 fairly strong Labour Party id	-1.825*** (0.213)	-0.710 (0.519)	-1.698*** (0.216)	-1.668*** (0.217)	-0.669 (0.526)

	Model 1	Model 2	Model 3	Model 4	Model 5
2015 very strong Labour Party id	-2.834*** (0.408)	-1.876 (0.968)	-2.718*** (0.419)	-2.623*** (0.408)	-1.736 (0.971)
2010 not very strong UKIP party id	0.414 (0.263)	0.0692 (0.628)	0.411 (0.265)	0.416 (0.263)	0.0663 (0.629)
2010 fairly strong UKIP party id	0.409 (0.303)	-0.0859 (0.522)	0.369 (0.305)	0.394 (0.305)	-0.0900 (0.537)
2010 very strong UKIP party id	2.477*** (0.652)	0.619 (1.205)	2.441*** (0.664)	2.396*** (0.657)	0.616 (1.202)
2010 not very strong Labour Party id	-0.110 (0.212)	-0.110 (0.486)	-0.0312 (0.216)	-0.0754 (0.215)	-0.180 (0.484)
2010 fairly strong Labour Party id	-0.198 (0.232)	0.274 (0.499)	-0.142 (0.235)	-0.113 (0.236)	0.0957 (0.500)
2010 very strong Labour Party id	-1.211** (0.460)	-1.089 (1.094)	-1.144* (0.466)	-1.098* (0.457)	-1.258 (1.065)
Constant	-1.176* (0.531)	-0.600 (1.293)	-0.901 (0.542)	-1.607** (0.549)	-0.327 (1.344)
N	4228	992	4218	4228	992

Green Party (base category = Labour)	Model 1	Model 2	Model 3	Model 4	Model 5
2010 Retrospective economic evaluation	-0.107 (0.0883)	-0.262 (0.216)	-0.104 (0.0884)	-0.0768 (0.0906)	-0.199 (0.224)
2015 Retrospective economic evaluation	-0.0123 (0.102)	-0.0917 (0.311)	-0.0427 (0.106)	-0.0431 (0.103)	-0.0886 (0.318)
Labour economic competence		-0.417 (0.261)			-0.434 (0.272)
Conservative economic competence		-0.0865 (0.282)			-0.0581 (0.307)
Attitude towards austerity			0.165 (0.137)		-0.00949 (0.367)
Labour responsible for Global Financial Crisis				0.225 (0.203)	0.560 (0.477)
Labour responsible for level of national debt				0.369 (0.202)	-0.207 (0.541)
Age	0.00179 (0.00760)	0.00910 (0.0187)	0.00203 (0.00764)	0.00262 (0.00763)	0.0106 (0.0188)
Female	0.136 (0.193)	0.0234 (0.455)	0.143 (0.193)	0.166 (0.194)	-0.0519 (0.472)
Education level (Base = no qualifications)					
Below GCSE	-1.090 (0.810)	-14.32 (1024.1)	-1.124 (0.810)	-1.080 (0.810)	-13.73 (722.9)
GCSE	0.152 (0.419)	-0.189 (0.883)	0.134 (0.419)	0.144 (0.421)	-0.269 (0.897)
A Level	0.0938 (0.430)	-1.142 (0.939)	0.0756 (0.430)	0.0624 (0.433)	-1.320 (0.970)
Undergraduate	0.0911 (0.408)	-1.278 (0.901)	0.0760 (0.408)	0.0414 (0.411)	-1.270 (0.902)
Postgraduate	0.688 (0.463)	-1.383 (1.097)	0.656 (0.464)	0.596 (0.466)	-1.296 (1.086)
Other	-0.960 (0.908)	-0.632 (1.458)	-0.926 (0.903)	-1.012 (0.910)	-0.543 (1.452)

Continued

Table A6.3 Continued

Green Party (base category = Labour)	Model 1	Model 2	Model 3	Model 4	Model 5
Income percentile	0.000135	−0.000611	5.64e−08	−0.000168	−0.00129
	(0.00378)	(0.00866)	(0.00378)	(0.00378)	(0.00871)
Missing income data dummy	−0.609	−0.658	−0.633	−0.637	−0.576
	(0.373)	(1.019)	(0.373)	(0.375)	(1.012)
Economic left–right values	−0.166	−0.487	−0.217	−0.176	−0.468
	(0.122)	(0.295)	(0.132)	(0.123)	(0.319)
Liberal–authoritarian values	−0.125	−0.578*	−0.146	−0.133	−0.576*
	(0.116)	(0.279)	(0.119)	(0.117)	(0.287)
Immigration attitudes	−0.239	−0.425	−0.244	−0.277	−0.468
	(0.143)	(0.360)	(0.143)	(0.144)	(0.368)
2015 not very strong Green Party id	1.743***	2.342**	1.737***	1.738***	2.282*
	(0.374)	(0.888)	(0.373)	(0.374)	(0.898)
2015 fairly strong Green Party id	2.190***	1.911*	2.175***	2.210***	2.126**
	(0.340)	(0.793)	(0.341)	(0.340)	(0.807)
2015 very strong Green Party id	4.303***	5.340***	4.253***	4.353***	5.817***
	(0.855)	(1.475)	(0.852)	(0.858)	(1.539)
2015 not very strong Labour Party id	−0.560*	−0.904	−0.557	−0.472	−0.945
	(0.286)	(0.775)	(0.286)	(0.290)	(0.802)
2015 fairly strong Labour Party id	−1.635***	−0.721	−1.608***	−1.558***	−0.682
	(0.304)	(0.669)	(0.304)	(0.305)	(0.684)
2015 very strong Labour Party id	−2.779***	−2.162	−2.747***	−2.668***	−2.150
	(0.600)	(1.276)	(0.601)	(0.602)	(1.261)
2010 not very strong Green Party id	−0.0178	0.505	0.0244	−0.0118	0.651
	(0.438)	(1.023)	(0.438)	(0.439)	(1.017)
2010 fairly strong Green Party id	−0.256	0.203	−0.259	−0.276	0.123
	(0.517)	(1.061)	(0.517)	(0.515)	(1.047)
2010 very strong Green Party id	1.792	0	1.803	1.817	0
	(1.503)	(.)	(1.484)	(1.540)	(.)
2010 not very strong Labour Party id	−0.361	−0.205	−0.347	−0.327	−0.166
	(0.293)	(0.648)	(0.294)	(0.295)	(0.658)
2010 fairly strong Labour Party id	−0.705*	−1.348	−0.693*	−0.647	−1.303
	(0.329)	(0.767)	(0.328)	(0.330)	(0.791)
2010 very strong Labour Party id	−0.993	−1.094	−0.980	−0.938	−1.082
	(0.573)	(1.255)	(0.572)	(0.577)	(1.257)
Constant	−1.194	0.673	−1.093	−1.492*	0.299
	(0.718)	(1.740)	(0.719)	(0.739)	(1.889)
N	4228	992	4218	4228	992

* $p<0.05$ ** $p<0.01$ *** $p<0.001$

Table A6.4 Graded response IRT Model of austerity attitudes

Necessity of deficit reduction	
Discrimination	−0.888***
	(0.0107)
Difficulty (base = It is completely unnecessary)	
≥ *It is not necessary but it would be desirable*	3.119***
	(0.0367)
≥ *It is important but not absolutely necessary*	0.991***
	(0.0156)
= *It is completely necessary*	−1.774***
	(0.0212)
How to reduce deficit	
Discrimination	−1.201***
	(0.0117)
Difficulty (base = Only by increasing taxes)	
≥ *Mainly by increasing taxes, but also by cutting spending*	1.633***
	(0.0166)
≥ *An equal balance of spending cuts and tax increases*	0.460***
	(0.00993)
≥ *Mainly by cutting spending, but with some tax increases*	−1.435***
	(0.0139)
= *Only by cutting spending*	−2.592***
	(0.0237)
Cuts too far: public spending	
Discrimination	4.710***
	(0.0584)
Difficulty (base = Not gone nearly far enough)	
≥ *Not gone far enough*	−2.177***
	(0.0134)
≥ *About right*	−1.339***
	(0.00758)
≥ *Gone too far*	−0.388***
	(0.00536)
= *Gone much too far*	0.617***
	(0.00585)
Cuts too far: NHS	
Discrimination	2.739***
	(0.0231)
Difficulty (base = Not gone nearly far enough)	
≥ *Not gone far enough*	−2.747***
	(0.0212)
≥ *About right*	−1.944***
	(0.0121)
≥ *Gone too far*	−0.949***
	(0.00713)
= *Gone much too far*	0.220***
	(0.00594)

Continued

Table A6.4 Continued

Cuts too far: Local services	
Discrimination	3.368***
	(0.0305)
Difficulty (base = Not gone nearly far enough)	
≥ *Not gone far enough*	−2.660***
	(0.0200)
≥ *About right*	−1.822***
	(0.0107)
≥ *Gone too far*	−0.422***
	(0.00579)
= *Gone much too far*	0.780***
	(0.00668)

* p<0.05 ** p<0.01 *** p<0.001

Note: The direction of the predicted score is then reversed to give a scale that runs from anti-austerity to pro-austerity.

Table A6.5 Multinomial Logistic regression model of 2017 vote

Base = Labour	Conservative	Liberal Democrat	UKIP	Green Party
2010 Retrospective economic evaluation	−0.0948 (0.0798)	0.0113 (0.0870)	0.0190 (0.155)	−0.164 (0.156)
2015 Retrospective economic evaluation	0.177 (0.0966)	0.238* (0.110)	0.0236 (0.163)	−0.208 (0.191)
2017 Retrospective economic evaluation	0.669*** (0.103)	−0.184 (0.125)	0.380* (0.170)	0.215 (0.207)
Age	0.0271*** (0.00738)	0.0343*** (0.00801)	0.0218 (0.0153)	0.00968 (0.0144)
Female	−0.106 (0.171)	−0.297 (0.196)	−0.257 (0.316)	−0.0956 (0.346)
Education level (Base = no qualifications)				
Below GCSE	0.358 (0.428)	0.839 (0.583)	−0.358 (0.759)	−15.39 (1363.3)
GCSE	−0.0727 (0.309)	0.258 (0.455)	0.0348 (0.456)	−0.752 (0.619)
A Level	0.0559 (0.333)	0.522 (0.454)	−0.680 (0.566)	−0.919 (0.665)
Undergraduate	−0.285 (0.317)	0.132 (0.436)	−0.384 (0.513)	−0.678 (0.585)
Postgraduate	−0.0345 (0.432)	0.699 (0.496)	−1.268 (1.159)	−0.595 (0.765)
Other	−0.372 (0.726)	0.151 (0.884)	0.304 (1.022)	−1.056 (1.530)
Income percentile	0.00221 (0.00353)	0.00899* (0.00377)	0.0108 (0.00654)	0.00142 (0.00687)
Economic left–right values	0.959*** (0.120)	0.520*** (0.128)	0.328 (0.197)	0.339 (0.222)
Liberal–authoritarian values	0.274* (0.118)	0.0458 (0.125)	0.0760 (0.213)	−0.267 (0.221)

Immigration attitudes	0.208	−0.104	0.511*	−0.104
	(0.119)	(0.143)	(0.223)	(0.257)
EU attitudes	1.073***	−0.286*	1.437***	0.236
	(0.132)	(0.141)	(0.274)	(0.251)
2017 not very strong outcome party id	1.100***	0.417	1.478**	1.026
	(0.269)	(0.321)	(0.496)	(0.954)
2017 fairly strong outcome party id	1.860***	1.009**	1.707***	1.152
	(0.311)	(0.378)	(0.425)	(0.706)
2017 very strong outcome party id	1.991***	3.232***	1.479*	2.214
	(0.601)	(0.922)	(0.584)	(1.133)
2017 not very strong Labour Party id	−1.032**	−0.681	−0.725	−0.876
	(0.316)	(0.364)	(0.635)	(0.668)
2017 fairly strong Labour Party id	−1.810***	−1.446***	−1.878*	−1.231*
	(0.330)	(0.345)	(0.729)	(0.544)
2017 very strong Labour Party id	−3.241***	−2.418***	−2.510*	−16.75
	(0.713)	(0.615)	(1.263)	(631.5)
2015 not very strong outcome party id	−0.304	0.696*	2.233***	1.945**
	(0.292)	(0.346)	(0.602)	(0.673)
2015 fairly strong outcome party id	0.143	1.092*	0.00548	0.691
	(0.335)	(0.461)	(0.500)	(0.739)
2015 very strong outcome party id	0.392	0.857	0.185	2.238
	(0.609)	(0.971)	(0.487)	(1.162)
2015 not very strong Labour Party id	−0.687*	0.214	−1.008	−0.651
	(0.309)	(0.347)	(0.700)	(0.725)
2015 fairly strong Labour Party id	−0.654*	0.0395	−0.160	0.182
	(0.319)	(0.368)	(0.613)	(0.563)
2015 very strong Labour Party id	−0.432	0.115	−0.184	−1.471
	(0.548)	(0.531)	(1.022)	(1.196)
2010 not very strong outcome party id	0.522*	0.0896	−1.385	−0.374
	(0.263)	(0.281)	(0.747)	(1.002)
2010 fairly strong outcome party id	0.0419	−0.544	−0.0475	2.062**
	(0.290)	(0.385)	(0.506)	(0.768)
2010 very strong outcome party id	−0.0965	−1.275	0.279	2.785
	(0.501)	(0.763)	(0.652)	(4.137)
2010 not very strong Labour Party id	0.267	−0.959*	0.0123	−0.209
	(0.294)	(0.383)	(0.574)	(0.644)
2010 fairly strong Labour Party id	0.269	−0.226	0.439	0.178
	(0.317)	(0.357)	(0.611)	(0.576)
2010 very strong Labour Party id	0.145	−1.131	−0.0352	1.458*
	(0.545)	(0.618)	(0.992)	(0.698)
Constant	−3.539***	−3.529***	−5.213***	−1.645
	(0.697)	(0.809)	(1.348)	(1.307)
N	2255			

* $p<0.05$ ** $p<0.01$ *** $p<0.001$

Appendix to Chapter 7

Table A7.1 Logistic model of attribution of responsibility for change in policy area to Conservatives and Liberal Democrats

	Economy		NHS		Education		Cost of Living		Immigration		Crime	
	Con	Lib Dem	Con	Lib Dem	Con	Lib Dem	Con	Lib Dem	Con	Lib Dem	Con	Lib Dem
Change	0.276*	-0.257	-0.417**	0.156	-0.411**	-0.0424	0.0175	-0.0201	0.177	0.147	0.0743	0.0988
	(0.112)	(0.135)	(0.133)	(0.160)	(0.130)	(0.160)	(0.111)	(0.153)	(0.121)	(0.171)	(0.119)	(0.162)
Party identity (base = none)												
Conservative	-3.098***	-0.00715	-3.122***	-0.224	-3.302***	0.388	3.479***	-0.310	2.819***	-0.0838	3.105***	-0.389
	(0.351)	(0.347)	(0.237)	(0.271)	(0.280)	(0.303)	(0.324)	(0.416)	(0.414)	(0.571)	(0.295)	(0.412)
Liberal Democrat	1.141**	-1.902***	1.760***	-1.993***	1.010**	-1.826***	-0.949*	2.549***	-0.242	1.882**	-0.671	2.115***
	(0.356)	(0.388)	(0.344)	(0.356)	(0.348)	(0.397)	(0.377)	(0.451)	(0.465)	(0.592)	(0.372)	(0.465)
Other party	1.920***	0.300	2.126***	0.565*	1.902***	0.410	-1.029***	0.413	-0.553	-0.190	-0.915***	-0.236
	(0.247)	(0.252)	(0.237)	(0.222)	(0.253)	(0.261)	(0.283)	(0.372)	(0.366)	(0.495)	(0.281)	(0.378)
Conservative X Change	1.189***	-0.132	1.266***	-0.0405	1.233***	-0.188	-0.964***	-0.0335	-0.769***	-0.0340	-0.881***	0.0580
	(0.111)	(0.102)	(0.100)	(0.113)	(0.102)	(0.113)	(0.0908)	(0.114)	(0.0953)	(0.127)	(0.0864)	(0.113)
Liberal Democrat X Change	-0.440***	0.794***	-0.640***	0.921***	-0.358**	0.785***	0.258*	-0.655***	0.0706	-0.498***	0.206	-0.608***
	(0.108)	(0.117)	(0.145)	(0.150)	(0.127)	(0.144)	(0.106)	(0.125)	(0.114)	(0.142)	(0.113)	(0.140)
Other party X Change	-0.666***	-0.120	-0.676***	-0.303*	-0.623***	-0.158	0.387***	-0.0979	0.244**	0.0482	0.360***	0.0912
	(0.0793)	(0.0849)	(0.101)	(0.105)	(0.0947)	(0.105)	(0.0786)	(0.0973)	(0.0856)	(0.111)	(0.0818)	(0.102)
Political attention	0.171***	0.172***	0.152***	0.163***	0.0647	0.165***	0.0603	-0.0258	-0.0227	-0.00175	-0.0512	-0.0283
	(0.0434)	(0.0469)	(0.0396)	(0.0423)	(0.0436)	(0.0477)	(0.0509)	(0.0679)	(0.0636)	(0.0906)	(0.0508)	(0.0709)
Political attention X Change	-0.00709	-0.00479	-0.00988	-0.0155	0.0214	-0.0160	0.0206	0.0465*	0.0169	0.0343	0.0364*	0.0426*
	(0.0143)	(0.0158)	(0.0168)	(0.0189)	(0.0162)	(0.0185)	(0.0139)	(0.0181)	(0.0147)	(0.0204)	(0.0146)	(0.0193)
Constant	-0.966**	-1.702***	0.654*	-2.604***	0.704*	-2.169***	-0.420	-2.392***	-0.927	-2.880***	-0.748	-2.713***
	(0.338)	(0.396)	(0.300)	(0.353)	(0.340)	(0.405)	(0.413)	(0.581)	(0.522)	(0.759)	(0.419)	(0.598)
N	5920	5920	5900	5900	5357	5357	5974	5974	5848	5848	5779	5779

* p<0.05 ** p<0.01 *** p<0.001

Table A7.2 Multinomial logistic model of 2015 vote choice of 2010 Liberal Democrat voters

Base = Liberal Democrats	Conservatives	Labour	UKIP	Green Party
Like Outcome Party	0.983***	0.661***	0.734***	0.720***
	(0.0910)	(0.0592)	(0.0703)	(0.0860)
Like Liberal Democrats	−0.565***	−0.597***	−0.340**	−0.566***
	(0.109)	(0.0894)	(0.117)	(0.117)
Like Clegg	−0.109	−0.0763	−0.225*	−0.0981
	(0.0892)	(0.0732)	(0.0968)	(0.101)
Change in economy	0.267	−0.230	−0.0213	−0.142
	(0.217)	(0.164)	(0.241)	(0.207)
Liberal Democrats responsible for change in economy	1.068 (1.567)	0.131 (1.064)	0.962 (1.459)	1.294 (1.276)
Liberal Democrats responsible X change in economy	−0.285 (0.429)	0.0158 (0.322)	−0.133 (0.444)	−0.497 (0.421)
Likelihood of Liberal Democrats winning constituency − likelihood of Conservatives winning constituency	−0.111** (0.0398)	−0.0396 (0.0336)	−0.0925* (0.0455)	−0.155*** (0.0470)
Likelihood of Liberal Democrats winning constituency − likelihood of Labour winning constituency	−0.107** (0.0360)	−0.280*** (0.0335)	−0.192*** (0.0448)	−0.185*** (0.0444)
Constant	−2.953**	0.00332	−1.994*	−2.398**
	(0.910)	(0.649)	(0.969)	(0.917)
N	875			

* p<0.05 ** p<0.01 *** p<0.001

Table A7.3 Linear regression model of change in feelings towards the Liberal Democrats between elections

	2015	2017
Liberal Democrat like at previous election	−0.594*** (0.0158)	−0.359*** (0.0164)
Liberal–authoritarian values	0.436*** (0.0311)	−0.189*** (0.0364)
Economic left–right values	−0.363*** (0.0336)	−0.458*** (0.0394)
2010 Liberal Democrat Party identity strength (base: no/other party id)		
Not very strong	0.933*** (0.116)	0.739*** (0.133)
Fairly strong	1.548*** (0.147)	1.152*** (0.162)
Very strong	2.161*** (0.308)	1.277*** (0.339)
Constant	0.813*** (0.0816)	1.542*** (0.0601)
N	4430	2757

* $p<0.05$ ** $p<0.01$ *** $p<0.001$

Table A7.4 Multinomial logistic model of 2017 vote choice

Base = Liberal Democrats	Conservatives	Labour	UKIP	Green Party
Like Outcome Party	0.739*** (0.0234)	0.566*** (0.0210)	0.641*** (0.0409)	0.509*** (0.0436)
Like Liberal Democrats	−0.590*** (0.0387)	−0.520*** (0.0360)	−0.509*** (0.0637)	−0.593*** (0.0627)
Like Farron	−0.138*** (0.0355)	−0.0179 (0.0319)	−0.128* (0.0587)	0.0185 (0.0597)
Likelihood of Liberal Democrats winning constituency – likelihood of Conservatives winning constituency	−0.0786*** (0.0168)	−0.0599*** (0.0141)	−0.0577* (0.0276)	−0.0598* (0.0269)
Likelihood of Liberal Democrats winning constituency – likelihood of Labour winning constituency	−0.156*** (0.0171)	−0.218*** (0.0154)	−0.160*** (0.0286)	−0.161*** (0.0282)
Constant	0.147 (0.223)	0.614** (0.194)	−2.076*** (0.402)	−1.903*** (0.380)
N	6302			

* $p<0.05$ ** $p<0.01$ *** $p<0.001$

Appendix to Chapter 8

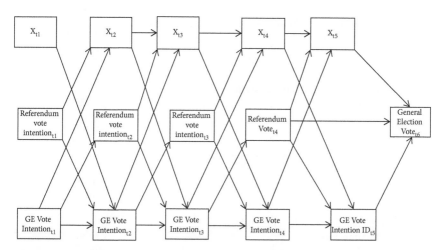

Figure A8.1 Simplified Illustration of the Cross–Lagged Model of Attitudes, Referendum Vote, And Party ID/Vote Intention used to Estimate The Impact of the Scottish Independence Refeferendum vote on General Election Vote Choice

X variables represent a vector of control variables (party ID, leader likes, Britishness, Scottishness, approval of Scottish government, devolution preferences, satisfaction with UK democracy). Additional controls are also used (without recursive effects from other variables) but not shown on the diagram: 2011 Holyrood SNP vote, 2010 Labour vote, age, political knowledge, and subjective class.

T1 = Feb/march (BESIP wave 1)
T2 = May 2014 (BESIP wave 2)
T3 = pre-referendum (SRS pre-referendum)
T4 = referendum (BESIP wave 3)
T5 = pre-election (BESIP wave 4)
T6 = Post general election 2015 (BESIP wave 6)

Table A8.1 Two parameter IRT model of Scottish devolution preferences (constant loading and varying preferences across waves)

Preference for devolution: Welfare benefits	
Discrimination	5.262***
	(0.121)
Difficulty	−0.303***
	(0.00783)
Preference for devolution: Defence & foreign affairs	
Discrimination	4.574***
	(0.116)
Difficulty	0.340***
	(0.0109)
Preference for devolution: Taxation	
Discrimination	5.221***
	(0.118)
Difficulty	−0.267***
	(0.00781)
Preference for devolution: Immigration[†]	
Discrimination	3.806***
	(0.174)
Difficulty	0.00725
	(0.0154)
Preference for devolution: Pensions[†]	
Discrimination	6.089***
	(0.350)
Difficulty	−0.0129
	(0.0129)
Preference for devolution: Energy[†]	
Discrimination	3.580***
	(0.170)
Difficulty	−0.397***
	(0.0178)
Preference for devolution: NHS	
Discrimination	3.980***
	(0.0904)
Difficulty	−0.706***
	(0.0102)
Preference for devolution: Schools	
Discrimination	4.810***
	(0.137)
Difficulty	−1.000***
	(0.0129)
Preference for devolution: Police	
Discrimination	3.425***
	(0.0741)
Difficulty	−0.854***
	(0.0118)

[†] Only asked in Scottish Referendum Study pre–referendum wave

* p<0.05 ** p<0.01 *** p<0.001

Table A8.2 Cross-lagged model of attitudes, referendum vote, and party ID/vote intention used to estimate the impact of the Scottish independence referendum vote on general election vote choice

Independent variables	Referendum Yes intention	Referendum Yes intention	Referendum Yes vote
(measured in previous wave)	t2	t3	t4
SNP Vote intention		−1.082	−1.078*
		(0.719)	(0.646)
Party ID Labour	0.379	0.00447	0.00194
	(0.443)	(0.399)	(0.407)
Party ID SNP	−0.498	0.858	0.570
	(0.805)	(1.078)	(1.581)
Like Salmond	0.225***	0.144***	0.136
	(0.0608)	(0.0558)	(0.0896)
Like Sturgeon			0.181**
			(0.0873)
Like Miliband	−0.168**	−0.136**	−0.106
	(0.0662)	(0.0608)	(0.0838)
Britishness	−0.0396	−0.154*	0.111
	(0.0896)	(0.0836)	(0.120)
Scottishness	0.00155	0.136*	0.0824
	(0.0822)	(0.0770)	(0.111)
Approve of Scottish Government	0.483	0.853***	0.0419
	(0.317)	(0.307)	(0.406)
Devolution Preferences	0.690***	0.208	0.834***
	(0.204)	(0.191)	(0.282)
Satisfaction with UK democracy	−0.115	−0.245	−0.456**
	(0.171)	(0.170)	(0.208)
2011 Holyrood SNP vote	0.358	−0.117	−0.554
	(0.383)	(0.398)	(0.510)
2010 Labour vote	0.320	−0.316	−0.242
	(0.310)	(0.298)	(0.390)
Economy better off independence	0.376	1.582***	−1.536***
	(0.335)	(0.364)	(0.389)
Personally worse off independence	−0.512	−0.784***	0.216
	(0.319)	(0.289)	(0.614)
Referendum Yes vote (intention)	3.822***	2.718***	3.531***
	(0.323)	(0.358)	(0.451)
Age	−0.0112	−0.0125	−0.0255*
	(0.0100)	(0.00951)	(0.0134)
Political knowledge	−0.0148	−0.147	−0.0708
	(0.165)	(0.159)	(0.224)
Working class (subjective)	0.118	−0.200	−0.0957
	(0.279)	(0.267)	(0.357)
Constant	−2.162**	−0.133	−0.514
	(0.851)	(0.841)	(1.121)

Table A8.2 Continued

Independent variables (measured in previous wave)	Vote SNP Intention t2	Vote SNP Intention t3	Vote SNP Intention t4	Vote SNP Intention t5	Vote SNP Intention t6	Party ID Lab t2	Party ID Lab t3	Party ID Lab t4	Party ID Lab t5	Party ID Lab t6	Party ID SNP t4	Party ID SNP t5	Party ID SNP t6
SNP vote intention		0.826 (0.656)	1.339*** (0.474)	3.118*** (0.536)	3.053*** (0.442)		-1.117* (0.573)	-0.587 (0.384)	-0.331 (0.396)	-1.020** (0.397)	0.793* (0.458)	0.801* (0.432)	1.209** (0.486)
Party ID Labour	-0.927* (0.481)	-0.602 (0.422)	0.435 (0.381)	-0.394 (0.453)	0.231 (0.461)	3.274*** (0.228)	2.335*** (0.239)	2.238*** (0.237)	2.963*** (0.259)	3.193*** (0.268)	0.916 (1.024)	1.770*** (0.417)	1.827*** (0.441)
Party ID SNP	-0.389 (0.679)	0.488 (0.726)	0.0615 (1.087)	0.707 (0.737)	4.262*** (1.407)								
Like Salmond	0.330*** (0.0832)	0.305*** (0.0707)	0.160* (0.0821)	0.112 (0.0799)		-0.0378 (0.0461)	-0.0935* (0.0439)	-0.0518 (0.0642)	0.0266 (0.0605)		0.259*** (0.0998)	0.144 (0.0925)	
Like Sturgeon			0.182** (0.0823)		0.149* (0.0772)			-0.0185 (0.0604)		-0.0917 (0.0594)	0.138 (0.0963)		0.198** (0.100)
Like Miliband	-0.306*** (0.0844)	-0.0420 (0.0773)	-0.282*** (0.0725)	-0.180** (0.0766)	-0.216*** (0.0814)	0.152*** (0.0488)	0.0598 (0.0429)	0.204*** (0.0498)	0.00883 (0.0526)	0.268*** (0.0535)	-0.254*** (0.0786)	0.0682 (0.0766)	-0.155** (0.0763)
Britishness	-0.309*** (0.106)	-0.0981 (0.0928)	0.00399 (0.0912)	-0.00821 (0.112)	-0.347*** (0.106)	0.106 (0.0701)	-0.0149 (0.0629)	-0.00979 (0.0733)	0.0802 (0.0792)	0.0756 (0.0848)	-0.0674 (0.0979)	-0.117 (0.104)	-0.167 (0.109)
Scottishness	0.343* (0.185)	0.143 (0.0988)	0.0846 (0.110)	0.164 (0.104)	0.242** (0.104)	-0.0730 (0.0568)	-0.0430 (0.0495)	-0.0636 (0.0623)	-0.107 (0.0660)	-0.0884 (0.0627)	0.317** (0.147)	0.384** (0.174)	0.236 (0.145)
Approve of Scottish Government	0.216 (0.449)	0.871** (0.373)	0.429 (0.363)	0.666* (0.396)	0.465 (0.389)	-0.0693 (0.269)	0.317 (0.274)	0.0508 (0.281)	0.579* (0.328)	0.638* (0.349)	0.397 (0.458)	-0.00237 (0.466)	-0.344 (0.499)
Devolution Preferences	-0.0259 (0.306)	0.467* (0.257)	0.779*** (0.271)	0.233 (0.295)	0.354 (0.275)	-0.0252 (0.160)	0.0871 (0.149)	-0.407** (0.192)	0.270 (0.193)	0.191 (0.215)	0.634** (0.314)	-0.143 (0.292)	0.211 (0.323)

Independent variables	Vote SNP Intention	Vote SNP Intention	Vote SNP Intention	Vote SNP Intention	Vote SNP Intention	Party ID Lab	Party ID Lab	Party ID Lab	Party ID Lab	Party ID Lab	Party ID SNP	Party ID SNP	Party ID SNP
Satisfaction with UK democracy	0.0305	0.110	-0.244	0.0583	0.304	0.122	-0.0773	0.0561	0.110	-0.166	-0.339	-0.306	-0.0218
	(0.230)	(0.198)	(0.185)	(0.210)	(0.201)	(0.128)	(0.120)	(0.132)	(0.140)	(0.157)	(0.209)	(0.224)	(0.229)
2011 Holyrood SNP vote	-0.501	1.312***	-0.900*	0.811*	0.842*	-0.386	-0.186	-0.0243	-0.777***	-0.586*	-1.008**	0.427	1.110***
	(0.447)	(0.330)	(0.480)	(0.421)	(0.431)	(0.282)	(0.291)	(0.326)	(0.307)	(0.339)	(0.484)	(0.390)	(0.394)
2010 Labour vote	0.0433	-1.025***	-0.126	0.320	-0.270	0.930***	0.587***	0.639***	0.961***	0.402	-0.891**	-0.0122	-0.0137
	(0.398)	(0.336)	(0.358)	(0.367)	(0.368)	(0.204)	(0.202)	(0.235)	(0.245)	(0.264)	(0.409)	(0.372)	(0.384)
Referendum Yes vote (intention)	0.571	0.725*	1.890***	2.104***	1.188***	-0.675**	0.603*	-1.112***	-1.090***	-0.608	1.936***	1.624***	1.327***
	(0.496)	(0.377)	(0.432)	(0.445)	(0.384)	(0.303)	(0.332)	(0.324)	(0.376)	(0.371)	(0.597)	(0.559)	(0.489)
Age	0.0100	-0.00149	-0.00389	-0.00709	0.00453	0.00519	0.0131*	0.0180**	0.0273***	-0.00167	0.0170	-0.0102	0.0260*
	(0.0129)	(0.0112)	(0.0123)	(0.0129)	(0.0136)	(0.00701)	(0.00669)	(0.00818)	(0.00865)	(0.00943)	(0.0134)	(0.0135)	(0.0139)
Political knowledge	0.0250	-0.0360	-0.142	0.460**	-0.484**	0.0612	0.311***	-0.0649	-0.0405	0.370**	-0.281	-0.488**	-0.803***
	(0.228)	(0.187)	(0.194)	(0.224)	(0.197)	(0.125)	(0.118)	(0.137)	(0.147)	(0.151)	(0.214)	(0.211)	(0.226)
Working class (subjective)	0.241	0.269	-0.201	0.138	0.168	0.258	0.393**	0.431*	0.503**	0.555**	-0.267	-0.481	-0.362
	(0.377)	(0.321)	(0.328)	(0.351)	(0.339)	(0.204)	(0.188)	(0.223)	(0.235)	(0.246)	(0.369)	(0.358)	(0.358)
Constant	-3.959***	-3.950***	-3.171***	-3.980***	-2.885***	-2.806***	-1.652***	-2.088***	-3.050***	-2.143***	-5.796***	-5.532***	-5.832***
	(1.430)	(0.969)	(1.081)	(1.139)	(1.107)	(0.606)	(0.595)	(0.707)	(0.734)	(0.753)	(1.414)	(1.441)	(1.323)

Continued

Table A8.2 Continued

	Britishness	Britishness	Britishness	Britishness	Scottishness	Scottishness	Scottishness	Scottishness
	t2	t3	t4	t5	t2	t3	t4	t5
Lagged dependent variable	0.692***	0.678***	0.687***	0.669***	0.871***	0.841***	0.919***	0.883***
	(0.0211)	(0.0242)	(0.0261)	(0.0287)	(0.0147)	(0.0176)	(0.0167)	(0.0170)
SNP vote intention		-0.481*	-0.495***	0.185		0.102	-0.0855	-0.0554
		(0.247)	(0.147)	(0.168)		(0.242)	(0.125)	(0.140)
Referendum Yes vote (intention)	-0.540***	-0.357***	-0.803***	-0.239**	0.0512	-0.0883	0.237***	0.0409
	(0.0867)	(0.0993)	(0.106)	(0.121)	(0.0758)	(0.0910)	(0.0861)	(0.0970)
Party ID Labour	0.126	-0.109	-0.00394	-0.0447	0.0185	-0.274***	0.0904	-0.125
	(0.0883)	(0.106)	(0.0900)	(0.126)	(0.0816)	(0.102)	(0.0773)	(0.105)
Party ID SNP	0.331	-0.214	-0.00808	-0.285	0.0838	-0.173	0.155	-0.0140
	(0.224)	(0.278)	(0.398)	(0.208)	(0.206)	(0.267)	(0.356)	(0.175)
Age	0.00752***	0.0123***	0.00876***	0.0104***	0.000678	0.00400*	-0.00157	0.00223
	(0.00217)	(0.00252)	(0.00276)	(0.00306)	(0.00194)	(0.00241)	(0.00233)	(0.00251)
Political knowledge	-0.00804	-0.0512	0.00276	0.0247	-0.0549	-0.0226	0.0169	-0.0945**
	(0.0374)	(0.0426)	(0.0459)	(0.0494)	(0.0349)	(0.0419)	(0.0399)	(0.0415)
Working class (subjective)	-0.0391	-0.173**	-0.00511	0.0709	0.0796	0.00679	0.0986	0.0101
	(0.0619)	(0.0703)	(0.0757)	(0.0811)	(0.0578)	(0.0686)	(0.0650)	(0.0682)
Constant	1.237***	1.356***	1.374***	1.510***	0.568***	1.001***	0.403***	0.600***
	(0.155)	(0.186)	(0.195)	(0.227)	(0.132)	(0.167)	(0.152)	(0.171)

	Approve of Scottish Government	Approve of Scottish Government	Approve of Scottish Government	Approve of Scottish Government	Devolution Preferences	Devolution Preferences	Devolution Preferences	Devolution Preferences
	t2	t3	t4	t5	t2	t3	t4	t5
Lagged dependent variable	0.551***	0.485***	0.464***	0.495***	0.543***	0.392***	0.477***	0.462***
	(0.0228)	(0.0344)	(0.0327)	(0.0308)	(0.0234)	(0.0307)	(0.0341)	(0.0348)
SNP vote intention		0.0346	0.118**	0.231***		0.160	0.0792	0.275***
		(0.0910)	(0.0536)	(0.0537)		(0.137)	(0.0807)	(0.0881)
Referendum Yes vote (intention)	0.222***	0.217***	0.210***	0.207***	0.402***	0.625***	0.284***	0.263***
	(0.0268)	(0.0387)	(0.0376)	(0.0382)	(0.0468)	(0.0591)	(0.0629)	(0.0662)
Party ID Labour	0.00794	0.0154	-0.0000190	0.0307	-0.0239	0.0696	0.0274	-0.0735
	(0.0264)	(0.0392)	(0.0319)	(0.0407)	(0.0453)	(0.0590)	(0.0489)	(0.0670)
Party ID SNP	0.156**	0.0849	0.00114	-0.000343	-0.0318	0.0461	0.379*	-0.0275
	(0.0675)	(0.101)	(0.135)	(0.0669)	(0.116)	(0.152)	(0.207)	(0.110)
Age	-0.00131**	-0.000757	-0.00282***	0.000429	-0.00105	-0.00271**	0.000353	-0.00157
	(0.000625)	(0.000901)	(0.000946)	(0.000960)	(0.00108)	(0.00136)	(0.00145)	(0.00157)
Political knowledge	0.00479	-0.0340**	0.00235	0.00285	0.0831***	-0.0781***	0.0859***	0.0580**
	(0.0112)	(0.0157)	(0.0163)	(0.0160)	(0.0194)	(0.0241)	(0.0249)	(0.0264)
Working class (subjective)	-0.0102	0.0628**	-0.00672	-0.00683	-0.0490	0.0600	-0.00353	0.0783*
	(0.0186)	(0.0259)	(0.0268)	(0.0262)	(0.0318)	(0.0390)	(0.0410)	(0.0431)
Constant	0.147***	0.173***	0.303***	0.0344	-0.0952	-0.186**	-0.180**	-0.150
	(0.0377)	(0.0573)	(0.0554)	(0.0615)	(0.0642)	(0.0857)	(0.0853)	(0.0999)

Continued

Table A8.2 Continued

	Like Salmond	Like Salmond	Like Salmond	Like Sturgeon	Like Miliband	Like Miliband	Like Miliband
	t2	t3	t4	t5	t2	t4	t5
Lagged dependent variable	0.783***	0.688***	0.795***	0.678***	0.693***	0.665***	0.690***
	(0.0174)	(0.0224)	(0.0286)	(0.0324)	(0.0220)	(0.0270)	(0.0292)
SNP vote intention		0.279	0.509**	0.858***		-0.639***	0.599**
		(0.378)	(0.243)	(0.295)		(0.242)	(0.271)
Referendum Yes vote (intention)	0.834***	1.535***	1.072***	1.405***	-0.188	-1.172***	0.000459
	(0.133)	(0.168)	(0.186)	(0.233)	(0.129)	(0.164)	(0.184)
Party ID Labour	-0.162	0.110	0.229	0.0636	0.308**	0.275*	0.527***
	(0.125)	(0.165)	(0.144)	(0.208)	(0.144)	(0.150)	(0.202)
Party ID SNP	0.398	0.967**	0.0321	-0.567	-0.140	-0.944	-0.146
	(0.318)	(0.420)	(0.633)	(0.355)	(0.354)	(0.632)	(0.330)
Age	-0.00197	-0.00793**	-0.0149***	0.00691	-0.000612	0.00115	0.00734
	(0.00295)	(0.00380)	(0.00425)	(0.0053)	(0.00331)	(0.00441)	(0.00482)
Political knowledge	-0.00632	-0.204***	-0.0473	0.054	0.0965	0.0429	0.0976
	(0.0539)	(0.0682)	(0.0754)	(0.0897)	(0.0606)	(0.0768)	(0.0816)
Working class (subjective)	0.0320	0.162	0.138	-0.375**	0.168*	-0.0107	0.0790
	(0.0875)	(0.109)	(0.120)	(0.144)	(0.0980)	(0.125)	(0.132)
Constant	0.578***	0.771***	1.139***	1.299***	1.441***	1.449***	1.247***
	(0.181)	(0.241)	(0.252)	(0.333)	(0.217)	(0.288)	(0.328)

	Satisfaction with UK democracy	Satisfaction with UK democracy	Satisfaction with UK democracy	Satisfaction with UK democracy
	t2	t3	t4	t5
Lagged dependent variable	0.524***	0.568***	0.539***	0.539***
	(0.0238)	(0.0317)	(0.0307)	(0.0305)
SNP vote intention		0.0715	-0.167	0.0176
		(0.169)	(0.103)	(0.105)
Referendum Yes vote (intention)	-0.268***	-0.334***	-0.428***	-0.0322
	(0.0537)	(0.0676)	(0.0719)	(0.0753)
Party ID Labour	0.0720	0.0661	0.0413	0.198**
	(0.0568)	(0.0766)	(0.0646)	(0.0814)
Party ID SNP	-0.134	-0.0785	0.258	0.00675
	(0.143)	(0.188)	(0.288)	(0.132)
Age	0.000300	-0.000311	0.000666	-0.00183
	(0.00134)	(0.00174)	(0.00187)	(0.00189)
Political knowledge	0.0349	-0.0839***	-0.0772**	-0.0449
	(0.0246)	(0.0313)	(0.0330)	(0.0325)
Working class (subjective)	-0.0477	-0.00191	0.0417	0.0189
	(0.0396)	(0.0495)	(0.0524)	(0.0516)
Constant	1.091***	1.067***	1.077***	0.985***
	(0.0966)	(0.135)	(0.136)	(0.141)

Table A8.3 Logistic regression model of SNP vote (intention) before and after the Scottish independence referendum among 2010 Labour voters used to estimate the counterfactual effect of change in attitude on voting for the SNP

	Pre-referendum	Post-referendum
Britishness	−0.214**	−0.238***
	(0.103)	(0.0923)
Scottishness	−0.0894	0.175*
	(0.121)	(0.104)
Approval of Scottish Government	0.358	0.778**
	(0.439)	(0.346)
Like Salmond (pre referendum)/	0.447***	0.251***
Sturgeon (post referendum)	(0.0942)	(0.0698)
Like Miliband	−0.327***	−0.195***
	(0.0861)	(0.0704)
Devolution preferences	−0.397	0.481*
	(0.281)	(0.258)
Satisfaction with UK democracy	0.0729	0.299
	(0.238)	(0.189)
Referendum Yes vote (intention)	0.954**	1.652***
	(0.466)	(0.356)
Labour party identity strength (base = non−identifier)		
Not very strong	−0.548	0.345
	(0.575)	(0.507)
Fairly strong	−0.789	−0.146
	(0.518)	(0.443)
Very strong	−0.640	−1.216*
	(0.787)	(0.621)
SNP party identity strength (base = non−identifier)		
Not very strong	1.095	0.769
	(0.710)	(0.844)
Fairly strong	1.573**	2.920***
	(0.633)	(0.943)
Very strong	1.751*	1.579
	(0.915)	(1.115)
Constant	−1.577	−2.841***
	(1.018)	(0.946)
N	708	708

Table A8.4 Hybrid (two parameter and graded response) IRT model of Scottish devolution preferences Across the 2014-17 panel (varying loading and constant preferences across waves)

	BESIP Wave						
	1	2	3	4	6	10	11
Devolution preference: **Welfare benefits**							
Discrimination	3.368***	3.158***	2.967***	3.680***	3.717***	3.431***	3.039***
	(0.112)	(0.100)	(0.108)	(0.131)	(0.134)	(0.155)	(0.126)
Difficulty	-0.366***	-0.354***	-0.727***	-0.511***	-0.542***	-0.543***	-0.540***
	(0.0162)	(0.0164)	(0.0191)	(0.0163)	(0.0164)	(0.0201)	(0.0204)
Devolution preference: NHS							
Discrimination	2.347***	2.298***	2.665***	3.253***	3.111***	3.082***	2.914***
	(0.0818)	(0.0803)	(0.112)	(0.128)	(0.125)	(0.145)	(0.131)
Difficulty	-0.847***	-0.941***	-1.310***	-1.000***	-1.059***	-0.808***	-0.890***
	(0.0221)	(0.0233)	(0.0293)	(0.0213)	(0.0227)	(0.0233)	(0.0237)
Devolution preference: Schools							
Discrimination	2.389***	2.352***	2.512***	3.369***	3.324***	3.302***	2.889***
	(0.0979)	(0.0972)	(0.120)	(0.150)	(0.152)	(0.173)	(0.140)
Difficulty	-1.405***	-1.506***	-1.741***	-1.329***	-1.408***	-1.124***	-1.203***
	(0.0324)	(0.0348)	(0.0424)	(0.0271)	(0.0291)	(0.0279)	(0.0293)
Devolution preference: Defence & foreign affairs							
Discrimination	3.473***	3.564***	3.098***	3.226***	3.035***	3.199***	3.442***
	(0.112)	(0.113)	(0.101)	(0.105)	(0.0983)	(0.134)	(0.141)
Difficulty	0.294***	0.283***	0.311***	0.285***	0.365***	0.285***	0.300***
	(0.0176)	(0.0172)	(0.0189)	(0.0182)	(0.0190)	(0.0226)	(0.0212)
Devolution preference: Taxation							
Discrimination	3.513***	3.254***	3.036***	3.739***	3.749***	3.451***	3.255***
	(0.117)	(0.104)	(0.110)	(0.132)	(0.133)	(0.155)	(0.136)
Difficulty	-0.314***	-0.351***	-0.687***	-0.467***	-0.465***	-0.488***	-0.494***
	(0.0160)	(0.0163)	(0.0186)	(0.0161)	(0.0162)	(0.0199)	(0.0196)

Continued

Table A8.4 Continued

				BESIP Wave			
	1	2	3	4	6	10	11
Devolution preference: Police							
Discrimination	2.083***	2.087***	2.204***	2.467***	2.548***	2.838***	2.559***
	(0.0791)	(0.0789)	(0.0922)	(0.0955)	(0.100)	(0.135)	(0.114)
Difficulty	−1.217***	−1.268***	−1.409***	−1.142***	−1.145***	−0.953***	−0.969***
	(0.0301)	(0.0307)	(0.0348)	(0.0268)	(0.0266)	(0.0265)	(0.0266)
Feelings if Scotland became independent							
Discrimination	2.650***	2.766***					2.015***
	(0.0601)	(0.0611)					(0.0526)
Difficulty (base = 0: Extremely disappointed)							
≥1	−0.560***	−0.591***					−1.019***
	(0.0181)	(0.0176)					(0.0161)
≥2	−0.379***	−0.403***					−0.712***
	(0.0174)	(0.0169)					(0.0130)
≥3	−0.222***	−0.227***					−0.350***
	(0.0172)	(0.0167)					(0.0105)
≥4	−0.0930***	−0.111***					−0.0515***
	(0.0174)	(0.0169)					(0.00966)
≥5	−0.0167	−0.0277					0.111***
	(0.0175)	(0.0171)					(0.00981)
≥6	0.202***	0.153***					0.703***
	(0.0182)	(0.0176)					(0.0133)
≥7	0.280***	0.239***					0.879***
	(0.0185)	(0.0179)					(0.0150)
≥8	0.428***	0.389***					1.089***
	(0.0193)	(0.0186)					(0.0172)
≥9	0.646***	0.608***					1.371***
	(0.0207)	(0.0198)					(0.0205)
= 10: Extremely happy	0.800***	0.752***					1.527***
	(0.0219)	(0.0209)					(0.0225)

Table A8.5 Graded response IRT Model of EU Integration attitudes

						Measured in wave:						
	1	2	3	4	6	7	8	9	10	11	12	13

Some people feel that Britain should do all it can to unite fully with the European Union. Other people feel that Britain should do all it can to protect its independence from the European Union.

Where would you place yourself on this scale?

	1	2	3	4	6	7	8	9	10	11	12	13
Discrimination	2.968***	2.791***	3.467***	3.544***	3.538***	3.886***	4.010***	4.274***	5.154***	5.466***	5.548***	5.345***
	(0.0403)	(0.0372)	(0.0465)	(0.0449)	(0.0444)	(0.0355)	(0.0350)	(0.0383)	(0.0502)	(0.0521)	(0.0523)	(0.0504)
Difficulty (base = 0: Unite fully with the European Union)												
≥ 1	-1.566***	-1.681***	-1.547***	-1.582***	-1.531***	-1.737***	-1.767***	-1.412***	-1.366***	-1.272***	-1.180***	-1.255***
	(0.0174)	(0.0193)	(0.0166)	(0.0159)	(0.0153)	(0.0131)	(0.0130)	(0.0100)	(0.00932)	(0.00852)	(0.00777)	(0.00843)
≥ 2	-1.381***	-1.454***	-1.355***	-1.391***	-1.345***	-1.544***	-1.562***	-1.223***	-1.188***	-1.100***	-1.011***	-1.089***
	(0.0153)	(0.0164)	(0.0143)	(0.0138)	(0.0133)	(0.0113)	(0.0110)	(0.00878)	(0.00823)	(0.00761)	(0.00701)	(0.00757)
≥ 3	-1.117***	-1.134***	-1.053***	-1.093***	-1.019***	-1.266***	-1.255***	-0.944***	-0.930***	-0.851***	-0.779***	-0.829***
	(0.0130)	(0.0135)	(0.0118)	(0.0114)	(0.0109)	(0.00934)	(0.00894)	(0.00751)	(0.00714)	(0.00672)	(0.00633)	(0.00667)
≥ 4	-0.839***	-0.816***	-0.740***	-0.796***	-0.727***	-0.933***	-0.919***	-0.635***	-0.643***	-0.582***	-0.528***	-0.539***
	(0.0113)	(0.0115)	(0.0102)	(0.00984)	(0.00960)	(0.00777)	(0.00745)	(0.00667)	(0.00637)	(0.00614)	(0.00590)	(0.00611)
≥ 5	-0.676***	-0.617***	-0.549***	-0.594***	-0.531***	-0.693***	-0.686***	-0.430***	-0.459***	-0.408***	-0.371***	-0.367***
	(0.0106)	(0.0106)	(0.00963)	(0.00916)	(0.00904)	(0.00703)	(0.00677)	(0.00637)	(0.00609)	(0.00575)	(0.00575)	(0.00594)
≥ 6	-0.288***	-0.245***	-0.207***	-0.249***	-0.173***	-0.343***	-0.356***	-0.111***	-0.157***	-0.120***	-0.117***	-0.0794***
	(0.00959)	(0.00977)	(0.00912)	(0.00860)	(0.00863)	(0.00646)	(0.00624)	(0.00621)	(0.00592)	(0.00584)	(0.00568)	(0.00587)
≥ 7	-0.121***	-0.0595***	-0.0350***	-0.0642***	0.0188*	-0.150***	-0.165***	0.0643***	0.00280	0.0358***	0.0359***	0.0723***
	(0.00946)	(0.00970)	(0.00907)	(0.00856)	(0.00866)	(0.00637)	(0.00614)	(0.00625)	(0.00595)	(0.00587)	(0.00571)	(0.00591)
≥ 8	0.139***	0.209***	0.226***	0.216***	0.299***	0.108***	0.0913***	0.291***	0.222***	0.260***	0.234***	0.305***
	(0.00958)	(0.00998)	(0.00929)	(0.00876)	(0.00899)	(0.00645)	(0.00619)	(0.00642)	(0.00610)	(0.00602)	(0.00582)	(0.00608)
≥ 9	0.366***	0.468***	0.432***	0.435***	0.529***	0.334***	0.334***	0.504***	0.435***	0.475***	0.428***	0.512***
	(0.0100)	(0.0107)	(0.00975)	(0.00922)	(0.00957)	(0.00670)	(0.00642)	(0.00674)	(0.00640)	(0.00631)	(0.00605)	(0.00639)
= 10: Protect our independence	0.507***	0.639***	0.562***	0.569***	0.676***	0.485***	0.501***	0.663***	0.571***	0.618***	0.558***	0.652***
	(0.0105)	(0.0114)	(0.0102)	(0.00968)	(0.0102)	(0.00701)	(0.00673)	(0.00713)	(0.00672)	(0.00663)	(0.00630)	(0.00673)

Continued

Table A8.5 Continued

					Measured in wave:							
	1	2	3	4	6	7	8	9	10	11	12	13
Some say European unification should be pushed further. Others say it has already gone too far. What is your opinion?												
Discrimination	−2.660***	−2.190***	−2.964***	−2.841***	−2.879***							
	(0.0383)	(0.0319)	(0.0418)	(0.0382)	(0.0384)							
Difficulty (base = 0: Unification has already gone too far)												
≥1	0.504***	0.634***	0.527***	0.557***	0.608***							
	(0.0116)	(0.0136)	(0.0114)	(0.0112)	(0.0114)							
≥2	0.299***	0.378***	0.325***	0.365***	0.429***							
	(0.0109)	(0.0125)	(0.0107)	(0.0105)	(0.0107)							
≥3	0.106***	0.141***	0.101***	0.139***	0.190***							
	(0.0105)	(0.0118)	(0.0103)	(0.0100)	(0.0101)							
≥4	−0.128***	−0.140***	−0.148***	−0.131***	−0.0769***							
	(0.0104)	(0.0115)	(0.0101)	(0.00984)	(0.00983)							
≥5	−0.317***	−0.349***	−0.350***	−0.333***	−0.296***							
	(0.0105)	(0.0117)	(0.0102)	(0.00996)	(0.00990)							
≥6	−0.981***	−1.066***	−0.949***	−1.008***	−0.969***							
	(0.0131)	(0.0148)	(0.0122)	(0.0123)	(0.0120)							
≥7	−1.267***	−1.358***	−1.225***	−1.296***	−1.239***							
	(0.0153)	(0.0175)	(0.0143)	(0.0146)	(0.0140)							
≥8	−1.636***	−1.714***	−1.551***	−1.642***	−1.547***							
	(0.0193)	(0.0219)	(0.0177)	(0.0184)	(0.0171)							
≥9	−1.904***	−1.985***	−1.803***	−1.890***	−1.822***							
	(0.0233)	(0.0262)	(0.0213)	(0.0221)	(0.0209)							
= 10: Unification should be pushed further	−2.044***	−2.183***	−1.932***	−2.010***	−1.929***							
	(0.0257)	(0.0300)	(0.0236)	(0.0243)	(0.0227)							

* p<0.05 ** p<0.01 *** p<0.001

Note: In waves 1–6, each question was asked to a randomly half of the sample. From waves 7 onward, one question was asked to the whole sample.

Table A8.6 Multinomial logistic model of 2015 and
2017 vote choice in Scotland

Base category = SNP	2015	2017
Conservative		
Economic left–right	1.347***	1.081***
	(0.0846)	(0.0897)
Liberal–authoritarianism	0.289**	0.324**
	(0.0982)	(0.104)
EU attitude	0.245*	1.300***
	(0.0993)	(0.111)
Immigration attitude	−0.0288	0.236*
	(0.107)	(0.116)
Scottish devolution attitude	−3.326***	−2.831***
	(0.118)	(0.114)
Constant	−2.321***	−0.542***
	(0.0983)	(0.0855)
Labour		
Economic left–right	−0.0724	−0.284***
	(0.0572)	(0.0664)
Liberal–authoritarianism	−0.289***	−0.180*
	(0.0678)	(0.0753)
EU attitude	−0.268***	0.117
	(0.0776)	(0.0892)
Immigration attitude	−0.0448	0.106
	(0.0799)	(0.0904)
Scottish devolution attitude	−2.954***	−2.144***
	(0.0932)	(0.0906)
Constant	−0.821***	−0.0376
	(0.0583)	(0.0713)
Liberal Democrat		
Economic left–right	0.596***	0.405***
	(0.0807)	(0.0980)
Liberal–authoritarianism	−0.209*	0.00223
	(0.0972)	(0.115)
EU attitude	−0.0333	0.169
	(0.104)	(0.130)
Immigration attitude	−0.192	−0.175
	(0.111)	(0.137)
Scottish devolution attitude	−2.889***	−2.319***
	(0.120)	(0.128)
Constant	−1.957***	−1.254***
	(0.0886)	(0.104)
UKIP		
Economic left–right	0.152	−0.341
	(0.138)	(0.366)
Liberal–authoritarianism	0.120	0.359
	(0.179)	(0.433)
EU attitude	1.437***	1.552**
	(0.207)	(0.527)
Immigration attitude	0.490**	1.169*
	(0.190)	(0.497)

Continued

Table A8.6 Continued

Base category = SNP	2015	2017
Scottish devolution attitude	−2.872***	−2.682***
	(0.184)	(0.366)
Constant	−4.468***	−6.088***
	(0.244)	(0.757)
Green Party		
Economic left–right	−0.290*	−0.0457
	(0.124)	(0.308)
Liberal–authoritarianism	−0.784***	0.179
	(0.137)	(0.336)
EU attitude	−0.294	0.292
	(0.173)	(0.408)
Immigration attitude	−0.0258	−0.446
	(0.170)	(0.406)
Scottish devolution attitude	−1.240***	−0.896*
	(0.149)	(0.357)
Constant	−3.362***	−3.957***
	(0.160)	(0.336)
N	5041	3424

* $p<0.05$ ** $p<0.01$ *** $p<0.001$

Appendix to Chapter 9

Table A9.1 Conditional logit model with alternative specific coefficients of 2017 vote choice

Base = Conservative	Labour	Liberal Democrats	UKIP	Green Party
2015 Voted Conservative	−1.464***	−0.847***	−2.769***	−1.818***
	(0.179)	(0.199)	(0.587)	(0.420)
2015 Voted Outcome party	1.188***	2.005***	0.893**	1.433***
	(0.135)	(0.179)	(0.328)	(0.259)
Economic left–right distance: Conservatives	0.357***	0.279***	0.108	0.256***
	(0.0363)	(0.0437)	(0.0628)	(0.0622)
Economic left–right distance: Outcome party	−0.258***	−0.273***	−0.0776	−0.281***
	(0.0302)	(0.0445)	(0.0654)	(0.0738)
EU distance: Conservatives	0.178***	0.202***	0.297***	0.178***
	(0.0334)	(0.0375)	(0.0530)	(0.0529)
EU distance: Outcome party	−0.113***	−0.203***	−0.0202	−0.145**
	(0.0248)	(0.0303)	(0.0600)	(0.0526)
Immigration distance: Conservatives	0.103**	0.0758	0.0214	0.0467
	(0.0377)	(0.0437)	(0.0566)	(0.0593)
Immigration distance: Outcome party	−0.177***	−0.175***	−0.263**	−0.0837
	(0.0256)	(0.0343)	(0.0841)	(0.0549)
Immigration competence: Conservatives	−0.814***	−0.685***	−0.947***	−0.718*
	(0.154)	(0.186)	(0.233)	(0.323)
Immigration competence: Outcome party	1.191***	0.919*	0.756**	−0.0759
	(0.295)	(0.402)	(0.294)	(1.117)
Constant	0.408	−0.199	−3.037***	−1.595***
	(0.215)	(0.254)	(0.489)	(0.406)
N	3648			

* p<0.05 ** p<0.01 *** p<0.001

Table A9.2 Graded response IRT model of Immigration attitudes

					Measured in wave:						
	1	2	3	4	7	8	9	10	11	12	13
Do you think immigration is good or bad for Britain's economy?											
Discrimination	3.220***	3.568***	3.538***	3.488***	3.688***	3.544***		3.220***	3.173***		3.527***
	(0.0268)	(0.0293)	(0.0300)	(0.0282)	(0.0299)	(0.0276)		(0.0267)	(0.0258)		(0.0287)
Difficulty (base = 0: Bad for economy)											
≥ 2	−0.978***	−0.992***	−0.869***	−1.091***	−1.035***	−1.084***		−1.374***	−1.502***		−1.396***
	(0.00859)	(0.00831)	(0.00814)	(0.00865)	(0.00825)	(0.00832)		(0.0105)	(0.0112)		(0.0101)
≥ 3	−0.550***	−0.574***	−0.470***	−0.679***	−0.648***	−0.712***		−0.969***	−1.108***		−1.047***
	(0.00722)	(0.00702)	(0.00702)	(0.00720)	(0.00703)	(0.00705)		(0.00851)	(0.00904)		(0.00837)
≥ 4	−0.181***	−0.193***	−0.108***	−0.303***	−0.272***	−0.339***		−0.581***	−0.723***		−0.668***
	(0.00673)	(0.00652)	(0.00666)	(0.00656)	(0.00646)	(0.00641)		(0.00732)	(0.00767)		(0.00717)
≥ 5	0.362***	0.337***	0.411***	0.219***	0.241***	0.224***		0.0144*	−0.104***		−0.0519***
	(0.00673)	(0.00669)	(0.00693)	(0.00652)	(0.00652)	(0.00641)		(0.00672)	(0.00671)		(0.00648)
≥ 6	0.971***	0.947***	1.020***	0.851***	0.845***	0.861***		0.611***	0.521***		0.558***
	(0.00846)	(0.00805)	(0.00846)	(0.00770)	(0.00764)	(0.00758)		(0.00744)	(0.00723)		(0.00705)
= 7: Good for economy	1.639***	1.609***	1.697***	1.529***	1.506***	1.525***		1.295***	1.235***		1.230***
	(0.0121)	(0.0114)	(0.0123)	(0.0108)	(0.0107)	(0.0106)		(0.0101)	(0.00965)		(0.00928)
And do you think that immigration undermines or enriches Britain's cultural life?											
Discrimination	3.476***	3.680***	3.687***	3.447***	3.768***	3.716***		3.673***	3.631***		3.712***
	(0.0294)	(0.0307)	(0.0317)	(0.0283)	(0.0309)	(0.0293)		(0.0310)	(0.0299)		(0.0307)
Difficulty (base = 0: Undermines cultural life)											
≥ 2	−0.762***	−0.780***	−0.695***	−0.860***	−0.818***	−0.861***		−0.981***	−1.046***		−0.959***
	(0.00765)	(0.00754)	(0.00751)	(0.00788)	(0.00752)	(0.00743)		(0.00828)	(0.00845)		(0.00799)
≥ 3	−0.375***	−0.390***	−0.319***	−0.471***	−0.422***	−0.473***		−0.594***	−0.640***		−0.588***
	(0.00671)	(0.00661)	(0.00669)	(0.00681)	(0.00656)	(0.00646)		(0.00700)	(0.00707)		(0.00685)
≥ 4	−0.0488***	−0.0617***	0.00550	−0.126***	−0.0696***	−0.121***		−0.259***	−0.306***		−0.249***
	(0.00646)	(0.00634)	(0.00648)	(0.00641)	(0.00628)	(0.00614)		(0.00647)	(0.00649)		(0.00637)
≥ 5	0.376***	0.345***	0.395***	0.277***	0.335***	0.310***		0.175***	0.121***		0.175***
	(0.00674)	(0.00658)	(0.00676)	(0.00655)	(0.00652)	(0.00635)		(0.00647)	(0.00642)		(0.00641)

≥6	0.868***	0.853***	0.898***	0.792***	0.843***	0.830***	0.650***	0.607***	0.652***
	(0.00785)	(0.00764)	(0.00789)	(0.00754)	(0.00755)	(0.00735)	(0.00716)	(0.00704)	(0.00710)
= 7: *Enriches cultural life*	1.432***	1.415***	1.463***	1.380***	1.392***	1.384***	1.169***	1.145***	1.177***
	(0.0104)	(0.0101)	(0.0105)	(0.0100)	(0.00993)	(0.00967)	(0.00899)	(0.00881)	(0.00891)

Some people think that the UK should allow *many more* immigrants to come to the UK to live and others think that the UK should allow *many fewer* immigrants.

Where would you place yourself this scale?

Discrimination	3.312***	3.348***	3.183***	3.363***	3.339***	3.374***
	(0.0280)	(0.0271)	(0.0264)	(0.0288)	(0.0279)	(0.134)

Difficulty (base = 0: Allow many fewer)

≥1	-0.598***	-0.566***	-0.656***	-0.671***	-0.719***	-0.668***	-0.570***
	(0.00744)	(0.00705)	(0.00756)	(0.00759)	(0.00764)	(0.0137)	(0.0297)
≥2	-0.417***	-0.393***	-0.495***	-0.503***	-0.562***	-0.490***	-0.424***
	(0.00704)	(0.00671)	(0.00716)	(0.00715)	(0.00720)	(0.0128)	(0.0282)
≥3	-0.161***	-0.145***	-0.239***	-0.248***	-0.310***	-0.247***	-0.197***
	(0.00678)	(0.00649)	(0.00681)	(0.00679)	(0.00680)	(0.0120)	(0.0270)
≥4	0.134***	0.129***	0.0558***	0.0560***	0.00131	0.0682***	0.0585*
	(0.00680)	(0.00652)	(0.00676)	(0.00671)	(0.00668)	(0.0117)	(0.0268)
≥5	0.377***	0.356***	0.282***	0.292***	0.241***	0.313***	0.284***
	(0.00704)	(0.00675)	(0.00695)	(0.00689)	(0.00683)	(0.0120)	(0.0275)
≥6	0.873***	0.874***	0.908***	0.913***	0.908***	0.982***	0.854***
	(0.00809)	(0.00782)	(0.00828)	(0.00820)	(0.00808)	(0.0146)	(0.0326)
≥7	1.168***	1.168***	1.187***	1.193***	1.188***	1.282***	1.116***
	(0.00922)	(0.00892)	(0.00943)	(0.00939)	(0.00921)	(0.0172)	(0.0374)
≥8	1.562***	1.548***	1.581***	1.565***	1.554***	1.691***	1.495***
	(0.0115)	(0.0110)	(0.0118)	(0.0117)	(0.0114)	(0.0224)	(0.0475)
≥9	1.907***	1.895***	1.951***	1.933***	1.913***	2.063***	1.763***
	(0.0145)	(0.0139)	(0.0152)	(0.0152)	(0.0146)	(0.0293)	(0.0579)
= 10: Allow many more	2.086***	2.043***	2.119***	2.082***	2.061***	2.207***	1.945***
	(0.0167)	(0.0156)	(0.0173)	(0.0171)	(0.0163)	(0.0329)	(0.0673)

* p<0.05 ** p<0.01 *** p<0.001

Note: The direction of the predicted score is then reversed to give a scale that runs from pro–immigration to anti–immigration

Table A9.3 Graded response IRT model of redistribution attitudes

Some people feel that government should make much greater efforts to make people's incomes more equal. Other people feel that government should be much less concerned about how equal people's incomes are.

Where would you place yourself on this scale?

	Measured in wave:									
	1	2	3	4	6	7	10	11	12	13
Discrimination	2.400***	2.081***	3.082***	3.032***	3.319***	2.708***	2.635***	2.872***	2.693***	2.862***
	(0.0245)	(0.0216)	(0.0316)	(0.0294)	(0.0326)	(0.0263)	(0.0282)	(0.0297)	(0.0479)	(0.0292)
Difficulty (base = 0: Government should try to make incomes equal)										
≥ 1	-1.088***	-1.335***	-1.004***	-1.072***	-1.047***	-1.619***	-1.052***	-1.083***	-1.218***	-1.107***
	(0.0113)	(0.0139)	(0.0101)	(0.00998)	(0.00967)	(0.0136)	(0.0109)	(0.0105)	(0.0195)	(0.0105)
≥ 2	-0.833***	-1.052***	-0.795***	-0.850***	-0.833***	-1.283***	-0.826***	-0.867***	-0.984***	-0.877***
	(0.0100)	(0.0121)	(0.00913)	(0.00896)	(0.00870)	(0.0113)	(0.00980)	(0.00943)	(0.0173)	(0.00940)
≥ 3	-0.532***	-0.736***	-0.508***	-0.570***	-0.536***	-0.906***	-0.508***	-0.579***	-0.676***	-0.561***
	(0.00891)	(0.0106)	(0.00820)	(0.00803)	(0.00777)	(0.00951)	(0.00868)	(0.00842)	(0.0151)	(0.00831)
≥ 4	-0.172***	-0.350***	-0.177***	-0.212***	-0.193***	-0.385***	-0.154***	-0.226***	-0.325***	-0.181***
	(0.00815)	(0.00923)	(0.00760)	(0.00735)	(0.00717)	(0.00790)	(0.00798)	(0.00766)	(0.0135)	(0.00756)
≥ 5	0.0720***	-0.0855***	0.0566***	0.0354***	0.0580***	0.0336***	0.0865***	-0.00862	-0.0708***	0.0653***
	(0.00800)	(0.00874)	(0.00747)	(0.00721)	(0.00704)	(0.00745)	(0.00784)	(0.00746)	(0.0128)	(0.00741)
≥ 6	0.526***	0.423***	0.458***	0.432***	0.455***	0.502***	0.533***	0.401***	0.357***	0.504***
	(0.00854)	(0.00893)	(0.00784)	(0.00753)	(0.00739)	(0.00793)	(0.00840)	(0.00770)	(0.0129)	(0.00787)
≥ 7	0.772***	0.673***	0.668***	0.660***	0.677***	0.825***	0.771***	0.623***	0.590***	0.731***
	(0.00930)	(0.00959)	(0.00833)	(0.00804)	(0.00789)	(0.00887)	(0.00915)	(0.00820)	(0.0137)	(0.00847)
≥ 8	1.189***	1.080***	1.037***	1.055***	1.039***	1.344***	1.182***	0.990***	1.001***	1.118***
	(0.0112)	(0.0114)	(0.00968)	(0.00947)	(0.00913)	(0.0113)	(0.0111)	(0.00952)	(0.0163)	(0.0100)
≥ 9	1.540***	1.427***	1.351***	1.381***	1.363***	1.781***	1.538***	1.318***	1.366***	1.458***
	(0.0135)	(0.0137)	(0.0114)	(0.0112)	(0.0108)	(0.0144)	(0.0134)	(0.0113)	(0.0198)	(0.0120)
= 10: Government should be less concerned about equal incomes	1.721***	1.626***	1.497***	1.541***	1.516***	2.001***	1.714***	1.489***	1.568***	1.627***
	(0.0149)	(0.0152)	(0.0124)	(0.0123)	(0.0118)	(0.0165)	(0.0149)	(0.0124)	(0.0224)	(0.0133)

* p<0.05 ** p<0.01 *** p<0.001

Table A9.4 Logistic models of 2015 and 2017 Conservative vs Labour (1=conservative) vote choice, examining the relative explanatory power of the economic and cultural dimensions

	2015			2017		
	Economic dimension	Cultural dimension	Both dimensions	Economic dimension	Cultural dimension	Both dimensions
Economic left–right values	1.283***		1.796***	0.809***		1.581***
	(0.0764)		(0.103)	(0.0596)		(0.0862)
Redistribution attitude	1.039***		0.878***	0.906***		0.741***
	(0.0858)		(0.104)	(0.0660)		(0.0872)
Liberal–authoritarian values		0.275***	0.757***		0.303***	0.725***
		(0.0591)	(0.0936)		(0.0563)	(0.0792)
EU attitude		0.912***	0.877***		1.182***	1.342***
		(0.0662)	(0.0931)		(0.0636)	(0.0878)
Immigration attitude		−0.0326	0.140		0.140*	0.394***
		(0.0712)	(0.0977)		(0.0702)	(0.0880)
Constant	−0.127**	0.0415	−0.399***	−0.0108	−0.142***	−0.560***
	(0.0486)	(0.0367)	(0.0584)	(0.0387)	(0.0357)	(0.0521)
N	7128			8454		
Pseudo R^2	0.330	0.115	0.441	0.228	0.205	0.448

* $p<0.05$ ** $p<0.01$ *** $p<0.001$

Table A9.5 Multinomial logistic models of 2015 and 2017 vote choice in England, examining the relative explanatory power of the economic and cultural dimensions

Base = Conservatives	2015			2017		
	Economic dimension	Cultural dimension	Both dimensions	Economic dimension	Cultural dimension	Both dimensions
Labour						
Economic left–right values	-1.264***		-1.715***	-0.851***		-1.575***
	(0.0663)		(0.0794)	(0.0504)		(0.0670)
Redistribution attitude	-0.911***		-0.893***	-0.879***		-0.678***
	(0.0709)		(0.0848)	(0.0564)		(0.0679)
Liberal–authoritarian values		-0.264***	-0.667***		-0.284***	-0.672***
		(0.0496)	(0.0686)		(0.0479)	(0.0611)
EU attitude		-0.902***	-0.830***		-1.194***	-1.281***
		(0.0634)	(0.0822)		(0.0570)	(0.0735)
Immigration attitude		0.0581	-0.190*		-0.132*	-0.413***
		(0.0634)	(0.0886)		(0.0630)	(0.0747)
Constant	-0.0670	-0.168***	0.202***	-0.106**	0.0615	0.456***
	(0.0437)	(0.0343)	(0.0489)	(0.0346)	(0.0318)	(0.0435)
Liberal Democrats						
Economic left–right values	-0.791***		-1.293***	-0.321***		-1.126***
	(0.0827)		(0.0997)	(0.0740)		(0.0931)
Redistribution attitude	-0.458***		-0.278**	-0.526***		-0.125
	(0.0770)		(0.103)	(0.0641)		(0.0938)
Liberal–authoritarian values		-0.378***	-0.750***		-0.394***	-0.784***
		(0.0892)	(0.112)		(0.0811)	(0.102)
EU attitude		-0.747***	-0.732***		-1.402***	-1.564***
		(0.0994)	(0.116)		(0.0889)	(0.107)
Immigration attitude		-0.271*	-0.477**		-0.208	-0.467***
		(0.125)	(0.147)		(0.109)	(0.127)
Constant	-1.245***	-1.583***	-1.006***	-1.269***	-1.357***	-0.839***
	(0.0548)	(0.0514)	(0.0621)	(0.0455)	(0.0500)	(0.0597)

UKIP

	(1)	(2)	(3)	(4)	(5)	(6)
Economic left–right values	-1.370***		-1.119***	-1.167***		-0.911***
	(0.0712)		(0.0782)	(0.0858)		(0.102)
Redistribution attitude	-0.00442		-0.0381	-0.105		-0.0514
	(0.0746)		(0.0676)	(0.110)		(0.0816)
Liberal–authoritarian values		0.0000816	-0.286***		-0.00517	-0.274**
		(0.0622)	(0.0761)		(0.0856)	(0.0952)
EU attitude		0.709***	0.807***		0.572***	0.551***
		(0.0784)	(0.0852)		(0.129)	(0.135)
Immigration attitude		0.725***	0.630***		0.762***	0.596***
		(0.0685)	(0.0793)		(0.109)	(0.117)
Constant	-0.694***	-2.021***	-1.531***	-2.508***	-3.787***	-3.316***
	(0.0498)	(0.0725)	(0.0816)	(0.0714)	(0.144)	(0.153)
Green Party						
Economic left–right values	-1.319***		-1.790***	-0.836***		-1.595***
	(0.0972)		(0.114)	(0.115)		(0.133)
Redistribution attitude	-0.890***		-0.786***	-0.560***		-0.283
	(0.0994)		(0.132)	(0.135)		(0.164)
Liberal–authoritarian values		-0.709***	-1.050***		-0.492***	-0.878***
		(0.112)	(0.115)		(0.117)	(0.117)
EU attitude		-1.135***	-1.046***		-1.004***	-1.119***
		(0.126)	(0.134)		(0.126)	(0.135)
Immigration attitude		-0.161	-0.366*		-0.123	-0.392*
		(0.138)	(0.142)		(0.156)	(0.155)
Constant	-2.282***	-2.672***	-2.256***	-3.004***	-2.911***	-2.424***
	(0.0734)	(0.0867)	(0.0882)	(0.0917)	(0.0941)	(0.102)
N	10135	10135	10135	10101	10101	10101
Pseudo R^2	0.148	0.134	0.282	0.132	0.155	0.297

* $p<0.05$ ** $p<0.01$ *** $p<0.001$

Table A9.6 Multinomial logistic models of 2015 and 2017 vote choice in Scotland, examining the relative explanatory power of the economic and cultural dimensions

Base = SNP	2015				2017			
	Economic dimension	Cultural dimension	Devolution Dimension	All dimensions	Economic dimension	Cultural dimension	Devolution Dimension	Both dimensions
Conservatives								
Economic left–right values	1.254***			1.200***	0.885***			0.948***
	(0.145)			(0.166)	(0.115)			(0.143)
Redistribution attitude	0.765***			0.0940	0.785***			0.167
	(0.149)			(0.175)	(0.113)			(0.139)
Liberal–authoritarian values		0.442***		0.547***		0.371***		0.382**
		(0.0990)		(0.154)		(0.0888)		(0.135)
EU attitude		0.658***		0.351*		1.079***		1.283***
		(0.108)		(0.151)		(0.100)		(0.140)
Immigration attitude		−0.140		−0.247		0.179		0.160
		(0.101)		(0.166)		(0.101)		(0.159)
Devolution attitude			−3.078***	−2.724***			−2.859***	−2.517***
			(0.167)	(0.182)			(0.126)	(0.135)
Constant	−1.590***	−1.284***	−2.255***	−2.586***	−0.355***	−0.364***	−0.628***	−0.720***
	(0.100)	(0.0723)	(0.118)	(0.142)	(0.0703)	(0.0643)	(0.0883)	(0.104)
Labour								
Economic left–right values	0.343**			0.0763	0.284***			−0.0243
	(0.108)			(0.137)	(0.0813)			(0.105)
Redistribution attitude	0.0741			−0.326*	0.0644			−0.228*
	(0.0987)			(0.140)	(0.0901)			(0.113)
Liberal–authoritarian values		0.0571		−0.166		0.0435		−0.121
		(0.0913)		(0.113)		(0.0879)		(0.102)
EU attitude		−0.0834		−0.198		0.0175		0.0551
		(0.0923)		(0.132)		(0.0995)		(0.118)
Immigration attitude		0.244*		0.0246		0.266*		0.112
		(0.107)		(0.135)		(0.104)		(0.126)

	(1)	(2)	(3)	(4)	(5)	(6)	(7)	(8)
Devolution attitude			-2.223*** (0.142)	-2.334*** (0.154)			-1.721*** (0.108)	-1.796*** (0.116)
Constant	-0.626*** (0.0667)	-0.728*** (0.0640)	-1.059*** (0.0873)	-1.155*** (0.0926)	-0.273*** (0.0664)	-0.324*** (0.0675)	-0.0194 (0.0728)	-0.0672 (0.0864)
Liberal Democrats								
Economic left–right values	0.768*** (0.142)			0.508** (0.174)	0.623*** (0.140)			0.267 (0.159)
Redistribution attitude	0.584*** (0.135)			0.161 (0.173)	0.590*** (0.146)			0.305 (0.165)
Liberal–authoritarian values		0.226* (0.0989)		0.0719 (0.143)		0.280* (0.117)		0.0768 (0.138)
EU attitude		0.286* (0.127)		0.0636 (0.158)		0.154 (0.124)		0.172 (0.146)
Immigration attitude		-0.309** (0.119)		-0.545** (0.169)		-0.114 (0.145)		-0.320 (0.183)
Devolution attitude			-2.428*** (0.187)	-2.395*** (0.209)			-2.257*** (0.139)	-2.159*** (0.150)
Constant	-1.874*** (0.0972)	-1.833*** (0.0894)	-2.331*** (0.126)	-2.437*** (0.142)	-1.614*** (0.0908)	-1.706*** (0.0980)	-1.613*** (0.108)	-1.575*** (0.126)
UKIP								
Economic left–right values	-0.208 (0.200)			-0.232 (0.252)	-0.618** (0.219)			-0.119 (0.238)
Redistribution attitude	0.985*** (0.202)			0.480* (0.229)	0.323 (0.517)			-0.00159 (0.568)
Liberal–authoritarian values		-0.119 (0.346)		-0.356 (0.399)		0.756 (0.424)		0.451 (0.333)
EU attitude		0.915** (0.354)		0.729 (0.381)		0.963 (0.842)		0.996 (0.790)

Continued

Table A9.6 Continued

Base = SNP	2015				2017			
	Economic dimension	Cultural dimension	Devolution Dimension	All dimensions	Economic dimension	Cultural dimension	Devolution Dimension	Both dimensions
Immigration attitude		0.793**		0.744*		1.678**		1.577**
		(0.298)		(0.356)		(0.578)		(0.528)
Devolution attitude			-2.789***	-2.360***			-2.300**	-2.236**
			(0.377)	(0.341)			(0.773)	(0.721)
Constant	-3.417***	-3.939***	-4.198***	-4.493***	-4.870***	-6.293***	-4.460***	-6.145***
	(0.180)	(0.309)	(0.405)	(0.459)	(0.461)	(0.692)	(0.584)	(0.902)
Green Party								
Economic left–right values	-0.155			-0.320	0.299			0.141
	(0.222)			(0.247)	(0.657)			(0.666)
Redistribution attitude	-0.114			-0.0942	0.153			-0.000833
	(0.186)			(0.237)	(0.446)			(0.490)
Liberal–authoritarian values		-0.515		-0.547*		0.315		0.214
		(0.263)		(0.258)		(0.302)		(0.305)
EU attitude		-0.659**		-0.677**		0.324		0.331
		(0.216)		(0.221)		(0.513)		(0.545)
Immigration attitude		0.0284		-0.0570		-0.684		-0.793
		(0.205)		(0.196)		(0.559)		(0.598)
Devolution attitude			-0.358*	-0.910***			-0.936*	-0.993**
			(0.171)	(0.214)			(0.370)	(0.346)
Constant	-3.842***	-4.287***	-3.606***	-4.226***	-4.443***	-4.691***	-4.186***	-4.287***
	(0.168)	(0.204)	(0.155)	(0.203)	(0.412)	(0.401)	(0.395)	(0.442)
N	4695	4695	4695	4695	3413	3413	3413	3413
Pseudo R²	0.095	0.039	0.215	0.281	0.092	0.094	0.222	0.317

* $p<0.05$ ** $p<0.01$ *** $p<0.001$

Table A9.7 Multinomial logistic models of 2015 and 2017 vote choice in Wales, examining the relative explanatory power of the economic and cultural dimensions

Base = Labour	2015				2017			
	Economic dimension	Cultural dimension	Devolution Dimension	All dimensions	Economic dimension	Cultural dimension	Devolution Dimension	Both dimensions
Conservatives								
Economic left–right values	1.287***			1.576***	0.883***			1.410***
	(0.166)			(0.180)	(0.119)			(0.145)
Redistribution attitude	0.841***			0.556***	0.658***			0.242
	(0.154)			(0.166)	(0.120)			(0.148)
Liberal–authoritarian values		0.340**		0.631***		0.390***		0.604***
		(0.122)		(0.169)		(0.112)		(0.148)
EU attitude		0.882***		0.690***		1.445***		1.547***
		(0.125)		(0.163)		(0.136)		(0.181)
Immigration attitude		-0.0553		0.0662		-0.0334		0.0974
		(0.137)		(0.189)		(0.133)		(0.167)
Devolution attitude			-1.203***	-0.719***			-1.212***	-0.750***
			(0.0958)	(0.123)			(0.0980)	(0.122)
Constant	-0.494***	-0.388***	-0.508***	-0.765***	-0.502***	-0.662***	-0.643***	-1.010***
	(0.1000)	(0.0770)	(0.0816)	(0.108)	(0.0808)	(0.0823)	(0.0747)	(0.107)
Liberal Democrats								
Economic left–right values	0.801***			0.763***	0.340*			0.317
	(0.176)			(0.182)	(0.165)			(0.173)
Redistribution attitude	0.352*			0.480**	0.424**			0.412*
	(0.151)			(0.185)	(0.149)			(0.170)
Liberal–authoritarian values		-0.202		-0.315		-0.0404		-0.157
		(0.157)		(0.162)		(0.142)		(0.164)
EU attitude		0.0577		-0.0560		0.120		0.0250
		(0.156)		(0.171)		(0.189)		(0.210)
Immigration attitude		-0.230		-0.261		-0.225		-0.250
		(0.188)		(0.214)		(0.171)		(0.198)

Continued

Table A9.7 Continued

Base = Labour	2015				2017			
	Economic dimension	Cultural dimension	Devolution Dimension	All dimensions	Economic dimension	Cultural dimension	Devolution Dimension	Both dimensions
Devolution attitude			-0.563*** (0.111)	-0.430*** (0.128)			-0.727*** (0.141)	-0.680*** (0.158)
Constant	-1.596*** (0.112)	-1.834*** (0.117)	-1.739*** (0.109)	-1.716*** (0.128)	-1.969*** (0.121)	-2.096*** (0.141)	-2.105*** (0.124)	-2.077*** (0.161)
Plaid Cymru								
Economic left–right values	-0.135 (0.145)			0.0159 (0.157)	-0.0289 (0.129)			0.203 (0.142)
Redistribution attitude	0.272 (0.142)			0.608*** (0.172)	0.228 (0.137)			0.267 (0.147)
Liberal–authoritarian values		-0.430** (0.152)		-0.247 (0.166)		0.0524 (0.141)		0.169 (0.138)
EU attitude		0.0698 (0.133)		0.0717 (0.147)		0.456** (0.141)		0.476*** (0.144)
Immigration attitude		0.115 (0.139)		0.114 (0.143)		-0.0485 (0.151)		-0.0854 (0.146)
Devolution attitude			0.846*** (0.133)	1.024*** (0.140)			0.609*** (0.120)	0.834*** (0.140)
Constant	-1.092*** (0.102)	-1.198*** (0.109)	-1.576*** (0.123)	-1.434*** (0.134)	-1.552*** (0.109)	-1.475*** (0.107)	-1.826*** (0.123)	-1.623*** (0.130)
UKIP								
Economic left–right values	-0.00228 (0.143)			0.509** (0.197)	-0.425 (0.232)			0.261 (0.333)
Redistribution attitude	0.967*** (0.162)			0.605*** (0.166)	0.558* (0.242)			0.371 (0.232)
Liberal–authoritarian values		0.438* (0.177)		0.550* (0.219)		0.198 (0.294)		0.0493 (0.322)
EU attitude		1.645*** (0.164)		1.587*** (0.173)		1.802*** (0.264)		1.853*** (0.285)

Immigration attitude		0.612**		0.780***		0.796*		0.889*
		(0.190)		(0.213)		(0.355)		(0.374)
Devolution attitude			−1.005***	−0.515***			−0.498	−0.152
			(0.135)	(0.151)			(0.291)	(0.252)
Constant	−0.845***	−2.137***	−1.096***	−2.100***	−2.855***	−3.908***	−2.778***	−3.789***
	(0.0949)	(0.154)	(0.100)	(0.175)	(0.182)	(0.374)	(0.168)	(0.388)
Green Party								
Economic left–right values	0.235			0.215	−0.134			0.103
	(0.233)			(0.244)	(0.559)			(0.351)
Redistribution attitude	0.128			0.209	−0.973**			−1.158***
	(0.206)			(0.266)	(0.328)			(0.342)
Liberal–authoritarian values		−0.554		−0.615*		0.511		0.272
		(0.286)		(0.299)		(0.433)		(0.307)
EU attitude		0.00959		−0.0210		1.180		0.953
		(0.213)		(0.217)		(1.254)		(0.857)
Immigration attitude		0.0926		0.106		−1.927		−1.417
		(0.297)		(0.291)		(1.254)		(0.865)
Devolution attitude			−0.150	−0.196			−0.179	−0.419*
			(0.202)	(0.217)			(0.215)	(0.204)
Constant	−2.473***	−2.745***	−2.578***	−2.591***	−5.137***	−4.780***	−4.366***	−5.267***
	(0.162)	(0.168)	(0.153)	(0.179)	(0.446)	(0.552)	(0.422)	(0.486)
N	2463	2463	2463	2463	2029	2029	2029	2029
Pseudo R²	0.114	0.125	0.090	0.267	0.092	0.145	0.081	0.269

* p<0.05 ** p<0.01 *** p<0.001

Table A9.8 Hybrid (two parameter and graded response) IRT model of Welsh devolution preferences across the 2014–17 panel (varying loading and constant preferences across waves)

	Measured in wave						
	1	2	3	4	6	7	11
Preference for devolution: Welfare benefits							
Discrimination	2.516***	2.580***	2.383***	2.393***	2.537***		
	(0.105)	(0.107)	(0.102)	(0.109)	(0.115)		
Difficulty	0.237***	0.383***	0.217***	0.383***	0.305***		
	(0.0247)	(0.0249)	(0.0260)	(0.0279)	(0.0265)		
Preference for devolution: NHS							
Discrimination	2.479***	2.562***	2.517***	2.705***	2.620***		
	(0.0996)	(0.0995)	(0.105)	(0.116)	(0.113)		
Difficulty	-0.350***	-0.213***	-0.343***	-0.211***	-0.258***		
	(0.0258)	(0.0243)	(0.0265)	(0.0253)	(0.0261)		
Preference for devolution: Schools							
Discrimination	2.800***	2.871***	2.572***	2.892***	2.829***		
	(0.115)	(0.113)	(0.110)	(0.127)	(0.124)		
Difficulty	-0.611***	-0.507***	-0.705***	-0.580***	-0.578***		
	(0.0266)	(0.0250)	(0.0295)	(0.0273)	(0.0277)		
Preference for devolution: Defence & foreign affairs							
Discrimination	2.569***	2.739***	2.726***	2.520***	2.754***		
	(0.133)	(0.144)	(0.156)	(0.148)	(0.166)		
Difficulty	1.290***	1.388***	1.449***	1.524***	1.478***		
	(0.0419)	(0.0429)	(0.0475)	(0.0530)	(0.0505)		
Preference for devolution: Taxation							
Discrimination	3.073***	3.501***	3.037***	3.038***	3.064***		
	(0.137)	(0.159)	(0.139)	(0.147)	(0.149)		
Difficulty	0.476***	0.564***	0.452***	0.572***	0.575***		
	(0.0244)	(0.0237)	(0.0250)	(0.0271)	(0.0270)		

Preference for devolution: Police

	(1)	(2)	(3)	(4)	(5)	(6)	(7)
Discrimination	2.185***	2.117***	1.871***	2.069***	1.911***		
	(0.0880)	(0.0827)	(0.0793)	(0.0898)	(0.0839)		
Difficulty	−0.215***	−0.153***	−0.276***	−0.156***	−0.167***		
	(0.0264)	(0.0261)	(0.0300)	(0.0284)	(0.0298)		
Preference for devolution: Justice							
Discrimination	2.564***	2.502***	2.085***	2.436***	2.545***		
	(0.112)	(0.109)	(0.0959)	(0.117)	(0.124)		
Difficulty	0.539***	0.689***	0.703***	0.715***	0.737***		
	(0.0268)	(0.0287)	(0.0332)	(0.0321)	(0.0319)		
Overall devolution preference							
Discrimination	3.721***	3.923***	3.807***	4.243***	3.996***	3.895***	3.458***
	(0.108)	(0.110)	(0.114)	(0.131)	(0.122)	(0.132)	(0.132)
Difficulty (base = There should be no devolved government in Wales)							
≥ *The National Assembly for Wales should have fewer powers*	−0.981***	−0.886***	−0.971***	−0.858***	−0.868***	−0.798***	−0.863***
	(0.0267)	(0.0250)	(0.0272)	(0.0257)	(0.0262)	(0.0271)	(0.0307)
≥ *We should leave things as they are now*	−0.697***	−0.554***	−0.705***	−0.562***	−0.619***	−0.564***	−0.550***
	(0.0239)	(0.0222)	(0.0245)	(0.0231)	(0.0239)	(0.0247)	(0.0273)
≥ *The National Assembly for Wales should have more powers*	0.137***	0.210***	0.0479*	0.125***	0.109***	0.267***	0.328***
	(0.0209)	(0.0204)	(0.0212)	(0.0209)	(0.0213)	(0.0229)	(0.0259)
= *Wales should become independent, separate from the UK*	1.430***	1.423***	1.541***	1.435***	1.422***	1.452***	1.495***
	(0.0350)	(0.0341)	(0.0386)	(0.0363)	(0.0370)	(0.0395)	(0.0447)

* p<0.05 ** p<0.01 *** p<0.001

Appendix to Chapter 10
Identity scale questions

Party identity

Generally speaking, do you think of yourself as Labour, Conservative, Liberal Democrat, or what?

Conservative, Labour, Liberal Democrat, Scottish National Party (SNP) [Scotland only], Plaid Cymru [Wales only], United Kingdom Independence Party (UKIP), Green Party, Other party, No – None

Earlier you said that you tend to identify as [party]. Thinking about this party, how much do you agree with these statements?

When I speak about this party, I usually say 'we' instead of 'they'. I am interested in what other people think about this party. When people criticize this party, it feels like a personal insult. I have a lot in common with other supporters of this party. If this party does badly in opinion polls, my day is ruined.* When I meet someone who supports this party, I feel connected with this person. When I speak about this party, I refer to them as 'my party'.* When people praise this party, it makes me feel good.

Strongly disagree – Disagree – Agree – Strongly agree

* No equivalent referendum identity question asked and so these items are excluded from the scales used to compare referendum identity strength.

EU referendum identity

Thinking about the EU referendum, do you think of yourself as closer to either the 'Leave' or 'Remain' side? If yes, which one?

The remain side – The leave side – Neither

You said that you feel closer to the [EU referendum side]. Thinking about this side, how much do you agree with these statements?

When I speak about the [EU referendum side], I usually say 'we' instead of 'they'. I am interested in what other people think about the [EU referendum side]. When people criticize the [EU referendum side], it feels like a personal insult. I have a lot in common with other supporters of the [EU referendum side]. When I meet someone who supports the [EU referendum side], I feel connected with this person. When people praise the

[EU referendum side], it makes me feel good. If the [EU referendum side] side does badly in opinion polls, my day is ruined*

Strongly disagree – Disagree – Agree – Strongly agree

*Waves 7–9 only and so excluded from the scales used to compare referendum identity strength.

Scottish independence referendum identity

Thinking about the Scottish independence debate, do you think of yourself as closer to either the 'Yes' (pro-independence) or 'No' (anti-independence) side? If yes, which one?

The Yes side – The No side – Neither

You said that you feel closer to the [Scottish referendum side]. Thinking about this side, how much do you agree with these statements?

When I speak about the [Scottish referendum side], I usually say 'we' instead of 'they'. I am interested in what other people think about the [Scottish referendum side]. When people criticize the [Scottish referendum side], it feels like a personal insult. I have a lot in common with other supporters of the [Scottish referendum side]. When I meet someone who supports the [Scottish referendum side], I feel connected with this person. When people praise the [Scottish referendum side], it makes me feel good.

Strongly disagree – Disagree – Agree – Strongly agree

Table A10.1 Linear regression model of feelings towards the Labour and Conservative parties as a function of party and referendum identity strength

	Like Labour	Like Conservatives
Conservative–Labour party identity strength	−1.026***	1.111***
	(0.0137)	(0.0144)
Leave–Remain referendum identity strength	−0.208***	0.312***
	(0.0105)	(0.0111)
Party X referendum identity strength	0.0261***	0.0207***
	(0.00499)	(0.00525)
Constant	4.258***	4.536***
	(0.0266)	(0.0279)
N	7186	7201

* $p<0.05$ ** $p<0.01$ *** $p<0.001$

References

Abramowitz, Alan. 2010. *The Disappearing Center: Engaged Citizens, Polarization, and American Democracy.* New Haven and London: Yale University Press.

Achen, Christopher H, and Larry M. Bartels. 2016. *Democracy for Realists: Why Elections Do Not Produce Responsive Government.* Princeton, New Jersey: Princeton University Press.

Adams, Greg D. 1997. 'Abortion: Evidence of an Issue Evolution.' *American Journal of Political Science* 41 (3): 718. doi:10.2307/2111673.

Adams, James, Jane Green, and Caitlin Milazzo. 2012. 'Who Moves? Elite and Mass-Level Depolarization in Britain, 1987–2001.' *Electoral Studies* 31 (4): 643–55. doi:10.1016/J.ELECTSTUD.2012.07.008.

Adams, James, Lawrence Ezrow, and Zeynep Somer-Topcu. 2014. 'Do Voters Respond to Party Manifestos or to a Wider Information Environment? An Analysis of Mass-Elite Linkages on European Integration.' *American Journal of Political Science* 58 (4): 967–78. doi:10.1111/ajps.12115.

Adams, James, Michael Clark, Lawrence Ezrow, and Garrett Glasgow. 2006. 'Are Niche Parties Different Fundamentally The Causes and the Parties' Western European Parties' Policy Shifts, 1976–1998.' *American Journal of Political Science* 50 (3): 513–29.

Alesina, Alberto, John Londregan, and Howard Rosenthal. 1993. 'A Model of the Political Economy of the United States.' *American Political Science Review* 87 (1): 12–33. doi:10.2307/2938953.

Anderson, Christopher J. 2000. 'Economic Voting and Political Context: A Comparative Perspective.' *Electoral Studies* 19 (2–3): 151–70. doi:10.1016/S0261-3794(99)00045-1.

Arzheimer, Kai. 2017. 'Explaining Electoral Support for the Radical Right.' In *The Oxford Handbook of the Radical Right,* edited by Jens Rydgren, 216–246. Oxford University Press.

Arzheimer, Kai, and Elisabeth Carter. 2006. 'Political Opportunity Structures and Right-Wing Extremist Party Success.' *European Journal of Political Research* 45 (3). Blackwell Publishing Ltd: 419–43. doi:10.1111/j.1475-6765.2006.00304.x.

Ascher, William, and Sidney Tarrow. 1975. 'The Stability of Communist Electorates: Evidence from a Longitudinal Analysis of French and Italian Aggregate Data.' *American Journal of Political Science* 19 (3): 475. doi:10.2307/2110540.

Bale, Tim. 2012. 'The Black Widow Effect: Why Britain's Conservative–Liberal Democrat Coalition Might Have an Unhappy Ending.' *Parliamentary Affairs* 65 (2): 323–37. doi:10.1093/pa/gsr033.

Bankert, Alexa, Leonie Huddy, and Martin Rosema. 2017. 'Measuring Partisanship as a Social Identity in Multi-Party Systems.' *Political Behavior* 39 (1): 103–32. doi:10.1007/s11109-016-9349-5.

Bara, Judith, and Ian Budge. 2001. 'Party Policy and Ideology: Still New Labour?' *Parliamentary Affairs* 54 (4): 590–606. doi:10.1093/parlij/54.4.590.

Bartels, Larry M. 1993. 'Messages Received: The Political Impact of Media Exposure.' *American Political Science Review* 87 (2): 267–85. doi:10.2307/2939040.

Bartels, Larry M. 2000. 'Partisanship and Voting Behavior, 1952–1996.' *American Journal of Political Science* 44 (1). Midwest Political Science Association: 35. doi:10.2307/2669291.

Bartels, Larry M. 2002. 'Beyond the Running Tally: Partisan Bias in Political Perceptions.' *Political Behavior* 24 (2): 117–50. http://www.jstor.org/stable/1558352.

Bartle, John. 2005. 'The Press, Television, and the Internet.' *Parliamentary Affairs* 58 (4): 699–711. doi:10.1093/pa/gsi059.

Baumgartner, Frank R., and Bryan D. Jones. 1993. *Agendas and Instability in American Politics*. Chicago: University of Chicago Press.

BBC News. 2010. 'Gordon Brown "Stepping down as Labour Leader."' *BBC News*. http://news.bbc.co.uk/1/hi/uk_politics/election_2010/8672859.stm.

Berglund, Frode, Sören Sören Holmberg, Hermann Schmitt, and Jacques Thomassen. 2005. 'Party Identification and Party Choice.' In *The European Voter*, edited by Jacques Thomassen, 106–124. Oxford and New York: Oxford University Press.

Bermeo, Nancy, and Jonas Pontusson, eds. 2012. *Coping with Crisis: Government Reactions to the Great Recession*. New York: Russell Sage Foundation.

Billig, Michael. 1978. *Fascists: A Social Psychological View of the National Front*. Harcourt.

Blais, André, Elisabeth Gidengil, Richard Nadeau, and Neil Nevitte. 2001. 'Measuring Party Identification: Britain, Canada, and the United States.' *Political Behavior* 23 (1): 5–22. doi:10.1023/A:1017665513905.

Blau, Peter M., Terry C. Blum, and Joseph E. Schwartz. 1982. 'Heterogeneity and Intermarriage.' *American Sociological Review* 47 (1): 45–62.

Bohman, Andrea, and Mikael Hjerm. 2016. 'In the Wake of Radical Right Electoral Success: A Cross-Country Comparative Study of Anti-Immigration Attitudes over Time.' *Journal of Ethnic and Migration Studies* 42 (11): 1729–1747. doi:10.1080/1369183X.2015.1131607.

Bølstad, Jørgen, Elias Dinas, and Pedro Riera. 2013. 'Tactical Voting and Party Preferences: A Test of Cognitive Dissonance Theory.' *Political Behavior* 35 (3): 429–52. doi:10.1007/s11109-012-9205-1.

Boomgaarden, Hajo G., and Rens Vliegenthart. 2007. 'Explaining the Rise of Anti-Immigrant Parties: The Role of News Media Content.' *Electoral Studies* 26 (2): 404–17. doi:10.1016/j.electstud.2006.10.018.

Boomgaarden, Hajo G., and Rens Vliegenthart. 2009. 'How News Content Influences Anti-Immigration Attitudes: Germany, 1993–2005.' *European Journal of Political Research* 48 (4): 516–42. doi:10.1111/j.1475-6765.2009.01831.x.

Brewer, Mark D. 2005. 'The Rise of Partisanship and the Expansion of Partisan Conflict within the American Electorate.' *Political Research Quarterly* 58 (2): 219. doi:10.2307/3595624.

Budge, Ian, and Dennis Farlie. 1983. *Explaining and Predicting Elections*. London: Allen and Urwin.

Buelens, Jo, and Airo Hino. 2008. 'The Electoral Fate of New Parties in Government.' In *New Parties in Government: In Power for the First Time*, edited by Kris Deschouwer, 157–74. London: Routledge. doi:10.4324/9780203938591.

Burnham, Walter Dean. 1970. *Critical Elections and the Mainsprings of American Politics*. New York: Norton.

Butler, David, and Donald Stokes. 1969. *Political Change in Britain: Forces Shaping Electoral Choice*. Harmondsworth: Palgrave Macmillan.

Butler, David, and Donald Stokes. 1974. *Political Change in Britain, 1963–1970 [Data Collection]*. UK Data Service. doi:10.5255/UKDA-SN-44-1.

Byrne, Liam. 2015. '"I'm Afraid There Is No Money." The Letter I Will Regret for Ever.' *The Guardian*, May 9. https://www.theguardian.com/commentisfree/2015/may/09/liam-byrne-apology-letter-there-is-no-money-labour-general-election.

Campbell, Angus, Philip E. Converse, Warren E. Miller, and Donald E. Stokes. 1960. *The American Voter*. New York, London: John Wiley & Sons.

Campbell, James E. 1992. 'Forecasting the Presidential Vote in the States.' *American Journal of Political Science* 36 (2): 386. doi:10.2307/2111483.

Carmines, Edward G., and James A. Stimson. 1989. *Issue Evolution: Race and the Transformation of American Politics.* Princeton, New Jersey: Princeton University Press.

Carsey, Thomas M., and Geoffrey C Layman. 2006. 'Changing Sides or Changing Minds? Party Identification and Policy Preferences in the American Electorate.' *American Journal of Political Science* 50 (2): 464–77.

Chzhen, Kat, Geoffrey Evans, and Mark Pickup. 2014. 'When Do Economic Perceptions Matter for Party Approval?: Examining the Endogeneity of Economic Perceptions Before and During the Economic Downturn.' *Political Behavior* 36 (2): 291–313. doi:10.1007/s11109-013-9236-2.

Clark, Terry Nichols, and Seymour Martin Lipset. 1991. 'Are Social Classes Dying?' *International Sociology* 6 (4): 397–410. doi:10.1177/026858091006004002.

Clarke, Harold D. 1983. 'The Parti Québécois and Sources of Partisan Realignment in Contemporary Quebec.' *The Journal of Politics* 45 (1): 64–85. doi:10.2307/2130325.

Clarke, Harold D., Peter Kellner, Marianne C. Stewart, Joe Twyman, and Paul Whiteley. 2016. *Austerity and Political Choice in Britain.* Palgrave Macmillan. doi:10.1057/9781137524935.0001.

Clarke, Harold, David Sanders, Marianne Stewart, and Paul Whiteley. 2006. 'British Election Study 2005 [Data Collection].' doi:10.5255/UKDA-SN-5494-1.

Clarke, Harold, David Sanders, Marianne Stewart, and Paul Whiteley. 2014. 'British Election Study Nine-Wave Panel Survey, 2005–2010 [Data Collection].' doi:10.5255/UKDA-SN-6607-2

Clarke, Harold D., and Matthew Lebo. 2003. 'Fractional (Co)Integration and Governing Party Support in Britain.' *British Journal of Political Science* 33 (2): 283–301. doi:10.1017/S0007123403000127.

Clarke, Harold D., and Marianne C. Stewart. 1998. 'The Decline of Parties in the Minds of Citizens.' *Annual Review of Political Science* 1 (1): 357–78. doi:10.1146/annurev.polisci.1.1.357.

Clements, Ben, and John Bartle. 2009. 'The European issue and party choice at British general elections, 1974–2005.' *Journal of Elections, Public Opinion and Parties* 19 (4): 377–411. doi:10.1080/17457280903275188.

Cowley, Philip, and Dennis Kavanagh. 2015. *The British General Election of 2015.* Houndmills, Basingstoke, Hampshire: Palgrave MacMillan.

Crewe, Ivor. 1985. '"Great Britain."' In *Electoral Change in Western Democracies: Patterns and Sources of Electoral Volatility*, edited by Ivor Crewe and David Denver, 100–150. London: Croom Helm.

Crewe, Ivor, and Anthony King. 1995. *SDP: The Birth, Life and Death of the Social Democratic Party.* Oxford and New York: Oxford University Press. doi:10.2307/2657978.

Crewe, Ivor, David Robertson, and Bo Särlvik. 1975. 'British Election Study: EEC Referendum Survey, 1975.' British Election Study. doi:10.5255/UKDA-SN-830-1.

Crewe, Ivor, David Robertson, and Bo Särlvik. 1976. 'British Election Study, 1969, June 1970, February 1974; Panel Survey.' https://beta.ukdataservice.ac.uk/datacatalogue/studies/study?id=422&type=Data catalogue.

Crewe, Ivor, Bo Särlvik, and James Alt. 1977. 'Partisan Dealignment in Britain 1964–1974.' *British Journal of Political Science* 7 (2): 129–90. doi:10.1017/S0007123400000922.

Curtice, John. 1989. 'The 1989 European Election: Protest or Green Tide?' *Electoral Studies* 8 (3): 217–30. doi:10.1016/0261-3794(89)90002-4.

Curtice, John. 2010. 'So What Went Wrong with the Electoral System? The 2010 Election Result and the Debate About Electoral Reform.' *Parliamentary Affairs* 63 (4): 623–38. doi:10.1093/pa/gsq018.

Curtice, John. 2016. 'How Deeply Does Britain's Euroscepticism Run?' *British Social Attitudes* 33. http://whatukthinks.org/eu/analysis/how-deeply-does-britains-euroscepticism-run/.

Curtice, John, Stephen D. Fisher, and Robert Ford. 2016. 'The Results Analysed.' In *The British General Election of 2015*, edited by Philip Cowley and Dennis Kavanagh, 387–431. Houndmills, Basingstoke, Hampshire: Palgrave Macmillan.

Cutts, David. 2014. 'Local Elections as a 'Stepping Stone': Does Winning Council Seats Boost the Liberal Democrats' Performance in General Elections?' *Political Studies* 62 (2): 361–80. doi:10.1111/1467-9248.12029.

Cutts, David, and Andrew Russell. 2015. 'From Coalition to Catastrophe: The Electoral Meltdown of the Liberal Democrats.' *Parliamentary Affairs* 68 (suppl 1): 70–87. doi:10.1093/pa/gsv028.

Dalton, Russel J., S. C. Flanagan, and P. A. Beck. 1985. *Electoral Change in Industrial Democracies: Realignment or Dealignment?* Princeton, New Jersey: Princeton University Press.

Dalton, Russell J. 1984. 'Cognitive Mobilization and Partisan Dealignment in Advanced Industrial Democracies.' *The Journal of Politics* 46 (1): 264–84.

Dalton, Russell J. 2012a. 'Apartisans and the Changing German Electorate.' *Electoral Studies* 31 (1): 35–45. doi:10.1016/j.electstud.2011.06.005.

Dalton, Russell J. 2012b. *The Apartisan American: Dealignment and the Transformation of Electoral Politics.* Washington, DC: CQ Press.

Dalton, Russell J, Ian McAllister, and Martin Wattenberg. 2000. 'The Consequences of Partisan Dealignment.' In *Parties without Partisans: Political Change in Advanced Industrial Democracies*, edited by Russell J. Dalton and Martin Wattenberg, 37–63. Oxford University Press.

Dalton, Russell J. 2000. 'The Decline of Party Identifications.' In *Parties without Partisans: Political Change in Advanced Industrial Democracies*, edited by Russell J. Dalton and Martin Wattenberg, 19–36. Oxford and New York: Oxford University Press.

Dassonneville, Ruth, Marc Hooghe, and Bram Vanhoutte. 2012. 'Age, Period and Cohort Effects in the Decline of Party Identification in Germany: An Analysis of a Two Decade Panel Study in Germany (1992–2009).' *German Politics* 21 (2): 209–27. doi:10.1080/0964 4008.2012.679659.

Denman, Roy. 1995. 'Missed Chances—Britain and Europe in the 20th-Century.' *Political Quarterly* 66 (1): 36–45.

Dinas, Elias. 2013. 'Why Does the Apple Fall Far from the Tree? How Early Political Socialization Prompts Parent-Child Dissimilarity.' *British Journal of Political Science* 44 (4): 1–26. doi:10.1017/S0007123413000033.

Dinas, Elias. 2014. 'Does Choice Bring Loyalty? Electoral Participation and the Development of Party Identification.' *American Journal of Political Science* 58 (2): 449–65. doi:10.1111/ajps.12044.

Druckman, James N, Erik Peterson, and Rune Slothus. 2013. 'How Elite Partisan Polarization Affects Public Opinion Formation.' *American Political Science Review* 107 (1): 57–79. doi:10.1017/S0003055412000500.

Duch, Raymond, Wojtek Przepiorka, and Randolph Stevenson. 2015. 'Responsibility Attribution for Collective Decision Makers.' *American Journal of Political Science* 59 (2): 372–89. doi:10.1111/ajps.12140.

Duch, Raymond, and Randolph Stevenson. 2008. *The Economic Vote: How Political and Economic Institutions Condition Election Results.* Cambridge and New York: Cambridge University Press.

Duch, Raymond, and Randolph Stevenson. 2013. 'Voter Perceptions of Agenda Power and Attribution of Responsibility for Economic Performance.' *Electoral Studies* 32 (3). Pergamon: 512–16. doi:10.1016/J.ELECTSTUD.2013.05.013.

Duck, Julie M., Michael A. Hogg, and Deborah J. Terry. 1995. 'Me, Us and Them: Political Identification and the Third-Person Effect in the 1993 Australian Federal Election.' *European Journal of Social Psychology* 25 (2): 195–215. doi:10.1002/ejsp.2420250206.

Dustmann, Christian, Maria Casanova, Michael Fertig, Ian Preston, and Christoph M. Schmidt. 2003. 'The Impact of EU Enlargement on Migration Flows.' *Home Office Online Report* 25. http://discovery.ucl.ac.uk/14332/1/14332.pdf.

Duverger, Maurice. 1954. *Political Parties, Their Organization and Activity in the Modern State*. London: Methuen.

Eichenberg, Richard C., and Russell J. Dalton. 2007. 'Post-Maastricht Blues: The Transformation of Citizen Support for European Integration, 1973–2004.' *Acta Politica* 42 (2–3): 128–52. doi:10.1057/palgrave.ap.5500182.

Eifert, Benn, Edward Miguel, and Daniel N. Posner. 2010. 'Political Competition and Ethnic Identification in Africa.' *American Journal of Political Science* 54 (2): 494–510. doi:10.1111/j.1540-5907.2010.00443.x.

Eijk, Cees van der, Mark Franklin, Froukje Demant, and Wouter van der Brug. 2007. 'The Endogenous Economy: "Real" Economic Conditions, Subjective Economic Evaluations and Government Support.' *Acta Politica* 42 (1): 1–22. doi:10.1057/palgrave.ap.5500172.

Elsas, Erika J. van, Emily M. Miltenburg, and Tom W.G. van der Meer. 2016. 'If I Recall Correctly. An Event History Analysis of Forgetting and Recollecting Past Voting Behavior.' *Journal of Elections, Public Opinion and Parties*, 26 (3): 253–272. doi:10.1080/17457289.2016.1150286.

Elsas, Erika van, and Wouter van der Brug. 2015. 'The Changing Relationship between Left–right Ideology and Euroscepticism, 1973–2010.' *European Union Politics* 16 (2): 194–215. doi:10.1177/1465116514562918.

Erisen, Cengiz, Milton Lodge, and Charles S. Taber. 2014. 'Affective Contagion in Effortful Political Thinking.' *Political Psychology* 35 (2): 187–206. doi:10.1111/j.1467-9221.2012.00937.x.

Europa.eu. 2011. 'Frequently Asked Questions: The End of Transitional Arrangements for the Free Movement of Workers on 30 April 2011.' *European Commission Press Release Database* MEMO/11/25. http://europa.eu/rapid/press-release_MEMO-11-259_en.htm.

Evans, Geoffrey. 1998. 'Euroscepticism and Conservative Electoral Support: How an Asset Became a Liability.' *British Journal of Political Science* 28 (4): 573–90. doi:10.1017/S0007123498000258.

Evans, Geoffrey. 1999a. 'Europe: A New Electoral Cleavage?' In *Critical Elections: British Parties and Voters in Long-Term Perspective*, edited by Geoffrey Evans and Pippa Norris, 207–22. London: Sage.

Evans, Geoffrey. 1999b. *The End of Class Politics?: Class Voting in Comparative Context*. Oxford University Press.

Evans, Geoffrey. 2002. 'European Integration, Party Politics and Voting in the 2001 Election.' *British Elections & Parties Review* 12 (1): 95–110. doi:10.1080/13689880208413072.

Evans, Geoffrey. 2003. 'Will We Ever Vote for the Euro?' In *British Social Attitudes: Continuity and Change Over Two Decades*, 215–32. London: Sage Publications.

Evans, Geoffrey, and Robert Andersen. 2006. 'The Political Conditioning of Economic Perceptions.' *Journal of Politics* 68 (1): 194–207. doi:10.1111/j.1468-2508.2006.00380.x.

Evans, Geoffrey, and Sarah Butt. 2007. 'Explaining Change in British Public Opinion on the European Union: Top down or Bottom Up?' *Acta Politica* 42 (2–3): 173–90. doi:10.1057/palgrave.ap.5500181.

Evans, Geoffrey, and Kat Chzhen. 2013. 'Explaining Voters' Defection from Labour over the 2005–10 Electoral Cycle: Leadership, Economics and the Rising Importance of Immigration.' *Political Studies* 61 (S1): 138–57. doi:10.1111/1467-9248.12009.

Evans, Geoffrey, Anthony Heath, and Mansur Lalljee. 1996. 'Measuring Left-Right and Libertarian-Authoritarian Values in the British Electorate.' *British Journal of Sociology* 47 (1): 93–112. doi:10.2307/591118.

Evans, Geoffrey, and Jonathan Mellon. 2016a. 'Social Class: Identity, Awareness and Political Attitudes: Why Are We Still Working Class?' *British Social Attitudes* 33: 1–19.

Evans, Geoffrey, and Jonathan Mellon. 2016b. 'Working Class Votes and Conservative Losses: Solving the UKIP Puzzle.' *Parliamentary Affairs* 69 (2): 464–79. doi:10.1093/pa/gsv005.

Evans, Geoffrey, and Jonathan Mellon. 2019. 'Immigration, Euroscepticism, and the Rise and Fall of UKIP.' *Party Politics* 25 (1): 76–87. doi:10.1177/1354068818816969.

Evans, Geoffrey, and Anand Menon. 2017. *Brexit and British Politics*. Cambridge: Polity Press.

Evans, Geoffrey, and Pippa Norris. 1999. *Critical Elections: British Parties and Voters in Long-term Perspective*. London: Sage Publications.

Evans, Geoffrey, and Mark Pickup. 2010. 'Reversing the Causal Arrow: The Political Conditioning of Economic Perceptions in the 2000–2004 U.S. Presidential Election Cycle.' *Journal of Politics* 72 (4): 1236–51. doi:10.1017/S0022381610000654.

Evans, Geoffrey, and James Tilley. 2017. *The New Politics of Class: The Political Exclusion of the British Working Class*. Oxford and New York: Oxford University Press.

Fairclough, Norman. 2000. *New Labour, New Language?* London and New York: Routledge.

Farrell, David M., Ian McAllister, and David Broughton. 1994. 'The Changing British Voter Revisited: Patterns of Election Campaign Volatility Since 1964.' *British Elections and Parties Yearbook* 4 (1): 110–27. doi:10.1080/13689889408412944.

Farrer, Benjamin. 2015. 'Connecting Niche Party Vote Change in First- and Second-Order Elections.' *Journal of Elections, Public Opinion and Parties* 25 (4): 482–503. doi:10.1080/17457289.2015.1063496.

Ferland, Benjamin. 2014. 'How Do Voters' Strategic Behaviors Mediate the Impact of Electoral Systems on the Effective Number of Electoral Parties? An Experimental Study.' *Journal of Elections, Public Opinion and Parties* 24 (3): 265–90. doi:10.1080/17457289.2013.846345.

Fieldhouse, Edward, and David Cutts. 2016. 'Shared Partisanship, Household Norms and Turnout: Testing a Relational Theory of Electoral Participation.' *British Journal of Political Science*, 48 (3): 807–832. doi:10.1017/S0007123416000089.

Fieldhouse, Edward, David Cutts, and Andrew Russell. 2006. 'Neither North nor South: The Liberal Democrat Performance in the 2005 General Election.' *Journal of Elections, Public Opinion and Parties* 16 (1): 77–92. doi:10.1080/13689880500505306.

Fieldhouse, Edward, Jane Green, Geoffrey Evans, Hermann Schmitt, Cees van der Eijk, Jonathan Mellon, and Christopher Prosser. 2015. 'British Election Study 2015 Face-to-Face Post-Election Survey [Data Collection].' doi:10.5255/UKDA-SN-7972-1.

Fieldhouse, Edward, Jane Green, Geoffrey Evans, Hermann Schmitt, Cees van der Eijk, Jonathan Mellon, and Christopher Prosser. 2017. 'British Election Study 2017 Face-to-Face Post-Election Survey [Data Collection].' doi:10.5255/UKDA-SN-8418-1.

Fieldhouse, Edward, Jane Green, Geoffrey Evans, Hermann Schmitt, Cees van der Eijk, Jonathan Mellon, and Christopher Prosser. 2018. 'British Election Study Internet Panel 2014–2018 [Data Collection].' doi:10.5255/UKDA-SN-8202-2.

Fieldhouse, Edward, and Christopher Prosser. 2018. 'The Limits of Partisan Loyalty: How the Scottish Independence Referendum Cost Labour.' *Electoral Studies* 52 (April): 11–25. doi:10.1016/j.electstud.2018.01.002.

Fieldhouse, Edward, N. Shryane, and A. Pickles. 2007. 'Strategic Voting and Constituency Context: Modelling Party Preference and Vote in Multiparty Elections.' *Political Geography* 26 (2). doi:10.1016/j.polgeo.2006.09.005.

Fielding, Nigel. 1981. *The National Front*. London: Routledge.

Fiorina, Morris P. 1981. *Retrospective Voting in American National Elections*. Yale University Press.

Fiorina, Morris P., and Samuel J. Abrams. 2008. 'Political Polarization in the American Public.' *Annual Review of Political Science* 11 (1): 563–88. doi:10.1146/annurev.polisci. 11.053106.153836.

Fiorina, Morris P., Samuel J. Abrams, and Jeremy C Pope. 2006. *Culture War? The Myth of a Polarized America*, 2nd ed., New York and London: Pearson Education.

Firebaugh, Glenn. 1990. 'Replacement Effects, Cohort and Otherwise: Response to Rodgers.' *Sociological Methodology* 20: 439–46.

Firebaugh, Glenn. 1997. *Analyzing Repeated Surveys*. Sage.

Fischer, Manuel. 2015. 'Collaboration Patterns, External Shocks and Uncertainty: Swiss Nuclear Energy Politics before and after Fukushima.' *Energy Policy* 86: 520–28. doi:10.1016/j.enpol.2015.08.007.

Fisher, Stephen D., and John Curtice. 2006. 'Tactical Unwind? Changes in Party Preference Structure and Tactical Voting in Britain between 2001 and 2005.' *Journal of Elections, Public Opinion & Parties* 16 (1): 55–76. doi:10.1080/13689880500505231.

Fisher, Stephen D., and Sara B Hobolt. 2010. 'Coalition Government and Electoral Accountability.' *Electoral Studies* 29 (3): 358–69. doi:10.1016/j.electstud.2010.03.003.

Ford, Robert, and Matthew Goodwin. 2014. *Revolt on the Right: Explaining Support for the Radical Right in Britain*. London and New York: Routledge.

Forster, Anthony. 2002. 'Anti-Europeans, Anti-Marketeers and Eurosceptics: The Evolution and Influence of Labour and Conservative Opposition to Europe.' *The Political Quarterly* 73 (3): 299–308. doi:10.1111/1467-923X.00470.

Fowler, Anthony, and Andrew B. Hall. 2018. 'Do Shark Attacks Influence Presidential Elections? Reassessing a Prominent Finding on Voter Competence.' *Journal of Politics* 80 (4): 1423–1437.

Fowler, Anthony, and B. Pablo Montagnes. 2015. 'College Football, Elections, and False-Positive Results in Observational Research.' *Proceedings of the National Academy of Sciences* 112 (45): 13800–804. doi:10.1073/pnas.1502615112.

Franklin, Mark N., and Anthony Mughan. 1978. 'The Decline of Class Voting in Britain: Problems of Analysis and Interpretation.' *American Political Science Review* 72 (2): 523–34. doi:10.2307/1954108.

Franklin, Mark N, Richard G. Niemi, and Guy D. Whitten. 1994. 'The Two Faces of Tactical Voting.' *American Journal of Political Science* 24 (4): 549–57. doi:10.2307/2111154.

Gaines, Brian J., James H. Kuklinski, Paul J. Quirk, Buddy Peyton, and Jay Verkuilen. 2007. 'Same Facts, Different Interpretations: Partisan Motivation and Opinion on Iraq.' *Journal of Politics* 69 (4): 957–74.

Gerard, Liz. 2016. 'The Press and Immigration: Reporting the News or Fanning the Flames of Hatred?' *SubScribe*. http://www.sub-scribe.co.uk/2016/09/the-press-and-immigration-reporting.html.

Gerber, Alan S., and Gregory A. Huber. 2009. 'Partisanship and Economic Behavior: Do Partisan Differences in Economic Forecasts Predict Real Economic Behavior?' *American Political Science Review* 103 (3): 407–26. doi:10.1017/S0003055409990098.

Glenn, Norval. 2005. *Cohort Analysis*. Sage.

Goertz, Gary, and Paul F. Diehl. 1995. 'The Initiation and Termination of Enduring Rivalries: The Impact of Political Shocks.' *American Journal of Political Science* 39 (1): 30–52. doi:10.2307/2111756.

Gonthier, Frederic. 2017. 'Parallel Publics? Support for Income Redistribution in Times of Economic Crisis.' *European Journal of Political Research* 56 (1): 92–114. doi:10.1111/1475-6765.12168.

Goodwin, Matthew, and Caitlin Milazzo. 2017. 'Taking Back Control? Investigating the Role of Immigration in the 2016 Vote for Brexit.' *The British Journal of Politics and International Relations* 19 (3): 450–64. doi:10.1177/1369148117710799.

Goren, Paul, and Christopher Chapp. 2017. 'Moral Power: How Public Opinion on Culture War Issues Shapes Partisan Predispositions and Religious Orientations.' *American Political Science Review* 111 (1): 110–28. doi:10.1017/S0003055416000435.

Grasso, Maria Teresa, Stephen Farrall, Emily Gray, Colin Hay, and Will Jennings. 2017. 'Thatcher's Children, Blair's Babies, Political Socialization and Trickle-down Value Change: An Age, Period and Cohort Analysis.' *British Journal of Political Science*, 1–20. doi:10.1017/S0007123416000375.

Green, Donald, Bradley Palmquist, and Eric Schickler. 2002. *Partisan Hearts and Minds: Political Parties and the Social Identities of Voters*. New Haven and London: Yale University Press.

Green, Jane. 2010. 'Strategic Recovery? The Conservatives Under David Cameron.' *Parliamentary Affairs* 63 (4): 667–88. doi:10.1093/pa/gsq027.

Green, Jane. 2007. 'When Voters and Parties Agree: Valence Issues and Party Competition.' *Political Studies* 55: 629–55. doi:10.1111/j.1467-9248.2007.00671.x.

Green, Jane. 2015. 'Party and Voter Incentives at the Crowded Centre of British Politics.' *Party Politics* 21 (1): 80–99. doi:10.1177/1354068812472569.

Green, Jane, Ed Fieldhouse, and Chris Prosser. 2015. 'Coalition in a Plurality System: Explaining Party System Fragmentation in Britain.' UC Berkeley British Politics Group Conference.

Green, Jane, and Sara B. Hobolt. 2008. 'Owning the Issue Agenda: Party Strategies and Vote Choices in British Elections.' *Electoral Studies* 27 (3): 460–76. doi:10.1016/j.electstud.2008.02.003.

Green, Jane, and Will Jennings. 2012. 'The Dynamics of Issue Competence and Vote for Parties in and out of Power: An Analysis of Valence in Britain, 1979–1997.' *European Journal of Political Research* 51 (4): 469–503. doi:10.1111/j.1475-6765.2011.02004.x.

Green, Jane, and Will Jennings. 2017. *The Politics of Competence: Parties, Public Opinion, and Voters*. Cambridge: Cambridge University Press. doi:10.1017/9781316662557.

Green, Jane, and Christopher Prosser. 2016. 'Party System Fragmentation and Single-Party Government: The British General Election of 2015.' *West European Politics* 39 (6): 1299–1310. doi:10.1080/01402382.2016.1173335.

Greene, Steven. 1999. 'Understanding Party Identification: A Social Identity Approach.' *Political Psychology* 20 (2): 393–403.

Greene, Steven. 2004. 'Social Identity Theory and Party Identification.' *Social Science Quarterly* 85 (1): 136–53. doi:10.1111/j.0038-4941.2004.08501010.x.

Grossman, Peter Z. 2015. 'Energy Shocks, Crises and the Policy Process: A Review of Theory and Application.' *Energy Policy* 77: 56–69. doi:10.1016/j.enpol.2014.11.010.

Hall, Peter A. 1993. 'Policy Paradigms, Social Learning, and the State: The Case of Economic Policymaking in Britain.' *Comparative Politics* 25 (3): 275. doi:10.2307/422246.

Harding, Roger. 2017. 'British Social Attitudes 34—A Kind-Hearted but Not Soft-Hearted Country,' 14. http://www.bsa.natcen.ac.uk/media/39195/bsa34_key-findings.pdf.

Haslam, S. Alexander, Stephen D. Reicher, and Michael J. Platow. 2010. *The New Psychology of Leadership: Identity, Influence and Power.* New Ed. Hove, East Sussex England; New York: Psychology Press.

Hazell, Robert, and Ben Yong. 2012. *Politics of Coalition: How the Conservative-Liberal Democrat Government Works.* Oxford: Hart Publishing.

Healy, A. J., N. Malhotra, and C. H. Mo. 2010. 'Irrelevant Events Affect Voters' Evaluations of Government Performance.' *Proceedings of the National Academy of Sciences* 107 (29): 12804–9. doi:10.1073/pnas.1007420107.

Healy, Andrew J., Mikael Persson, and Erik Snowberg. 2017. 'Digging into the Pocketbook: Evidence on Economic Voting from Income Registry Data Matched to a Voter Survey.' *American Political Science Review* 111 (4): 1–15. doi:10.1017/S0003055417000314.

Heath, Anthony, Geoffrey Evans, and Jean Martin. 1994. 'The Measurement of Core Beliefs and Values: The Development of Balanced Socialist / Laissez Faire and Libertarian / Authoritarian Scales.' *British Journal of Political Science* 24 (1): 115–32.

Heath, Anthony, Roger Jowell, and John Curtice. 1985. *How Britain Votes.* Oxford: Pergamon.

Heath, Anthony, Roger Jowell, and John Curtice. 1998. 'British Election Panel Study, 1992–1997 [Data Collection].' doi:10.5255/UKDA-SN-3888-1

Heath, Anthony, Roger Jowell, and John Curtice. 1999. 'British Election Study Panel, 1983, 1986, 1987 [Data Collection].' doi:10.5255/UKDA-SN-4000-1

Heath, Anthony, Roger Jowell, and John Curtice. 2002. 'British Election Panel Study, 1997–2001 [Data Collection].' doi:10.5255/UKDA-SN-4028-1

Heath, Anthony, Roger Jowell, John Curtice, Jack Brand, and John C. Mitchell. 1993. 'British General Election Panel Study, 1987–1992 [Data Collection].' doi:10.5255/UKDA-SN-2983-1

Heath, Anthony, Roger Jowell, John Curtice, and Geoffrey Evans. 1990. 'The Rise of the New Political Agenda?' *European Sociological Review* 6 (1). http://esr.oxfordjournals.org/content/6/1/31.short.

Heath, Anthony, Roger Jowell, Bridget Taylor, and Katarina Thomson. 1998. 'Euroscepticism and the Referendum Party.' *British Elections & Parties Review* 8 (1): 95–110. doi:10.1080/13689889808413007.

Heath, Oliver. 2015. 'Policy Representation, Social Representation and Class Voting in Britain.' *British Journal of Political Science* 45 (1): 173–93. doi:10.1017/S0007123413000318.

Hellwig, Timothy, and Dani M. Marinova. 2015. 'More Misinformed than Myopic: Economic Retrospections and the Voter's Time Horizon.' *Political Behavior* 37 (4): 865–87. doi:10.1007/s11109-014-9295-z.

Henderson, Ailsa, James Mitchell, Robert Johns, and Christopher Carman. 2014. 'Scottish Referendum Study: Pre-Referendum Wave [Computer File].' doi:10.5255/UKDA-SN-8402-1

Hetherington, Marc, and Jonathan Weiler. 2009. *Authoritarianism and Polarization in American Politics.* Cambridge and New York: Cambridge University Press.

Hino, Airo. 2012. *New Challenger Parties in Western Europe: A Comparative Analysis.* Abingdon: Routledge.

Hobolt, Sara B. 2016. 'The Brexit Vote: A Divided Nation, a Divided Continent.' *Journal of European Public Policy* 23 (9): 1259–77. doi:10.1080/13501763.2016.1225785.

Hobolt, Sara B., Thomas J. Leeper, and James Tilley. 2018. 'Divided by the Vote: Affective Polarization in the Wake of Brexit.' http://ukandeu.ac.uk/emerging-brexit-identities/.

Hobolt, Sara B, and James Tilley. 2016. 'Fleeing the Centre: The Rise of Challenger Parties in the Aftermath of the Euro Crisis.' *West European Politics* 39 (5): 971–91. doi:10.1080/01 402382.2016.1181871.

Hogg, Michael A. 2001. 'A Social Identity Theory of Leadership.' *Personality and Social Psychology Review* 5 (3): 184–200. doi:10.1207/S15327957PSPR0503_1.

Hooghe, L., G. Marks, and C. J. Wilson. 2002. 'Does Left/Right Structure Party Positions on European Integration?' *Comparative Political Studies* 35 (8): 965–89. doi:10.1177/ 001041402236310.

Hopmann, David Nicolas, Rens Vliegenthart, Claes de Vreese, and Erik Albæk. 2010. 'Effects of Election News Coverage: How Visibility and Tone Influence Party Choice.' *Political Communication* 27 (4): 389–405. doi:10.1080/10584609.2010.516798.

Huckfeldt, Robert, and John D. Sprague. 1995. *Citizens, Politics, and Social Communication: Information and Influence in an Election Campaign*. Cambridge: Cambridge University Press.

Huddy, Leonie. 2001. 'From Social to Political Identity: A Critical Examination of Social Identity Theory.' *Political Psychology* 22 (1): 127–56. doi:10.1111/0162-895X.00230.

Huddy, Leonie. 2013. 'From Group Identity to Political Cohesion and Commitment.' In *The Oxford Handbook of Political Psychology*, edited by Leonie Huddy, David O. Sears, and Jack S. Levy, 2nd ed., 737–73. Oxford: Oxford University Press.

Huddy, Leonie, Lilliana Mason, and Lene Aarøe. 2015. 'Expressive Partisanship: Campaign Involvement, Political Emotion, and Partisan Identity.' *American Political Science Review* 109 (1): 1–17. doi:10.1017/S0003055414000604.

Ignazi, Piero. 2003. *Extreme Right Parties in Western Europe*. Oxford: Oxford University Press.

Inglehart, Ronald. 1981. 'Post-Materialism in an Environment of Insecurity.' *American Political Science Review* 75 (4): 880–900.

Ivarsflaten, Elisabeth. 2005. 'Threatened by Diversity: Why Restrictive Asylum and Immigration Policies Appeal to Western Europeans.' *Journal of Elections, Public Opinion & Parties* 15 (1): 21–45. doi:10.1080/13689880500064577.

Jennings, Will. 2009. 'The Public Thermostat, Political Responsiveness and Error-Correction: Border Control and Asylum in Britain, 1994–2007.' *British Journal of Political Science* 39 (4): 847–70. doi:10.1017/S000712340900074X.

Jennings, Will, and Gerry Stoker. 2017. 'Tilting Towards the Cosmopolitan Axis? Political Change in England and the 2017 General Election.' *Political Quarterly* 88 (3): 359–69. doi:10.1111/1467-923X.12403.

Jensen, Christian B., and Jae Jae Spoon. 2010. 'Thinking Locally, Acting Supranationally: Niche Party Behaviour in the European Parliament.' *European Journal of Political Research* 49 (2): 174–201. doi:10.1111/j.1475-6765.2009.01875.x.

Johnson, Craig. 2014. 'The Importance of Local Parties and Incumbency to the Electoral Prospects of the Liberal Democrats.' *Politics* 34 (3): 201–12. doi:10.1111/1467-9256.12049.

Johnston, R J. 1987. 'Dealignment, Volatitility, and Electoral Geography.' *Studies in Comparative International Development* 22 (3): 3–25.

Johnston, Ron, and Charles Pattie. 2011. 'Where Did Labour's Votes Go? Valence Politics and Campaign Effects at the 2010 British General Election.' *British Journal of Politics and International Relations* 13 (3): 283–303. doi:10.1111/j.1467-856X.2011.00454.x.

Kaufmann, Eric. 2016. 'It's NOT the Economy, Stupid: Brexit as a Story of Personal Values.' *LSE European Politics and Policy (EUROPP) Blog*, 1–5. http://blogs.lse.ac.uk/ politicsandpolicy/personal-values-brexit-vote/%5Cnhttp://eprints.lse.ac.uk/71585/.

Kaufmann, Eric. 2017. 'Levels or Changes?: Ethnic Context, Immigration and the UK Independence Party Vote.' *Electoral Studies* 48: 57–69. doi:10.1016/j.electstud.2017.05.002.

Kawalerowicz, Juta. 2016. 'Too Many Immigrants: What Shapes Perceptions and Attitudes towards Immigrants in England and Wales?' https://www.academia.edu/15012421/Too_many_immigrants_What_shapes_peoples_perception_and_attitudes_towards_immigrants_in_the_United_Kingdom.

Kayser, Mark Andreas, and Christopher Wlezien. 2011. 'Performance Pressure: Patterns of Partisanship and the Economic Vote.' *European Journal of Political Research* 50 (3): 365–94. doi:10.1111/j.1475-6765.2010.01934.x.

Kellstedt, Paul M. 2003. *The Mass Media and the Dynamics of American Racial Attitudes*. *The Mass Media and the Dynamics of American Racial Attitudes*. Cambridge and New York: Cambridge University Press. doi:10.1017/CBO9780511615634.

Kernell, Samuel. 1978. 'Explaining Presidential Popularity: How Ad Hoc Theorizing, Misplaced Emphasis, and Insufficient Care in Measuring One's Variables Refuted Common Sense and Led Conventional Wisdom Down the Path of Anomalies.' *American Political Science Review* 72 (2): 506–22. doi:10.2307/1954107.

Key, V. O. 1955. 'A Theory of Critical Elections.' Journal of Politics 17 (1): 3–18. doi:10.2307/2126401.

King, Gary, and Margaret E. Roberts. 2015. 'How Robust Standard Errors Expose Methodological Problems They Do Not Fix, and What to Do about It.' *Political Analysis* 23 (2): 159–79. doi:10.1093/pan/mpu015.

King, Gary, Benjamin Schneer, and Ariel White. 2017. 'How the News Media Activate Public Expression and Influence National Agendas.' *Science* 358 (6364): 776–80. doi:10.1126/science.aao1100.

Kitschelt, Herbert. 1988. 'Left-Libertarian Parties: Explaining Innovation in Competitive Party Systems.' *World Politics* 40 (2): 194–234.

Kitschelt, Herbert. 1995. *The Radical Right in Western Europe*. Ann Arbor: University of Michigan Press.

Klingeren, Marijn Van, Hajo G. Boomgaarden, Rens Vliegenthart, and Claes H. De Vreese. 2015. 'Real World Is Not Enough: The Media as an Additional Source of Negative Attitudes toward Immigration, Comparing Denmark and the Netherlands.' *European Sociological Review* 31 (3): 268–83. doi:10.1093/esr/jcu089.

Kramer, Gerald H. 1971. 'Short-Term Fluctuations in U. S. Voting Behavior, 1896–1964.' *American Political Science Review* 65 (1): 131–43.

Laakso, Markku, and Rein Taagepera. 1979. "Effective' Number of Parties: A Measure with Application to West Europe.' *Comparative Political Studies* 12 (1): 3–27. doi:10.1177/001041407901200101.

Lau, Richard R., and David P. Redlawsk. 2001. 'Advantages and Disadvantages of Cognitive Heuristics in Political Decision Making.' *American Journal of Political Science* 45 (4): 951–71. doi:10.2307/2669334.

Lewis-Beck, Michael S. 1990. *Economics and Elections: The Major Western Democracies*. Ann Arbor: University of Michigan Press.

Lewis-Beck, Michael S., and Mary Stegmaier. 2000. 'Economic Determinants of Electoral Outcomes.' *Annual Review of Political Science* 3 (1): 183–219. doi:10.1146/annurev.polisci.3.1.183.

Lindaman, Kara, and Donald P. Haider-Markel. 2002. 'Issue Evolution, Political Parties, and the Culture Wars.' *Political Research Quarterly* 55 (1): 91. doi:10.2307/3088067.

Lipset, Seymour Martin, and Stein Rokkan, eds. 1967. *Party Systems and Voter Alignemets*. New York: Free Press.

Lodge, Milton, and Charles S. Taber. 2005. 'The Automaticity of Affect for Political Leaders, Groups, and Issues: An Experimental Test of the Hot Cognition Hypothesis.' *Political Psychology* 26 (3): 455–82.

Lodge, Milton, and Charles S. Taber. 2013. *The Rationalizing Voter*. Cambridge and New York: Cambridge University Press.

Lubbers, Marcel, Merove Gijsberts, and Peer Scheepers. 2002. 'Extreme Right-Wing Voting in Western Europe.' *European Journal of Political Research* 41 (3): 345–78. doi:10.1111/1475-6765.00015.

MacAllister, Iain, Edward Fieldhouse, and Andrew Russell. 2002. 'Yellow Fever? The Political Geography of Liberal Voting in Great Britain.' *Political Geography* 21 (4): 421–47. doi:10.1016/S0962-6298(01)00077-4.

Mader, Matthias, and Harald Schoen. 2018. 'The European Refugee Crisis, Party Competition, and Voters' Responses in Germany.' *West European Politics* 42 (1): 67–90. doi:10.1080/01402382.2018.1490484.

Markus, Gregory B., and Philip E. Converse. 1979. 'A Dynamic Simultaneous Equation Model of Electoral Choice.' *The American Political Science Review* 73 (4): 1055–70.

Martin, Lanny W., and Georg Vanberg. 2008. 'Coalition Government and Political Communication.' *Political Research Quarterly* 61 (3): 502–16. doi:10.1177/1065912907308348.

Martin, Nicole, and Jonathan Mellon. 2018. 'The Puzzle of High Political Partisanship among Ethnic Minority Young People in Great Britain.' *Journal of Ethnic and Migration Studies*. doi:10.1080/1369183X.2018.1539285.

Martin, Ron. 2012. 'Regional Economic Resilience, Hysteresis and Recessionary Shocks.' *Journal of Economic Geography* 12 (1): 1–32. doi:10.1093/jeg/lbr019.

Mason, Lilliana. 2015. ' " I Disrespectfully Agree": The Differential Effects of Partisan Sorting on Social and Issue Polarization.' *American Journal of Political Science* 59 (1): 128–45. doi:10.1111/ajps.12089.

Mason, Lilliana. 2016. 'A Cross-Cutting Calm: How Social Sorting Drives Affective Polarization.' *Public Opinion Quarterly* 80 (S1): 351–77. doi:10.1093/poq/nfw001.

Mayhew, David R. 2000. 'Electoral Realignments.' Annual Review of Political Science 3 (1): 449–74. doi:10.1146/annurev.polisci.3.1.449.

McEnhill, Libby. 2015. 'Unity and Distinctiveness in UK Coalition Government: Lessons for Junior Partners.' *The Political Quarterly* 86 (1): 101–9. doi:10.1111/1467-923X.12147.

McEwen, Nicola. 2018. 'Brexit and Scotland: Between Two Unions.' *British Politics* 13 (1): 65–78. doi:10.1057/s41293-017-0066-4.

McFadden, Daniel. 1979. 'Quantitative Methods for Analyzing Travel Behaviour on Individuals.' In *Behavioural Travel Modelling*, edited by David Hensher and Peter Stopher, 279–318. London: Croom Helm.

McGrath, Mary C. 2017. 'Economic Behavior and the Partisan Perceptual Screen.' *Quarterly Journal of Political Science* 11 (4): 363–83. doi:10.1561/100.00015100.

McHarg, Aileen, and James Mitchell. 2017. 'Brexit and Scotland.' *The British Journal of Politics and International Relations* 19 (3): 512–26. doi:10.1177/1369148117711674.

McLaren, Lauren M. 2002. 'Public Support for the European Union: Cost/Benefit Analysis or Perceived Cultural Threat?' *The Journal of Politics* 64 (2): 551–66. doi:10.1111/1468-2508.00139.

McLaren, Lauren M. 2006. *Identity, Interests and Attitudes to European Integration*. Basingstoke: Palgrave Macmillan. doi:10.1057/9780230504240.

Meguid, Bonnie M. 2008. *Party Competition between Unequals: Strategies and Electoral Fortunes in Western Europe*. Cambridge and New York: Cambridge University Press.

Mellon, Jonathan, Geoffrey Evans, Edward Fieldhouse, Jane Green, and Christopher Prosser. 2018a. 'Brexit or Corbyn? Campaign and Inter-Election Vote Switching in the 2017 UK General Election.' *Parliamentary Affairs* 71 (4): 719–37. doi:10.1093/pa/gsy001

Mellon, Jonathan, Geoffrey Evans, Edward Fieldhouse, Jane Green, and Christopher Prosser. 2018b. 'Aggregate Turnout Is Mismeasured.' https://papers.ssrn.com/sol3/papers.cfm?abstract_id=3098436.

Mellon, Jonathan, and Christopher Prosser. 2017. 'Missing Non-Voters and Misweighted Samples: Explaining the 2015 Great British Polling Miss.' *Public Opinion Quarterly* 81 (3): 661–687. doi:10.1093/poq/nfx015.

Mellon, Jonathan, Christopher Prosser, Jordan Urban, and Adam Feldman. 2018. 'Which Promises Actually Matter? Understanding Promissory Representation with Conjoint Analysis of Election Pledges.' https://papers.ssrn.com/sol3/papers.cfm?abstract_id=3283813.

Meyer, Marco, and Harald Schoen. 2017. 'Avoiding Vote Loss by Changing Policy Positions: The Fukushima Disaster, Party Responses, and the German Electorate.' *Party Politics* 23 (4): 424–36. doi:10.1177/1354068815602145.

Meyer, Thomas M., and Daniel Strobl. 2016. 'Voter Perceptions of Coalition Policy Positions in Multiparty Systems.' *Electoral Studies* 41: 80–91. doi:10.1016/j.electstud.2015.11.020.

Michelitch, Kristin, and Stephen Utych. 2018. 'Electoral Cycle Fluctuations in Partisanship: Global Evidence from Eighty-Six Countries.' *Journal of Politics* 80 (2). doi:10.1086/694783.

Miller, W. L., S. Tagg, and K. Britto. 1986. 'Partisanship and Party Preference in Government and Opposition: The Mid-term Perspective.' *Electoral Studies* 5 (1): 31–46. https://www.sciencedirect.com/science/article/pii/0261379486900272.

Mueller, John E. 1970. 'Presidential Popularity from Truman to Johnson.' *American Political Science Review* 64 (1): 18–34. doi:10.2307/1955610.

Mullen, Brian, Rupert Brown, and Colleen Smith. 1992. 'Ingroup Bias as a Function of Salience, Relevance, and Status: An Integration.' *European Journal of Social Psychology* 22 (2): 103–22. doi:10.1002/ejsp.2420220202.

Muller-Rommel, Ferdinand. 1993. *Grüne Parteien in Westeuropa*. Wiesbaden: Westdeutscher Verlag.

Murphy, Justin, and Daniel Devine. 2018. 'Does Media Coverage Drive Public Support for UKIP or Does Public Support for UKIP Drive Media Coverage?' *British Journal of Political Science*: 1–18. doi:10.1017/S0007123418000145.

Murray, James. 2010. 'Election 2010: Green Party Downplays Talk of 'Rainbow Coalition.'' *The Guardian*. https://www.theguardian.com/environment/2010/may/11/green-party-downplay-rainbow-coalition.

Nadeau, Richard, Richard G. Niemi, David P. Fan, and Timothy Amato. 1999. 'Elite Economic Forecasts, Economic News, Mass Economic Judgments, and Presidential Approval.' *Journal of Politics* 61 (1): 109–35. doi:10.2307/2647777.

Nairn, Tom. 1972. 'The European Problem.' *New Left Review* 75: 5–120.

NatCen Social Research, and Social and Community Planning Research. 2017. 'British Social Attitudes 1983–2017. [Data Collection].' doi:10.5255/UKDA-SN-8450-1.

Newman, Benjamin J. 2013. 'Acculturating Contexts and Anglo Opposition to Immigration in the United States.' *American Journal of Political Science* 57 (2): 374–90. doi:10.1111/j.1540-5907.2012.00632.x.

Nieuwbeerta, Paul, and Nan Dirk De Graaf. 1999. 'Traditional Class Voting in Twenty Postwar Societies.' In *The End of Class Politics?*, edited by Geoffrey Evans, 23–56. Oxford: Oxford University Press.

Norris, Pippa. 1997. *Electoral Change since 1945.* Oxford: Blackwell.

Oppermann, Kai. 2008. 'The Blair Government and Europe: The Policy of Containing the Salience of European Integration.' *British Politics* 3 (2): 156–82. doi:10.1057/bp.2008.1.

Oppermann, Kai. 2013. 'The Politics of Discretionary Government Commitments to European Integration Referendums.' *Journal of European Public Policy* 20 (5): 684–701. doi:10.1080/13501763.2012.751715.

Ostrom, Charles W., and Dennis M. Simon. 1985. 'Promise and Performance: A Dynamic Model of Presidential Popularity.' *American Political Science Review* 79 (2): 334–58. doi:10.2307/1956653.

Pedersen, Mogens N. 1979. 'The Dynamics of European Party Systems: Changing Patterns of Electoral Volatility.' *European Journal of Political Research* 7 (1): 1–26. doi:10.1111/j.1475-6765.1979.tb01267.x.

Petrocik, John R. 1996. 'Issue Ownership in Presidential Elections, with a 1980 Case Study.' *American Journal of Political Science* 40 (3): 825–50. doi:10.1111/j.1540-5907.2005.00144.x.

Pickard, Jim, and George Parker. 2017. 'Labour Draws up Most Leftwing Manifesto since Michael Foot Years.' *Financial Times.* https://www.ft.com/content/0914c192-24cc-11e7-a34a-538b4cb30025.

Pickup, Mark, and Geoffrey Evans. 2013. 'Addressing the Endogeneity of Economic Evaluations in Models of Political Choice.' *Public Opinion Quarterly* 77 (3): 735–54. doi:10.1093/poq/nft028.

Pierson, Paul. 2000. 'Increasing Returns, Path Dependence, and the Study of Politics.' *American Political Science Review* 94 (2): 251–67. doi:10.2307/2586011.

Plutzer, Eric. 2002. 'Becoming a Habitual Voter: Inertia, Resources, and Growth in Young Adulthood.' *American Political Science Review* 96 (1).

Prindle, David F. 2012. 'Importing Concepts from Biology into Political Science: The Case of Punctuated Equilibrium.' *Policy Studies Journal* 40 (1): 21–44. doi:10.1111/j.1541-0072.2011.00432.x.

Prosser, Christopher. 2016a. 'Calling European Union Treaty Referendums: Electoral and Institutional Politics.' *Political Studies* 64 (1): 182–99. doi:10.1111/1467-9248.12176.

Prosser, Christopher. 2016b. 'Second Order Electoral Rules and National Party Systems: The Duvergerian Effects of European Parliament Elections.' *European Union Politics* 17 (3): 366–86. doi:10.1177/1465116516633300.

Prosser, Christopher. 2016c. 'Do Local Elections Predict the Outcome of the next General Election? Forecasting British General Elections from Local Election National Vote Share Estimates.' *Electoral Studies* 41: 274–78. doi:10.1016/j.electstud.2015.11.008.

Prosser, Christopher. 2016d. 'Dimensionality, Ideology and Party Positions towards European Integration.' *West European Politics* 39 (4): 731–54. doi:10.1080/01402382.2015.1116199.

Prosser, Christopher. 2017. 'What Was It All about? The 2017 Election Campaign in Voters' Own Words.' *British Election Study.* http://www.britishelectionstudy.com/bes-findings/what-was-it-all-about-the-2017-election-campaign-in-voters-own-words.

Prosser, Christopher. 2018. 'The Strange Death of Multi-Party Britain: The UK General Election of 2017.' *West European Politics* 41 (5). doi:10.1080/01402382.2018.1424838.

Prosser, Christopher, Edward A. Fieldhouse, Jane Green, Jonathan Mellon, and Geoffrey Evans. 2018. 'Tremors But No Youthquake: Measuring Changes in the Age and Turnout

Gradients at the 2015 and 2017 British General Elections.' https://papers.ssrn.com/sol3/papers.cfm?abstract_id=3111839.

Prosser, Christopher, Jonathan Mellon, and Jane Green. 2016. 'What Mattered Most to You When Deciding How to Vote in the EU Referendum?' http://www.britishelectionstudy.com/bes-findings/what-mattered-most-to-you-when-deciding-how-to-vote-in-the-eu-referendum/#.WzUJtqdKhaQ.

Quinn, Thomas, Judith Bara, and John Bartle. 2011. 'The UK Coalition Agreement of 2010: Who Won?' *Journal of Elections, Public Opinion and Parties* 21 (2): 295–312. doi:10.1080/17457289.2011.562610.

Rattinger, Hans, and Elena Wiegand. 2014. 'Volatility on the Rise? Attitudinal Stability, Attitudinal Change, and Voter Volatility.' In *Voters on the Move or on the Run?*, 287–308. Oxford: Oxford University Press. doi:10.1093/acprof:oso/9780199662630.003.0013.

Redlawsk, David P. 2002. 'Hot Cognition or Cool Consideration? Testing the Effects of Motivated Reasoning on Political Decision Making.' *Journal of Politics* 64 (04): 1021–44. doi:10.1111/1468-2508.00161.

RePass, David E. 1971. 'Issue Salience and Party Choice.' *American Political Science Review* 65 (2): 389–400. doi:10.2307/1954456.

Rodgers, Willard L. 1990. 'Interpreting the Components of Time Trends.' *Sociological Methodology* 20: 421–38.

Rodrik, Dani. 1999. 'Where Did All the Growth Go? External Shocks, Growth Collapses and Social Conflicts.' *Journal of Economic Growth* 4: 385–412.

Rosenbaum, Paul R. 1984. 'The Consequences of Adjustment for a Concomitant Variable That Has Been Affected by the Treatment.' *Journal of the Royal Statistical Society. Series A (General)* 147 (5): 656. doi:10.2307/2981697.

Rosenstone, Steven J, and John Mark Hansen. 1993. *Mobilization, Participation, and Democracy in America*. New York: Macmillan.

Russell, Andrew. 2010. 'Inclusion, Exclusion or Obscurity? The 2010 General Election and the Implications of the Con–Lib Coalition for Third-Party Politics in Britain.' *British Politics* 5 (4): 506–24. doi:10.1057/bp.2010.24.

Russell, Andrew, and Edward Fieldhouse. 2005. *Neither Left nor Right?: The Liberal Democrats and the Electorate*. Manchester: Manchester University Press.

Russell, Andrew, Edward Fieldhouse, and Iain MacAllister. 2002. 'The Anatomy of Liberal Support in Britain, 1974–1997.' *Political Studies* 4 (1): 49–74. doi:10.1111/1467-856X.41070.

Sanders, David, and Paul Whiteley. 2014a. 'British Election Study, 2010: Face-to-Face Survey [Data Collection].' doi:10.5255/UKDA-SN-7529-1.

Sanders, David, and Paul Whiteley. 2014b. 'British Election Study Continuous Monitoring Survey Cumulative File, 2004–2013 [Data Collection].' http://www.bes2009-10.org/. http://www.bes2009-10.org/updec13z.zip.

Sanders, David, Paul Whiteley, Harold Clarke, and Marianne Stewart. 2002. 'British Election Study Cross-Section 2001 [Data Collection].' doi:10.5255/UKDA-SN-4619-1.

Särlvik, Bo, and Ivor Crewe. 1983. *Decade of Dealignment: The Conservative Victory of 1979 and Electoral Trends in the 1970s*. Cambridge: Cambridge University Press.

Särlvik, Bo, David Robertson, and Ivor Crewe. 1981. 'British Election Study, February 1974, October 1974, June 1975, May 1979; Panel Survey [Data Collection].' doi:10.5255/UKDA-SN-1614-1

Saunders, Robert. 2016. 'A Tale of Two Referendums: 1975 and 2016.' *Political Quarterly* 87 (3): 318–22. doi:10.1111/1467-923X.12286.

Scarrow, Susan. 2004. 'Embracing Dealignment, Combating Realignment: German Parties Respond.' In *Political Parties and Electoral Change: Party Responses to Electoral Markets*, edited by Peter Mair, Wolfgang Muller, and Fritz Plasser, 86–110. London: Sage Publications.

Shipman, Tim. 2016. *All Out War: The Full Story of How Brexit Sank Britain's Political Class*. London: William Collins.

Singer, Matthew. 2018. 'Personal Economic Struggles and Heterogeneous Government Approval after the Great Recession.' *Public Opinion Quarterly* 82 (3): 524–52. doi:10.1093/poq/nfy039.

Somer-Topcu, Zeynep. 2015. 'Everything to Everyone: The Electoral Consequences of the Broad-Appeal Strategy in Europe.' *American Journal of Political Science* 59 (4): 841–54. doi:10.1111/ajps.12165.

Studlar, Donley T. 1978. 'Policy Voting in Britain: The Colored Immigration Issue in the 1964, 1966, and 1970 General Elections.' *American Political Science Review* 72 (1): 46–64.

Sturgis, Patrick, Jouni Kuha, Nick Baker, Mario Callegaro, Stephen Fisher, Jane Green, Will Jennings, Benjamin E. Lauderdale, and Patten Smith. 2018. 'An Assessment of the Causes of the Errors in the 2015 UK General Election Opinion Polls.' *Journal of the Royal Statistical Society: Series A (Statistics in Society)*, 181 (3): 757–781. doi:10.1111/rssa.12329.

Surridge, Paula. 2018. 'Brexit, British Politics, and the Left-Right Divide.' *Political Insight* 9 (4): 4–7. doi:10.1177/2041905818815189.

Tajfel, Henri. 1981. *Human Groups and Social Categories*. Cambridge: Cambridge University Press.

Tajfel, Henri, and John Turner. 1979. 'An Integrative Theory of Intergroup Conflict.' In *The Social Psychology of Intergroup Relations*, edited by William G. Austin and Stephen Worchel. Monterey, CA: Brooks-Cole.

Thesen, Gunnar. 2018. 'News Content and Populist Radical Right Party Support. The Case of Denmark.' *Electoral Studies* 56: 80–9. doi:10.1016/j.electstud.2018.09.003.

Tilley, James. 2005. 'Libertarian-Authoritarian Value Change in Britain, 1974–2001.' *Political Studies* 53 (2): 442–53. doi:10.1111/j.1467-9248.2005.00537.x.

Tilley, James, and Sara B. Hobolt. 2011. 'Is the Government to Blame? An Experimental Test of How Partisanship Shapes Perceptions of Performance and Responsibility.' *Journal of Politics* 73 (2): 316–30. doi:10.1017/S0022381611000168.

Tillman, E. R. 2013. 'Authoritarianism and Citizen Attitudes towards European Integration.' *European Union Politics* 14 (4): 566–589. doi:10.1177/1465116513483182.

Tufte, Edward R. 1978. *Political Control of the Economy*. Princeton, New Jersey: Princeton University Press. https://press.princeton.edu/titles/786.html.

Turner, John. 2000. *The Tories and Europe*. Manchester: Manchester University Press.

Turner, John, Michael A. Hogg, Penelope J. Oakes, Stephen D. Reicher, and Margaret S. Whetherell. 1987. *Rediscovering the Social Group: A Self-Categorization Theory*. Oxford: Basil Blackwell.

UK Independence Party. 2016. 'UKIP Local Manifesto 2016.'

Vargas-Silva, Carlos, and Yvonni Markaki. 2015. 'EU Migration to and from the UK.' *Migration Observatory Briefing*. https://www.geo-europa.nl/wp-content/uploads/2016/06/EU-Migration-to-and-from-the-UK-Migratory-Observatory-Okt-15.pdf.

Volkens, Andrea, Pola Lehmann, Theres Matthiess, Nicolas Merz, Sven Regel, and Annika Werner. 2015. *The Manifesto Data Collection. Manifesto Project. Manifesto Project (MRG/CMP/MARPOR)*. Berlin: Wissenschaftszentrum Berlin für Sozialforschung (WZB). https://manifesto-project.wzb.eu/.

Vries, Catherine E. de, and Sara B Hobolt. 2012. 'When Dimensions Collide: The Electoral Success of Issue Entrepreneurs.' *European Union Politics* 13 (2): 246–68. doi:10.1177/1465116511434788.

Wagner, Markus. 2012. 'Defining and Measuring Niche Parties.' *Party Politics* 18 (6): 845–64. doi:10.1177/1354068810393267.

Wardt, Marc van de. 2014. 'Putting the Damper on: Do Parties de-Emphasize Issues in Response to Internal Divisions among Their Supporters?' *Party Politics* 20 (3): 330–40. doi:10.1177/1354068811436047.

Webb, Paul. 2000. *The Modern British Party System*. London: Sage Publications.

Weir, Blair T. 1975. 'The Distortion of Voter Recall.' *American Journal of Political Science* 19 (1): 53. doi:10.2307/2110693.

Weßels, Bernhard, Hans Rattinger, Sigrid Roßteutscher, and Rüdiger Schmitt-Beck, eds. 2014. *Voters on the Move or on the Run?* Oxford: Oxford University Press. doi:10.1093/acprof:oso/9780199662630.001.0001.

Whiteley, Paul, Harold D. Clarke, David. Sanders, and Marianne C. Stewart. 2013. *Affluence, Austerity and Electoral Change in Britain*. Cambridge: Cambridge University Press. doi:10.1017/CBO9781139162517.

Wlezien, Christopher. 1995. 'The Public as Thermostat: Dynamics of Preferences for Spending.' *American Journal of Political Science* 39 (4): 981–1000.

Wlezien, Christopher. 2015. 'The Myopic Voter? The Economy and US Presidential Elections.' *Electoral Studies* 39: 195–204. doi:10.1016/j.electstud.2015.03.010.

Wlezien, Christopher, Mark Franklin, and Daniel Twiggs. 1997. 'Economic Perceptions and Vote Choice: Disentangling the Endogeneity.' *Political Behavior* 19 (1). Springer: 7–17. doi:10.2307/586547.

YouGov. 2017. 'YouGov/ The Times Survey Results, 12th–13th April 2017.' https://d25d2506sfb94s.cloudfront.net/cumulus_uploads/document/zs2ifb9u3g/TimesResults_170413_VI_Trackers.pdf.

Ysmal, Colette, and Roland Cayrol. 1996. 'France: The Midwife Comes to Call.' In *Choosing Europe? The European Electorate and National Politics in the Face of Union*, edited by Cees Van der Eijk and Mark N. Franklin, 115–36. Ann Arbor: University of Michigan Press.

Zaller, John R. 1991. 'Information, Values, and Opinion.' *American Political Science Review* 85 (4): 1215–37.

Zaller, John R. 1992. *The Nature and Origins of Mass Opinion*. Cambridge: Cambridge University Press.

Zuckerman, Alan S., Josip Dasovic, and Jennifer Fitzgerald. 2007. *Partisan Families: The Social Logic of Bounded Partisanship in Germany and Britain*. Cambridge: Cambridge University Press.

Index